Honda XL125V Varadero and VT125C Shadow
Service and Repair Manual

by Phil Mather

(4899 - 7AP1 -288)

Models covered

XL125V Varadero   2001 to 2014
VT125C Shadow   1999 to 2009

© Haynes Group Limited 2016

ABCDE
FGHIJ
K

A book in the **Haynes Service and Repair Manual Series**

All rights reserved. No part of this book may be reproduced or
transmitted in any form or by any means, electronic or mechanical,
including photocopying, recording or by any information storage or
retrieval system, without permission in writing from the copyright
holder.

ISBN **978 1 78521 363 2**

British Library Cataloguing in Publication Data
A catalogue record for this book is available from the British Library.

Printed in India

Haynes Group Limited
Sparkford, Yeovil, Somerset BA22 7JJ, England

Haynes North America, Inc
2801 Townsgate Road, Suite 340, Thousand Oaks, CA 91361

Contents

LIVING WITH YOUR HONDA

MAINTENANCE

REPAIRS & OVERHAUL

REFERENCE

VT125C Shadow

The VT125C is a cruiser-styled machine with a low seat height, forward footrests, deeply valanced mudguards and a tank mounted instrument panel.

Introduced in 1999, it is powered by a liquid-cooled, 125 cc V-twin engine with one overhead camshaft per cylinder. The camshafts are driven by chains from the left-hand side of the crankshaft.

The clutch is a conventional, cable operated, multi-plate unit and the gearbox is 5-speed. Drive to the rear wheel is by chain and sprockets.

Twin 22 mm CV carburettors supply the fuel and air mixture to the engine. A fully transistorised electronic system ignites the mixture via one spark plug per cylinder. A catalytic converter is incorporated in the exhaust system.

An all-steel, twin downtube, cradle frame houses the engine. Front suspension is by conventional, oil-damped telescopic forks. Rear suspension is by swingarm with pre-load adjustable twin shock absorbers.

The front brake is a single, 276 mm hydraulically operated disc, the rear brake is a rod operated 130 mm drum. Both front and rear wheels are wire spoked with chromed steel rims.

A carburettor heating system was introduced on the 2004 model to prevent icing in extreme conditions, otherwise changes to the VT125C have been limited to colour and graphics.

XL125V Varadero

The XL125V is styled after the 1000 cc Honda Varadero dual purpose trail machine with a large fuel tank, twin headlight fairing, luggage rack and high level exhaust.

Introduced in 2001, it is powered by the

The 2001 VT125C-1

same liquid-cooled, 125 cc V-twin engine as the VT125C Shadow. However, the frame design is revised to provide greater ground clearance and rear suspension features a box-section swingarm. Suspension travel is increased and the centrally mounted single rear shock has seven spring pre-load settings.

The front brake is a single, 276 mm hydraulically operated disc with twin piston sliding caliper. The rear brake is a single, 220 mm hydraulically operated disc with single piston sliding caliper. Both front and rear wheels are three-spoke alloys.

Apart from colour and graphics and the addition of a carburettor warmer system in 2004 the XL125V didn't receive significant modification until 2007. The new model features fuel injection with twin throttle bodies and an all-new engine management system. A fuel pump is located in the fuel tank and oxygen sensors are mounted in the exhaust header pipes for the front and rear cylinders. A new instrument cluster has a coolant temperature gauge, low fuel level warning light and LED illumination. The fairing is restyled with new mirrors, headlight and turn signals, and the brake/tail light unit incorporates the rear turn signals. The licence plate is illuminated by a separate light.

The 2001 XL125V-1

The 2007 XL125V-7

Our thanks are due to Bridge Motorcycles of Exeter and Hatfields Motorcycles of Crowthorne who supplied the machines featured in the illustrations throughout this manual. We would also like to thank NGK Spark Plugs (UK) Ltd for supplying the colour spark plug condition photographs, the Avon Rubber Company for supplying information on tyre fitting and Draper Tools Ltd for some of the workshop tools shown.

About this Manual

The aim of this manual is to help you get the best value from your motorcycle. It can do so in several ways. It can help you decide what work must be done, even if you choose to have it done by a dealer; it provides information and procedures for routine maintenance and servicing; and it offers diagnostic and repair procedures to follow when trouble occurs.

We hope you use the manual to tackle the work yourself. For many simpler jobs, doing it yourself may be quicker than arranging an appointment to get the motorcycle into a dealer and making the trips to leave it and pick it up. More importantly, a lot of money can be saved by avoiding the expense the shop must pass on to you to cover its labour and overhead costs. An added benefit is the sense of satisfaction and accomplishment that you feel after doing the job yourself.

References to the left or right side of the motorcycle assume you are sitting on the seat, facing forward.

We take great pride in the accuracy of information given in this manual, but motorcycle manufacturers make alterations and design changes during the production run of a particular motorcycle of which they do not inform us. No liability can be accepted by the authors or publishers for loss, damage or injury caused by any errors in, or omissions from, the information given.

Dimensions and weights

	VT125C	XL125V
Overall length	2300 mm	2150 mm
Overall width.	890 mm	850 mm
Overall height	1110 mm	1250 mm
Wheelbase	1530 mm	1450 mm
Seat height	680 mm	802 mm
Ground clearance.	145 mm	190 mm
Weight (dry)	145 kg	154 kg
Weight (with fuel, oil and coolant).	160 kg	167 kg
Maximum weight (with passenger and luggage)	180 kg	180kg

Engine

Type	Four-stroke V-twin
Capacity	125 cc
Bore	42.0 mm
Stroke	45.0 mm
Compression ratio	11.8 to 1
Cooling system.	Liquid-cooled
Clutch	Wet multi-plate
Transmission.	Five-speed constant mesh
Final drive.	Chain and sprockets
Camshaft	SOHC, chain-driven
Fuel system	
VT125C and XL125V-1 to XL125V-6	22 mm twin CV carburettors
XL125V-7 onwards	Fuel injection
Ignition system	Digital transistorised with electronic advance

Chassis

Frame type	Steel double cradle
Rake and Trail	
VT125C.	32°, 122 mm
XL125V.	28°, 97 mm
Fuel tank	
VT125C	
Capacity (inc. reserve)	14.0 litres
Reserve capacity	2.1 litres
XL125V-1 to XL125V-6	
Capacity (inc. reserve)	17.5 litres
Reserve capacity	2.0 litres
XL125V-7 onwards	
Capacity (inc. reserve)	17.0 litres
Reserve capacity	3.0 litres
Front suspension	
Type	35 mm oil-damped telescopic forks (non-adjustable)
Travel	
VT125C.	110 mm
XL125V.	132 mm
Rear suspension	
Type	
VT125C.	Twin shock absorbers (pre-load adjustable), box-section swingarm
XL125V.	Single shock absorber (pre-load adjustable), box-section swingarm
Travel (at axle)	
VT125C.	81 mm
XL125V.	150 mm
Wheels	
VT125C.	17 inch front, 15 inch rear, wire spoked steel rims
XL125V.	18 inch front, 17 inch rear, 3-spoke alloys
Tyres	
VT125C	
Front	100/90-17 MC (56P)
Rear	130/90-15 MC (66P)
XL125V	
Front.	100/90-18 MC (56P)
Rear	130/80-17 MC (65P)
Front brake.	Single 276 mm disc with twin piston Nissin sliding caliper
Rear brake	
VT125C.	130 mm drum
XL125V.	Single 220 mm disc with single piston Nissin sliding caliper

Frame and engine numbers

The frame serial number is stamped into the right-hand side of the steering head. The engine number is stamped into the crankcase on the left-hand side. Both of these numbers should be recorded and kept in a safe place so they can be given to law enforcement officials in the event of a theft.

There is also a VIN plate on the right-hand side of the frame and a colour code label on the right-hand side of the frame underneath the seat.

The carburettors or fuel injector throttle bodies (as applicable) have an ID number stamped into the body.

The frame serial number, engine serial

Model code	Production year
VT125C-X	1999
VT125C-Y	2000
VT125C-1	2001/2002
VT125C-21	2001/2002
VT125C-3	2003
VT125C-4	2004 to 2005
VT125C-6	2006 to 2009
XL125V-1	2001
XL125V-2	2002
XL125V-3	2003
XL125V-4	2004
XL125V-5	2005
XL125V-6	2006
XL125V-7	2007
XL125V-8	2008
XL125V-9	2009
XL125V-A	2010
XL125V-B	2011 to 2014

number, and colour code should also be kept in a handy place (such as with your driver's licence) so they are always available when purchasing or ordering parts for your machine.

Models are identified by their model code suffix (e.g. V-4, V-5, or C-X, C-Y). The model code or production year is printed on the colour code label.

Buying spare parts

Once you have found all the identification numbers, record them for reference when buying parts. Since the manufacturers change specifications, parts and vendors (companies that manufacture various components on the machine), providing the ID numbers is the only way to be reasonably sure that you are buying the correct parts.

Whenever possible, take the worn part to the dealer so direct comparison with the new component can be made. Along the trail from the manufacturer to the parts shelf, there are numerous places that the part can end up with the wrong number or be listed incorrectly.

The two places to purchase new parts for your motorcycle – the franchised or main dealer and the parts/accessories store – differ in the type of parts they carry. While dealers can obtain every single genuine part for your motorcycle, the accessory store is usually limited to normal high wear items such as chains and sprockets, brake pads, spark plugs and cables.

Used parts can be obtained from breakers yards for roughly half the price of new ones, but you can't always be sure of what you're getting. Once again, take your worn part to the breaker for direct comparison, or when ordering by mail order make sure that you can return it if you are not happy.

Whether buying new, used or rebuilt parts, the best course is to deal directly with someone who specialises in your particular make.

The frame number is stamped into the right-hand side of the steering head

The engine number is stamped into the left-hand side of the crankcase

VIN plate on VT125C models

VIN plate on XL125V models

The colour code label is on the right-hand side of the frame underneath the seat

Professional mechanics are trained in safe working procedures. However enthusiastic you may be about getting on with the job at hand, take the time to ensure that your safety is not put at risk. A moment's lack of attention can result in an accident, as can failure to observe simple precautions.

There will always be new ways of having accidents, and the following is not a comprehensive list of all dangers; it is intended rather to make you aware of the risks and to encourage a safe approach to all work you carry out on your bike.

Asbestos

● Certain friction, insulating, sealing and other products - such as brake pads, clutch linings, gaskets, etc. - contain asbestos. Extreme care must be taken to avoid inhalation of dust from such products since it is hazardous to health. If in doubt, assume that they do contain asbestos.

Fire

● Remember at all times that petrol is highly flammable. Never smoke or have any kind of naked flame around, when working on the vehicle. But the risk does not end there - a spark caused by an electrical short-circuit, by two metal surfaces contacting each other, by careless use of tools, or even by static electricity built up in your body under certain conditions, can ignite petrol vapour, which in a confined space is highly explosive. Never use petrol as a cleaning solvent. Use an approved safety solvent.

● Always disconnect the battery earth terminal before working on any part of the fuel or electrical system, and never risk spilling fuel on to a hot engine or exhaust.

● It is recommended that a fire extinguisher of a type suitable for fuel and electrical fires is kept handy in the garage or workplace at all times. Never try to extinguish a fuel or electrical fire with water.

Fumes

● Certain fumes are highly toxic and can quickly cause unconsciousness and even death if inhaled to any extent. Petrol vapour comes into this category, as do the vapours from certain solvents such as trichloro-ethylene. Any draining or pouring of such volatile fluids should be done in a well ventilated area.

● When using cleaning fluids and solvents, read the instructions carefully. Never use materials from unmarked containers - they may give off poisonous vapours.

● Never run the engine of a motor vehicle in an enclosed space such as a garage. Exhaust fumes contain carbon monoxide which is extremely poisonous; if you need to run the engine, always do so in the open air or at least have the rear of the vehicle outside the workplace.

The battery

● Never cause a spark, or allow a naked light near the vehicle's battery. It will normally be giving off a certain amount of hydrogen gas, which is highly explosive.

● Always disconnect the battery ground (earth) terminal before working on the fuel or electrical systems (except where noted).

● If possible, loosen the filler plugs or cover when charging the battery from an external source. Do not charge at an excessive rate or the battery may burst.

● Take care when topping up, cleaning or carrying the battery. The acid electrolyte, evenwhen diluted, is very corrosive and should not be allowed to contact the eyes or skin. Always wear rubber gloves and goggles or a face shield. If you ever need to prepare electrolyte yourself, always add the acid slowly to the water; never add the water to the acid.

Electricity

● When using an electric power tool, inspection light etc., always ensure that the appliance is correctly connected to its plug and that, where necessary, it is properly grounded (earthed). Do not use such appliances in damp conditions and, again, beware of creating a spark or applying excessive heat in the vicinity of fuel or fuel vapour. Also ensure that the appliances meet national safety standards.

● A severe electric shock can result from touching certain parts of the electrical system, such as the spark plug wires (HT leads), when the engine is running or being cranked, particularly if components are damp or the insulation is defective. Where an electronic ignition system is used, the secondary (HT) voltage is much higher and could prove fatal.

Remember...

✗ **Don't** start the engine without first ascertaining that the transmission is in neutral.

✗ **Don't** suddenly remove the pressure cap from a hot cooling system - cover it with a cloth and release the pressure gradually first, or you may get scalded by escaping coolant.

✗ **Don't** attempt to drain oil until you are sure it has cooled sufficiently to avoid scalding you.

✗ **Don't** grasp any part of the engine or exhaust system without first ascertaining that it is cool enough not to burn you.

✗ **Don't** allow brake fluid or antifreeze to contact the machine's paintwork or plastic components.

✗ **Don't** siphon toxic liquids such as fuel, hydraulic fluid or antifreeze by mouth, or allow them to remain on your skin.

✗ **Don't** inhale dust - it may be injurious to health (see Asbestos heading).

✗ **Don't** allow any spilled oil or grease to remain on the floor - wipe it up right away, before someone slips on it.

✗ **Don't** use ill-fitting spanners or other tools which may slip and cause injury.

✗ **Don't** lift a heavy component which may be beyond your capability - get assistance.

✗ **Don't** rush to finish a job or take unverified short cuts.

✗ **Don't** allow children or animals in or around an unattended vehicle.

✗ **Don't** inflate a tyre above the recommended pressure. Apart from overstressing the carcass, in extreme cases the tyre may blow off forcibly.

✔ **Do** ensure that the machine is supported securely at all times. This is especially important when the machine is blocked up to aid wheel or fork removal.

✔ **Do** take care when attempting to loosen a stubborn nut or bolt. It is generally better to pull on a spanner, rather than push, so that if you slip, you fall away from the machine rather than onto it.

✔ **Do** wear eye protection when using power tools such as drill, sander, bench grinder etc.

✔ **Do** use a barrier cream on your hands prior to undertaking dirty jobs - it will protect your skin from infection as well as making the dirt easier to remove afterwards; but make sure your hands aren't left slippery. Note that long-term contact with used engine oil can be a health hazard.

✔ **Do** keep loose clothing (cuffs, ties etc. and long hair) well out of the way of moving mechanical parts.

✔ **Do** remove rings, wristwatch etc., before working on the vehicle - especially the electrical system.

✔ **Do** keep your work area tidy - it is only too easy to fall over articles left lying around.

✔ **Do** exercise caution when compressing springs for removal or installation. Ensure that the tension is applied and released in a controlled manner, using suitable tools which preclude the possibility of the spring escaping violently.

✔ **Do** ensure that any lifting tackle used has a safe working load rating adequate for the job.

✔ **Do** get someone to check periodically that all is well, when working alone on the vehicle.

✔ **Do** carry out work in a logical sequence and check that everything is correctly assembled and tightened afterwards.

✔ **Do** remember that your vehicle's safety affects that of yourself and others. If in doubt on any point, get professional advice.

● If in spite of following these precautions, you are unfortunate enough to injure yourself, seek medical attention as soon as possible.

Engine oil level

Before you start:

✔ Start the engine and let it idle for 3 to 5 minutes.
Caution: Do not run the engine in an enclosed space such as a garage or workshop.
✔ Stop the engine and support the motorcycle upright on level ground. Allow it to stand for a few minutes for the oil level to stabilise.
✔ On VT125C models, the oil level is measured using a dipstick attached to the filler cap that screws into the cover on the right-hand side of the engine. Wipe the area around the filler cap clean before unscrewing it from the cover.
✔ On XL125V models, the oil level is marked on the inspection window located in the bottom of the cover on the right-hand side of the engine. If necessary wipe the window so that it is clean.

The correct oil:

● Always top up with a good quality motorcycle oil of the specified type and

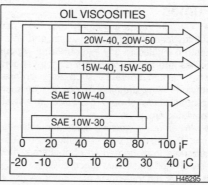

OIL VISCOSITIES

20W-40, 20W-50
15W-40, 15W-50
SAE 10W-40
SAE 10W-30

| ºF | 0 | 20 | 40 | 60 | 80 | 100 |
| ºC | -20 -10 | 0 | 10 | 20 | 30 | 40 |

H46295

viscosity and do not overfill the engine. Do not use engine oil designed for car use.

Oil type	API grade SE, SF or SG
Oil viscosity	SAE 10W40 (see viscosity chart for alternatives)

Caution: Do not use chemical additives or oils labelled 'ENERGY CONSERVING' – such additives or oils could cause clutch slip.

Bike care:

● If you have to add oil frequently, check the engine joints, oil seals and gaskets for oil leakage. If not, the engine could be burning oil, in which case there will be white smoke coming out of the exhaust (see *Fault Finding*).

VT125C

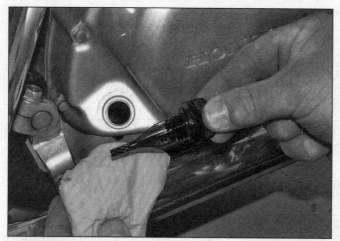

1 Unscrew the filler cap, withdraw the dipstick and wipe it clean.

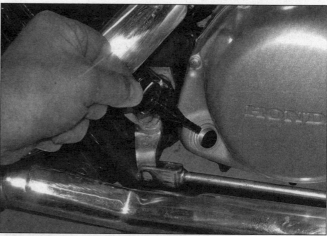

2 Insert the dipstick into its hole and rest the filler cap on the cover, but do not screw it in.

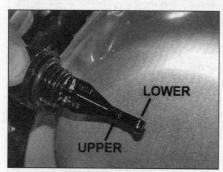

LOWER

UPPER

3 Withdraw the dipstick – the oil level should lie between the upper and lower level lines on the dipstick.

4 If the level is on or below the lower line, top-up with the recommended grade and type of oil to the upper line. Do not overfill. If necessary, drain off any excess (see Chapter 1).

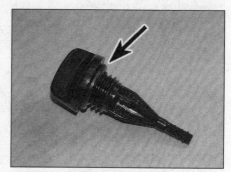

5 On completion, make sure the O-ring (arrowed) on the filler cap is in good condition and properly seated. Fit a new one if necessary and smear it with oil. Install the cap securely.

XL125V

1 The oil level should lie between the upper and lower level lines on the window.

2 If the level is on or below the lower line, unscrew the oil filler cap.

3 Top-up the with the recommended grade and type of oil almost up to the upper line on the inspection window. **Do not overfill**. If necessary, drain off any excess (see Chapter 1).

4 On completion, make sure the O-ring on the filler cap is in good condition and properly seated. Fit a new one if necessary and smear it with oil. Install the cap securely.

Brake fluid levels

⚠️ **Warning: Brake hydraulic fluid can harm your eyes and damage painted surfaces, so use extreme caution when handling and pouring it and cover surrounding surfaces with rag. Do not use fluid that has been standing open for some time, as it is hygroscopic (absorbs moisture from the air) which can cause a dangerous loss of braking effectiveness.**

Before you start:

✔ The front brake fluid reservoir is on the right-hand handlebar. On XL125V models, the rear brake fluid reservoir is located under the seat on the right-hand side. VT125C models are not fitted with an hydraulic rear brake.

✔ Make sure you have a supply of DOT 4 brake fluid.

✔ Wrap a rag around the reservoir being worked on to ensure that any spillage does not come into contact with painted surfaces.

Bike care:

● The fluid in the front and rear brake master cylinder reservoirs will drop very gradually as the brake pads wear down. If the fluid level is low check the brake pads for wear (see Chapter 1), and replace them with new ones if necessary (see Chapter 7). Do not top the reservoir(s) up until the new pads have been fitted, and then check to see if topping up

is still necessary – when the caliper pistons are pushed back to accommodate the extra thickness of the pads some fluid will be displaced back into the reservoir.

● If either fluid reservoir requires repeated topping-up there is a leak somewhere in the system, which must be investigated immediately.

● Check for signs of fluid leakage from the brake hoses and/or brake system components – if found, rectify immediately (see Chapter 7).

● Check the operation of both brakes before taking the machine on the road; if there is evidence of air in the system (spongy feel to lever or pedal), it must be bled out (see Chapter 7).

FRONT

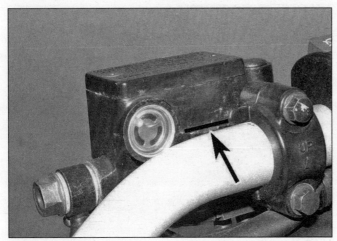

1 With the bike on its sidestand set the handlebars so the reservoir is level and check the fluid level through the window in the reservoir body – it must be above the LOWER level line (arrowed).

2 If the level is on or below the LOWER line, undo the two reservoir cover screws (arrowed) and remove the cover, diaphragm plate and diaphragm.

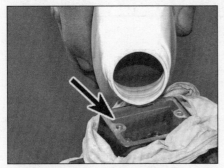

3 Top up with new clean DOT 4 brake fluid, until the level is up to the UPPER line (arrowed) on the inside of the reservoir. Do not overfill and take care to avoid spills (see **Warning** above).

4 Wipe any moisture off the diaphragm with a paper towel.

5 Ensure that the diaphragm is correctly seated before installing the plate and cover. Secure the reservoir cover with its screws.

REAR

1 Remove the seat for access (see Chapter 8). The brake fluid level is visible through the reservoir body – it must be between the UPPER and LOWER level lines (arrowed).

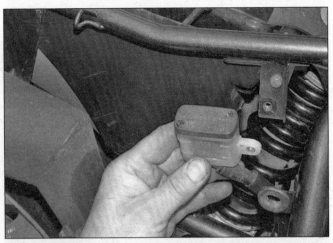

2 If the level is on or below the LOWER line, first remove the side panel (see Chapter 8) then undo the bolt securing the fluid reservoir to the frame and draw the reservoir out.

3 Undo the two reservoir cover screws and remove the cover, diaphragm plate and diaphragm.

4 Top up with new DOT 4 brake fluid, until the level is up to the UPPER line. Do not overfill and take care to avoid spills (see **Warning** on page 0•10).

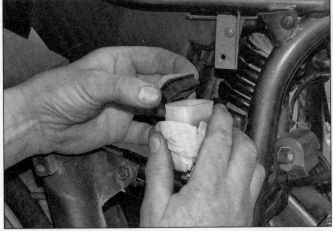

5 Wipe any moisture off the diaphragm with a paper towel and ensure that the diaphragm is correctly seated before installing the plate and cover. Secure the cover with its screws.

6 Fit the reservoir onto its mount and tighten the bolt.

Coolant level

⚠️ **Warning: DO NOT remove the radiator pressure cap to add coolant. Topping up is done via the coolant reservoir tank filler. DO NOT leave open containers of coolant about, as it is poisonous.**

Before you start:

✔ Make sure you have a supply of coolant available (use either an ethylene glycol based pre-mixed coolant, or prepare a mix of 50% distilled water and 50% corrosion inhibited ethylene glycol anti-freeze).

✔ Always check the coolant level when the engine is at normal working temperature. Take the motorcycle on a short run to allow it to reach normal temperature.

Caution: Do not run the engine in an enclosed space such as a garage or workshop.

✔ Stop the engine and support the motorcycle upright on level ground.

Bike care:

● It is important that anti-freeze is used in the system all year round, and not just in the winter. Do not top the system up using only water, as the system will become too diluted.

● Do not overfill the reservoir tank. If the coolant is significantly above the UPPER level line at any time, the surplus should be siphoned or drained off to prevent the possibility of it being expelled out of the overflow hose.

● If the coolant level falls steadily, check the system for leaks (see Chapter 1). If no leaks are found and the level continues to fall, it is recommended that the machine is taken to a Honda dealer for a pressure test.

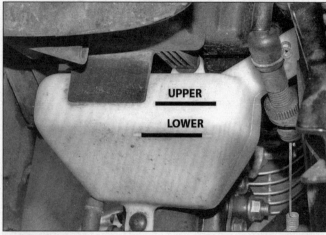

1 On VT125C models, the coolant reservoir is visible from the rear, right-hand side.

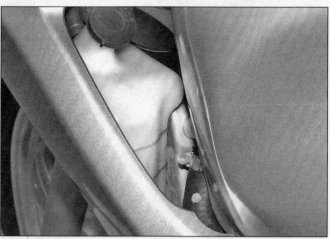

2 On XL125V models, the coolant reservoir is visible from the left-hand side.

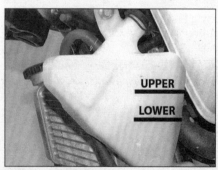

3 With the motorcycle vertical, the coolant level should lie between the upper and lower level lines marked on the reservoir.

4 If the coolant level is on or below the LOWER line, remove the reservoir filler cap. On VT125C models, remove the right-hand side panel for access (see Chapter 8).

5 Top the reservoir up with the recommended coolant mixture to the UPPER level line, using a suitable funnel if required. On completion, fit the cap securely.

Tyre checks

The correct pressures:

● The tyres must be checked when **cold**, not immediately after riding. Note that incorrect tyre pressures will cause abnormal tread wear and unsafe handling. Low tyre pressures may cause the tyre to slip on the rim or come off.

● Use an accurate pressure gauge. Many forecourt gauges are wildly inaccurate. If you buy your own, spend as much as you can justify on a quality gauge.

● Proper air pressure will increase tyre life and provide maximum stability and ride comfort.

Tyre care:

● Check the tyres carefully for cuts, tears, embedded nails or other sharp objects and excessive wear. Operation of the motorcycle with excessively worn tyres is extremely hazardous, as traction and handling are directly affected.

● Check the condition of the tyre valve and ensure the dust cap is in place.

● Pick out any stones or nails which may have become embedded in the tyre tread. If left, they will eventually penetrate through the casing and cause a puncture.

● If tyre damage is apparent, or unexplained loss of pressure is experienced, seek the advice of a tyre fitting specialist without delay.

Tyre tread depth:

● At the time of writing UK law requires that tread depth must be at least 1 mm over 3/4 of the tread breadth all the way around the tyre, with no bald patches. Many riders, however, consider 2 mm tread depth minimum to be a safer limit. Honda recommend a minimum of 1.5 mm on the front and 2 mm on the rear. Refer to the tyre tread legislation in your country.

● Many tyres now incorporate wear indicators in the tread. Identify the location marking on the tyre sidewall to locate the indicator bar and replace the tyre if the tread has worn down to the bar.

	Front	Rear
VT125C	29 psi (2.0 Bar)	29 psi (2.0 Bar)
XL125V:		
Rider only	29 psi (2.0 Bar)	29 psi (2.0 Bar)
Rider and passenger	29 psi (2.0 Bar)	33 psi (2.25 Bar)

1 Remove the dust cap from the valve and do not forget to fit it after checking the pressure.

2 Check the tyre pressures when the tyres are cold.

3 Measure tread depth at the centre of the tyre using a depth gauge.

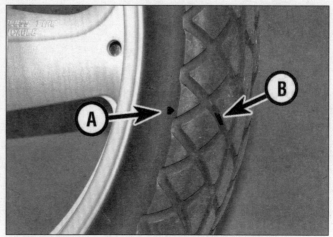

4 Tyre tread wear indicator (B) and its location marking (A) on the edge or sidewall (according to manufacturer).

Suspension, steering and drive chain

Suspension and Steering:

● Check that the front and rear suspension operates smoothly without binding (see Chapter 1).
● Check that the steering moves smoothly from lock-to-lock.

Drive chain:

● Check that the chain isn't too loose or too tight, and adjust it if necessary (see Chapter 1).
● If the chain looks dry, lubricate it (see Chapter 1).

Legal and safety

Lighting and signalling:

● Take a minute to check that the headlight, tail light, brake light, licence plate light, instrument lights and turn signals all work correctly.
● Check that the horn sounds when the button is pressed.
● A working speedometer, graduated in mph, is a statutory requirement in the UK.

Safety:

● Check that the throttle grip rotates smoothly when opened and snaps shut when released, in all steering positions. Also check for the correct amount of freeplay (see Chapter 1).
● Check that the brake lever and pedal, clutch lever and gearchange lever operate smoothly. Lubricate them at the specified intervals or when necessary (see Chapter 1).
● On VT125 C models, check that the rear brake operates correctly. If there appears to be too much freeplay in the pedal, refer to Chapter 1, Section 3 and check the adjustment.
● Check that the engine shuts off when the kill switch is operated. Check the starter interlock circuit (see Chapter 1).
● Check that the sidestand return springs hold the stand up securely when retracted.

Fuel:

● This may seem obvious, but check that you have enough fuel to complete your journey. If you notice signs of fuel leakage – rectify the cause immediately.
● Ensure you always use unleaded fuel, minimum 91 RON (Research Octane Number).

Chapter 1
Routine maintenance and servicing

Contents

Degrees of difficulty

| **Easy,** suitable for novice with little experience | | **Fairly easy,** suitable for beginner with some experience | | **Fairly difficult,** suitable for competent DIY mechanic | | **Difficult,** suitable for experienced DIY mechanic | | **Very difficult,** suitable for expert DIY or professional | |

Engine

Spark plug type	
Standard	
NGK	CR8EH-9
Denso	U24FER-9
Electrode gap	0.8 to 0.9 mm
Engine idle speed	1500 ± 100 rpm
Carburettor synchronisation – difference between carburettors	0.04 bar max
Valve clearances (COLD engine)	
VT125C	
Intake valve	0.15 ± 0.02 mm
Exhaust valve	0.20 ± 0.02 mm
XL125V	
Intake valve	0.15 ± 0.02 mm
Exhaust valve	0.24 ± 0.02 mm

Cycle parts

Clutch cable freeplay	10 to 20 mm at lever end
Drive chain slack	
VT125C	20 to 30 mm
XL125V	25 to 35 mm
Rear brake pedal freeplay (VT125C)	20 to 30 mm
Steering head bearing pre-load	0.10 to 0.15 kgf (0.22 to 0.33 lbf)
Throttle cable freeplay	2 to 6 mm at twistgrip flange

Lubricants and fluids

Engine oil type and viscosity	see *Pre-ride checks*
Engine oil capacity	
Oil change	1.3 litres
Following engine overhaul	1.5 litres
Coolant type	see *Pre-ride checks*
Brake fluid	DOT 4
Drive chain	SAE 80 or 90 gear oil or aerosol chain lubricant suitable for O-ring chains
Steering head bearings	Lithium-based grease with NLGI 2
Bearing seal lips	Multi-purpose grease
Gearchange lever/rear brake pedal/footrest pivots	Multi-purpose grease
Clutch lever pivot	Multi-purpose grease
Stand pivots	Multi-purpose grease
Throttle twistgrip	Multi-purpose grease
Front brake lever pivot and piston tip	Silicone grease
Cables	Aerosol cable lubricant

Torque settings

Alternator cover centre cap	8 Nm
Engine oil drain plug	25 Nm
Front fork clamp bolts in top yoke	27 Nm
Fuel valve nut	22 Nm
Rear axle nut	88 Nm
Spark plugs	12 Nm
Steering stem nut	103 Nm
Timing inspection cap	10 Nm
Valve clearance adjuster locknuts	17 Nm

Note: *The Pre-ride checks outlined in the owner's manual cover those items which should be inspected before every ride. Also perform the pre-ride inspection at every maintenance interval (in addition to the procedures listed). The intervals listed below are the intervals recommended by the manufacturer for the models covered in this manual.*

Pre-ride
☐ See *Pre-ride checks* at the beginning of this manual.

After the initial 600 miles (1000 km)
Note: *This check is usually performed by a Honda dealer after the first 600 miles (1000 km) from new. Thereafter, maintenance is carried out according to the following intervals of the schedule.*

Every 600 miles (1000 km)
☐ Check, adjust, clean and lubricate the drive chain (Section 1)

Every 2500 miles (4000 km) or 6 months
☐ Check and adjust the engine idle speed – VT125C and XL125V-1 to V-6 (Section 2)
☐ Check the brakes and brake system (Section 3)
☐ Check the fuel system and hoses (Section 4)
☐ Check and adjust the throttle and choke cables (Section 5)
☐ Check and adjust the clutch cable (Section 6)
☐ Check the sidestand and starter safety circuit (Section 7)
☐ Check the front and rear suspension (Section 8)
☐ Check the condition of the wheels and wheel bearings (Section 9)
☐ Lubricate the handlebar lever pivots, gearchange lever, brake pedal and stand pivots (Section 10)
☐ Lubricate the clutch, throttle and choke cables (Section 11)
☐ Check the steering head bearings (Section 12)
☐ Check the headlight aim (Chapter 9)

Every 5000 miles (8000 km) or 12 months
Carry out all the items under the 2500 mile (4000 km) check, plus the following:
☐ Fit new spark plugs (Section 13)
☐ Check the cooling system (Section 14)
☐ Check the tightness of all nuts, bolts and fasteners (Section 15)

Every 7500 miles (12,000 km) or 18 months
Carry out all the items under the 2500 mile (4000 km) check, plus the following:
☐ Change the engine oil and filter (Section 16)
☐ Check and adjust the valve clearances (Section 17)
☐ Check the secondary air system (Section 18)
☐ Fit a new air filter element* (Section 19)
☐ Check carburettor synchronisation – VT125C and XL125V-1 to V-6 (Section 20)
***Note:** If the machine is continually ridden in wet or dusty conditions, the filter should be changed more frequently.*

Every two years
☐ Change the brake fluid (Chapter 7)
☐ Change the coolant (Chapter 3)

Non-scheduled maintenance
☐ Check the battery (Chapter 9)
☐ Change the front fork oil (Chapter 6)
☐ Lubricate the swingarm bearings and pivot bolt (Chapter 6)
☐ Lubricate the steering head bearings (Chapter 6)
☐ Clean the fuel strainer – XL125V-7 onwards (Section 4 and Chapter 4B)
☐ Renew the brake hoses (Section 3 and Chapter 7)
☐ Renew the brake caliper seals and master cylinder seals (Section 3 and Chapter 7)

1 This Chapter is designed to help the home mechanic maintain his/her motorcycle for safety, economy, long life and peak performance.

2 Deciding where to start or plug into the routine maintenance schedule depends on several factors. If your motorcycle has been maintained according to the warranty standards and has just come out of warranty, start routine maintenance as it coincides with the next mileage or calendar interval. If you have owned the machine for some time but have never performed any maintenance on it, start at the nearest interval and include some additional procedures to ensure that nothing important is overlooked. If you have just had a major engine overhaul, then start the maintenance routine from the beginning. If you have a used machine and have no knowledge of its history or maintenance record, combine all the checks into one large service initially and then settle into the specified maintenance schedule.

3 Before beginning any maintenance or repair, the machine should be cleaned thoroughly, especially around the oil drain plug, valve covers, body panels, drive chain, suspension, wheels, etc. Cleaning will help ensure that dirt does not contaminate the engine and will allow you to detect wear and damage that could otherwise easily go unnoticed.

4 Certain maintenance information is sometimes printed on labels attached to the motorcycle. If the information on the labels differs from that included here, use the information on the label.

1 Drive chain and sprockets

Check, adjust, clean and lubricate the chain

Check chain slack

1 A neglected drive chain won't last long and will quickly damage the sprockets. Routine chain adjustment and lubrication isn't difficult and will ensure maximum chain and sprocket life.

2 To check the chain, support the bike on its sidestand and shift the transmission into neutral.

3 Hold a ruler midway between the two sprockets, then push up on the bottom run of the chain and measure the slack **(see illustrations)**. Compare your measurement to that listed in this Chapter's Specifications. As the chain stretches with wear, periodic adjustment will be necessary (see below).

4 Since the chain will rarely wear evenly, roll the bike forward so that another section of chain can be checked. Do this several times to check the entire length of chain, and mark the tightest spot.

Caution: Riding the bike with excess slack in the chain could lead to damage.

5 In some cases, where lubrication has been neglected, corrosion and dirt may cause the links to bind and kink, which effectively shortens the chain's length and makes it tight **(see illustration)**. Thoroughly clean and work

free any such links, then highlight them with a marker pen or paint. Take the bike for a ride.

6 After the bike has been ridden, repeat the measurement for slack in the highlighted area. If the chain has kinked again and is still tight, replace it with a new one (see Chapter 7). A rusty, kinked or worn chain will damage the sprockets and can damage transmission bearings. If in any doubt as to the condition of a chain, it is far better to install a new one than risk damage to other components and possible injury to yourself.

7 Check the entire length of the chain for damaged rollers, loose links and pins, and missing O-rings and replace it with a new one if necessary. **Note:** *Never install a new chain on old sprockets, and never use the old chain if you install new sprockets – replace the chain and sprockets as a set.*

Adjust chain slack

8 Move the bike so that the chain is positioned with the tightest point at the centre of its bottom run, then support the bike on its sidestand.

9 Loosen the rear axle nut **(see illustration)**.

10 Loosen the locknut on the left and right-hand chain adjusters, then turn both adjuster nuts evenly and a little at a time until the amount of freeplay specified at the beginning of the Chapter is obtained at the centre of the bottom run of the chain **(see illustration 1.9)**. If the chain was slack, turn the adjuster nuts clockwise; if the chain was tight turn them anti-clockwise, then move the wheel forwards in the swingarm to take up the gap between the nuts and the swingarm end caps.

11 Following adjustment, check that the chain adjusters are in the same position on both sides by ensuring that the same number of index marks are visible through both axle slots **(see illustration)**.

12 If the adjustment is not the same on both sides, the rear wheel will be out of alignment with the front (see *Wheel alignment* in Chapter 7). If there is a difference in the positions of the chain adjusters, adjust one so that its position is exactly the same as the other, then check the chain freeplay again and readjust if necessary.

13 Also check the alignment of the

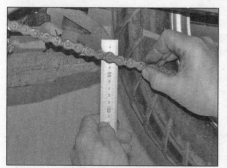

1.3a Hold a ruler midway between the two sprockets . . .

1.3b . . . then push the chain up to measure the slack

1.5 Neglect has caused the links in this chain to kink

1.9 Rear axle nut (A), locknut (B) and adjuster nut (C)

1.11 Adjustment index marks (arrowed)

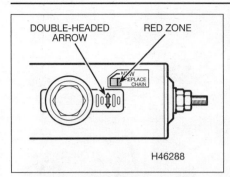

1.13 Check the alignment of the double-headed arrow with the wear decal

1.16a Using a dedicated chain cleaner . . .

1.16b . . . and a special chain cleaning brush

double-headed arrow on the adjustment marker with the wear decal on the left-hand side of the swingarm **(see illustration)**. When the arrow meets the red REPLACE CHAIN zone, the drive chain has stretched excessively and must be replaced with a new one (see Chapter 7).

14 When adjustment is complete, counter-hold the adjuster nuts to prevent them turning and tighten the locknuts **(see illustration 1.9)**. Tighten the axle nut to the torque setting specified at the beginning of this Chapter. Recheck the chain adjustment as above.

15 On VT125C models, check the adjustment of the rear brake (see Section 3).

Clean and lubricate the chain

16 Clean the chain using a dedicated aerosol cleaner that will not damage the O-rings, or paraffin (kerosene), using a soft brush to work out any dirt **(see illustrations)**. Wipe the cleaner off the chain and allow it to dry, using compressed air if available. If the chain is excessively dirty, follow the procedure in Chapter 7 to remove it from the machine and allow it to soak in the paraffin or solvent.

Caution: Don't use petrol (gasoline), an unsuitable solvent or other cleaning fluids which might damage the internal sealing properties of the chain. Don't use high-pressure water to clean the chain. The entire process shouldn't take longer than ten minutes, otherwise the O-rings could be damaged.

17 The best time to lubricate the chain is after the motorcycle has been ridden. When the chain is warm, the lubricant will penetrate the joints between the sideplates better than when cold. **Note:** *Honda specifies SAE 80 or 90 gear oil or an aerosol chain lube that is suitable for O-ring (sealed) chains; do not use any other chain lubricants – the solvents could damage the chain's sealing rings.* Apply the lubricant to the area where the sideplates overlap – not the middle of the rollers **(see illustration)**.

Apply the lubricant to the top of the lower chain run, so centrifugal force will work the oil into the chain when the bike is moving. After applying the lubricant, let it soak in a few minutes before wiping off any excess.

⚠ *Warning: Take care not to get any lubricant on the tyre or brake system components. If any of the lubricant inadvertently contacts them, clean it off thoroughly using a suitable solvent or dedicated brake cleaner before riding the machine.*

Check sprocket and chain slider wear

18 Remove the front sprocket cover (see Chapter 7).

19 Check the teeth on the front and the rear sprockets for wear **(see illustrations)**. If the sprocket teeth are worn excessively, replace the chain and both sprockets with a new set.

20 Inspect the drive chain slider on the front of the swingarm for excessive wear and damage **(see illustration)**, and replace it with a new one if necessary (see Chapter 5).

1.17 Apply the lubricant to the points where the sideplates overlap

1.19a Examine the teeth on the front . . .

1.19b . . . and rear sprockets

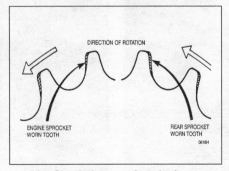

1.19c Check the sprockets in the area indicated

1.20 Check the drive chain slider

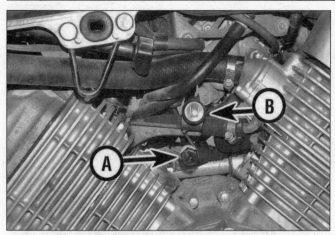

2.1 Idle speed adjuster (A) and choke knob (B)

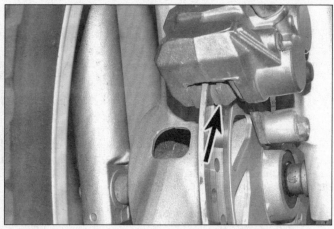

3.1a Location of the wear indicator on front brake pads

2 Idle speed – VT125C and XL125V-1 to V-6

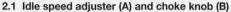

1 The engine idle speed can be adjusted manually on all models fitted with carburettors. The idle speed adjuster knob is located on the left-hand side below the choke knob **(see illustration)**. **Note:** *On fuel injected models the idle speed is controlled by the idle air control valve (IACV) – refer to Chapter 4B for details.*
2 The engine should be at normal operating temperature, which is usually reached after 10 to 15 minutes of stop-and-go riding. Support the bike on its sidestand, and make sure the transmission is in neutral. Ensure that the throttle cable is correctly adjusted (see Section 5).
3 With the engine running, turn the adjuster knob until the engine idles at the speed specified at the beginning of this Chapter. Turn the knob clockwise to increase idle speed, and anti-clockwise to decrease it.
4 Snap the throttle open and shut a few times, then recheck the idle speed. If necessary, repeat the adjustment procedure.

5 If a smooth, steady idle can't be achieved, check the spark plugs, air filter element and valve clearances (Sections 13, 19 and 17). If the problem persists, there could be an air leak in the manifolds between the carburettors and the cylinder heads, or a problem with one or both of the carburettors – refer to *Fault Finding* at the end of the manual and to Chapter 4A.

3 Brakes and brake system

Brake wear check

Disc brake

1 Each brake pad has a wear indicator line in the friction material. The indicator lines should be visible by looking at the edges of the friction material – on the front brake look at the bottom edge of each pad from below the caliper, and on the rear brake look at the rear edge of each pad from behind the caliper **(see illustrations)**. **Note:** *Some after-market pads*

may use different indicators to those fitted as original equipment.
2 If the indicators aren't visible due to an accumulation of road dirt or brake dust, or if you are in doubt as to the amount of friction material remaining, remove the pads for inspection (see Chapter 7). Honda doesn't specify a minimum thickness for the friction material, but anything less than 2 mm should be considered worn to the service limit and new pads should be fitted.
3 If any of the pads are excessively worn, check the corresponding brake disc for scoring and wear (see Chapter 7). If the pads appear to be wearing unevenly, disassemble the caliper and check the operation of the piston(s) and the condition of the slider pins (see Chapter 7).

Drum brake – VT125C rear

4 Check the rear brake pedal freeplay and compare the result with the specification at the beginning of this Chapter **(see illustration)**. To adjust the freeplay, turn the nut on the end of the brake rod – turn the nut clockwise to reduce freeplay and anti-clockwise to increase it **(see illustration)**.
5 Use an auxiliary stand to support the bike

3.1b Location of the wear indicator on rear brake pads

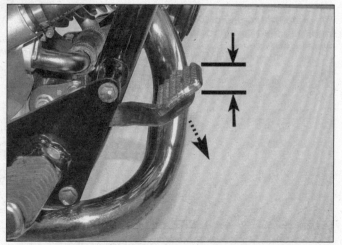

3.4a Press the pedal down to check the freeplay

3.4b Adjusting the brake pedal freeplay

3.6 Wear indicator (A) and reference mark (B)

3.7 Location of the brake pedal stop bolt

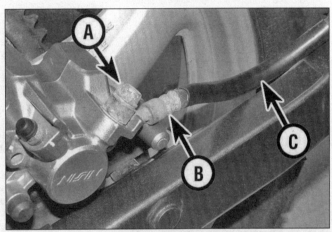

3.9 Brake union banjo bolt (A), banjo union (B) and brake hose (C)

with the rear wheel off the ground. Rotate the wheel by hand and ensure the rear brake is not binding. If it is, either there is insufficient freeplay in the pedal, the brake actuating cam is binding or the brake linings have worn unevenly – follow the procedure in Chapter 7 to check the condition of the rear brake.

6 To check the brake linings for wear, have an assistant apply the brake and check the position of the wear indicator on the brake arm **(see illustration)**. If the indicator aligns with the reference mark on the brake plate the linings are worn to the service limit and new brake shoes must be fitted (see Chapter 7).

7 If required, the height of the brake pedal can be altered by turning the stop bolt on the rear of the footrest bracket **(see illustration)**. Don't forget to tighten the stop bolt locknut after adjustment and check the rear brake pedal freeplay.

Brake system check

8 Check the brake lever and pedal for loose fixings, improper or rough action, excessive play, bends, and other damage. Replace any damaged parts with new ones (see Chapter 6). Clean and lubricate the lever and pedal pivots

if their action is stiff or rough (see Section 10). If the lever or pedal action is spongy, bleed the brakes (see Chapter 7).

9 Make sure all brake fasteners, caliper bolts and banjo union bolts are tight (see *Torque settings* at the beginning of Chapter 7). Look for leaks at the hose unions and check for cracks in the hoses **(see illustration)**. Check potential areas, such as around the steering head and suspension, for hose wear.

10 Make sure the brake light operates when the front brake lever is pulled in. The front

brake light switch is located on the underside of the lever bracket **(see illustration)**. The switch is not adjustable – if it fails to operate properly, check it (see Chapter 9).

11 Make sure the brake light is activated after about 10 mm of pedal travel and just before the rear brake takes effect. On VT125C models, the switch is located behind the right-hand side panel **(see illustration)** – if adjustment is necessary, remove the panel for access (see Chapter 8). On XL125V models, the switch is located behind the right-hand

3.10 Location of the front brake light switch

3.11a Location of the rear brake light switch – VT125C models

3.11b Location of the rear brake light switch – XL125V models. Note the adjuster (arrowed)

footrest bracket **(see illustration)** – if adjustment is necessary, displace the bracket for access (see Chapter 6). Hold the switch and turn the adjuster in the retaining bracket. If the brake light comes on too late, turn the adjuster clockwise. If the brake light comes on too soon or is permanently on, turn the adjuster anti-clockwise. If the switch doesn't operate the brake light, check the bulb, the switch and the circuit (see Chapter 9).

Brake fluid change

12 The brake fluid should be changed at the specified service interval or whenever a master cylinder or caliper overhaul is carried out. Refer to Chapter 7 for details. Ensure that

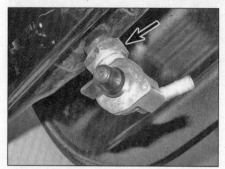

4.4 Ensure the fuel tap retaining nut is tight

all the old fluid is pumped from the system and that the level in the fluid reservoir is checked and the brakes tested before riding the motorcycle.

Brake hoses

13 The hoses will deteriorate with age and should be replaced with new ones if they show signs of hardening, cracking or abrasion (see Chapter 7).

14 Always renew the banjo union sealing washers when fitting new hoses. Refill the system with new brake fluid and bleed the system as described in Chapter 7.

Brake caliper and master cylinder seals

15 Brake system seals will deteriorate with age and lose their effectiveness. They should be replaced with new ones immediately if fluid leakage or a sticking action is apparent.

16 Renew the seals in the brake caliper as a set. Master cylinder seals are supplied as a kit along with a new piston and spring (see Chapter 6). Use all the parts supplied.

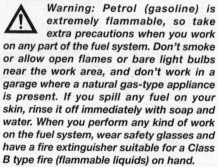

4   Fuel system

⚠️ **Warning: Petrol (gasoline) is extremely flammable, so take extra precautions when you work on any part of the fuel system. Don't smoke or allow open flames or bare light bulbs near the work area, and don't work in a garage where a natural gas-type appliance is present. If you spill any fuel on your skin, rinse it off immediately with soap and water. When you perform any kind of work on the fuel system, wear safety glasses and have a fire extinguisher suitable for a Class B type fire (flammable liquids) on hand.**

1 Remove the fuel tank (see Chapter 4A or 4B) and check the tank, the fuel hose and the tank breather hose for damage and deterioration.

2 Replace any hose that is cracked

or deteriorated with a new one. Where appropriate, secure each new hose to its unions using new clips.

3 In particular check that there are no leaks from the fuel hose unions. On models fitted with carburettors (VT125C and XL125V-1 to V-6), renew any of the hose clips if they are sprained or corroded (see Chapter 4A). On models fitted with fuel injection (XL125V-7 onwards), there are O-ring seals inside the unions – if they damaged or hardened a new fuel hose must be fitted (see Chapter 4B).

Carburettor models

4 If the fuel tap to tank joint is leaking, tightening the retaining nut may help **(see illustration)**. Hold the tap to prevent it twisting while tightening the nut. If leakage persists, renew the tap O-ring seal (see Chapter 4A).

5 Remove the air filter housing (see Chapter 4A) and inspect the carburettor assembly **(see illustration)**. Check the general condition of the throttle and choke cables (see Section 5), the carburettor heater hoses (see Section 14) and the secondary air system components (see Section 18).

6 Inspect the carburettors, particularly around the float chambers on the underside, for signs of fuel leakage. If there are any leaks, remove the carburettors and fit new seals (see Chapter 4A).

7 Cleaning and inspection of the fuel filter is advised after a particularly high mileage has been covered, although no service interval is specified. It is also necessary if fuel starvation is suspected. The filter is located on the fuel tap inside the fuel tank – remove the tap for access (see Chapter 4A).

Fuel injected models

8 If the joint between the fuel pump mounting plate and the tank is leaking, ensure the mounting bolts are tightened to the specified torque setting (see Chapter 4B). If the leak persists, remove the pump and fit a new gasket.

9 Remove the air filter housing (see Chapter 4B) and inspect the throttle body assembly **(see illustration)**. Check the general condition of the throttle cables (see Section 5), the secondary air system components

4.5 Check the carburettor assembly, cables and hoses

4.9 Check the throttle body assembly, cables, hoses and wiring

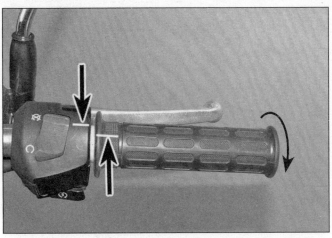

5.5 Throttle cable freeplay is measured in terms of twistgrip rotation

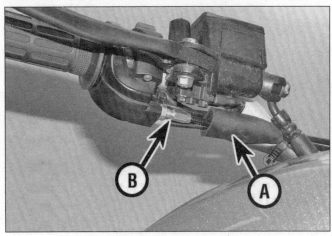

5.7 Throttle cable boot (A) and adjuster (B)

(see Section 18) and the engine management system wiring connectors (see Chapter 4B).

10 Inspect the area around the fuel injectors for signs of fuel leakage. If there are any leaks, remove the injectors and fit new seals (see Chapter 4B).

11 Cleaning of the fuel strainer is advised after a particularly high mileage has been covered, although no service interval is specified. It is also necessary if fuel starvation is suspected. The strainer is located on the end of the fuel pump assembly inside the tank – remove the pump for access (see Chapter 4B).

5   Throttle and choke cables

Throttle cables

Note: *Two cables are fitted to all models – a throttle opening and a throttle closing cable. All adjustment is made on the throttle opening cable.*

1 Make sure the throttle twistgrip rotates smoothly and freely from fully closed to fully open with the front wheel turned at various angles. The twistgrip should return automatically from fully open to fully closed when released.

2 If the throttle sticks, this is probably due to a cable fault. Remove the cables (see Chapter 4A or 4B) and lubricate them (see Section 11). Check that the inner cables slide freely in the outer cables. If not, replace the cables with new ones.

3 With the cables removed, check that the twistgrip turns smoothly around the handlebar – dirt combined with a lack of lubrication can cause the action to be stiff. Remove, clean and lightly grease the twistgrip pulley and the inside of the twistgrip housing if necessary (see Chapter 6, Section 5).

4 Install the lubricated or new cables, making sure they are correctly routed (see Chapter 4A or 4B). If this fails to improve the operation of the throttle, the fault could lie in the carburetor assembly or throttle bodies. Remove the air filter housing and check the action of the throttle pulley (see Chapter 4A or 4B).

5 With the throttle operating smoothly, check for a small amount of freeplay in the opening cable, measured in terms of the amount of twistgrip rotation before the throttle pulley begins to turn. Compare the result with the specification at the beginning of this Chapter **(see illustration)**.

6 Initial cable adjustment is made at the lower end of the cable when it is installed (see Chapter 4A or 4B). Further adjustment, when required, is made at the handlebar end as follows.

7 On XL125V models, pull back the boot to expose the cables where they connect to the throttle twistgrip **(see illustration)**.

8 Loosen the adjuster locknut, then screw the adjuster in or out as required **(see illustrations)** to obtain the correct amount of cable freeplay (see *Specifications* at the beginning of this Chapter). Tighten the locknut on completion. On XL125V models, don't forget to install the boot over the cables.

9 If the cable cannot be adjusted as specified, replace it with a new one (see Chapter 4A or 4B).

⚠ *Warning: Turn the handlebars all the way through their travel with the engine idling. Idle speed should not change. If it does, the cables may be routed incorrectly. Correct this condition before riding the bike.*

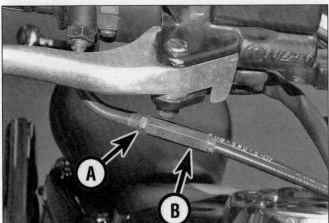

5.8a Loosen the locknut (A), then turn the adjuster (B) . . .

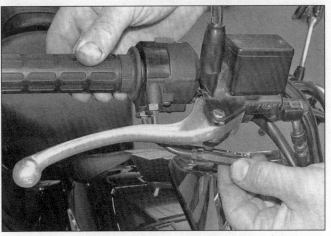

5.8b . . . to obtain the correct amount of cable freeplay

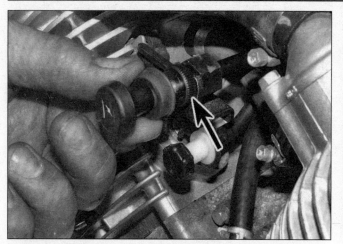

5.11 Knurled ring (arrowed) adjusts choke knob friction

6.3 Checking clutch lever freeplay

Choke cables – carburettor models

10 Manually operated choke cables are fitted – one for each carburettor, connected to the choke knob via a cable splitter.

11 The choke knob should move smoothly out and in, and should stay in the out (choke ON) position without being held **(see illustration 2.1)**. To adjust the friction on the knob, pull back the cover and screw the knurled ring clockwise to increase the friction and anti-clockwise to reduce the friction **(see illustration)**.

12 If the choke is stiff or seized, remove the cable assembly (see Chapter 4A) and lubricate it (see Section 11). Check that the inner cables slide freely in the outer cables. If not, renew the cable assembly.

13 If the choke is still stiff, the fault is in one or both of the choke plungers (see Chapter 4A).

6 Clutch cable

1 Check that the clutch lever operates smoothly and easily.

2 If the clutch lever operation is heavy or stiff, remove the cable (see Chapter 2) and lubricate it (see Section 11). If the cable is still stiff, replace it with a new one. Install the lubricated or new cable (see Chapter 2).

3 With the cable operating smoothly, check that it is correctly adjusted. Periodic adjustment is necessary to compensate for wear in the clutch plates and stretch of the cable. Check the amount of freeplay at the clutch lever ball end by pulling lightly on the lever until resistance is felt **(see illustration)**. Compare the result with the specification at the beginning of this Chapter. If required, adjust the cable as follows.

4 Initial cable adjustment is made at the lower end of the cable – ensure that the adjuster at the upper end is screwed fully into the lever bracket, then turn it out one full turn **(see illustration)**.

5 The lower cable adjuster is located in a bracket above the cover on the right-hand side of the engine **(see illustration)**. Loosen the upper or lower adjuster locknut as required, turn the opposite locknut until the specified amount of freeplay is obtained at the lever, then tighten the locknuts against the bracket. Note that the bracket itself is not threaded.

6 Subsequent adjustments can be made at the upper end of the cable when required. Loosen the adjuster lockring, then turn the adjuster in or out of the lever bracket until

the specified amount of freeplay is obtained **(see illustration 6.3)**. Don't forget to tighten the lockring. **Note:** *Ensure that the slot in the adjuster is facing downwards to prevent the ingress of water.* Ensure the slot in the adjuster is not aligned with the slot in the lever bracket. These slots are to facilitate cable removal – if they are aligned the cable could jump out while the bike is in use. Also ensure the adjuster is not threaded too far out of the handlebar bracket – this will leave it unstable and the threads could be damaged.

7 Sidestand and starter safety circuit

1 Check the stand springs – there are two, one inside the other – for damage and distortion **(see illustration)**. The springs must be capable of retracting the stand fully and holding it retracted when the motorcycle is in use. If a spring is sagged or broken it must be replaced with a new one (see Chapter 6).

2 Lubricate the stand pivot regularly (see Section 10).

3 Check the stand and its mount for bends and cracks. Stands can often be repaired by welding.

6.4 Set the handlebar end adjuster as described

6.5 Clutch cable adjuster locknuts (arrowed)

7.1 Examine the stand springs for damage

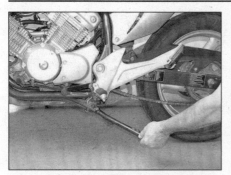

7.4 Lowering the sidestand should stop the engine

8.1 Checking the operation of the front suspension

8.2 Damage to the surface of the fork inner tubes will cause seal failure

4 Check the operation of the starter safety circuit as follows:

● Make sure the transmission is in neutral, then retract the stand and start the engine. Pull in the clutch lever and select a gear. Extend the sidestand. The engine should stop as the sidestand is extended **(see illustration)**. Turn the ignition OFF.

● Make sure the transmission is in neutral and the sidestand is down, then start the engine. Pull the clutch lever in and select a gear. The engine should stop.

● Check that when the sidestand is down the engine can only be started if the transmission is in neutral.

● Check that when the sidestand is up and the transmission is in gear the engine can only be started if the clutch lever is pulled in.

5 If the circuit does not operate as described, check the neutral switch, sidestand switch, clutch switch, diode, and the circuit wiring between them (see Chapter 9).

8 Suspension

Note: *The suspension components must be maintained in top operating condition to ensure rider safety. Loose, worn or damaged suspension parts decrease the motorcycle's stability and control.*

Front suspension check

1 While standing alongside the motorcycle, apply the front brake and push on the handlebars to compress the forks several times **(see illustration)**. See if they move up-and-down smoothly without binding. If binding is felt, the forks should be disassembled and inspected (see Chapter 6).

2 Inspect the surface of the fork inner tubes for scratches, corrosion and pitting which will cause premature seal failure **(see illustration)**. Minor blemishes can be polished out, but if the damage is excessive, new tubes should be installed (see Chapter 6).

3 Carefully lever up the dust seals using a flat-bladed screwdriver and inspect the area around the top of the fork seals. If oil leaks are evident, the fork seals must be replaced with new ones (see Chapter 6). If there is evidence of corrosion between the seal retaining ring and its groove in the fork outer tube, spray the area with a penetrative lubricant, otherwise the ring will be difficult to remove when required. Press the dust seals back into the tops of the fork outer tubes on completion.

4 Check the tightness of all suspension nuts and bolts to be sure none have worked loose, referring to the torque settings specified at the beginning of Chapter 6.

5 The front forks are not adjustable. If the suspension is poor it may be necessary to change the fork oil or renew the fork springs (see Chapter 6).

Front fork oil change

6 Although there is no specified service interval for changing the fork oil, note that the oil will degrade over a period of time and lose its damping qualities. Follow the procedure in Chapter 6 to change the fork oil. The forks do not need to be completely disassembled to change the oil.

Rear suspension check

7 Inspect the rear shock absorber(s) for fluid leaks and tightness of the mountings. If leakage is found, the shock(s) must be renewed – on VT125C models, always renew the rear shocks in pairs (see Chapter 6).

8 On XL125V models, clean the rear shock regularly and apply a corrosion inhibitor to the pre-load adjuster to prevent it seizing **(see illustration)**. Do not use a pressure washer – water will penetrate the lower shock mounting seals and corrode the bearing.

9 With the aid of an assistant to support the bike, compress the rear suspension several times. It should move up-and-down freely without binding. If any binding is felt, the worn or faulty component must be identified and checked (see Chapter 6). The problem could be caused by the shock absorber(s) or the swingarm components.

10 Support the motorcycle on an auxiliary stand so that the rear wheel is off the ground. Grasp the top of the rear wheel and pull it upwards – there should be no discernible freeplay before the shock absorber begins to compress **(see illustration)**. Any freeplay indicates a worn spring or shock absorber mountings. The worn components must be replaced with new ones (see Chapter 6).

11 Grasp the rear of the swingarm and rock it from side-to-side – there should be no discernible movement **(see illustration)**. If

8.8 Keep the pre-load adjuster clean to deter corrosion

8.10 Checking for play in the rear shock mountings

8.11 Checking for play in the swingarm bearings

8.17a Pre-load positions on VT125C rear shock

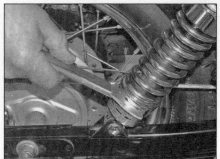

8.17b Adjusting the pre-load with a C-spanner

8.18 Location of the cam on the spring seat – pre-load position 2 (XL125V)

there's a little movement or a slight clicking can be heard, check the tightness of the swingarm pivot bolt, referring to the torque setting specified at the beginning of Chapter 6. If there is still movement with the pivot bolt tightened correctly it is likely the swingarm bearings are worn.

12 To make an accurate assessment of the swingarm bearings, first remove the rear wheel (see Chapter 7). Remove the lower shock mounting bolt(s) and secure the shock(s) clear of the swingarm (see Chapter 6).

13 Grasp the rear of the swingarm with one hand and place your other hand at the junction of the swingarm and the frame. Try to move the rear of the swingarm from side-to-side. Any wear (play) in the bearings should be felt as movement between the swingarm and the frame at the front. If there is any play the swingarm will be felt to move forward and backward at the front (not from side-to-side).

14 Next, move the swingarm up and down through its full travel. It should move freely, without any binding or rough spots.

15 If the swingarm bearings are worn or if the swingarm does not move freely, new bearings must be fitted (see Chapter 6).

Rear suspension adjustment

16 The rear shock absorbers are adjustable

for spring pre-load. Adjustment is made using a suitable C-spanner (one is provided in the bike's toolkit) to turn the spring seat on the bottom of the shock absorber.

17 On VT125C models there are five pre-load positions. Position 1 is the softest setting, position 5 is the hardest **(see illustration)**. The standard setting is position 2. Align the setting required with the arrow on the lower shock mount – to increase the pre-load, turn the spring seat anti-clockwise; to decrease the pre-load, turn the spring seat clockwise **(see illustration)**. **Note:** *Always ensure both shock absorber pre-load adjusters are adjusted equally.*

18 On XL125V models there are seven pre-load positions. Position 1 is the softest setting, position 7 is the hardest. The standard setting is position 2. Align the setting required with the cam on the spring seat – to increase the pre-load, turn the spring seat anti-clockwise; to decrease the pre-load, turn the spring seat clockwise **(see illustration)**. Do not attempt to turn the spring seat directly from setting 1 to setting 7.

Rear suspension lubrication

19 Although there is no specified service interval for lubricating the swingarm and, on XL125V models, the lower shock absorber

mounting bearing, note that any grease will gradually disperse or harden, allowing accelerated wear and the ingress of dirt and water. Periodically remove the swingarm and clean and re-grease the bearings and swingarm pivot bolt (see Chapter 6).

9 Wheels and wheel bearings

General

1 Check that any wheel balance weights are fixed firmly to the wheel rim or spokes **(see illustrations)**. If there are signs that a weight has fallen off, have the wheel rebalanced by a motorcycle tyre specialist.

2 Check the wheel runout and front/rear wheel alignment as described in Chapter 7.

Cast wheels – XL125V

3 Cast wheels are virtually maintenance free, but they should be kept clean and checked periodically for cracks and other damage. Look very closely for dents in the area where the tyre bead contacts the rim. Dents in this area may prevent complete sealing of the tyre against the rim, which leads to deflation of the tyre over a period of time.

9.1a Balance weights fixed to the wheel rim

9.1b Balance weight fixed to a wheel spoke

9.5 Checking the spoke tension by 'tone'

9.7 Spokes can be tightened with a spoke key

4 If damage is evident, or if runout in either direction is excessive, the wheel will have to be renewed. Never attempt to repair a damaged cast alloy wheel.

Wire spoked wheels – VT125C

5 Check each spoke in both wheels for looseness by tapping it gently with a small spanner or screwdriver and listening to the sound **(see illustration)**. The 'tone' of each spoke should sound the same.
6 If a spoke sounds dull or rattles, try to pull it backwards and forwards to confirm that it is loose.
7 A loose spoke can be tightened with a spoke key **(see illustration)**. Tighten the spoke carefully until the 'tone' is the same as the others.
8 If several spokes are loose it is possible that the wheel will be out of true – follow the procedure in Chapter 7 to check the radial and axial runout. If necessary, take the wheel to a wheel building expert for correction.
9 If a spoke is bent it must be replaced with a new one. First remove the tyre and check the wheel runout (see Chapter 7). If the wheel is true, undo the spoke nipple and draw the damaged spoke out from the hub, noting its alignment with adjacent spokes. Insert the new spoke through the hub and screw it into

the nipple in the wheel rim. Tighten the spoke with a spoke key (see Step 6). Make sure the new spoke doesn't protrude too far into the well of the wheel rim to cause a puncture and always ensure that the rim tape in in place to protect the inner tube from chaffing on the spoke ends.
10 If a spoke is damaged, inspect the wheel rim for damage and flat spots also.

 Warning: If you doubt your ability to change a wheel spoke, seek advise from a wheel building expert.

Wheel bearings

11 Wheel bearings will wear over a considerable mileage and should be checked periodically to avoid handling problems.
12 Support the motorcycle upright using an auxiliary stand so that the wheel being examined is off the ground. Check for any play in the bearings by pushing and pulling the wheel against the hub **(see illustrations)**. Also rotate the wheel and check that it turns smoothly and without any grating noises.
13 If any play is detected in the hub, or if the wheel does not rotate smoothly (and this is not due to brake or transmission drag), remove the wheel and inspect the bearings for wear or damage (see Chapter 7).

10 Stand and lever pivot lubrication

1 Since the components of a motorcycle are exposed to the elements, they should be checked and lubricated periodically to ensure safe and trouble-free operation.
2 The clutch and brake lever pivots, footrest pivots, brake pedal and gearchange lever linkages and stand pivots should be cleaned, inspected and lubricated. In order for the lubricant to be applied where it will do the most good, the component should be disassembled (see Chapter 6).
3 The lubricant recommended by Honda for each application is listed at the beginning of this Chapter. If a dry-film aerosol lubricant is used, it can be applied to the pivot joint gaps and will usually work its way into the areas where friction occurs, so less disassembly of the component is needed (however it is always better to do so and clean off all corrosion, dirt and old lubricant first).
4 If motor oil or light grease is being used, apply it sparingly as it may attract dirt (which could cause the controls to bind or wear at an accelerated rate).

11 Cable lubrication

Special tool: *A cable lubricating adapter is necessary for this procedure (see Step 3).*
1 Cable lubrication not only ensures smooth operation of the cable, but prevents wear and deters corrosion.
2 Disconnect the cable at its upper end – see Chapter 2 for the clutch cable removal procedure and Chapter 4A or 4B for the throttle and choke cables.
3 Attach the pressure adapter and aerosol

9.12a Checking for play in the front wheel bearings

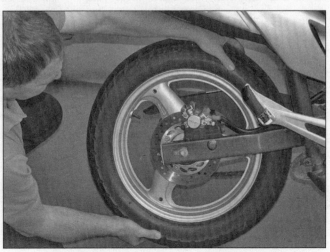

9.12b Checking for play in the rear wheel bearings

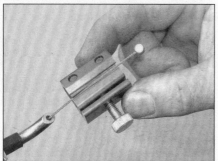

11.3a Fitting the adapter onto the inner cable

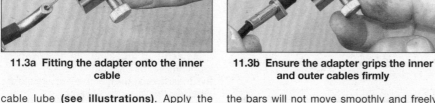

11.3b Ensure the adapter grips the inner and outer cables firmly

11.3c Connect the can of cable lubricant to the adapter

cable lube **(see illustrations)**. Apply the lubricant – if the adapter leaks, check the installation of the cable and ensure the adapter is tightened securely.

4 On completion, check the operation of the cable and adjust the freeplay as specified – see Section 5 (throttle and choke cables) and 6 (clutch cable).

12 Steering head bearings

Freeplay check and adjustment

1 Steering head bearings can become dented, rough or loose over a period of time, especially if the machine has bumped up against curbs for example. In extreme cases, worn or loose steering head bearings can cause steering wobble – a condition that is potentially dangerous.

Check

2 Raise the front wheel off the ground using an auxiliary stand placed under the engine. Always make sure that the bike is properly supported and secure.

3 Point the front wheel straight-ahead and slowly move the handlebars from lock to lock. Any dents or roughness in the bearing races will be felt and if the bearings are too tight

the bars will not move smoothly and freely. If the bearings are damaged they should be replaced with new ones (see Chapter 6). If the bearings are too tight, adjust them as described below.

4 If available, attach one end of a spring balance to one of the fork inner tubes, midway between the top and bottom yokes – note that on XL125V models it will first be necessary to remove the fairing (see Chapter 8). With the steering pointing straight-ahead, hold the spring balance at right angles to the forks and pull **(see illustration)**. Note the reading at which the steering starts to turn and compare the result to the specification for steering head bearing pre-load at the beginning of this Chapter. If the result is below the minimum value specified, the steering head bearings are too loose; if the result is higher than the maximum value specified, the bearings are too tight. If required, adjust the bearings as described below.

5 Next, grasp the bottom of the forks and try to move them forwards and backwards **(see illustration)**. Any looseness or freeplay in the steering head bearings will be felt as front-to-rear movement of the forks. If play is felt, adjust the bearings as described below.

Adjustment

Special tool: *A C-spanner will be required to locate in the notches of the bearing adjuster nut (see Step 9).*

HAYNES HiNT *Make sure you are not mistaking any movement between the bike and stand, or between the stand and the ground, for freeplay in the bearings. Do not pull and push the forks too hard – a gentle movement is all that is needed. Freeplay between the fork tubes due to worn bushes can also be misinterpreted as steering head bearing play – do not confuse the two.*

6 On XL125V models, if not already done, remove the fairing (see Chapter 8). On all models, remove the fuel tank (see Chapter 4A or 4B).

7 Loosen the steering stem nut and both fork clamp bolts in the top yoke **(see illustration)**.

12.4 Checking steering head bearing pre-load

12.5 Checking for play in the steering head bearings

12.7 Steering stem nut (A) and fork clamp bolt (B)

12.9a Steering head bearing adjuster (arrowed)

12.9b Using a C-spanner to adjust the bearings

13.3 Pull the cap off the spark plug

Access to the steering stem nut is restricted – if required, displace the handlebars (see Chapter 6).

8 Raise the front wheel off the ground (see Step 2).

9 Using a C-spanner (the rear shock spring pre-load adjuster spanner in the bike's toolkit is ideal), turn the adjuster clockwise to tighten the head bearings or anti-clockwise to loosen them **(see illustrations)**. Move the adjuster a small amount at a time, then check the freeplay before making further adjustments. The object is to set the adjuster so that any freeplay in the bearings is removed, not to tighten it so that the steering does not move freely from side-to-side. If you have a spring balance, check the pre-load as described in Step 4.

Caution: Take great care not to apply excessive pressure because this will cause premature failure of the bearings.

10 Once the bearings seem to be correctly adjusted, turn the steering from lock to lock several times to settle the bearings, then recheck the adjustment.

11 If the bearings cannot be correctly adjusted, disassemble the steering head and check the bearings and races for wear (see Chapter 6).

12 With the bearings correctly adjusted, tighten the steering stem nut, then the fork clamp bolts, to the torque settings specified at the beginning of this chapter **(see illustration 12.7)**. If applicable, install the handlebars.

13 Install the remaining components in the reverse order of removal.

Lubrication

14 Although there is no specified service interval for lubricating the steering head bearings, note that any grease will gradually disperse or harden, allowing accelerated wear and the ingress of dirt and water. Periodically remove the steering stem and clean and re-grease the bearings (see Chapter 6).

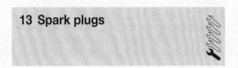

13 Spark plugs

Removal

1 Make sure your spark plug socket is the correct size (16 mm) before attempting to remove the plugs – a suitable one is supplied in the motorcycle's tool kit which is stored under the seat.

2 On XL125V models, access to the front spark plug is restricted. If required, remove the trim clips securing the right-hand side of the fairing inner panel, undo the lower fairing mounting bolt and release the peg on the inside of the fairing from the grommet on the lower edge of the fuel tank (see Chapter 8). The right-hand side of the fairing can now be eased out to gain access to the plug.

3 Pull the cap off the spark plug **(see illustration)**.

4 Clean the area around the base of the plug to prevent any dirt falling into the engine.

5 Using either the plug socket supplied in the bike's toolkit or a deep spark plug socket, unscrew and remove the plug from the cylinder head **(see illustrations)**.

Check

6 New spark plugs should be fitted at the specified service interval. However, if a running problem develops between services, check the plugs as follows.

7 Remember which plug goes in which cylinder; if either plug shows up a problem it will then be easy to identify the troublesome cylinder.

8 Make sure the plugs are the correct type and heat range as specified at the beginning of this Chapter.

9 Look for excessive deposits and evidence of a cracked or chipped insulator around the centre electrode. Compare your spark plugs to the colour spark plug reading chart on the inside rear cover. Inspect the ceramic insulator body for cracks and other damage. Check the threads and the sealing washer.

10 Clean each plug with a wire brush. Examine the tips of the electrodes; if a tip has rounded off, the plug is worn. Measure the gap between the two electrodes using a feeler gauge or a wire type gauge **(see illustration)**. The gap should be as given in the specifications at the beginning of this Chapter

13.5a Using the bike's plug socket . . .

13.5b . . . to unscrew the spark plug

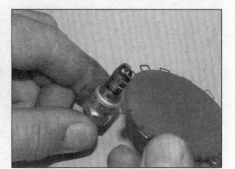

13.10a Using a wire type gauge to measure the spark plug gap

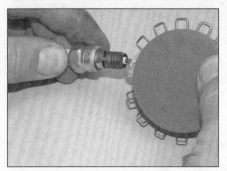
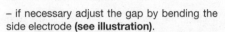

13.10b Bend the side electrode to adjust the gap

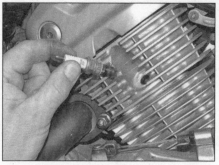

13.14 Thread the plug in by hand to avoid cross-threading

13.16 Push the caps down firmly onto the plugs

– if necessary adjust the gap by bending the side electrode **(see illustration)**.

11 If either plug is worn or damaged, or if any deposits cannot be cleaned off, renew both plugs.

Installation

12 Always install the correct type and heat range of spark plug for your machine (see *Specifications* at the beginning of this Chapter).

13 Check the gap between the electrodes (see Step 10) and make sure the sealing washer is in place on the plug.

14 Thread the plug into the cylinder head until the washer seats. Since the cylinder head is made of aluminium, which is soft and easily damaged,

thread the plug as far as possible by hand **(see illustration)**. Once the plug is finger-tight, the job can be finished with the spark plug socket **(see illustration 13.5a and b)**.

15 If a torque wrench is available, tighten the spark plugs to the torque setting specified at the beginning of this Chapter. Otherwise, tighten them according the instructions on the box – generally if new plugs are being used, tighten them by 1/2 a turn after the washer has seated, and if the old plugs are being reused, tighten them by 1/8 to 1/4 turn after they have seated. Do not over-tighten the spark plugs.

16 Fit the spark plug caps, making sure they locate correctly onto the plugs **(see illustration)**.

17 On XL125V models, if applicable, secure the right-hand side of the fairing (see Chapter 8).

> **HAYNES HINT** *Stripped plug threads in the cylinder head can be repaired with a Heli-Coil wire thread insert – see 'Tools and Workshop Tips' in the Reference Section.*

14 Cooling system

> ⚠ *Warning: The engine must be cool before beginning this procedure.*

1 Check the coolant level in the reservoir (see *Pre-ride checks*).

2 Remove the fuel tank (see Chapter 4A or 4B). On VT125C models, remove the right-hand engine cover **(see illustrations)**. On XL125V models, remove the fairing (see Chapter 8).

3 Check the cooling system for evidence of leaks. Examine each coolant hose along its entire length. The hoses will deteriorate with age – look for cracks, abrasions and other damage. Squeeze the hoses at various points to see whether they are dried out or hard **(see illustration)**. They should feel firm, yet pliable, and return to their original shape when released. If necessary, replace them with new ones (see Chapter 3).

4 Check for evidence of leaks at each cooling system joint, including the pipe elbows

14.2a Undo the screws (arrowed) . . .

14.2b . . . and remove the cover – VT125C

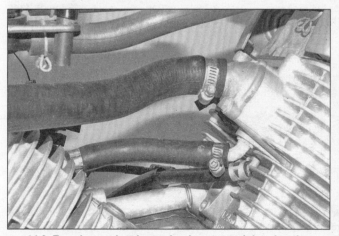

14.3 Examine coolant hoses for damage and deterioration

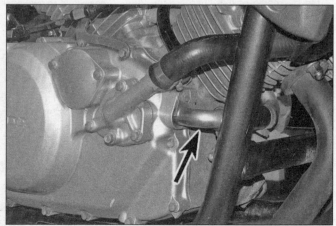

14.4 Check the pipe elbow (arrowed) joints for leaks

14.6 Check the water pump cover for leaks

14.7a Water pump drain hole – VT125C

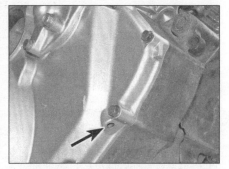

14.7b Water pump drain hole – XL125V

between the front cylinder and the right-hand crankcase cover **(see illustration)**, and the pipe between the front and rear cylinders **(see illustration 14.3)**. Where fitted, tighten the hose clips carefully to prevent future leaks. If any of the pipe unions is leaking, new O-rings will have to be fitted (see Chapter 3).

5 On models fitted with carburettors (VT125C and XL125V-1 to V-6), check the carburettor heater system for evidence of leaks (see Chapter 4A).

6 Check the water pump cover on the right-hand side of the engine **(see illustration)**. If the cover is leaking, check that the bolts are tight. If they are, remove the cover and replace the seal with a new one (see Chapter 3).

7 The water pump housing is integral with the right-hand crankcase cover. To prevent leakage of coolant from the cooling system to the lubrication system and vice versa, two seals are fitted on the pump shaft. On the front of the crankcase cover, below the pump, there is a drain hole **(see illustrations)**. If either seal fails, the drain allows the coolant or oil to escape and prevents them mixing. The outer seal on the pump shaft is a mechanical-type water seal which bears on the rear face of the impeller. The inner seal, which is mounted behind the water seal, is a conventional feathered-lip oil seal. If on inspection the drain shows signs of leakage, remove the pump and renew the seals (see Chapter 3).

8 Check the radiator for leaks and damage **(see illustration)**. Leaks leave tell-tale scale deposits or coolant stains on the outside of the core below the leak. If leaks are noted, remove the

radiator (see Chapter 3) and have it repaired or replace it with a new one – do not use a liquid leak stopping compound to try to repair leaks.

9 Check the fins for mud, dirt and insects, which may impede the flow of air through the radiator core. If the fins are clogged, remove the radiator (see Chapter 3) and clean it using water or low pressure compressed air directed through the fins from the back – remove the cooling fan first, if necessary. If the fins are bent or distorted, straighten them carefully with a screwdriver **(see illustration)**. If airflow is restricted by bent or damaged fins over more than 20% of the radiator's surface area, replace the radiator with a new one.

> ⚠ **Warning: Do not remove the pressure cap when the engine is hot. Even when the engine has cooled, it is good practice to cover the cap with a heavy cloth and turn the cap slowly anti-clockwise. If you hear a**

hissing sound (*indicating that there is still pressure in the system*), *wait until it stops, then continue turning the cap until it can be removed.*

10 Remove the pressure cap from the radiator filler neck by undoing the locking screw, then turning the cap anti-clockwise until it reaches the stop **(see illustrations)**. Now press down on the cap and continue turning it until it can be removed **(see illustrations)**. Check the cap seal for cracks and other damage. If in doubt about the pressure cap's condition, have it tested by a Honda dealer or fit a new one.

11 The coolant should be level with the lower edge of the radiator filler neck. Check the condition of the coolant. If it is rust-coloured or if accumulations of scale are visible, drain, flush and refill the system with new coolant (see Chapter 3).

12 Check the antifreeze content of the coolant with an antifreeze hydrometer (**see

14.8 Examine the radiator for leaks and damage

14.9 Radiator fins can be straightened with a small screwdriver

14.10a Undo the locking screw (arrowed) . . .

14.10b . . . then turn the cap anti-clockwise

14.10c Press down and turn to release the cap

illustration). If the system has not been topped-up with the correct coolant mixture (see *Pre-ride checks*) the coolant will be too weak to offer adequate protection. If the hydrometer indicates a weak mixture, drain, flush and refill the system (see Chapter 3).

13 If necessary, top the radiator up with the recommended coolant mixture. Fit the radiator cap by turning it clockwise until it reaches the first stop then push down on it and continue turning until it can turn no further. Don't forget to tighten the locking screw **(see illustration 14.10a)**.

14 Start the engine and let it reach normal operating temperature, then check for leaks again. As the coolant temperature increases, the electric fan (mounted on the back of the radiator) should come on automatically and the temperature should begin to drop. If it does not, refer to Chapter 3 and check the fan and appropriate fan circuit.

15 If the coolant level is consistently low, and no evidence of leaks can be found, have the entire system pressure checked by a Honda dealer.

15 Nuts and bolts

1 Since vibration of the machine tends to loosen fasteners, all nuts, bolts, screws, etc. should be periodically checked for proper tightness.
2 Pay particular attention to the following, referring to the relevant Chapter:
● *Exhaust system bolts/nuts*
● *Engine mounting bolts*
● *Engine oil and coolant drain bolts*
● *Spark plugs*
● *Front axle and axle clamp bolt*
● *Rear axle nut and split pin*
● *Front sprocket bolts and rear sprocket nuts*
● *Handlebar clamp bolts*
● *Lever and pedal bolts*
● *Brake caliper and master cylinder mounting bolts*
● *Brake hose banjo bolts and caliper bleed valves*

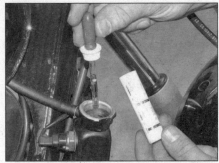

14.12 Checking the coolant with an antifreeze hydrometer

● *Brake disc bolts*
● *Front fork clamp bolts (top and bottom yoke)*
● *Steering stem bolt*
● *Swingarm pivot bolt*
● *Shock absorber and mounting bolts*
● *Footrest and sidestand bolts*

3 If a torque wrench is available, use it together with the torque settings given at the beginning of this and other Chapters.

16 Engine oil and filter

⚠ *Warning: Be careful when draining the oil, as the exhaust pipe, the engine, and the oil itself can cause severe burns.*

1 Regular oil changes are the single most important maintenance procedure you can perform. The oil not only lubricates the internal parts of the engine, transmission and clutch, but it also acts as a coolant, a cleaner, a sealant, and a protector. Because of these demands, the oil takes a terrific amount of abuse and should be replaced as specified with new oil of the recommended grade and type.
2 Before changing the oil, warm up the engine so the oil will drain easily. Support the bike on its sidestand on level ground.
3 Position a drain tray below the engine – the

16.3 Location of the oil drain plug

> **HAYNES HINT** *Saving a little money on the difference in cost between a good oil and a cheap oil won't pay off if the engine is damaged*

oil drain plug is on the underside of the engine on the left-hand side **(see illustration)**.
4 Unscrew the oil filler cap to vent the crankcase and to act as a reminder that there is no oil in the engine (see *Pre-ride checks*).
5 Unscrew the drain plug and allow the oil to drain into the tray **(see illustration)**. Note the location of the sealing washer on the drain plug and discard it as a new one must be fitted – you may have to cut the old one off **(see illustration)**.

> **HAYNES HINT** *To help determine whether any abnormal or excessive engine wear is occurring, place a strainer between the engine and the drain tray so that any debris in the oil is filtered out and can be examined. If there are flakes or chips of metal in the oil or on the drain plug magnet, then something is drastically wrong internally and the engine will have to be disassembled for inspection and repair. If there are pieces of fibre-like material in the oil, the clutch is wearing excessively and should be checked.*

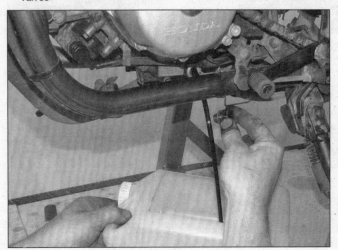

16.5a Drain the oil into a suitable tray

16.5b The sealing washer may need to be cut off

16.6 Always use a new sealing washer on the drain plug

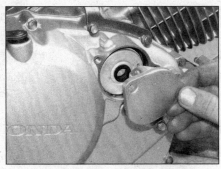

16.8 Remove the oil filter cover

16.9a Draw out the filter element . . .

16.9b . . . and the spring

16.10 Ensure the filter element is fitted correctly

Note: It is illegal and anti-social to dump oil down the drain. To find the location of your local oil recycling bank in the UK, call 03708 506 506 or visit www.oilbankline.org.uk

6 When the oil has completely drained, install the drain plug using a new sealing washer and tighten it to the torque setting specified at the beginning of this Chapter **(see illustration)**. Do not overtighten it as the threads in the crankcase are easily damaged.

7 On VT125C models, undo the bolts securing the right-hand engine cover and remove the cover **(see illustrations 14.2a and b)**.

8 Place the drain tray below the oil filter cover, then undo the bolts securing the cover and remove it **(see illustration)**. Discard the O-ring as a new one must be fitted.

9 Draw out the filter element, noting how it fits, and spring **(see illustrations)**.

10 Wipe any residual oil out of the filter housing with a clean cloth, then install the spring and the new filter element, making sure it is the correct way round **(see illustration)**.

11 Install a new O-ring on the filter cover, ensuring it is located in its groove **(see illustrations)**. Lubricate the O-ring with a smear of engine oil.

12 Install the cover and tighten the bolts securely. On VT125C models, install the right-hand engine cover.

13 Refill the engine to the correct level using the recommended grade and type of oil (see *Pre-ride checks*). Check the

condition of the O-ring on the filler cap and renew it if necessary. Install the filler cap securely.

14 Start the engine and let it run for two or three minutes. Shut it off, wait a few minutes, then check the oil level. If necessary, add more oil to bring it up to the correct level.

15 Check around the drain plug for leaks.

16 The old oil drained from the engine cannot be re-used and should be disposed of properly. Check with your local refuse disposal company, disposal facility or environmental agency to see whether they will accept the used oil for recycling. Don't pour used oil into drains or onto the ground.

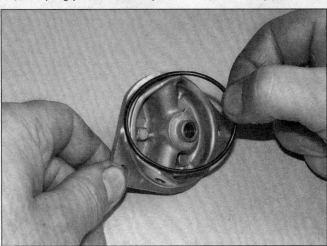

16.11a Install a new O-ring . . .

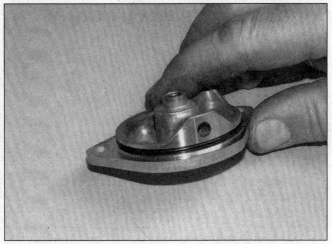

16.11b . . . into the groove in the cover

17.4a Unscrew the timing inspection cap . . .

17.4b . . . and the centre cap from the cover

17 Valve clearances

Special tool: *A set of feeler gauges is necessary for this job (see Step 8).*

1 The engine must be completely cool for this

maintenance procedure, so let the bike stand overnight before beginning.

2 Remove the front and rear cylinder valve covers (see Chapter 2).

3 Remove the spark plugs (see Section 13).

4 Unscrew the timing inspection cap and the centre cap from the alternator cover on the left-hand side of the engine **(see illustrations)**.

17.5 Turn the engine in an anti-clockwise direction

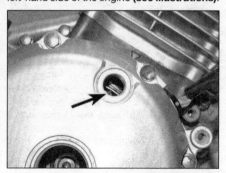

17.6a Location of the static timing mark

Note the location of the O-rings and discard them if they are damaged or distorted.

5 To check the valve clearances the engine must be turned to position the appropriate piston at top dead centre (TDC) on its compression stroke – at this point both valves for that cylinder will be closed. The engine can be turned using a suitable socket on the alternator nut and turning it in an anti-clockwise direction **(see illustration)**.

6 Check the valves for the rear cylinder first. Turn the engine anti-clockwise until the line next to the RT mark on the alternator rotor aligns with the static timing mark – the arrow in the timing inspection hole **(see illustrations)**. The rear piston will now be at TDC. Check for a small amount of freeplay in both rocker arms on the rear cylinder head i.e. they are not in direct contact with the valve stems **(see illustration)**.

7 If the exhaust rocker arm is in contact with the valve stem, the piston is TDC on its exhaust stroke. Turn the engine anti-clockwise

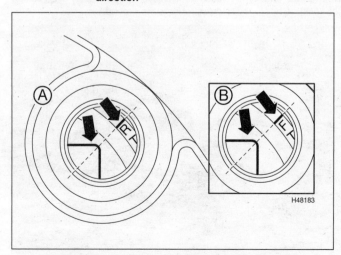

17.6b Timing mark alignment for rear cylinder (A) and front cylinder (B)

17.6c Check for freeplay in both rocker arms

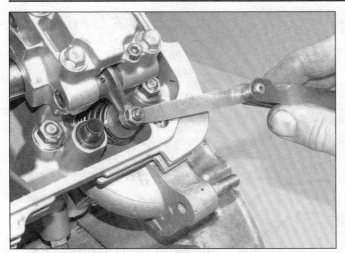

17.8 Checking the valve clearance with a feeler gauge

17.9a Valve adjuster locknut (arrowed)

one full turn (360°) until the line next to the RT mark again aligns with the static timing mark. The piston is now at TDC on its compression stroke and there should be freeplay in the rockers.

8 Check the clearance of each valve by inserting a feeler gauge of the same thickness as the correct valve clearance (see *Specifications* at the beginning of this Chapter) in the gap between the rocker arm and the valve stem **(see illustration)**. The exhaust valve is on the back of the cylinder head and the intake valve is on the front. If the clearance is correct, the gauge should be a firm sliding fit – you should feel a slight drag when you pull the gauge out. **Note:** *The intake and exhaust valve clearances are different.*

9 If the clearance is either too large or too small, slacken the locknut on the adjuster in the rocker arm **(see illustration)**. Using a screwdriver, turn the adjuster until the gap is as specified, then hold the adjuster still and

tighten the locknut **(see illustration)**. Recheck the clearance after tightening the locknut.

10 Now turn the engine anti-clockwise one full turn plus a further 90° (450° in total) so that the line next to the FT mark on the alternator rotor aligns with the static timing mark. The front piston will now be at TDC on its compression stroke – follow the procedure above to check the valves for the front cylinder, noting that the exhaust valve is on the front of the cylinder head and the intake valve is on the rear.

11 When the clearances are correct install the valve covers (see Chapter 2)

12 Install the timing inspection cap and the centre cap using new O-rings if required **(see illustration)**. Smear the O-rings with engine oil and tighten the caps to the torque settings specified at the beginning of this Chapter.

13 Install the remaining components in the reverse order of removal.

14 On completion, on models fitted with carburettors, check and adjust the idle speed (see Section 2).

18 Secondary air system

Carburettor models – VT125C and XL125V-1 to V-6

Description

1 To reduce the amount of unburned hydrocarbons released in the exhaust gases, a secondary air supply system is fitted. The system consists of the control valve (mounted under the fuel tank), the reed valves (fitted in the valve covers) and the hoses linking them.

2 Negative pressure pulses in the exhaust system draw filtered air through the control valve and the reed valves into the exhaust ports. The air mixes with the exhaust gases, causing any unburned particles of fuel to be burnt in the exhaust port/pipe. This process changes a considerable amount of

17.9b Adjust the valve clearance as described

17.12 Fit new O-rings if required

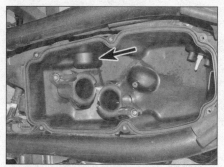

18.5 Location of the air supply hose port
– XL125V

18.6a Check the condition of the hoses
and hose clips – VT125C

18.6b Check the condition of the hoses
and hose clips – XL125V

18.7a Location of the air supply hose –
VT125C

hydrocarbons and carbon monoxide into relatively harmless carbon dioxide and water.

3 The reed valves prevent the reverse flow of exhaust gases back up the cylinder head passages and into the control valve and air filter housing.

4 The control valve is actuated by high intake vacuum in the cylinder head side of the rear carburettor bore. During engine deceleration, when the throttle is closed, the valve shuts off the air supply to the exhaust ports, preventing backfiring in the exhaust system.

Check

5 To ensure that the system is operating correctly, on VT125C models remove the carburettor cover (see Chapter 4A, Section 4). On XL125V models, remove the top of the air filter housing and lift out the filter element (see Section 19). Check that the port for the air supply hose is clean **(see illustration)** – if there are carbon deposits around the port, one or both of the reed valves is not closing fully (see Chapter 2, Section 11). Note that on VT125C models, the port for the air supply hose is in the carburettor cover **(see illustration 18.7a)**.

6 Check that the hoses are not kinked or pinched, are in good condition and are securely connected at each end **(see illustration)**.

Renew any hoses that are cracked, split or generally deteriorated.

7 If the control valve is thought to be faulty, reassemble the carburettor cover and air filter housing if applicable, then disconnect the air supply hose from the carburettor cover/air filter housing **(see illustrations)**. Angle the open end of the hose downwards. Lower the fuel tank. Start the engine, open the throttle slightly and check that air is being drawn into the open end of the hose. Now close the throttle – the air flow should stop. If not, check the operation of the control valve (see Chapter 4A).

Fuel injected models – XL125V-7 onwards

Description

8 The system performs the same function as on carburettor models (see above), the only difference being that the control valve is actuated by a solenoid which, in turn, is activated by the electronic control unit (ECM).

Check

9 To ensure that the system is operating correctly, remove the air filter element (see Section 19). Check that the port for the air supply hose is clean – if there are carbon deposits around the port, one or both of the reed valves is not closing fully (see Chapter 2, Section 11).

10 Check that the hoses are not kinked or pinched, are in good condition and are securely connected at each end **(see illustration 18.6b)**. Renew any hoses that are cracked, split or generally deteriorated.

11 Disconnect the air supply hose from the air filter housing **(see illustration)** and angle the open end of the hose downwards. Install the air filter element and lower the fuel tank. Start the engine, open the throttle slightly and check that air is being drawn into the open end of the hose. Now close the throttle – the air flow should stop. If not, check the operation of the control valve (see Chapter 4B).

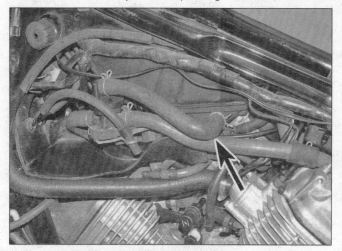

18.7b Location of the air supply hose – XL125V

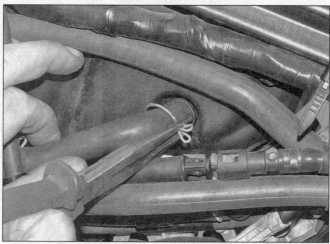

18.11 Release the clip and disconnect the hose

19.1a Undo the screw . . .

19.1b . . . and remove the chrome trim

19.1c Undo the screws (arrowed) . . .

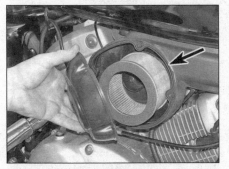

19.1d . . . and lift off the filter cover, noting the seal (arrowed)

19.2 Withdraw the air filter element

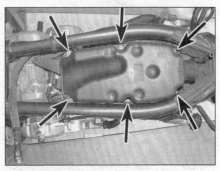

19.8 Screws (arrowed) secure air filter cover

19 Air filter

Note: *The paper filter elements fitted to the machines covered in this manual are treated with a dust adhesive and cannot be cleaned. If the machine is continually ridden in wet or dusty conditions, the filter should be changed more frequently.*

VT125C models

1 Undo the screw securing the filter cover trim and remove it, then undo the screws securing the filter cover and lift it off **(see illustrations)**.
2 Draw out the filter element, noting how it fits **(see illustration)**.
3 Note the location of the cover seal and renew it if it is damaged or deteriorated **(see illustration 19.1d)**.
4 Clean the inside of the filter housing and cover. Check that the housing is securely attached via the air intake elbow to the carburettor cover – if necessary, remove the fuel tank (see Chapter 4A) to ensure all the fixings are secure.
5 Install the new filter element, making sure it is properly seated, then fit the cover and secure it with its screws **(see illustrations 19.1d and c)**.
6 Fit the cover trim.

XL125V models

7 Remove the fuel tank on V-1 to V-6 models (see Chapter 4A). Raise and support the fuel tank on V-7 models onward (see Chapter 4B).
8 Undo the screws securing the air filter cover and lift it off **(see illustration)**.

9 Lift out the filter element from the housing, noting how it fits **(see illustration)**.
10 Clean the inside of the filter housing and cover. Check that the housing is securely attached to the carburettor assembly (XL125V-1 to V-6 models) or throttle body

assembly (XL125V-7 onwards) as applicable **(see illustrations)**.
11 Install the new filter element, making sure it is properly seated **(see illustration)**. Fit the cover and secure it with its screws.
12 Install/lower the fuel tank.

19.9 Lift out the filter element

19.10a Check that the housing is securely attached to the carburettor assembly

19.10b Check that the housing is securely attached to the throttle body assembly

19.11 Ensure the filter element is fitted correctly – underside shown

20.4 Vacuum port blanking screw (arrowed)

20.5 Secondary air system hose connection (arrowed)

20.6 Connect the vacuum gauges to the vacuum ports

20 Carburettor synchronisation – VT125C and XL125V-1 to V-6

⚠ **Warning: Petrol (gasoline) is extremely flammable, so take extra precautions when you work on any part of the fuel system.** Don't smoke or allow open flames or bare light bulbs near the work area, and don't work in a garage where a natural gas-type appliance is present. If you spill any fuel on your skin, rinse it off immediately with soap and water. When you perform any kind of work on the fuel system, wear safety glasses and have a fire extinguisher suitable for a Class B type fire (flammable liquids) on hand.

⚠ **Warning: Take great care not to burn your hand on the hot engine unit when accessing the gauge take-off points on the intake manifolds.** Do not allow exhaust gases to build up in the work area; either perform the check outside or use an exhaust gas extraction system.

Special tools: *A pair vacuum gauges or manometer and an adapter for the front cylinder vacuum port are necessary for this job (see Step 6). An angled screwdriver with flexible drive is required to adjust the synchronising screw (see Step 9).*

1 Carburettor synchronisation is simply the process of adjusting the carburettors so they pass the same amount of fuel/air mixture to each cylinder. This is done by measuring the vacuum produced in each cylinder. Carburettors that are out of synchronisation will result in decreased fuel mileage, increased engine temperature, less than ideal throttle response and higher vibration levels. Before synchronising the carburettors, make sure the valve clearances are correct.

2 The equipment used should come complete with the necessary adapter and hoses to fit the carburettor vacuum ports.

3 Support the machine upright on level ground using an auxiliary stand. Start the engine and let it run until it reaches normal operating temperature, then shut it off.

4 Remove the blanking screw from the vacuum port on the right-hand side of the front carburettor **(see illustration)**. Install the take-off adapter provided with the vacuum gauges or manometer.

5 Disconnect the secondary air system vacuum hose from the vacuum port on the left-hand side of the rear carburettor **(see illustration)**.

6 Connect the vacuum gauge or manometer hoses to the vacuum ports of both cylinders **(see illustration)**. Make sure the hoses are a good fit because any air leaks will result in false readings.

7 Start the engine and make sure the idle speed is correct (see Section 2). If using vacuum gauges, set their damping adjustment so that the needle flutter is just eliminated but so that they can still respond to small changes in pressure.

8 The vacuum readings for both cylinders should be the same, or at least within the tolerance listed in this Chapter's *Specifications*. If the vacuum readings vary, adjust the carburettors as follows. **Note:** *Incorrect valve clearances (see Section 17) and poor cylinder compression (see Chapter 2, Section 3) will affect the vacuum readings).*

9 The carburettors are adjusted by turning the synchronising screw situated on the right-hand side of the rear carburettor **(see illustration)**. To avoid pressing on the screw and giving a false vacuum reading, use the angled screwdriver with flexible drive as shown **(see illustrations)**. This tool is designed for pilot air screw adjustment, but is equally suitable for adjusting the synchronising screw due to its restricted location.

10 When the carburettors are synchronised, open and close the throttle quickly to settle the linkage, and recheck the gauge readings, readjusting if necessary.

11 When the adjustment is complete, check the idle speed and adjust as required (see Section 2), then stop the engine.

12 Remove the test equipment. Remove the adapter from the front carburettor vacuum port and fit the blanking screw. Connect the secondary air system vacuum hose to the vacuum port on the rear carburettor.

20.9a Location of the synchronisng screw (arrowed)

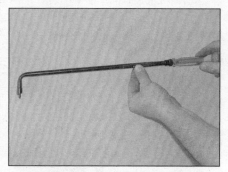

20.9b Use this special screwdriver . . .

20.9c . . . to adjust the carburettor synchronisation

Chapter 2
Engine, clutch and transmission

Contents

Degrees of difficulty

Easy, suitable for novice with little experience	**Fairly easy,** suitable for beginner with some experience	**Fairly difficult,** suitable for competent DIY mechanic	**Difficult,** suitable for experienced DIY mechanic	**Very difficult,** suitable for expert DIY or professional

Specifications

General

Type	Four-stroke V-twin
Capacity	125 cc
Bore	42.0 mm
Stroke	45.0 mm
Compression ratio	11.8 to 1
Cylinder compression	227 psi (16.0 Bar)
Cooling system	Liquid-cooled
Lubrication	Wet sump, trochoid pump
Clutch	Wet multi-plate
Transmission	Five-speed constant mesh
Final drive	Chain and sprockets

Camshafts and followers

Intake lobe height
    Standard . . . .   28.853 to 29.093 mm
    Service limit (min) . . . .   28.82 mm
Exhaust lobe height
    Standard . . . .   28.885 to 29.125 mm
    Service limit (min) . . . .   28.85 mm
Rocker arm bore diameter
    Standard . . . .   10.000 to 10.015 mm
    Service limit (max) . . . .   10.05 mm
Rocker arm shaft diameter
    Standard . . . .   9.972 to 9.987 mm
    Service limit (min) . . . .   9.92 mm
Rocker arm-to-shaft clearance
    Standard . . . .   0.013 to 0.043 mm
    Service limit (max) . . . .   0.10 mm

Cylinder head

Warpage (max) . . . .   0.05 mm

Valves, guides and springs

Valve clearances . . . .   see Chapter 1
Stem diameter
    Intake valve
        Standard . . . .   4.975 to 4.990 mm
        Service limit (min) . . . .   4.965 mm
    Exhaust valve
        Standard . . . .   4.955 to 4.970 mm
        Service limit (min) . . . .   4.945 mm
Guide bore diameter – intake and exhaust valves
    Standard . . . .   5.000 to 5.012 mm
    Service limit (max) . . . .   5.030 mm
Stem-to-guide clearance
    Intake valve
        Standard . . . .   0.010 to 0.037 mm
        Service limit . . . .   0.065 mm
    Exhaust valve
        Standard . . . .   0.030 to 0.057 mm
        Service limit . . . .   0.085 mm
Seat width – intake and exhaust valves
    Standard . . . .   0.90 to 1.10 mm
    Service limit (max) . . . .   1.50 mm
Valve guide height above cylinder head . . . .   12.10 mm
Valve spring free length
    VT125C-X to C-3 – intake valves
        Standard . . . .   38.0 mm
        Service limit (min) . . . .   36.5 mm
    VT125C-X to C-3 – exhaust valves
        Standard . . . .   38.51 mm
        Service limit (min) . . . .   37.0 mm
    VT125C-4 and all XL125V – intake and exhaust valves
        Standard . . . .   38.0 mm
        Service limit (min) . . . .   36.5 mm

Cylinder

Bore
    Standard . . . .   42.000 to 42.015 mm
    Service limit (max) . . . .   42.10 mm
Ovality (out-of-round) (max) . . . .   0.06 mm
Taper (max) . . . .   0.06 mm
Warpage (max) . . . .   0.05 mm

Piston

Piston diameter (see text)
Standard	41.97 to 41.99 mm
Service limit (min)	41.90 mm

Piston-to-bore clearance
Standard	0.010 to 0.040 mm
Service limit	0.10 mm
With oversize piston (after rebore)	
VT125C and XL125V-1 to V-6	0.020 to 0.060 mm
XL125V-7 onwards	0.010 to 0.045 mm

Piston pin diameter
Standard	12.994 to 13.000 mm
Service limit (min)	12.98 mm

Piston pin bore diameter in piston
Standard	13.002 to 13.008 mm
Service limit (max)	13.04 mm

Piston-to-piston pin clearance
Standard	0.002 to 0.014 mm
Service limit	0.04 mm

Piston rings

Ring end gap (installed)
Top ring	
Standard	0.05 to 0.15 mm
Service limit (max)	0.30 mm
Second ring	
Standard	0.20 to 0.35 mm
Service limit (max)	0.50 mm
Oil ring side-rail	
Standard	0.10 to 0.60 mm
Service limit (max)	0.80 mm

Ring-to-groove clearance
Top and second ring	
Standard	0.015 to 0.050 mm
Service limit (max)	0.080 mm

Starter clutch

Driven gear hub OD
Standard	45.657 to 45.673 mm
Service limit (min)	45.64 mm
Housing ID service limit (min)	62.33 mm

Clutch

Friction plates	5
Plain plates	4

Friction plate thickness
Standard	2.92 to 3.08 mm
Service limit (min)	2.60 mm
Plain plate warpage (max)	0.30 mm

Spring free length
Standard	42.1 mm
Service limit (min)	41.2 mm

Clutch housing centre ID
Standard	26.000 to 26.021 mm
Service limit (min)	26.04 mm

Clutch sleeve OD
Standard	25.959 to 25.980 mm
Service limit (min)	25.94 mm

Clutch sleeve ID
Standard	20.010 to 20.035 mm
Service limit (max)	20.05 mm

Input shaft OD at clutch sleeve
Standard	19.959 to 19.980 mm
Service limit (max)	19.94 mm

Oil pump

Inner rotor tip-to-outer rotor clearance
    Standard . . . . 0.15 mm
    Service limit (max) . . . . 0.20 mm
Outer rotor-to-body clearance
    Standard . . . . 0.15 to 0.21 mm
    Service limit (max) . . . . 0.26 mm
Rotor end-float
    Standard . . . . 0.03 to 0.10 mm
    Service limit (max) . . . . 0.15 mm

Crankshaft

Runout (max) . . . . 0.05 mm

Connecting rod

Small-end internal diameter
    Standard . . . . 13.016 to 13.034 mm
    Service limit (max) . . . . 13.044 mm
Small-end-to-piston pin clearance
    Standard . . . . 0.016 to 0.040 mm
    Service limit . . . . 0.060 mm
Big-end side clearance
    Standard . . . . 0.05 to 0.70 mm
    Service limit (max) . . . . 0.80 mm
Big-end radial clearance
    Standard . . . . 0.00 mm
    Service limit (max) . . . . 0.02 mm

Selector drum and forks

Selector fork end thickness
    Standard . . . . 4.93 to 5.00 mm
    Service limit (min) . . . . 4.90 mm
Selector fork bore ID
    Standard . . . . 12.000 to 12.018 mm
    Service limit (max) . . . . 12.03 mm
Selector fork shaft OD
    Standard . . . . 11.957 to 11.968 mm
    Service limit (min) . . . . 11.95 mm
Selector drum left-hand journal OD
    Standard . . . . 13.966 to 13.984 mm
    Service limit (min) . . . . 13.94 mm

Transmission

Gear ratios (no. of teeth)
    Primary reduction . . . . 3.722 to 1 (67/18T)
    Final reduction
        VT125C . . . . 2.928 to 1 (41/14T)
        XL125V . . . . 3.142 to 1 (44/14T)
    1st gear . . . . 3.083 to 1 (37/12T)
    2nd gear . . . . 1.933 to 1 (29/15T)
    3rd gear . . . . 1.428 to 1 (30/21T)
    4th gear . . . . 1.173 to 1 (27/23T)
    5th gear . . . . 1.000 to 1 (25/25T)
Input shaft (service limits)
    4th and 5th gears ID (max) . . . . 23.04 mm
    4th and 5th gears bush OD (min) . . . . 22.94 mm
    4th gear bush ID (max) . . . . 20.06 mm
    Shaft OD at 4th gear point (min) . . . . 19.94 mm
Output shaft (service limits)
    1st and 2nd gears ID (max) . . . . 23.04 mm
    3rd gear ID (max) . . . . 25.06 mm
    1st and 2nd gears bush OD (min) . . . . 22.94 mm
    3rd gear bush OD (min) . . . . 24.96 mm
    1st gear bush ID (max) . . . . 18.04 mm
    2nd gear bush ID (max) . . . . 20.04 mm
    3rd gear bush ID (max) . . . . 22.04 mm
    Shaft OD at 1st gear point (min) . . . . 17.95 mm
    Shaft OD at 2nd gear point (min) . . . . 19.95 mm
    Shaft OD at 3rd gear point (min) . . . . 21.94 mm

Torque settings

Cam chain tensioner bolts	12 Nm
Camshaft holder bolts	12 Nm
Camshaft sprocket bolts	20 Nm
Clutch centre nut	108 Nm
Clutch spring bolts	12 Nm
Crankcase bolts	12 Nm
Cylinder head nuts	
8 mm	32 Nm
6 mm	12 Nm
Cylinder head side cover bolts	10 Nm
Engine mounting bolt nuts	
VT125C-X and C-Y	
Front mounting bolt	39 Nm
Rear mounting bolts	29 Nm
VT125C-1 to C-6 and all XL125V	
Front and rear mounting bolts	39 Nm
Engine mounting bracket bolts	27 Nm
VT125C-X and C-Y	
Front bracket bolt	27 Nm
Rear bracket bolt	20 Nm
VT125C-1 to C-6	
Front and rear bracket bolts	27 Nm
XL125V-1 to V-6	
Rear bracket bolts	18 Nm
XL125V-7 onwards	
Rear bracket bolts	27 Nm
Front sprocket bolts	12 Nm
Gearchange cam centre bolt	23 Nm
Gearchange pedal pinch bolt	17 Nm
Gearchange stopper arm bolt	12 Nm
Oil pump bolts	14 Nm
Primary drive gear nut (left-hand thread)	88 Nm
Rocker shaft retainer bolts	5 Nm
Secondary air system reed valve cover bolts	5 Nm
Selector drum bearing retainer screws	10 Nm
Transmission shaft bearing retainer screws	10 Nm
Valve cover bolts	10 Nm

1 General information

The engine/transmission unit is a liquid-cooled single cylinder of unit construction. The two valves are operated by rocker arms actuated by a single overhead camshaft which is chain driven off the left-hand end of the crankshaft. The crankcase divides vertically.

The crankcase incorporates a wet sump, pressure-fed lubrication system which uses a twin rotor trochoidal oil pump that is gear-driven off the primary drive gear on the right-hand end of the crankshaft. Oil is filtered by a strainer in the bottom of the crankcase.

The alternator is on the left-hand end of the crankshaft. The ignition timing trigger is on the outside of the alternator rotor, and the pulse generator coil is mounted in the alternator cover along with the stator.

The water pump is on the right-hand side of the engine, and is gear driven off the primary drive gear on the right-hand end of the crankshaft.

Power from the crankshaft is routed to the transmission via the clutch. The clutch is of the wet, multi-plate type and is gear-driven off the crankshaft. The clutch is operated by cable. The transmission is a five-speed constant-mesh unit. Final drive to the rear wheel is by chain and sprockets.

2 Component access

Operations possible with the engine in the frame

The components and assemblies listed below can be removed without having to remove the engine from the frame. If however, a number of areas require attention at the same time, removal of the engine is recommended.

Valve covers
Cam chains, tensioners and blades
Camshafts and rockers
Cylinder heads
Cylinders and pistons
Clutch
Gearchange mechanism
Starter clutch
Oil pump
Starter motor and alternator (see Chapter 9)
Water pump (see Chapter 3)

Operations requiring engine removal

It is necessary to remove the engine from the frame to gain access to the following components.

Crankshaft, connecting rods and bearings
Oil scavenge pipe and strainer
Transmission shafts and bearings
Selector drum and forks

3 Cylinder compression check

Special tool: *A compression gauge with a 10 mm thread adapter is required for this test (see Step 4).*

1 Poor engine performance, exhaust smoke, heavy oil consumption and poor starting are indications of low compression. This may be

3.4 Compression test set-up

caused by leaking valve stem seals, incorrect valve clearances, a leaking head gasket, or worn pistons, rings and/or cylinder walls.

2 Before you start, make sure the valve clearances are correctly set (see Chapter 1).

3 Run the engine until it reaches normal operating temperature. Stop the engine and remove both spark plug caps.

4 Check the compression on one cylinder at a time. Remove the spark plug from either the front or rear cylinder and fit the adaptor and gauge into the spark plug hole **(see illustration)**.

 Warning: Take care not to burn your hands on the hot components.

5 Turn the ignition ON and open the throttle fully. Crank the engine over on the starter motor for a few seconds until the gauge reading stabilises and take a note of the reading. Turn the ignition OFF.

6 Remove the test equipment and install the spark plug, then transfer the adapter and compression gauge to the other cylinder and repeat the procedure.

7 Compare the readings obtained with those in the *Specifications* at the beginning of this Chapter. If they fall within the specified range and are relatively equal, the engine is in good condition. Install the second spark plug and reconnect the plug caps.

8 If the readings are close to or below the minimum limit, or one cylinder differs markedly from the other, further investigation is required. To determine the cause of low compression, inject a small quantity of engine oil into the spark plug hole of the suspect cylinder with a pump-type oil can – this will temporarily seal the piston rings. Repeat the compression test. If the result shows a noticeable increase in pressure this confirms that the cylinder bore, piston or rings are worn (see Sections 16 to 18). If there is no change in the reading, the cylinder head gasket or valves are leaking (see Sections 14 and 15).

9 Although unlikely with the use of modern fuels, a high compression reading indicates excessive carbon deposits in the combustion chamber. Remove the cylinder head(s) and clean all carbon off the piston, head and valves (see Sections 14 and 15).

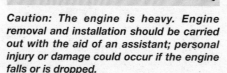

4 Engine removal and installation

Caution: The engine is heavy. Engine removal and installation should be carried out with the aid of an assistant; personal injury or damage could occur if the engine falls or is dropped.

Special tools: *A motorcycle jack or trolley jack will be required to support the engine.*

1 Support the bike securely in an upright position using an auxiliary stand. Work can be made easier by raising the machine to a suitable working height on an hydraulic ramp or a suitable platform.

2 During the removal procedure, make a careful note of the routing of all cables, wiring and hoses and of any ties, clips or clamps that secure or guide them, so everything can be returned to its original location. Keep nuts, bolts and washers with the parts they secure.

VT125C models

Removal

3 Remove the seat and side panels (see Chapter 8).

4 Disconnect the negative (-ve) lead from the battery (see Chapter 9).

5 Remove the fuel tank (see Chapter 4A).

6 Remove the right-hand footrest bracket and brake pedal linkage (see Chapter 6).

7 Remove the exhaust system (see Chapter 4A).

8 Remove the front sprocket cover (see Chapter 7).

9 If the engine is dirty, particularly around its mountings, clean it thoroughly before starting any major dismantling. This will make work much easier and rule out the possibility of dirt falling into some vital component.

10 Drain the engine oil – if required remove the oil filter (see Chapter 1).

11 Drain the coolant and remove the radiator and radiator hoses (see Chapter 3).

12 Remove the carburettor assembly (see Chapter 4A). Plug the engine intake manifolds with clean rag.

13 Remove the cylinder head side covers (see Section 11).

14 Remove the secondary air system control valve and hoses (see Chapter 4A).

15 Disconnect the thermo-switch and coolant temperature sensor wiring connectors **(see illustration)**.

16 Disconnect the lower end of the clutch cable from the actuating arm and secure the cable clear of the engine unit (see Section 8).

17 Pull the spark plug caps off the plugs and secure them clear of the engine (see Chapter 1).

18 Trace the alternator wiring and ignition pulse generator wiring from the rear of the alternator cover and disconnect it at the connectors (see Chapter 9, Section 27). Trace the speed sensor wiring from the rear of the crankcase and disconnect it at the connector (see Chapter 9, Section 15). Free the wiring from any clips or ties and secure it clear of the frame.

19 Disconnect the neutral switch wiring connector and the starter motor terminal lead (see Chapter 9). Release the wiring from the guides secured by the crankcase bolts.

20 Undo the bolt securing the earth (ground) lead to the rear of the crankcase and detach the lead **(see illustration)**. Temporarily install the bolt.

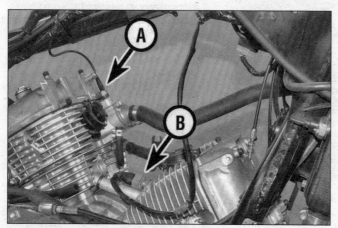

4.15 Thermo-switch (A) and coolant temperature sensor (B)

4.20 Detach the earth lead (arrowed) from the crankcase

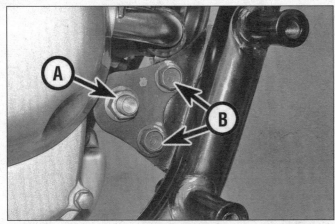

4.24a Undo the nut (A). Note the mounting bracket bolts (B)

4.24b Note the location of the spacer (arrowed)

4.25 Note the location of the spacer on the back of the bracket

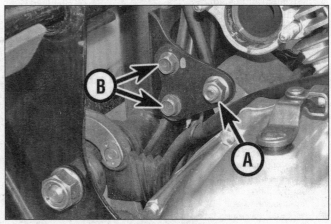

4.26 Undo the nut (A). Note the mounting bracket bolts (B)

21 Undo the pinch bolt securing the gearchange arm and draw the arm off the shaft, noting the alignment of the register marks (see Chapter 6).

22 Remove the front sprocket (see Chapter 7). Rest the drive chain over the chain slider on the swingarm.

23 At this point, position an hydraulic or mechanical jack under the engine with a block of wood between the jack head and sump. Make sure the jack is centrally positioned so the engine will not topple in any direction when the last mounting bolt is removed. Take the weight of the engine on the jack.

24 Undo the nut on the engine front mounting bolt (see illustration). As the bolt is withdrawn, remove the spacer located between the frame and the engine on the left-hand side (see illustration).

25 Undo the bolts securing the front right-hand mounting bracket (see illustration 4.24a). Remove the bracket, noting the location of the integral spacer (see illustration).

26 Undo the nut on the engine upper rear mounting bolt and withdraw the bolt (see illustration).

27 Undo the bolts securing the rear right-hand mounting bracket and remove the bracket, noting how it fits (see illustration 4.26).

28 Undo the nut on the rear lower mounting bolt (see illustration).

29 Make sure the engine is properly supported on the jack and have an assistant support it as well. Check that all wiring, cables and hoses are disconnected and clear of the engine.

30 Withdraw the rear lower mounting bolt.

31 Manoeuvre the engine unit out of the frame towards the right-hand side (see illustration).

Installation

32 Clean the threads of the engine mounting

bolts. As a precaution against damage, cover the lower right-hand frame tube with masking tape.

33 With the aid of an assistant, lift the engine unit into position from the right-hand side and support it on the jack. Ensure no wires, cables or hoses are trapped between the engine and the frame.

34 Align the bolt holes and slide the lower rear engine mounting bolt through from the left-hand side (see illustration 4.28). Tighten the nut finger-tight. Note: All nuts and bolts should be installed finger-tight to begin with.

4.28 Location of the rear lower mounting bolt

4.31 Manoeuvre the engine out towards the right-hand side

4.56 Detach the earth lead from the crankcase

4.60a Undo the nut (arrowed) . . .

4.60b . . . and withdraw the engine front mounting bolt

35 Install the rear right-hand mounting bracket, then slide the upper rear mounting bolt through from the left-hand side and fit the nut **(see illustration 4.26)**.

36 Install the front right-hand mounting bracket **(see illustration 4.25)**. Slide the front mounting bolt through from the left-hand side – don't forget to fit the spacer between the frame and the engine on the left-hand side **(see illustration 4.24b)**. Fit the nut on the mounting bolt **(see illustration 4.24a)**.

37 Once the engine unit, frame and mounting brackets are all correctly aligned, tighten the nuts and bolts in the following order to the torque settings specified at the beginning of this Chapter. **Note:** *Counter-hold the mounting bolts when tightening the nuts.*

● Front mounting bracket bolts.
● Rear mounting bracket bolts.
● Front mounting bolt nut.
● Rear lower mounting bolt nut.
● Rear upper mounting bolt nut.

38 The remainder of the installation procedure is the reverse of removal, noting the following:

● Make sure all wires, cables and hoses are correctly routed and connected, and secured by the relevant clips or ties.
● Tighten all bolts to the specified torque settings where given.
● Adjust the throttle and clutch cable freeplay (see Chapter 1).
● Adjust the drive chain (see Chapter 1).
● Refilll the engine with oil and coolant (see Chapter 1 and *Pre-ride checks*).
● Start the engine and check that there is no coolant or oil leakage.
● Adjust the idle speed if necessary (see Chapter 1).

XL125V

Removal

39 Remove the fairing, seat and side panels (see Chapter 8).

40 Disconnect the negative (-ve) lead from the battery (see Chapter 9).

41 Remove the fuel tank and the exhaust system (see Chapter 4A or 4B).

42 Remove the front sprocket cover (see Chapter 7).

43 If the engine is dirty, particularly around its mountings, clean it thoroughly before starting any major dismantling. This will make work

much easier and rule out the possibility of dirt falling into some vital component.

44 Drain the engine oil – if required remove the oil filter (see Chapter 1).

45 Drain the coolant and remove the radiator and radiator hoses (see Chapter 3).

46 On XL125V-1 to V-6 models, remove the carburettor assembly (see Chapter 4A).

47 On XL125V-7 onwards, remove the throttle body assembly (see Chapter 4B).

48 On all models, plug the engine intake manifolds with clean rag.

49 Remove the cylinder head side covers (see Section 11).

50 Remove the secondary air system control valve and hoses (see Chapter 4A or 4B as applicable).

51 On carburettor models, disconnect the thermo-switch and engine coolant temperature sensor wiring connectors **(see illustration 4.15)**.

52 Disconnect the lower end of the clutch cable from the actuating arm and secure the cable clear of the engine unit (see Section 8).

53 Pull the spark plug caps off the plugs and secure them clear of the engine (see Chapter 1).

54 Trace the alternator wiring and ignition pulse generator or crankshaft position sensor wiring from the rear of the alternator cover and disconnect it at the connectors (see Chapter 9, Section 27). As applicable, trace the speed sensor wiring from the rear of the crankcase and disconnect it at the connector (see Chapter 9, Section 15). Note that on most XL125V-1 to V-6 models the speed sensor is located on the front wheel. Free the wiring

from any clips or ties and secure it clear of the frame.

55 Disconnect the neutral switch wiring connector and the starter motor terminal lead (see Chapter 9). Release the wiring from the guides secured by the crankcase bolts.

56 Undo the bolt securing the earth (ground) lead to the rear of the crankcase and detach the lead **(see illustration)**. Temporarily install the bolt.

57 Undo the pinch bolt securing the gearchange arm and draw the arm off the shaft, noting the alignment of the register marks (see Chapter 6).

58 Remove the front sprocket (see Chapter 7). Rest the drive chain over the chain slider on the swingarm.

59 At this point, position an hydraulic or mechanical jack under the engine with a block of wood between the jack head and sump. Make sure the jack is centrally positioned so the engine will not topple in any direction when the last mounting bolt is removed. Take the weight of the engine on the jack.

60 Undo the nut on the engine front mounting bolt **(see illustration)**. As the bolt is withdrawn, remove the spacer located between the frame and the engine on the right-hand side **(see illustration)**.

61 Undo the nut on the rear upper engine mounting bolt and withdraw the bolt **(see illustrations)**.

62 Undo the bolts securing the rear right-hand mounting bracket and remove the bracket, noting how it fits **(see illustration 4.61a)**.

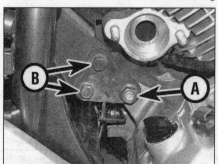

4.61a Undo the nut (A). Note the mounting bracket bolts (B)

4.61b Withdraw the rear upper engine mounting bolt

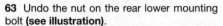

4.63 Undo the nut on the engine lower rear mounting bolt

4.65 Withdraw the engine lower rear mounting bolt

4.66 Manoeuvre the engine out towards the right-hand side

63 Undo the nut on the rear lower mounting bolt **(see illustration)**.
64 Make sure the engine is properly supported on the jack and have an assistant support it as well. Check that all wiring, cables and hoses are disconnected and clear of the engine.
65 Withdraw the rear lower mounting bolt **(see illustration)**.
66 Manoeuvre the engine unit out of the frame towards the right-hand side **(see illustration)**.

Installation

67 Clean the threads of the engine mounting bolts. **Note:** *On V-7 models onward, lubricate the threads of the mounting bolts with engine oil.*
68 As a precaution against damage, cover the lower right-hand frame tube with masking tape. With the aid of an assistant, lift the engine unit into position and support it on the jack. Ensure no wires, cables or hoses are trapped between the engine and the frame.
69 Align the bolt holes.
70 Slide the engine lower rear mounting bolt through from the left-hand side **(see illustration 4.65)**. Tighten the nut finger-tight. **Note:** *All nuts and bolts should be installed finger-tight to begin with.*
71 Install the rear right-hand mounting bracket, then slide the upper rear mounting bolt through from the left-hand side and fit the nut **(see illustrations)**.
72 Slide the front mounting bolt through from the left-hand side **(see illustration 4.60b)**. Don't forget to fit the spacer between the frame and the engine on the right-hand

side. Fit the nut on the mounting bolt **(see illustration 4.60a)**.
73 Once the engine unit, frame and mounting brackets are all correctly aligned, tighten the nuts and bolts in the following order to the torque settings specified at the beginning of this Chapter. **Note:** *Counter-hold the mounting bolts when tightening the nuts.*
V-1 to V-6 models:
● *Rear lower mounting bolt nut.*
● *Rear mounting bracket bolts.*
● *Rear upper mounting bolt nut.*
● *Front mounting bolt nut.*
V-7 models onward:
● *Rear lower mounting bolt nut.*
● *Front mounting bolt nut.*
● *Rear mounting bracket bolts.*
● *Rear upper mounting bolt nut.*
74 The remainder of the installation procedure is the reverse of removal, noting the following:
● Make sure all wires, cables and hoses are correctly routed and connected, and secured by the relevant clips or ties.
● Tighten all bolts to the specified torque settings where given.
● Adjust the throttle and clutch cable freeplay (see Chapter 1).
● Adjust the drive chain (see Chapter 1).
● Refilll the engine with oil and coolant (see Chapter 1 and *Pre-ride checks*).
● Start the engine and check that there is no coolant or oil leakage.
● On carburettor models, adjust the idle speed if necessary (see Chapter 1).

5 Engine overhaul –
general information

1 Before disassembling the engine, the external surfaces of the unit should be thoroughly cleaned and degreased. This will prevent contamination of the engine internals, and will also make working a lot easier and cleaner. A high flash-point solvent, such as paraffin (kerosene) can be used, or better still, a proprietary engine cleaner such as Gunk. Use a paraffin brush or old paintbrush to work the solvent into the recesses of the engine casings. Take care to exclude solvent or water from the electrical components and intake and exhaust ports.

⚠ *Warning: The use of petrol (gasoline) as a cleaning agent should be avoided because of the risk of fire.*

2 When the engine is clean and dry, clear a suitable area for working – a workbench is desirable for all operations once a component has been removed from the machine. Gather a selection of small containers and plastic bags so that parts can be grouped together in an easily identifiable manner. Some paper and a pen should be at hand so that notes can be made and labels attached where necessary. A supply of clean rag is also required. If the engine has been removed from the bike, have an assistant help you lift it onto the workbench.
3 Before commencing work, read through the appropriate section so that some idea of the necessary procedure can be gained. When removing components it should be noted that great force is seldom required. In many cases, a component's reluctance to be removed is indicative of an incorrect approach or removal method – if in any doubt, re-check with the text. In cases where fasteners have corroded, apply penetrating oil or WD-40 before disassembly.
4 When disassembling the engine, keep 'mated' parts together (e.g. camshafts and rockers, valve assemblies, pistons and connecting rods, clutch plates etc. that have been in contact with each other during engine operation). These 'mated' parts must be reused or renewed as assemblies.

4.71a Install the rear right-hand mounting bracket

4.71b Install the upper rear mounting bolt and fit the nut

5 A complete engine/transmission disassembly should be done in the following general order with reference to the appropriate Sections.

Remove the starter motor (see Chapter 9)
Remove the water pump (see Chapter 3)
Remove the oil pump
Remove the clutch
Remove the starter clutch drive gears
Remove the gearchange mechanism
Remove the alternator (see Chapter 9)
Remove the valve covers
Remove the cam chain tensioners
Remove the camshafts
Remove the cylinder heads
Remove the cylinders and pistons
Remove the cam chains and blades
Separate the crankcase halves
Remove the selector drum and forks
Remove the transmission shafts
Remove the crankshaft and connecting rods

6 Oil pump

Note: *The oil pump can be removed with the engine in the frame. If the engine has been removed, ignore the steps which don't apply.*

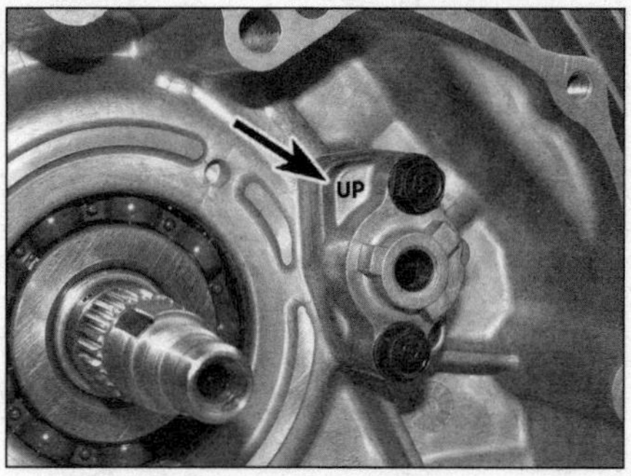

6.4a Note the UP mark then undo the bolts . . .

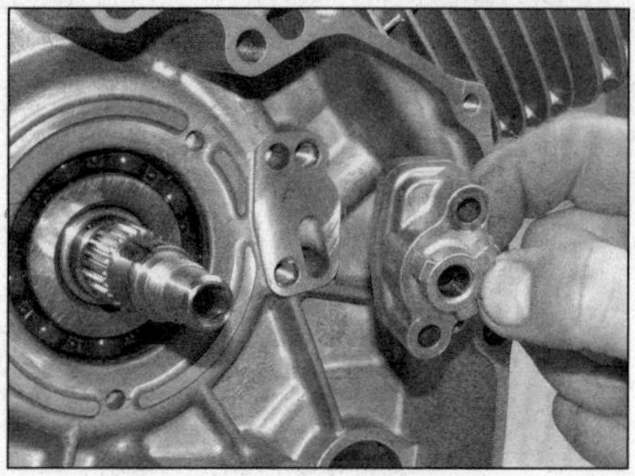

6.4b . . . and remove the cover

Removal

1 Drain the engine oil (see Chapter 1).
2 Drain the coolant (see Chapter 3).
3 Remove the right-hand crankcase cover (see Section 7).
4 Note the UP mark on the pump cover, then undo the mounting bolts and remove the pump **(see illustrations)**.
5 Undo the screw and lift off the back of the pump, noting how it fits **(see illustrations)**.
6 Remove the dowels **(see illustration)**.
7 Lift out the inner and outer pump rotors noting how they fit. **Note:** *The rotors are not marked – keep them in the correct order so that they can be installed in their original positions.*

Inspection

8 Clean all the components in a suitable solvent.
9 Inspect the pump body and rotors for scoring and wear **(see illustration)**. If any damage is evident, replace the components with new ones.
10 Fit the inner and outer rotors into the pump body as noted on removal.
11 Measure the clearance between the inner rotor tip and the outer rotor with a feeler gauge and compare it to the specification listed at the beginning of this Chapter **(see illustration)**. If the clearance is greater than the service limit, renew the rotors.

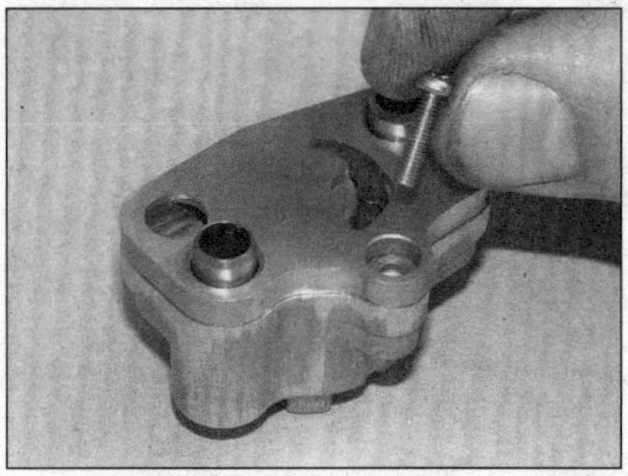

6.5a Undo the screw . . .

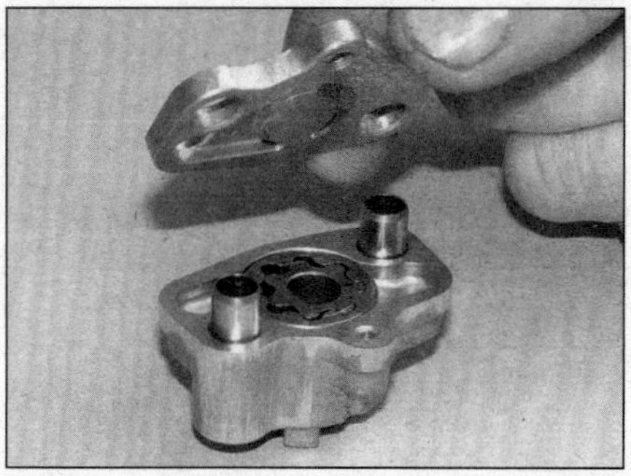

6.5b . . . and lift off the back of the pump

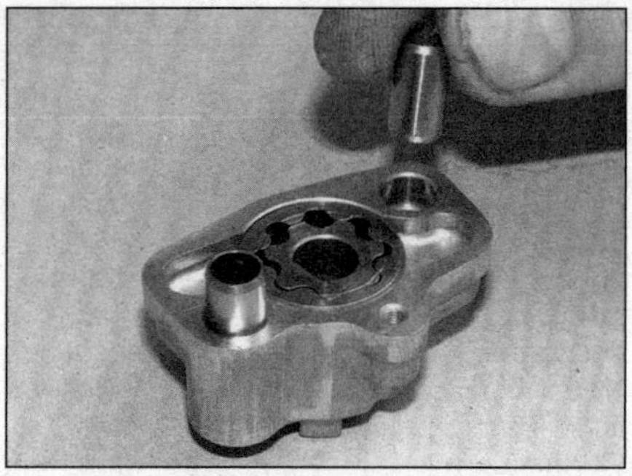

6.6 Remove the dowels

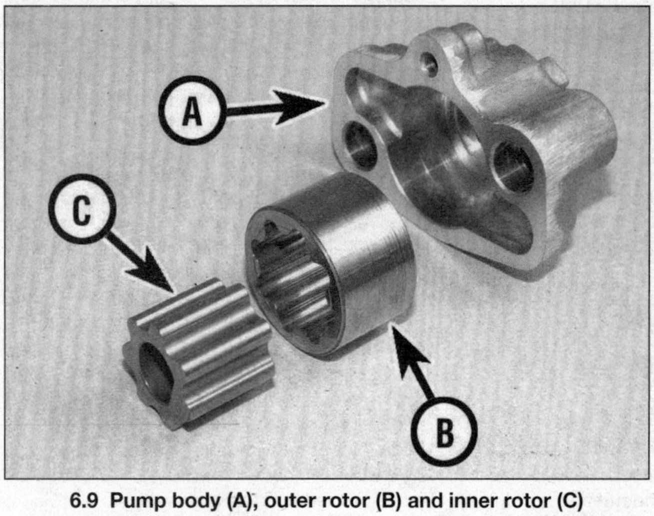

6.9 Pump body (A), outer rotor (B) and inner rotor (C)

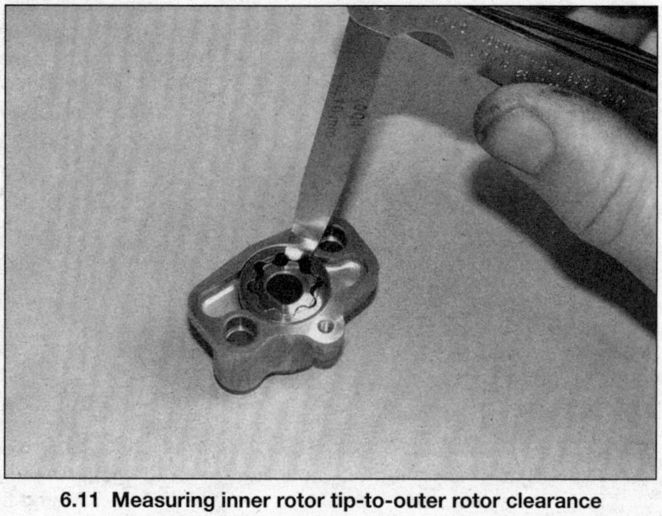

6.11 Measuring inner rotor tip-to-outer rotor clearance

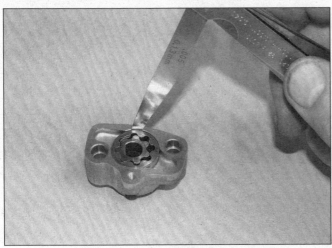

6.12a Measuring outer rotor-to-body clearance

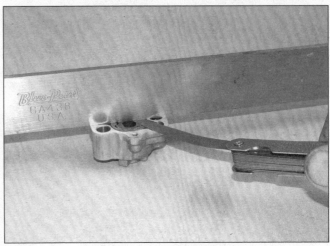

6.12b Measuring rotor end-float

12 Measure the clearance between the outer rotor and the pump body and compare it to the specification listed at the beginning of this Chapter (see illustration). Lay a straight-edge across the rotors and the pump body and, using a feeler gauge, measure the rotor end-float (the gap between the rotors and the straight-edge (see illustration). If either measurement is greater than the service limit, fit a new oil pump.

Installation

Note: *Prior to installation, lubricate the rotors with plenty of clean engine oil.*
13 Install the inner and outer rotors in the pump body as noted on removal.
14 Fit the dowels and the back of the pump and secure it with the screw (see illustrations 6.6, 5b and 5a).
15 Ensure the mating surfaces of the pump and crankcase are clean, then install the pump with the UP mark facing up and secure it with the

mounting bolts (see illustration 6.4a). Tighten the bolts to the specified torque setting.
16 Install the right-hand crankcase cover (see Section 7).
17 Install the remaining components in the reverse order of removal.
18 Refill the cooling system (see Chapter 3).
19 Refill the engine with the recommended grade and type of oil (see Chapter 1).

7 Clutch

Note 1: *The clutch can be removed with the engine in the frame. If the engine has been removed, ignore the steps which don't apply.*
Note 2: *The clutch centre nut must be discarded and a new one used on installation – it is best to obtain the new nut in advance.*

Special tool: *A clutch centre locking tool is required for this procedure (see Step 13).*

Removal

1 Drain the engine oil (see Chapter 1).
2 Drain the coolant (see Chapter 3).
3 On VT125C models, remove the right-hand footrest bracket and brake pedal linkage (see Chapter 6).
4 Disconnect the lower end of the clutch cable from the actuating arm and secure the cable clear of the engine unit (see Section 8). Undo the bolts securing the clutch cable bracket and remove he bracket (see illustration).
5 Remove the water pump cover and disconnect the coolant elbow from the front of the crankcase cover (see Chapter 3, Section 7).
6 Position a suitable receptacle underneath the right-hand crankcase cover to catch any residual oil when the cover is removed. Undo the cover bolts (see illustration). Pull the clutch arm back (anti-clockwise) towards the rear of the bike to disengage the actuating

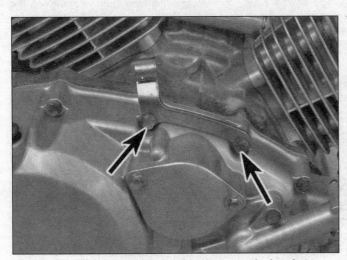

7.4 Undo the bolts (arrowed) and remove the bracket

7.6a Location of the crankcase cover bolts

7.6b Remove the cover . . .

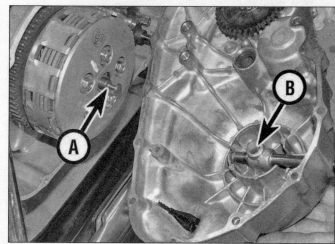

7.6c . . . disengaging the pull-rod (A) from the actuating shaft (B)

7.7 Location of the cover dowels

7.8 Remove the spring bolts, washers and springs

shaft from the pull-rod and draw the cover off **(see illustrations)**.

7 Remove the cover gasket and discard it; note the location of the cover dowels and remove them for safe-keeping if they are loose **(see illustration)**.

8 Undo the clutch spring bolts a little at a time in a criss-cross pattern, then remove the bolts, washers and the springs **(see illustration)**. **Note:** *The washers are integral with the bolts.*

9 Lift off the pressure plate and remove the pull-rod, either from the back of the pressure plate or the end of the transmission input shaft **(see illustrations)**.

10 Note the location of the outer friction plate tabs, then withdraw the clutch plates from the clutch housing **(see illustration)**. Keep the plates in their original order, even if they are being replaced with new ones. There are five friction plates and four plain plates. Note that the innermost friction plate has a larger inside

7.9a Remove the pressure plate . . .

7.9b . . . and the pull-rod

7.10a Note how the outer friction plate fits

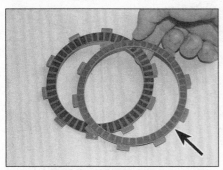

7.10b Innermost friction plate (arrowed) has a larger inside diameter

7.11a Withdraw the anti-judder spring . . .

7.11b . . . and spring seat

7.12 Unstake the centre nut carefully to avoid damage

7.13 Holding tool locks onto the clutch centre splines

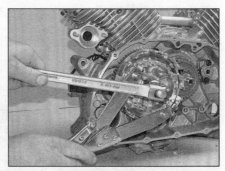

7.14a Unscrew the clutch centre nut . . .

diameter than the others to allow it to fit over the anti-judder spring and spring seat (see illustration).

11 Withdraw the anti-judder spring and spring seat (see illustrations).

12 Using a small chisel, unstake the clutch centre nut carefully to avoid damaging the transmission input shaft (see illustration).

13 To loosen the clutch centre nut the input shaft must be locked using one of the following methods:

● Use the Honda service tool (Part No. 07724-0050002) to engage the clutch centre splines.

● Use a commercially available clutch holding tool which will engage the clutch centre splines (see illustration).

Caution: The clutch centre nut is extremely tight. If a clutch holding tool is used, ensure it does not slip and damage the clutch.

14 Unscrew the centre nut and discard it as a new one must be fitted (see illustration). Remove the Belleville washer, noting how it fits, and the plain washer (see illustrations).

15 Draw the clutch centre off the shaft then

7.14b . . . then remove the Belleville washer . . .

7.14c . . . and plain washer

7.15a Draw off the clutch centre . . .

7.15b . . . then remove the thrust washer . . .

7.15c . . . and clutch housing

7.15d Draw off the input shaft sleeve

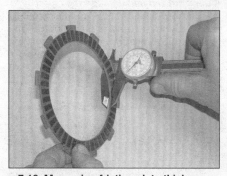

7.16 Measuring friction plate thickness with a Vernier caliper

remove the thrust washer and clutch housing (see illustrations). Slide off the input shaft sleeve (see illustration).

Inspection

16 After an extended period of service the clutch friction plates will wear and promote clutch slip. Measure the thickness of each friction plate using a Vernier caliper (see illustration). If any plate has worn to or beyond the service limits given in the Specifications at the beginning of this Chapter, or if any of the plates smell burnt or are glazed, the friction plates must be replaced with a new set.

17 The plain plates should not show any signs of excess heating (bluing). Check for warpage using a flat surface and feeler gauges (see illustration). If any plate exceeds the maximum permissible warpage, or shows signs of bluing, all plain plates must be replaced with a new set.

18 Inspect the clutch assembly for burrs and indentations in the slots in the housing and on the corresponding tabs on the friction plates (see illustration). Similarly check for wear between the slots in the clutch centre and the inner tongues of the plain plates (see illustration). Wear of this nature will cause clutch drag and slow disengagement during gear changes, since the plates will snag when

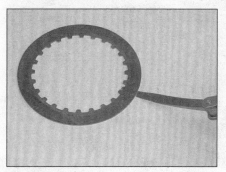

7.17 Checking a plain plate for warpage

7.18a Inspect the clutch housing and friction plate tabs

7.18b Inspect the clutch centre and plain plate tongues

7.20 Measuring clutch spring free length

7.22a Inspect the bearing surfaces of the clutch housing (A) and input shaft sleeve (B)

7.22b Measuring the external diameter of the input shaft with a micrometer

7.23 Check the cush drive springs and primary driven gear teeth

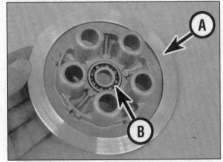

7.25 Check the surface (A) of the pressure plate and the pull-rod bearing (B)

7.26a Note the location of the shaft return spring . . .

the pressure plate is lifted. With care, a small amount of wear can be corrected by dressing with a fine file, but if this is excessive the worn components should be renewed.

19 Ensure the threads for the spring bolts in the clutch centre are in good condition.

20 Measure the free length of each clutch spring using a Vernier caliper (see illustration). Stand each spring upright on a flat surface and check it for bend by placing a set square against it. If any spring is shorter than the specified service limit, or if the bend in any spring is excessive, replace all the springs as a set.

21 Check the anti-judder spring and spring seat for damage or distortion and replace them with new ones if necessary.

22 Inspect the bearing surfaces of the clutch housing and the input shaft sleeve for wear (see illustration). Measure the external

and internal diameters of the sleeve and the external diameter of the input shaft where the sleeve sits (see illustration), and compare the results to the specifications at the beginning of this Chapter. If there are any signs of wear, pitting or other damage the affected parts must be replaced with new ones.

23 The clutch housing incorporates a cush-drive mechanism – check that the springs are not loose or broken and that there is no backlash between the housing and the primary driven gear, otherwise replace the housing with a new one (see illustration).

24 Check the teeth of the primary driven gear on the back of the clutch housing (see illustration 7.23) and the corresponding teeth of the primary drive gear on the crankshaft. Renew the clutch housing and the primary drive gear if the teeth are worn or chipped – refer to Section 9 for the primary drive gear.

25 Check the surface of the pressure plate and the pull-rod bearing for signs of wear, damage or roughness and renew any parts as necessary (see illustration). Refer to Tools and Workshop Tips in the Reference section for details of bearing removal and installation.

26 Inspect the outer end of the pull-rod (see illustration 7.9b) and the lower end of the clutch actuating shaft where it engages for wear – note the location of the shaft return spring, then draw the shaft out to see it more clearly (see illustrations).

27 If there is evidence of oil leakage at the top of the shaft, pull the shaft all the way out of the cover. Using a flat-bladed screwdriver, carefully lever out the seal to avoid damaging the cover (see illustration). Lubricate the new seal with a smear of engine oil, then press it into place with a suitably-sized socket (see illustration). Install the shaft carefully to avoid

7.26b . . . then draw the shaft out for inspection

7.27a Remove the old seal with a flat-bladed screwdriver

7.27b Install the new seal with a suitably-sized socket

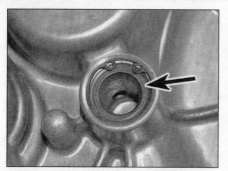

7.28a Location of the crankshaft oil seal

7.28b Remove the circlip . . .

7.28c . . . and lever out the old seal

7.28d Lubricate the new seal with engine oil

7.33a Raised rim on the nut should face out

7.33b Tighten the nut to the specified torque setting

damaging the seal and ensure the ends of the return spring locate correctly.

28 Check the condition of the crankshaft oil seal in the cover and replace it with a new one if necessary **(see illustration)**. It is good practice to renew the seal whenever the cover is removed. Using circlip pliers, remove the circlip, then lever out the old seal **(see illustrations)**. Lubricate the new seal with a smear of engine oil, then press it into place with a suitably-sized socket **(see illustration)**. Don't forget to fit the circlip, using a new one if necessary, making sure it locates in its groove.

Installation

29 Remove all traces of old gasket from the crankcase and cover surfaces.

30 Lubricate the input shaft sleeve with clean engine oil, then slide it onto the shaft **(see illustration 7.15d)**.

31 Install the clutch housing, ensuring the primary driven gear engages correctly with the primary drive gear **(see illustration 7.15c)**. Install the thrust washer and clutch centre **(see illustrations 7.15b and a)**.

32 Install the plain washer and Belleville washer with the OUT SIDE mark facing out **(see illustrations 7.14c and b)**.

33 Lubricate the seating surface of the new centre nut and install it finger-tight – the raised rim on the nut should face out **(see illustration)**. Using the method employed on removal to lock the input shaft (see Step 13), tighten the nut to the torque setting specified at the beginning of this Chapter **(see illustration)**.

34 Using a small punch, stake the rim of the nut into the notch in the end of the shaft **(see illustrations)**.

7.34a Use a small punch to stake the nut onto the shaft

7.34b The staked nut should look like this

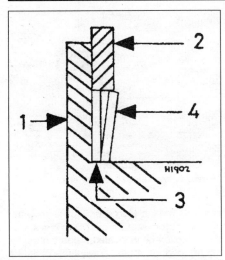

7.35 Correct fitting of anti-judder spring

1 *Clutch centre*
2 *Friction plate*
3 *Spring seat*
4 *Anti-judder spring*

35 Install the spring seat and anti-judder spring **(see illustration)**.
36 Coat each clutch plate with engine oil, then build up the plates in the housing, starting with the innermost friction plate with the larger internal diameter **(see illustration)**. Next, fit a plain plate followed by a friction plate and continue to alternate plain and friction plates to build up the clutch, finishing with the outermost friction plate, locating its tabs in the shallow slots in the housing **(see illustration)**.
37 Lubricate the pull-rod with engine oil and install it in the end of the input shaft **(see illustration 7.9b)**.
38 Lubricate the pull-rod bearing, then install the pressure plate, clutch springs, bolts and washers **(see illustrations 7.9a and 8)**. Tighten the bolts evenly in a criss-cross pattern to the specified torque setting **(see illustration)**.
39 If removed, install the cover dowels, then fit the new cover gasket, making sure it locates correctly onto the dowels **(see illustration 7.7)**.
40 Lubricate the end of the crankshaft with oil.
41 Install the cover – at the front, rotate the water pump impeller to engage the flat on the pump shaft with the oil pump inner rotor and the teeth on the water pump driven gear with the primary drive gear. Pull the clutch arm back (anti-clockwise), then rotate it forwards so that it engages behind the end of the pull-rod as the cover is pressed into position **(see illustration 7.6c and b)**.
42 Install the cover bolts finger-tight, not forgetting the clutch cable bracket, then tighten the bolts evenly in a criss-cross pattern **(see illustration 7.6a)**.
43 Install the remaining components in the reverse order of removal.
44 Refill the cooling system (see Chapter 3).

7.36a Start with the innermost friction plate

45 Refill the engine with the recommended grade, quantity and type of oil (see Chapter 1).

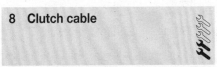

8 Clutch cable

1 On XL125V models, if required, remove the fairing for access (see Chapter 8).
2 Start at the handlebar end of the cable. Loosen the adjuster lockring, then thread the adjuster fully into the lever bracket to make freeplay in the cable **(see illustration)**.
3 At the lower end of the cable, slacken the upper locknut on the cable adjuster, then thread the lower locknut off the adjuster **(see illustration)**. Free the cable end from the

8.2 Thread the adjuster (arrowed) fully into the lever bracket

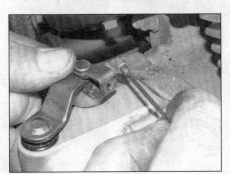

8.3b Free the cable end from the actuating arm . . .

7.36b Tabs on outermost plate locate in shallow slots

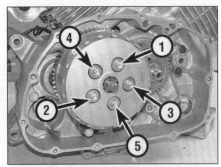

7.38 Tighten the bolts evenly in a criss-cross pattern

actuating arm then draw the cable forward out of the bracket **(see illustrations)**.
4 Align the slots in the adjuster and lockring at the handlebar end of the cable with the slot

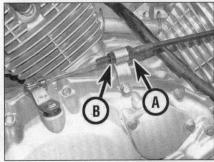

8.3a Upper locknut (A) and lower locknut (B)

8.3c . . . then draw the cable out of the bracket

8.4a Align the slots in the adjuster, lockring and lever bracket

8.4b Pull the outer cable end from the socket in the adjuster . . .

8.4c . . . and release the inner cable from the lever

in the lever bracket **(see illustration)**. Pull the outer cable end from the socket in the adjuster and release the inner cable from the lever **(see illustrations)**.

5 Remove the cable from the machine, noting its routing.

Before removing the cable from the bike, tape the lower end of the new cable to the upper end of the old cable. Slowly pull the lower end of the old cable out, guiding the new cable down into position. Using this method will ensure the cable is routed correctly.

6 Installation is the reverse of removal. Apply grease to the cable ends. Make sure the cable is correctly routed. Adjust the clutch lever freeplay (see Chapter 1).

9 Starter clutch and drive gears

Note: *The starter clutch can be removed with the engine in the frame.*

Check

1 The operation of the starter clutch can be checked while it is in situ. First remove the starter motor (see Chapter 9). Check that the reduction gear, located inside the starter motor aperture, rotates freely anti-clockwise (as you look at it from the left-hand side), but locks when rotated clockwise. If not, the starter clutch or one of the intermediate gears is faulty and should be removed for inspection.

Removal

2 Remove the right-hand crankcase cover (see Section 7).

3 Note how the idler gear engages with the driven gear on the starter clutch and the smaller pinion on the reduction gear **(see illustration)**. Withdraw the idler gear shaft and remove the gear **(see illustration)**.

4 Withdraw the reduction gear shaft and remove the gear, noting how the larger pinion engages with the starter motor pinion **(see illustration)**.

5 Check the operation of the starter clutch – the driven gear on the starter clutch should rotate freely anti-clockwise as you look at it, but should lock when rotated clockwise **(see illustration)**. If not the starter clutch is faulty and should be removed for inspection.

9.3a Idler gear (A), starter clutch driven gear (B) and reduction gear (C)

9.3b Withdraw the shaft and remove the idler gear

9.4 Withdraw the shaft and remove the reduction gear

9.5 Starter clutch driven gear should rotate freely anti-clockwise

9.6a Drive gear nut (arrowed) has a left-hand thread

9.6b Lock the gears with a piece of soft aluminium

9.7a Remove the nut . . .

6 Remove the clutch (see Section 7), but before removing the clutch housing, lock the primary driven gear on the housing with the primary drive gear on the crankshaft so that the drive gear nut can be loosened. Honda provides a service tool to do this (Part No. 07724-0010200). Alternatively, wedge a piece of soft aluminium between the teeth of the two gears. The drive gear nut has a left-hand thread – turn it *clockwise* to loosen it **(see illustrations)**. Remove the clutch housing

7 Unscrew the nut and remove the plain washer **(see illustrations)**.

8 Draw the primary drive gear off the crankshaft, noting how it locates on the Woodruff key, then remove the key from its slot in the shaft **(see illustrations)**.

9 Draw off the starter clutch assembly **(see illustration)**.

Inspection

10 Withdraw the driven gear from the starter clutch, rotating it anti-clockwise as you do **(see illustration)**.

11 Lift out the needle bearing **(see illustration)**.

12 Using circlip pliers, remove the two circlips securing the sprag assembly in the clutch housing, noting how they fit **(see illustrations)**.

9.7b . . . and the plain washer

9.8a Draw off the primary drive gear . . .

9.8b . . . and remove the Woodruff key

9.9 Draw off the starter clutch assembly

9.10 Withdraw the driven gear from the starter clutch

9.11 Lift out the needle bearing

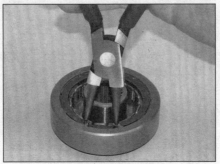

9.12a Use circlip pliers . . .

9.12b . . . to remove both circlips from the housing

9.13 Note which way round the sprag assembly fits

9.16 Inspect the needle bearing and the bearing surfaces

9.17 Check the gear teeth and the gear shafts

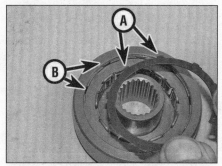

9.18 Align the tabs (A) on the first circlip with the gaps (B)

13 Lift out the sprag assembly, noting which way round it fits **(see illustration)**.

14 Inspect the condition of the sprags and the sprag cage. Clean the assembly with a suitable solvent, dry it thoroughly, then lubricate it with clean engine oil. The sprags should turn freely inside the cage – if they are damaged or worn, the corresponding surfaces of the housing and the driven gear are likely to be worn also.

15 Measure the inside diameter of the housing and the outside diameter of the driven gear hub, then compare the results to the specifications at the beginning of this Chapter. If either item is worn it must be renewed.

16 Refer to *Tools and Workshop Tips* in the *Reference* section and inspect the bearing and the bearing surfaces of the housing hub and the driven gear hub **(see illustration)**.

17 Inspect the teeth of the driven gear,

reduction and idler gears **(see illustration)**. Renew the gears as a set if worn or chipped teeth are discovered on related gears. Also check the idler and reduction gear shafts for damage, and check that the gears are not a loose fit on them. Check the teeth on the starter motor shaft (see Chapter 9).

Installation

18 Lubricate the sprag assembly with engine oil and install it in the clutch housing **(see illustration 9.13)**. Using circlip pliers, install the first circlip – align the tabs on the outer edge with the gaps in the sprag cage **(see illustration)**. Install the second circlip in the groove around the top inside edge of the housing. Position the open end of the second circlip directly opposite the open end of the first circlip.

19 Lubricate the needle bearing with engine oil and install it in the clutch housing **(see illustration 9.11)**.

20 Install the driven gear, rotating it anti-clockwise as you do **(see illustration 9.10)**. Check that the driven gear rotates freely anti-clockwise, but locks against the housing when turned clockwise **(see illustration)**.

21 Slide the assembly onto the crankshaft **(see illustration 9.9)**.

22 Install the Woodruff key, then align the slot in the primary drive gear with the key and press it into place **(see illustrations 9.8b and a)**.

23 Install the plain washer and tighten the drive gear nut finger-tight **(see illustrations 9.7b and a)**. Don't forget the nut has a left-hand thread – turn it *anti-clockwise* to tighten it.

24 Install the clutch housing, then using the method employed on removal to lock the primary driven gear with the primary drive gear (see Step 6), tighten the nut to the torque setting specified at the beginning of this Chapter **(see illustration)**.

25 Install the remainder of the clutch components (see Section 7).

26 Lubricate the idler and reduction gear shafts with engine oil. Install the reduction gear with the smaller pinion outermost, then install the idler gear **(see illustrations 9.4, 3b and a)**. **Note:** *The larger pinion on the reduction gear should engage with the teeth on the starter motor shaft.*

27 Install the right-hand crankcase cover (see Section 7).

10 Gearchange mechanism

Note: *The gearchange mechanism can be removed with the engine in the frame.*

Removal

1 Make sure the transmission is in neutral. Undo the bolts securing the front sprocket cover and remove the cover (see Chapter 7).

2 Undo the pinch bolt securing the gearchange arm and draw the arm off the shaft, noting the alignment of the register marks (see Chapter 6). Clean the exposed length of the gearchange shaft thoroughly **(see illustration)** – this will rule out the possibility

9.20 Driven gear should rotate freely anti-clockwise

9.24 Tighten the nut to the specified torque setting – note the location of the aluminium strip

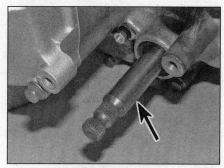

10.2 Clean the exposed length of the gearchange shaft

10.4a Note how the return spring fits each side of the locating pin (arrowed)

10.4b Note how the pawls locate onto the pins on the selector cam (arrowed)

10.4c Draw the gearchange shaft assembly out

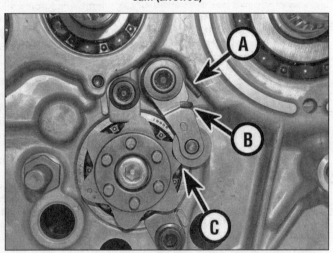

10.5a Note the ends of the stopper arm spring (A) and (B), and neutral detent (C)

of dirt entering the engine unit when the shaft is withdrawn. Clean off any corrosion with wire wool.

3 Remove the clutch (see Section 7).

4 Note how the ends of the gearchange shaft return spring fit on each side of the locating pin in the casing, and how the pawls on the selector arm locate onto the pins on the end of the selector cam, then draw the shaft assembly out **(see illustrations)**. Note the location of the thrust washer on the shaft.

5 Note how the ends of the stopper arm spring locate and how the roller on the arm locates in the neutral detent on the selector cam **(see illustration)**. Unscrew the stopper arm pivot bolt and remove the arm, washer and spring, noting how they fit **(see illustration)**.

6 Unscrew the bolt securing the gearchange cam and lift the cam off, noting how it locates onto the pin in the end of the selector drum **(see illustrations)**.

10.5b Unscrew the pivot bolt and remove the assembly

10.6a Unscrew the bolt (arrowed) . . .

10.6b . . . and lift off the gearchange cam, noting the locating pin (arrowed)

10.6c Remove the pin for safekeeping

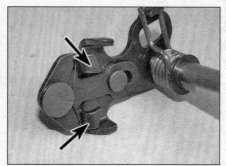

10.7a Inspect the selector arm pawls (arrowed) for wear

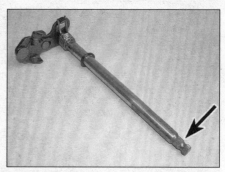

10.7b Ensure the shaft is straight. Check the splines (arrowed)

Remove the pin for safekeeping **(see illustration)**.

Inspection

7 Check the selector arm for cracks, distortion and wear of its pawls **(see illustration)**. Check for any corresponding wear on the pins on the selector cam. Check that the gearchange shaft is straight and that the splines on the end of the shaft are undamaged **(see illustration)**. If necessary, fit a new gearchange shaft and selector arm assembly.

8 Inspect the shaft return spring for fatigue, wear or damage **(see illustration)**. To remove the spring, first slide the thrust washer off the shaft, then slide off the circlip and discard it as a new one must be fitted. Note how the ends of the spring locate either side of the tab on the selector arm, then ease the spring off. Install the new spring and secure it with a new circlip – open the circlip only enough to slide it along the shaft and ensure it is correctly located in its groove. Fit the thrust washer.

9 Check the stopper arm return spring for fatigue and wear and ensure that the stopper arm roller turns freely **(see illustration)**. Renew any components that are worn or damaged. Also check the detents in the selector drum cam for wear.

10 Check the condition of the shaft oil seal in the left-hand side of the crankcase. If it is damaged, deteriorated or shows signs of leakage it must be replaced with a new one. Lever out the old seal with a seal hook or flat-bladed screwdriver. Lubricate the new seal with a smear of engine oil and press it squarely into place using your fingers or suitable socket.

Installation

11 Make sure the transmission is still in neutral. Clean the threads of the gearchange cam bolt and apply a suitable non-permanent thread-locking compound. Install the pin in the end of the selector drum, install the cam and secure it with the bolt **(see illustrations 10.6c, b and a)**. Tighten the bolt to the torque setting specified at the beginning of this Chapter.

12 Assemble the stopper arm, washer and spring on the stopper arm bolt and install the assembly **(see illustration 10.5b)**. Ensure the straight end of the spring is against the casing, the hooked end is around the arm, and the roller is located in the neutral detent on the cam **(see illustration 10.5a)**. Tighten the pivot bolt to the specified torque setting. Check that the arm moves freely.

13 Ensure the thrust washer is in place on the gearchange shaft, then install the shaft carefully to avoid damaging the seal on the left-hand side **(see illustration 10.4c)**. Fit the ends of the return spring on each side of the locating pin in the casing and align the pawls on the selector arm with the pins on the end of the selector cam **(see illustration 10.4b and a)**.

14 Install the remaining components in the reverse order of removal.

11 Valve covers

Note: *The valve covers can be removed with the engine in the frame. If the engine has been removed, ignore the steps which don't apply.*

Removal

1 On XL125V models, remove the fairing (see Chapter 8).

2 Remove the fuel tank and air filter housing (see Chapter 4A or 4B).

3 Pull the spark plug caps off the plugs, then remove the two-piece cylinder head side covers. On VT125C models, the covers are fitted to both front and rear cylinder heads – note the location of the seal between the front

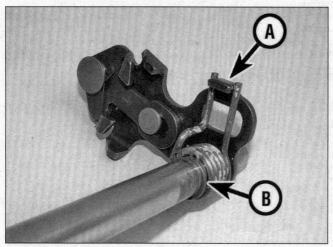

10.8 Note arrangement of spring ends on tab (A). Circlip (B) secures spring

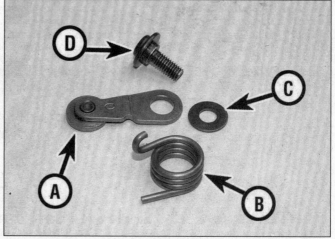

10.9 Stopper arm roller (A), return spring (B), washer (C) and pivot bolt (D)

11.3a Note the seal (arrowed) between the covers

11.3b Remove the screws and washers . . .

11.3c . . . and lift the covers off

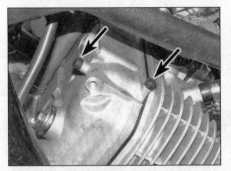

11.3d Note the location of the rubber buttons . . .

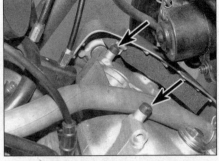

11.3e . . . on the cylinder heads

11.3f Note the sound deadening material

covers, then undo the screws securing the covers, noting the location of the washers, and lift the covers off **(see illustrations)**. Note how the covers locate on the rubber buttons on the valve covers **(see illustrations)**. Note the location of the sound deadening material on the inside of the side covers **(see illustration)**. **Note:** *On XL125V models, the side covers are fitted on the rear cylinder only.*

4 Remove the secondary air system control valve and hoses (see Chapter 4A or 4B).

5 If required, the secondary air system reed valves can be removed at this stage. Working on one cylinder at a time, undo the bolts securing the reed valve cover and lift the cover off **(see illustrations)**. Lift out the reed valve, noting which way round it fits **(see illustration)**. Take care not to damage the sealing surface of the valves as no gasket is fitted.

6 Inspect the reed valves for damage and gum and carbon deposits. If necessary, clean the reeds and stopper plates carefully with a suitable solvent **(see illustration)**. The reeds should lay flat against the valve body **(see illustration)** – if the reeds have become distorted, fit a new valve assembly.

7 Unscrew the valve cover bolts, noting

11.5a Undo the bolts . . .

11.5b . . . and remove the reed valve cover

11.5c Lift out the reed valve

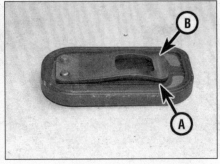

11.6a Reed (A) and stopper plate (B)

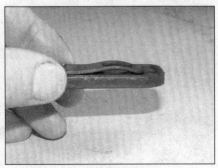

11.6b Reed should lay flat against the valve body

11.7a Remove the cover bolts and washers . . .

11.7b . . . and the seals

11.8 Lift off the valve cover

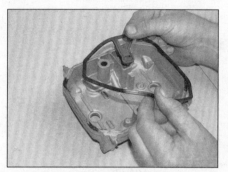

11.9 Remove the old gasket only if it is damaged

11.10 Note the location of the O-ring

the cover is being fitted, then lay the gasket in place **(see illustrations)**.

13 Install new O-rings on the secondary air system dowels and lubricate them with a smear of engine oil **(see illustration 11.10)**.

14 Position the valve cover on the cylinder head, making sure the gasket stays in place **(see illustration)**.

15 Install the seals, cover bolts and washers **(see illustrations 11.7b and a)**. Tighten the bolts to the specified torque setting.

16 Install the remaining components in the reverse order of removal. Tighten the cylinder head side cover bolts to the specified torque.

12 Cam chain tensioners

Note: *The cam chain tensioners can be removed with the engine in the frame. If the engine has been removed, ignore the steps which don't apply.*

Front cylinder

Removal

1 Remove both spark plugs (see Chapter 1).

2 Unscrew the timing inspection cap and the centre cap from the alternator cover on the

the location of the washers and seals **(see illustrations)**. Discard the seals if they are damaged or deteriorated.

8 Lift the cover off **(see illustration)**. If it is stuck, do not lever it off with a screwdriver as this will damage the sealing surface. Tap the cover gently around the sides with a rubber hammer or block of wood to dislodge it.

9 The cover gasket is normally glued into the groove in the cover, and is best left there if it is reusable. If there are signs of oil leakage, or the gasket is in any way damaged, deformed or deteriorated, peel it off and remove any traces of sealant with a suitable solvent **(see illustration)**.

10 Note the O-ring on the dowel that links the secondary air system passage between the valve cover and cylinder head and discard it as a new one must be fitted **(see illustration)**.

Installation

11 If removed, install the secondary air system reed valves, ensuring they are fitted the correct way round **(see illustrations 11.5c, b and a)**. Tighten the cover bolts to the torque setting specified at the beginning of this Chapter.

12 If a new cover gasket is being fitted, apply sealant in a few places around the groove in the cover to hold the gasket in position while

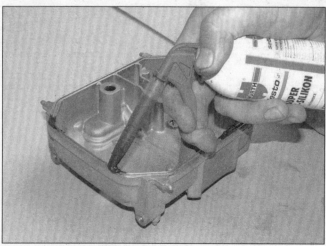

11.12 Secure a new gasket with dabs of sealant

11.14 Ensure the gasket remains in position

12.2 Timing inspection cap (A) and centre cap (B)

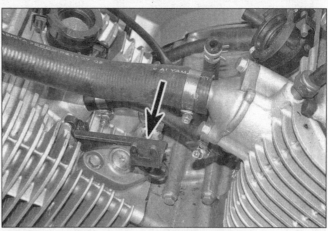

12.4 Remove the bracket (arrowed)

12.6a Tensioner cap screw (A) and mounting bolts (B)

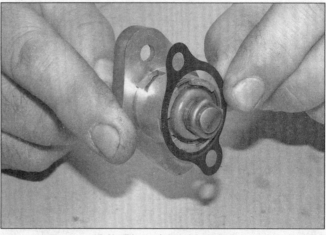

12.6b Discard the old gasket

left-hand side of the engine **(see illustration)**. Note the location of the O-rings and discard them if they are damaged or distorted.

3 Remove the front cylinder valve cover (see Section 11).

4 On carburettor models (VT125C and XL125V-1 to V-6) displace the idle speed adjuster knob and the choke knob from the bracket on the front cylinder head (see Chapter 4A), then undo the bolt securing the bracket and lift it off **(see illustration)**.

5 Before removing the cam chain tensioner, the engine must be turned to position the piston at

top dead centre (TDC) on its compression stroke. Follow the procedure in Chapter 1, Section 17, to position the front piston at TDC and check for a small amount of freeplay in both rocker arms.

6 On carburettor models, loosen the tensioner cap screw, then undo the mounting bolts evenly, a little at a time **(see illustration)**. Withdraw the tensioner and discard the gasket as a new one must be fitted **(see illustration)**.

7 On fuel injected models, undo the tensioner cap screw and remove the O-ring **(see illustration)**.

8 If the Honda service tool (Part No. 070MG-0010100) is available, insert it into the

tensioner, turn it clockwise and then push it in to lock the tensioner plunger in the retracted position. Undo the mounting bolts, withdraw the tensioner and discard the gasket as a new one must be fitted. Remove the service tool.

9 Alternatively, insert a small flat-bladed screwdriver into the tensioner and turn it clockwise to retract the tensioner plunger. Hold the screwdriver in this position, then undo the mounting bolts and withdraw the tensioner **(see illustrations)**. Release the screwdriver – the plunger will spring back out, but can be easily reset on installation.

12.7 Remove the O-ring

12.9a Use a screwdriver to retract the plunger . . .

12.9b . . . then remove the tensioner

Check

10 If not already done, unscrew the tensioner cap screw and remove the O-ring.

11 Check that the plunger cannot be pushed back into the tensioner body. Insert a small flat-bladed screwdriver into the tensioner and turn it clockwise to retract the tensioner plunger **(see illustrations 12.15a and b)**. Now release the screwdriver – the plunger should spring back out freely. If the tensioner fails either of these checks replace it with a new one.

Installation

12 Clean the mating surfaces of the tensioner body and cylinder.

13 Ensure that the front piston at TDC on its compression stroke (see Step 5).

14 Fit a new gasket onto the tensioner body **(see illustration 12.6b)**.

15 On carburettor models, insert a small flat-bladed screwdriver into the tensioner and turn it clockwise until the plunger is fully retracted **(see illustrations)**. Hold the screwdriver in this position, then install the tensioner with its mounting bolts and tighten them to the torque setting specified at the beginning of this Chapter. Remove the screwdriver.

16 On fuel injected models, if the Honda service tool is available, use it to lock the tensioner plunger in the retracted position (see Step 8). Install the tensioner and tighten the mounting bolts to the specified torque setting, then remove the service tool. Alternatively, follow the procedure in Step 15.

17 Lubricate a new O-ring with engine oil and install it in its groove **(see illustration 12.7)**, then tighten the cap screw securely.

18 Install the remaining components in the reverse order of removal.

Rear cylinder

19 To remove the rear cylinder cam chain tensioner, first remove the front sprocket cover and chain guide (see Chapter 7).

20 The procedure for removal, checking and installation is the same as for the front cam chain tensioner, noting the following:

● Remove the rear cylinder valve cover.
● There is no need to displace the idle speed adjuster knob and the choke knob.

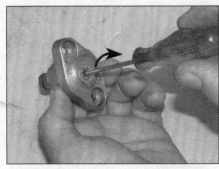

12.15a Turn the screwdriver clockwise . . .

● Follow the procedure in Chapter 1, Section 17, to position the rear piston at TDC on its compression stroke.

13 Camshafts and rocker arms

Note 1: *The camshafts and rocker arms can be removed with the engine in the frame. If the engine has been removed, ignore the steps which don't apply.*
Note 2: *The procedures are the same for both front and rear cylinders.*

Removal

1 Remove the valve covers (see Section 11).

13.2a Undo the bolts . . .

12.15b . . . to retract the plunger

2 To remove the front camshaft, undo the bolts securing the camshaft end holder and lift it off, noting the location of the dowels **(see illustrations)**.

3 Follow the procedure in Section 12 and remove the front cylinder's cam chain tensioner. Note that if the alternator cover has been removed as part of a general overhaul procedure, the appropriate line on the alternator rotor (front cylinder FT, rear cylinder RT) can be aligned with the static timing mark on the crankcase below the rear cylinder **(see illustration)**. With the piston at top dead centre (TDC) on its compression stroke the F and R lines on the camshaft sprocket should be aligned with the sealing surface of the valve cover and the UP mark should be visible **(see illustration)**.

13.2b . . . and remove the camshaft end holder. Note the dowels (arrowed)

13.3a Align the rotor mark (circled) with the static mark (arrowed)

13.3b Alignment of camshaft timing marks

13.4a Undo the bolts . . .

13.4b . . . and remove the camshaft holder

4 The front camshaft holder is marked FR – undo the bolts securing the camshaft holder and lift it off, noting the location of the dowels **(see illustrations)**.

5 Grip the camshaft securely and undo the upper sprocket bolt **(see illustration)**. Carefully turn the engine anti-clockwise one full turn (360°) and undo the other sprocket bolt.

6 Displace the camshaft sprocket and lift out the camshaft **(see illustration)**. Lift the chain off the sprocket and secure it with a piece of wire to prevent it falling into the cam chain tunnel. Note the location of the camshaft stopper pin and remove it for safekeeping **(see illustration)**.

7 If required, follow the same procedure to remove the rear camshaft, noting the following:

● The rear camshaft holder is marked RR **(see illustration)**.
● When turning the engine, take care to prevent the front cam chain falling into the cam chain tunnel.

8 With the camshafts removed, avoid turning the crankshaft – the cam chains may drop down and bind between the crankshaft and case. Place a clean rag over the cylinder heads to prevent anything falling inside.

9 Before removing the rocker arms, mark them so that they can be installed in their original locations if required.

10 Working on one assembly at a time, undo the rocker shaft retainer bolts, then use one of the bolts to draw the shafts out from the camshaft holder **(see illustrations)**. Note

13.4c Note the dowels (arrowed)

13.5 Grip the camshaft to undo the sprocket bolts

13.6a Displace the sprocket and lift out the camshaft

13.6b Remove the stopper pin for safekeeping

13.7 Identification marks RR on rear camshaft holder

13.10a Undo the stopper bolts

13.10b Draw out the rocker shafts

13.10c Note how the rocker arm fits . . .

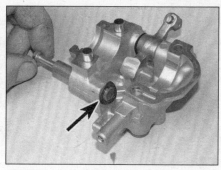

13.10d . . . and the wave washer (arrowed)

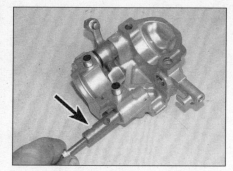

13.10e Note alignment of cut-out (arrowed)

the location of the rocker arm and the wave washer, and the alignment of the cut-out in the shaft (see illustrations). Keep related components together – slide each rocker arm back onto its shaft to aid inspection and installation.

Inspection

11 The camshaft bearings should be an interference fit on the shaft – if they are loose a new camshaft and bearing assembly will have to be fitted (see illustration). Also check that the bearings turn smoothly and freely, and that there is no freeplay between the inner and outer races. Check that the bearing housings in the holder are not worn or damaged.

12 Inspect the camshaft lobes for heat discoloration (blue appearance), score marks, chipped areas, flat spots and pitting. Measure

the height of each lobe with a micrometer (see illustration) and compare the results to the minimum height listed in this Chapter's *Specifications*. If damage is noted or wear is excessive, the camshaft must be replaced with a new one.

13 Inspect the rocker arms for heat discoloration, score marks, chipped areas, flat spots and pitting where they contact the camshaft lobes (see illustration). Similarly check the bottom of each valve clearance adjuster and the top of each valve stem. If damage is noted or wear is excessive, the rocker arms, adjusters and valves must be renewed as required.

14 Check for freeplay between each rocker arm and its shaft (see illustration). Measure the internal diameter of the arm bores and the corresponding diameter of the shaft and

compare the results with the specifications. Renew any component that is worn beyond its service limit.

15 Check the sprockets for wear and replace them with new ones if necessary (see illustration). If the sprockets are worn, it is likely that the cam chain will also be worn, and so too the sprocket on the crankshaft (see Section 19).

Installation

16 Lubricate each rocker shaft and arm with molybdenum disulphide oil (a 50/50 mixture of molybdenum disulphide grease and engine oil).

17 Slide the first rocker shaft into the holder and locate the wave washer on the shaft (see illustrations 13.10e and d). Position the rocker arm in the holder with the adjuster on the outside, then slide the shaft all the way through and secure it with the retainer bolt (see illustrations 13.10c, b and a). Tighten the retainer bolts to the torque setting specified at the beginning of this Chapter.

18 Follow the same procedure to install the remaining rocker arms.

Installing both camshafts

19 If both camshafts have been removed, install the rear one first. Turn the engine anti-clockwise to align the RT mark on the alternator rotor with the static timing mark (see Chapter 1, Section 17). The rear piston should now be at TDC.

20 Install the camshaft stopper pin (see

13.11 Camshaft and bearings are supplied as an assembly

13.12 Measuring the cam lobe height with a micrometer

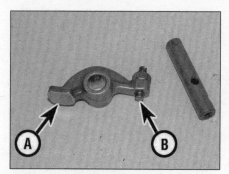

13.13 Check for wear on the rocker arm (A) and adjuster (B)

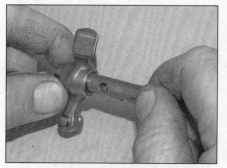

13.14 Check for freeplay between the rocker arm and shaft

13.15 Examine the camshaft sprockets for wear

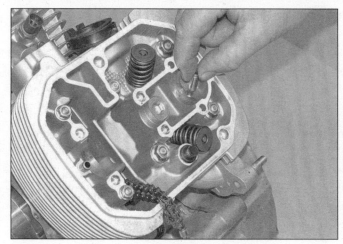

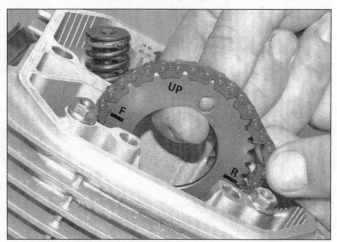

13.20a Install the camshaft stopper pin

13.20b Align the camshaft sprocket as shown

illustration). Hold the camshaft sprocket in position with the UP mark visible and the F and R lines aligned with the sealing surface of the valve cover **(see illustration)**. Install the camshaft with the lobes facing down, aligning the holes for the sprocket bolts with the holes in the sprocket **(see illustration)**. Press the camshaft bearings into their housings.

21 Clean the threads of the sprocket bolts and temporarily install the upper bolt finger tight **(see illustration)**.

22 Fill the pocket around the cam lobes with engine oil. Loosen the valve clearance adjusters fully and ensure the dowels are in position in the camshaft holder (marked RR), then fit the holder over the camshaft ensuring it seats correctly on the bearing and the cylinder head **(see illustration)**.

23 Install the camshaft holder bolts and tighten them to the specified torque setting **(see illustration)**.

24 Check that the camshaft sprocket is still correctly aligned **(see illustration)**, then apply a suitable non-permanent thread-locking compound to the sprocket bolts. Tighten the upper bolt lightly. Carefully turn the engine anti-clockwise one full turn (360°) and tighten

13.20c Fit the camshaft into the sprocket

13.21 Temporarily install the upper sprocket bolt

13.22 Fit the camshaft holder over the right-hand bearing

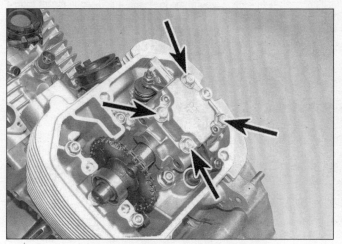

13.23 Install the camshaft holder bolts

13.24 Alignment of camshaft timing marks

the other sprocket bolt to the specified torque setting. Turn the engine anti-clockwise another full turn and tighten the first bolt to the specified torque setting.

25 Install the rear cam chain tensioner (see Section 12).

26 Before installing the front camshaft, carefully turn the engine anti-clockwise 1 1/4 turns (450°) – the FT mark on the alternator rotor should align with the static timing mark (see Chapter 1, Section 17) and the front piston should now be at TDC on its compression stroke.

27 Follow the procedure in Steps 20 to 25 to install the front camshaft.

28 Finally check that the alignment of the marks on the alternator rotor and the camshaft sprockets coincide. With the rear cylinder at TDC on its compression stroke the line next to the RT mark on the alternator rotor should align with the static timing mark, the UP mark on the rear camshaft sprocket should be visible and the F and R lines should align with the sealing surface of the rear valve cover. With the front cylinder at TDC on its compression stroke the line next to the FT mark on the alternator rotor should align with the static timing mark, the UP mark on the front camshaft sprocket should be visible and the F and R lines should align with the sealing surface of the front valve cover.

Caution: If the marks are not aligned exactly as described, the valve timing will be incorrect and the valves may strike the pistons, causing extensive damage to the engine.

29 If for any reason the timing marks do not align, remove the appropriate cam chain tensioner and camshaft sprocket. Move the camshaft and/or crankshaft round as required to correct the alignment, then reassemble the components as described.

30 Install the front and rear camshaft end holders with the flat side facing the camshaft sprocket **(see illustration 13.2a and b)**. Tighten the camshaft holder bolts to the specified torque setting.

31 Adjust the valve clearances (see Chapter 1).

32 Install the remaining components in the reverse order of removal. Check the engine oil level and top-up as necessary (see *Pre-ride checks*).

Installing the rear camshaft only

33 Before installing the rear camshaft the position of the front camshaft must be verified as follows.

34 If not already done, remove the front cylinder's valve cover (see Section 11) and the front camshaft end holder (see Step 2). Following the procedure in Chapter 1, Section 17, turn the engine anti-clockwise until the FT mark on the alternator rotor aligns with the static timing mark, the UP mark on the front camshaft sprocket is visible and the F and R lines align with the sealing surface of the front valve cover **(see illustration 13.3b)**. The front cylinder is now at TDC on the compression stroke.

35 Now turn the engine anti-clockwise 3/4 turn (270°) so that the line next to the RT mark on the alternator rotor aligns with the static timing mark. The rear cylinder is now at TDC on the compression stroke. Follow the procedure in Steps 20 to 25 to install the rear camshaft.

36 Check that the timing marks for the front and rear camshafts coincide and adjust them if necessary (see Steps 28 and 29), then follow Steps 30 to 32.

Installing the front camshaft only

37 Before installing the front camshaft the position of the rear camshaft must be verified as follows.

38 If not already done, remove the rear cylinder's valve cover (see Section 11) and the rear camshaft end holder (see Step 2). Following the procedure in Chapter 1, Section 17, turn the engine anti-clockwise until the RT mark on the alternator rotor aligns with the static timing mark, the UP mark on the rear camshaft sprocket is visible and the F and R lines align with the sealing surface of the rear valve cover **(see illustration 13.24)**. The rear cylinder is now at TDC on the compression stroke.

39 Now turn the engine anti-clockwise 1 1/4 turns (450°) so that the line next to the FT mark on the alternator rotor aligns with the static timing mark. The front cylinder is now at TDC on the compression stroke. Follow the procedure in Steps 20 to 25 to install the front camshaft.

40 Check that the timing marks for the front and rear camshafts coincide and adjust them if necessary (see Steps 28 and 29), then follow Steps 30 to 32.

14 Cylinder head – removal and installation

Note: *The cylinder heads can be removed with the engine in the frame. If the engine has been removed, ignore the steps which don't apply.*

Removal

1 Drain the coolant and, for access to the front cylinder head, remove the radiator (see Chapter 3).

2 Drain the engine oil (see Chapter 1).

3 Remove the carburettor or throttle body assembly; remove the exhaust system (see Chapter 4A or 4B).

4 Disconnect the coolant hoses from the front and rear cylinder heads and remove the thermostat as required (see Chapter 3).

5 Remove the horn for access to the front cylinder head (see Chapter 9).

6 On XL125V models, remove the rear cylinder ignition coil for access to the rear cylinder head (see Chapter 4B or 5).

7 On carburettor models, disconnect the thermo-switch wiring connector **(see illustration 4.15)**.

8 Remove the valve covers (see Section 11).

9 The remaining steps of the procedure are the same for both front and rear cylinder heads. If only one head is being removed, ignore the steps that don't apply.

10 Remove the camshaft(s) (see Section 13). Secure the cam chain to the guide blade with an elastic band to prevent it falling into the cam chain tunnel.

11 Undo the two 6 mm cylinder head nuts on the left-hand side next to the cam chain tunnel, then undo the four 8 mm nuts evenly **(see illustration)**.

12 Pull the cylinder head up off the cylinder **(see illustration)**. Note that the cylinder is held against the crankcase by the cylinder head nuts – if the cylinder lifts with the head the cylinder base gasket seal will be broken and the cylinder will have to be removed and a new base gasket fitted (see Section 16). If the head is stuck, tap around the joint with a soft-faced mallet to free it. Do not attempt to free the head by levering it off – you'll damage the sealing surfaces.

13 Remove the cylinder head gasket **(see illustration)**. Ensure the cam chain is held

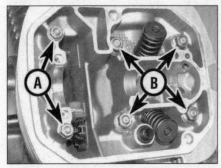

14.11 Cylinder head 6 mm nuts (A) and 8 mm nuts (B)

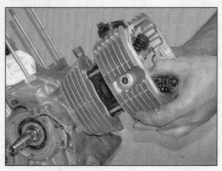

14.12 Lift off the cylinder head

14.13 Remove the cylinder head gasket

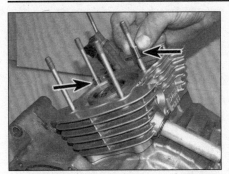

14.14 Remove the dowels for safekeeping

14.19 Note gasket UP mark. Cam chain secured with elastic band (arrowed)

14.20 Lower cylinder head carefully over the dowels

securely **(see illustration 14.19)** and stuff a clean rag into the cam chain tunnel to prevent any debris falling in.

14 If they are loose, remove the dowels from the front and rear edges of the cylinder for safekeeping **(see illustration)**. If either appears to be missing it is probably stuck in the underside of the cylinder head.

15 Inspect the cylinder head gasket and the mating surfaces on the head and cylinder for signs of leakage, which could indicate that the head is distorted. If necessary, check the cylinder head with a straight-edge (see Section 15). Discard the old head gasket as a new one must be fitted on reassembly.

16 Clean any traces of old gasket material from the head and cylinder. If a scraper is used, take care not to scratch or gouge the soft aluminium. Be careful not to let any of the gasket material fall into the cylinder bore or coolant passages.

Installation

17 If removed, fit the dowels into the cylinder **(see illustration 14.14)**.

18 Remove any rag from the cam chain tunnel. Ensure the cam chain is held securely **(see illustration 14.19)**

19 Ensure both cylinder head and cylinder mating surfaces are clean. Lay the *new* head gasket over the studs, the cam chain and blades and onto the cylinder, locating it over the dowels with the UP mark facing up **(see illustration)**. Never reuse the old gasket.

20 Carefully fit the cylinder head over the studs and the cam chain and lower it onto the

cylinder, making sure it locates correctly onto the dowels **(see illustration)**.

21 Lubricate the threads of the studs and the undersides of the cylinder head nuts with engine oil **(see illustration)** then install the nuts finger-tight.

22 Tighten the 8 mm nuts evenly in a criss-cross pattern to the torque setting specified at the beginning of this Chapter, then tighten the 6 mm nuts to the specified torque **(see illustration)**.

23 Install the remaining components in the reverse order of removal.

24 Refill the engine with the recommended grade and type of oil (see Chapter 1).

15 Cylinder head – valve overhaul

1 Because of the complex nature of this job and the special tools and equipment required, most owners leave servicing of the valves, valve seats and valve guides to a professional. However, you can make an initial assessment of whether the valves are seating correctly, and therefore sealing, by pouring a small amount of solvent into each of the valve ports. If the solvent leaks past any valve into the combustion chamber area the valve is not seating correctly and sealing.

2 With the correct tools (a valve spring compressor is essential – make sure it is suitable for motorcycle work), you can also remove the valves and associated components

from the cylinder head, clean them and check them for wear to assess the extent of the work needed, and, unless seat cutting or guide replacement is required, grind in the valves and reassemble them in the head.

3 A dealer service department or specialist engineer can renew the guides and re-cut the valve seats.

4 After the valve service has been performed, be sure to clean it very thoroughly before installation on the engine to remove any metal particles or abrasive grit that may still be present from the valve service operations. Use compressed air, if available, to blow out all the holes and passages.

Disassembly

Special tool: *A valve spring compressor suitable for motorcycle work is absolutely necessary for this procedure (see Step 8).*

5 Before proceeding, arrange to label and store the valves along with their related components in such a way that they can be returned to their original locations without getting mixed up **(see illustration)**. A container with four compartments is ideal. Alternatively, labelled plastic bags will do just as well.

6 If required, remove the thermostat from the left-hand side of the rear cylinder head, and, on carburettor models, unscrew the thermo-switch (see Chapter 3).

7 If required, loosen the lower clamps securing the intake manifolds to the heads and pull the manifolds off, noting how they fit.

14.21 Lubricate the stud threads and nuts before tightening

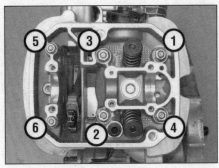

14.22 Tightening sequence for the cylinder head nuts

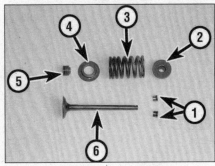

15.5 Valve components

1 *Collets*   4 *Spring seat*
2 *Spring retainer*   5 *Valve stem seal*
3 *Spring*   6 *Valve*

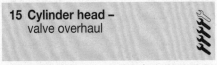

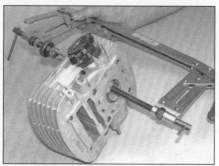

15.8 Install the valve spring compressor

15.9 Removing the collets with a small screwdriver

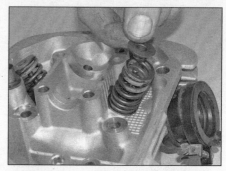

15.10a Remove the spring retainer . . .

15.10b . . . the valve spring . . .

15.10c . . . and the spring seat

15.11a Pull out the valve

If the manifolds are cracked or hardened, new ones must be fitted on reassembly.

8 Working on one cylinder head at a time, install the valve spring compressor, making sure it is correctly located onto each end of the valve assembly (see illustration). On the underside of the head, make sure the compressor only contacts the valve and not the soft aluminium of the head – if necessary, fit a spacer between them. On the top of the valve the compressor needs to be about the same size as the spring retainer – if it is too small it will be difficult to remove and install the collets (see illustration 15.9).

9 Compress the spring just enough to free the collets, then remove them using a magnet or a screwdriver with a dab of grease on it (see illustration).

10 Carefully release the valve spring compressor and remove the spring retainer, the spring and the spring seat, noting which way up each component fits (see illustrations).

11 Pull the valve out from the underside of the head (see illustration). If the valve binds in the guide and won't pull through, push it back into the head and deburr the area around the collet groove with a very fine file (see illustration).

12 Pull the valve stem seal off the top of the valve guide with pliers and discard it (see illustration) – never reuse the old seals.

13 Repeat the procedure for the remaining valve. Remember to keep the parts for each valve together so they can be reinstalled in the same location.

14 Clean the cylinder head with solvent and dry it thoroughly. Compressed air will speed the drying process and ensure that all holes and recessed areas are clean. Note: Do not use a wire brush mounted in a drill motor to clean the combustion chambers as the head material is soft and may be scratched or eroded away by the wire brush.

15 Clean all the valve springs, collets, retainers and spring seats with solvent and dry them thoroughly. Do the parts from one valve at a time so that no mixing of parts between valves occurs.

16 Remove any carbon deposits that may have formed on the valve heads using a scraper or a motorised wire brush. Again, make sure the valves do not get mixed-up.

Inspection

17 Working on one cylinder head at a time, check very carefully for cracks and other damage, especially around the valve seats and spark plug hole. If cracks are found, a new head will be required.

18 Using a precision straight-edge and a feeler gauge, check the head gasket mating surface for warpage (see illustration). Refer to Tools and Workshop Tips in the Reference section for details of how to use the straight-

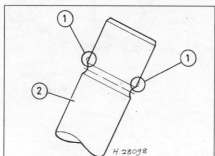

15.11b If necessary, deburr the valve stem (2) above the collet groove (1)

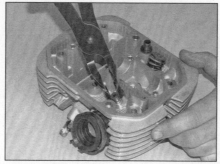

15.12 Pull the stem seal off with pliers

15.18 Check the head gasket mating surface for warpage

edge. If the head is warped beyond the limit specified at the beginning of this Chapter, consult a Honda dealer or take it to a specialist repair shop for rectification.

19 Examine the valve seats in the combustion chamber. If they are pitted, cracked or burned, the head will require work beyond the scope of the home mechanic. Measure the valve seat width and compare it to this Chapter's *Specifications* **(see illustration)**. If it exceeds the service limit, or if it varies around its circumference, overhaul is required.

20 Examine the head of each valve for cracks, pits and burned spots, then check the valve stem and the collet groove area for wear and damage **(see illustration)**. Rotate the valve and check for any obvious indication that it is bent. Check the end of the stem for pitting and excessive wear. Renew the valve if necessary.

21 Clean the valve guides to remove any carbon build-up. Working on one valve and guide at a time, measure the valve stem diameter and note the results – take measurements in three different places to check for uneven wear **(see illustration)**. Now measure the inside diameter of the guide (at both ends and in the centre of the guide) with a small hole gauge (see *Tools and Workshop Tips* in the *Reference* section). Subtract the stem diameter from the guide diameter to obtain the stem-to-guide clearance. If the clearance is greater than the service limit listed in this Chapter's *Specifications*, renew whichever component is worn beyond its service limit. If the valve guide is within specifications, but is worn unevenly, it should be renewed.

22 Check the end of each valve spring for wear and pitting. Measure the spring free length and compare the result to the specifications **(see illustration)**. If any spring is shorter than specified it has sagged and must be replaced with a new one.

23 Stand each spring upright on a flat surface and check it for bend with a set square **(see illustration)**. If the bend in any spring is excessive, it must be replaced with a new one.

24 Check the spring seats, retainers and collets for obvious wear and cracks. Any questionable parts should not be reused, as

15.19 Measure the valve seat width

15.21 Measuring the valve stem diameter with a micrometer

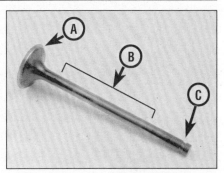

15.20 Examine the valve head (A), stem (B) and collet groove (C)

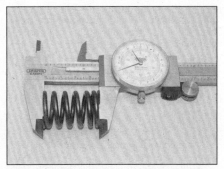

15.22 Measuring valve spring free length

extensive damage will occur in the event of failure during engine operation.

25 If the inspection indicates that no overhaul work is required, the valve components can be reinstalled in the head.

Reassembly

26 Ensure the cylinder heads are clean and blow through all passages with compressed air.

27 Working on one valve at a time, lubricate the *new* valve stem seal with engine oil and fit it onto the top of the valve guide **(see illustration)**. Use an appropriate size deep socket to push the seal squarely over the end of the guide until it is felt to clip into place **(see illustration)**.

28 Lubricate the valve stem with engine oil, then install the valve in its guide, rotating it slowly to avoid damaging the seal **(see illustration 15.11a)**.

29 Lay the spring seat in place with its shouldered side facing up, then install the spring, with the closer-wound coils facing down, followed by the spring retainer, with its shouldered side facing down so that it fits into the top of the spring **(see illustrations 15.10c, b and a)**.

30 Apply a small amount of grease to the collets to help hold them in place. Compress the spring with the valve spring compressor and install the collets **(see illustrations 15.8 and 15.9)**. When compressing the spring, depress it only as far as is absolutely necessary to slip the collets into place. Make certain that the collets are securely located in the collet groove and release the spring compressor.

31 Repeat the procedure for the remaining valves. Remember to keep the parts for each valve together and separate from the other valves so they can be reinstalled in the correct location.

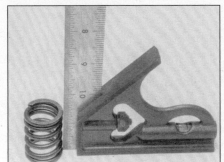

15.23 Check that the springs are not bent

15.27a Lubricate the new seal with engine oil . . .

15.27b . . . and press it on with a suitably-sized socket

15.32 Tap each valve stem lightly to seat the collets

32 Support the cylinder head on blocks so the valves can't contact the work surface, then tap the end of each valve stem lightly with a hammer and punch to seat the collets in their grooves (see illustration).

Check for proper sealing of the valves by pouring a small amount of solvent into each of the valve ports. If the solvent leaks past either valve into the combustion chamber the valve grinding operation on that valve should be repeated.

33 If removed, install the intake manifolds. Align the slot on the underside of each manifold with the lug on the cylinder head and push the manifold on firmly. Align the lower manifold clamps as shown (see illustrations).

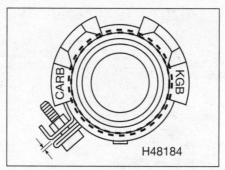

15.33a Position of lower manifold clamp – VT125C and XL125V-1 to V-6 models. End clearance is 0 to 2 mm

34 If removed, install the thermostat and the thermo-switch (see Chapter 3).

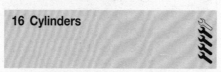

16 Cylinders

Note: *The cylinders can be removed with the engine in the frame. If the engine has been removed, ignore the steps which don't apply.*

Removal

1 Remove the cylinder head(s) (see Section 14). Note: *If only one cylinder is being removed, only remove the relevant cylinder head.*
2 Disconnect the coolant pipe from the front of the crankcase cover and the front cylinder (see Chapter 3).

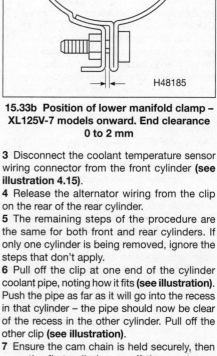

15.33b Position of lower manifold clamp – XL125V-7 models onward. End clearance 0 to 2 mm

3 Disconnect the coolant temperature sensor wiring connector from the front cylinder (see illustration 4.15).
4 Release the alternator wiring from the clip on the rear of the rear cylinder.
5 The remaining steps of the procedure are the same for both front and rear cylinders. If only one cylinder is being removed, ignore the steps that don't apply.
6 Pull off the clip at one end of the cylinder coolant pipe, noting how it fits (see illustration). Push the pipe as far as it will go into the recess in that cylinder – the pipe should now be clear of the recess in the other cylinder. Pull off the other clip (see illustration).
7 Ensure the cam chain is held securely, then ease the first cylinder up off the crankcase (see illustration). If the cylinder is stuck, tap around the joint with a soft-faced mallet to free it. Do not attempt to free the cylinder by levering it off – you'll damage the sealing surfaces.
8 Support the piston as the cylinder is lifted off to prevent the connecting rod or piston skirt hitting the crankcase (see illustration).
9 Remove the cylinder coolant pipe and discard the O-rings as new ones must be fitted (see illustration).

16.6a Pull off the first coolant pipe clip

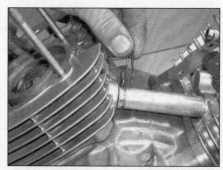

16.6b Pull off the other coolant pipe clip

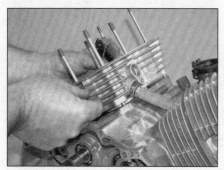

16.7 Ease the cylinder up off the crankcase

16.8 Support the piston as the cylinder is lifted

16.9 Discard the coolant pipe O-rings

10 Remove the cylinder base gasket and discard it as a new one must be used **(see illustration)**. If they are loose, remove the dowels from the crankcase for safekeeping **(see illustration)**. If either appears to be missing it is probably stuck in the underside of the cylinder.

11 Stuff clean rag into the cam chain tunnel and around the connecting rod to protect and support it and the piston and to prevent anything falling into the crankcase.

12 Clean all traces of old gasket material and sealant from the cylinder and crankcase. If a scraper is used, take care not to scratch or gouge the soft aluminium. Be careful not to let any of the gasket material fall into the engine.

13 If required, unscrew the coolant temperature sensor from the front cylinder (see Chapter 3).

Inspection

14 Working on one cylinder at a time, use a precision straight-edge and a feeler gauge to check the top surface of the cylinder for warpage **(see illustration 15.18)**. Refer to *Tools and Workshop Tips* in the Reference section for details of how to use the straight-edge. If the cylinder is warped beyond the limit specified at the beginning of this Chapter, consult your Honda dealer or take it to a specialist repair shop for rectification.

15 Inspect the cylinder wall carefully for scratches and score marks **(see illustration)**.

16 Using a telescoping bore gauge and a micrometer, check the dimensions of the cylinder bore to assess the amount of wear, taper and ovality. Measure near the top (but below the level of the top piston ring at TDC), centre and bottom (but above the level of the oil ring at BDC) of the bore, both parallel to and across the crankshaft axis **(see illustrations)**. Compare the results to the specifications at the beginning of this Chapter. If the bore is worn, oval or tapered beyond the service limit it can be re-bored and an oversize piston and ring set fitted. Two sizes of oversize piston (+0.25 mm and +0.50 mm) are available. Note that the engineer carrying out the re-bore must be aware of the required piston-to-bore clearance (see *Specifications*).

17 If the precision measuring tools are not available, take the pistons and cylinders to

16.10a Remove the cylinder base gasket

16.10b Remove the dowels for safekeeping

16.15 Inspect the cylinder wall (arrowed) for damage

16.16a Measure the cylinder bore with a telescoping gauge . . .

a Honda dealer or specialist repair shop for assessment and advice.

18 Check that all the cylinder studs are tight in the crankcase. If any are loose, or damaged and need to be renewed, remove them, noting where they fit – the length and diameter of the studs differs depending on their location in the crankcase **(see illustration)**.

19 Before installing a stud, ensure that the threads on the stud and in the crankcase are clean. If an old stud is being re-tightened, lubricate the threads with engine oil then tighten it securely. If a new stud is being fitted, apply a suitable non-permanent thread-locking compound then tighten it securely. When fitting the studs always screw the end with the longest thread into the crankcase. To avoid marking the studs when they are fitted, lock

two nuts together on the upper thread, then tighten the stud using a spanner on the upper nut. Check the installed length of the studs by measuring the distance between the top and the crankcase surface **(see illustration)**.

Installation

20 If removed, fit the dowels over the studs and press them down firmly **(see illustration 16.10b)**.

21 Remove the rags from around the piston and the cam chain tunnel, taking care not to

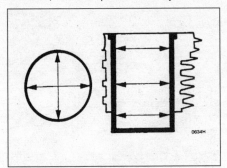

16.16b . . . in the directions shown

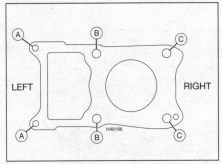

16.18 Cylinder stud locations
6 mm diameter x 160 mm overall length (A)
8 mm diameter x 146 mm overall length (B)
8 mm diameter x 146 mm overall length (C)

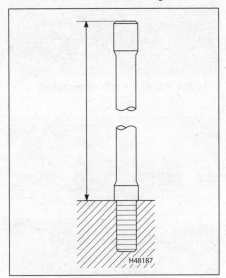

16.19 Installed length of the cylinder studs (A) 145 mm, (B) 137.4 mm, (C) 132.4 mm

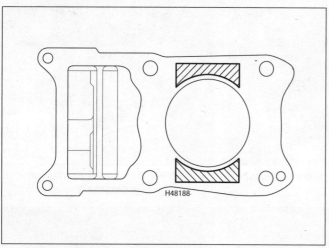

16.22 Apply sealant to the crankcase mating surface in the shaded areas

16.23 Install the new base gasket. Note the UP mark

let the connecting rod fall against the rim of the crankcase.

22 Ensure both cylinder and crankcase mating surfaces are clean. On VT125C-4 models and XL125V-4 models onward, apply suitable sealant (Three-Bond 1207B or equivalent RTV sealant – ask your Honda dealer) to the area shown on the crankcase sealing surfaces **(see illustration)**.

23 Lay the *new* base gasket over the studs, the cam chain and blades and onto the crankcase, locating it over the dowels with the UP mark facing up **(see illustration)**. Never reuse the old gasket.

24 Ensure the piston ring end gaps are correctly staggered **(see illustration 18.11)** then lubricate the piston, rings and cylinder bore with engine oil.

25 Rotate the crankshaft so that the piston is at its highest point – if possible, have an assistant support the piston. Fit the cylinder over the studs and the cam chain and lower it onto the top of the piston **(see illustrations)**.

26 Carefully compress and feed the top ring into the bore as the cylinder is pressed down – use your finger-tips and a small screwdriver to do this **(see illustration)**. Don't press the cylinder down too hard as this will only

cause the ring to snag and take care not to score the surface of the piston skirt with the screwdriver.

27 Gradually lower the cylinder over the piston and feed the second ring and oil ring in using the same method.

28 Once all the rings are safely inside the bore, lower the cylinder onto the base gasket – ensure the dowels at the front and rear are aligned with their holes in the cylinder and press the cylinder down firmly **(see illustration)**.

29 At this stage, if both cylinders have been removed, it is advisable to install the corresponding cylinder head (see Section 14). Until the cylinder head is in place and the head nuts have been tightened, the installed cylinder may lift off the base gasket while the second cylinder is being fitted.

30 Before fitting the second cylinder, lubricate two new coolant pipe O-rings with coolant. Install the O-rings in the outer grooves on both ends of the pipe, then push the pipe as far as it will go into the recess in the installed cylinder **(see illustration)**.

31 Follow the procedure in Steps 20 to 28 and install the second cylinder.

32 With the cylinder in place, fit the clip to

16.25a Install the cylinder carefully . . .

16.25b . . . then lower it onto the piston

16.26 Feed the top ring into the cylinder bore

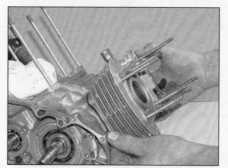

16.28 Press the cylinder down onto the base gasket

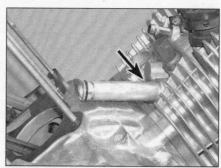

16.30 Push the coolant pipe all the way into the installed cylinder

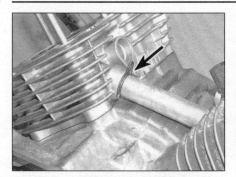

16.32 Push the pipe in as far as the clip (arrowed) will allow

17.3 Note markings on the top of the piston

17.4a Insert a screwdriver into the notch . . .

the inner groove in the free end of the coolant pipe, then push that end of the pipe into its recess **(see illustration)**. Fit the other clip to the inner groove in the other end of the pipe.
33 Install the remaining components in the reverse order of removal.

17 Pistons

Note: *The pistons can be removed with the engine in the frame.*

Removal

1 The procedure for removing the pistons is the same for both front and rear cylinders.
2 Remove the cylinder(s) (see Section 16). Ensure that the crankcase and the cam chain tunnel are completely blocked with clean rag to prevent anything falling inside.
3 Note that the pistons are marked F (front cylinder) and R (rear cylinder) **(see illustration)**. They are also marked IN – this mark faces the intake side of the cylinder in both cases. The marks may not be clearly visible until the pistons are cleaned.
4 Carefully prise out the circlip on one side of the piston using needle-nose pliers or a small flat-bladed screwdriver inserted into the notch **(see illustrations)**. Push the piston pin óut from the other side to free the piston from the connecting rod **(see illustration)**. When the piston has been removed, remove the other circlip and discard them both as new ones must be used. Slide the piston pin back

17.4b . . . then prise out the circlip . . .

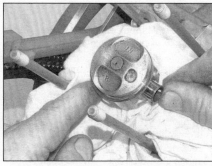

17.4c . . . and push out the piston pin

into the piston so that related parts don't get mixed up.

> **HAYNES HiNT**
>
> *If a piston pin is a tight fit, heat the piston gently with a hot air gun – this will expand the alloy piston sufficiently to release its grip on the pin. If the piston pin is particularly stubborn, extract it using a drawbolt tool, but be careful to protect the piston's working surfaces – see Tools and Workshop Tips in the Reference section.*

5 Using your thumbs or a thin blade, carefully remove the rings from the piston **(see illustrations)**. Do not nick or gouge the piston in the process. Note which way up each ring fits and in which groove as they must be installed in their original positions if being re-used (see Section 18). The oil control ring (lowest on the piston) is composed of three

separate components – the expander and the upper and lower side rails. **Note:** *It is good practice to fit new piston rings when an engine is being overhauled.*
6 Clean all traces of carbon from the top of the piston. A hand-held wire brush or a piece of fine emery cloth can be used once most of the deposits have been scraped away. Do not, under any circumstances, use a wire brush mounted in a drill motor; the piston material is soft and will be eroded away by the brush.
7 Use a piston ring groove cleaning tool to remove any carbon deposits from the ring grooves. If a tool is not available, a piece broken off an old ring will do the job. Be very careful to remove only the carbon deposits. Do not remove any metal and do not nick or gouge the sides of the ring grooves.
8 Once the carbon has been removed, clean the piston with a suitable solvent and dry it thoroughly. Make sure the oil return holes at the back of the oil ring groove are clear **(see illustration)**.

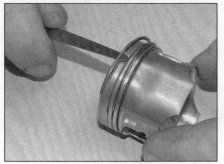

17.5a Using a thin blade . . .

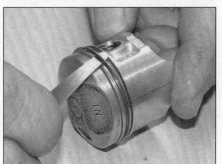

17.5b . . . to ease off the piston rings

17.8 Ensure the oil holes (arrowed) are clear

17.11 Measuring the piston diameter

17.12 Measuring the ring-to-groove clearance

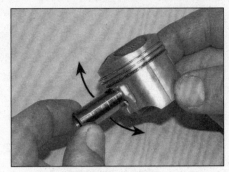

17.13a Checking the piston pin for freeplay in the piston

Inspection

9 Carefully inspect each piston for cracks around the skirt, at the pin bosses and at the ring lands (between the ring grooves). Also check that the circlip grooves are not damaged. Normal piston wear appears as even, vertical wear on the thrust surfaces of the piston. If the skirt is scored or scuffed, the engine may have been suffering from overheating and/or abnormal combustion, which causes excessively high operating temperatures. The oil pump should be checked thoroughly.

10 In extreme cases, a hole in the top of the piston or burned areas around the edge of the piston crown indicate that pre-ignition or knocking under load have occurred, although the ignition control unit (ECM) should detect over-heating problems long before serious damage takes place. Check the symptoms of

poor running in *Fault Finding* in the *Reference* section.

11 Check the piston-to-bore clearance by measuring the cylinder bore (see Section 16) and the piston diameter. Make sure the piston is matched to its correct cylinder. Measure the piston 14 mm up from the bottom of the skirt and at 90° to the piston pin axis **(see illustration)**. Subtract the piston diameter from the bore diameter to obtain the clearance. If it is greater than the figure specified at the beginning of this Chapter, check whether it is the bore or piston, or both, that is worn beyond the service limit. If just the piston is worn, a new piston and ring set should be fitted. If the bore is worn the cylinder will have to be re-bored and an oversize piston fitted (see Section 16).

12 Measure the piston ring-to-groove clearance by fitting each ring in its groove

and slipping a feeler gauge in beside it **(see illustration)**. Make sure you have the correct ring for the groove (see Step 5). Check the clearance at three or four locations around the groove. If the clearance is greater than specified, replace both the piston and rings as a set. If new rings are being used, measure the clearance using the new rings. If the clearance is greater than that specified, the piston is worn and must be replaced with a new one.

13 Apply clean engine oil to the piston pin, insert it into the piston and check for any freeplay between the two **(see illustration)**. Measure the pin external diameter at each end **(see illustration)**, and the pin bores in the piston **(see illustration)**. Calculate the difference to obtain the piston-to-piston pin clearance and compare the result to the specifications at the beginning of this Chapter. If the clearance is greater than specified, replace the components that are worn beyond their specified limits.

14 Repeat the check and measurements between the middle of the pin and the connecting rod small-end **(see illustrations)**.

Installation

15 Inspect and install the piston rings (see Section 18).

16 Working on one piston at a time, install a *new* circlip into one side of the piston – never re-use old circlips. When installing the circlips, compress them only just enough to fit them in the piston, and make sure they are

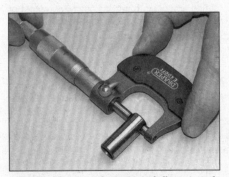

17.13b Measure the external diameter of the pin at both ends . . .

17.13c . . . and the internal diameter of the pin bore

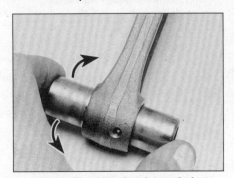

17.14a Checking the piston pin for freeplay in the small-end

17.14b Measure the external diameter of the pin at the centre . . .

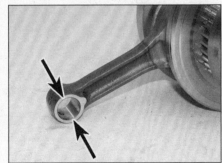

17.14c . . . and the internal diameter of the small-end

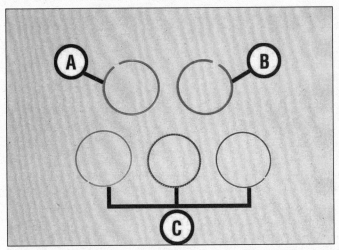

18.2 Piston ring set – top ring (A), second ring (B) and oil control ring (C)

18.3 Measuring piston ring installed end gap

properly seated in their grooves with the open end away from the removal notch **(see illustration 17.4a)**.

17 Lubricate the piston pin, the piston pin bore and the connecting rod small-end bore with engine oil, then install the piston on its correct connecting rod (see Step 3). Ensure the piston is fitted the correct way round **(see illustration 17.3)**.

18 Insert the piston pin from the side without the circlip and push it all the way in. Secure the pin with the other *new* circlip.

19 Remove the rag from the crankcase openings and install the cylinder (see Section 16).

18 Piston rings

Inspection

1 It is good practice to fit new piston rings when an engine is being overhauled. Before installing the new rings, measure the end gaps as follows.

2 Lay out each piston with its ring set so the rings will be matched with the same piston and cylinder during the measurement procedure. The upper surface of the top and second rings should have a manufacturer's mark at one end – the top ring is marked 'R' and the second ring is marked 'RN' **(see illustration)**. Also note that the rings can be identified by their different cross-sections **(see illustration 18.11)**.

3 The end gaps are measured with the rings fitted inside the cylinder bore – insert a ring into the bottom of the bore and square it up with the cylinder walls by pushing it down with the top of the piston. The ring should be about 15 mm below the edge of the cylinder. Slip a feeler gauge between the ends of the ring to measure the gap and compare the result to *Specifications* at the beginning of this Chapter **(see illustration)**. Note that the gaps for each ring are different.

4 If the gap is larger or smaller than specified, check that you have the correct rings before proceeding. Excess end gap is not critical unless it exceeds the service limit.

5 Repeat the procedure for all the rings. Remember to keep the rings together with their matched pistons.

Installation

6 The oil control ring (lowest on the piston) is installed first. It is composed of three separate components – the expander and the upper and lower side rails. Slip the expander into the groove, positioning its ends so that they touch but do not overlap **(see illustration)**.

7 Install the lower side rail. Do not use a piston ring installation tool on the oil ring side rails as they may be damaged. Instead, place one end of the side rail into the groove between the expander and the ring land **(see illustration)**. Hold it firmly in place and slide a finger or thin blade around the piston while pushing the rail into the groove. Next, install the upper side rail in the same manner.

8 After the oil control ring has been installed, check that both its upper and lower side rails can be turned smoothly in the ring groove.

9 Fit the second ring into the middle groove in the piston with its RN mark facing up (see Step 2). Do not expand the ring any more than is necessary to slide it into place **(see illustrations)**. If required, use a piston ring installation tool to avoid breaking the ring.

10 Follow the same procedure to install the top ring into the top groove in the piston

11 Once the rings are correctly installed,

18.6 Installing the oil ring expander

18.7 Installing the lower side rail

18.9 Installing the second ring using a thin blade

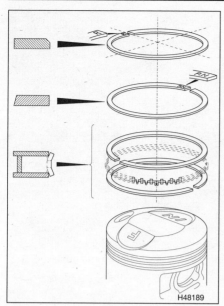

18.11 Stagger the ring end gaps as shown

check they move freely without snagging and stagger their end gaps as shown **(see illustration)**.

19 Cam chains, tensioner blades and guide blades

Note: *The cam chains and their blades can be removed with the engine in the frame.*

Removal

1 Remove the cylinder heads (see Section 14).
2 Remove the alternator rotor (see Chapter 9).
3 Note the arrangement of the front and rear cylinder cam chains, tensioner blades and guide blades, then undo the bolt securing

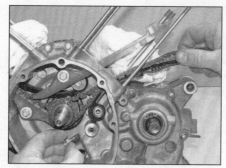

19.3 Remove the rear cylinder tensioner blade

the rear cylinder tensioner blade and lift it out **(see illustration)**. Note the location of the shouldered spacer in the lower end of the blade **(see illustration 19.10)**.
4 Undo the bolt securing the rear cylinder guide blade and lift it out **(see illustration)**. Note the location of the shouldered spacer in the lower end of the blade **(see illustration 19.10)**.
5 Mark the outer face of the cam chain with a dab of paint so that is can be assembled the same way round if it is to be reused, then slip it off the crankshaft sprocket and lift it out of the engine **(see illustration)**.
6 Follow the same procedure to remove the front cylinder guide blade, tensioner blade and cam chain **(see illustration)**.

Inspection

7 Except in cases of oil starvation, the cam chains should wear very little. If they have stretched excessively, and can no longer be correctly tensioned by the cam chain tensioners, it is likely that the guide and tensioner blades will be worn and in need of renewal as well.
8 Check all round the chain – if there is any discernible slack between the links, or if it is stiff or the links are binding or kinking, replace both chains.

19.4 Remove the rear cylinder guide blade

19.5 Remove the rear cylinder cam chain

9 Also check the condition of the camshaft sprockets (see Section 13) and crankshaft sprocket. If the crankshaft sprocket is worn or damaged a new crankshaft will have to be fitted – the sprocket is an integral part of the crankshaft assembly (see Section 25). **Note:** *Check the operation of the appropriate cam chain tensioner if either chain is slack but appears to be in good condition.*
10 Examine the sliding surfaces of the guide and tensioner blades for signs of wear or damage **(see illustration)**. Check them carefully for cracks in the surface and along the edges. Install new components if necessary.

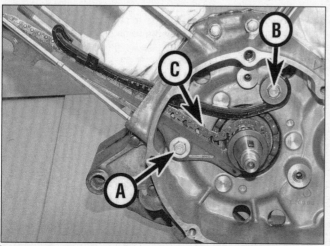

19.6 Remove the front cylinder guide blade (A), tensioner blade (B) and chain (C)

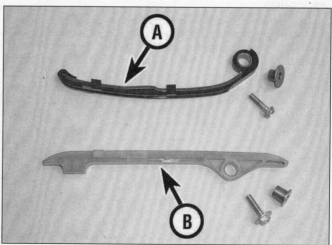

19.10 Tensioner blade, shouldered spacer and bolt (A), guide blade, shouldered spacer and bolt (B)

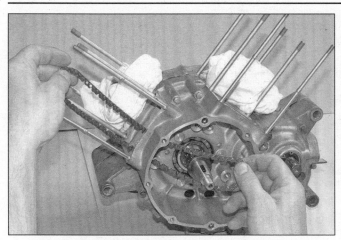

19.11a Installing the front cylinder cam chain

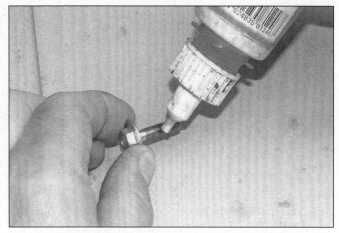

19.11b Thread-lock the tensioner blade mounting bolts

Installation

11 Installation is the reverse of removal, noting the following:

● If the original chains are being used, fit them as noted on removal (see Step 5) **(see illustration)**.

● Clean the threads of the tensioner blade mounting bolts and apply a suitable non-permanent thread-locking compound **(see illustration)**.

● Install the spacers in the chain guide blades from the rear (as assembled) and in the chain tensioner blades from the front (as assembled).

● Tighten the blade mounting bolts securely.

● Lubricate the chains with engine oil.

| 20 | Crankcase separation and reassembly |

Note: *To separate the crankcase halves, the engine must be removed from the frame.*
Special tool: *A puller is required to install the*

crankshaft in the left-hand crankcase half (see Section 25).

Separation

1 To access the crankshaft and connecting rod assembly, transmission shafts, selector drum and forks, and their associated bearings, the crankcase halves must be separated.

2 Before the crankcases can be separated the following components must be removed:

Starter motor and alternator (Chapter 9)
Oil pump (Section 6)
Clutch (Section 7)
Starter clutch and drive gears (Section 9)
Gearchange mechanism (Section 10)
Cylinder heads (Section 14)
Cylinders (Section 16)
Pistons (Section 17)
Cam chains and blades (Section 19)

3 Make a cardboard template punched with holes to match all the crankcase bolts – as each bolt is removed, store it in its relative position in the template. This will ensure all bolts and washers are installed in the correct location on reassembly. **Note:** *New sealing*

washers should be used on reassembly where fitted – keep the old ones with the bolts as a guide to reassembly.

4 Support the crankcases on wooden blocks, left-hand side uppermost. Loosen the crankcase bolts evenly in a criss-cross pattern until they are finger-tight, then remove them and store them in the template, noting the position of the wiring clips and sealing washers **(see illustration)**.

5 Turn the crankcases over so that the right-hand side is uppermost. Carefully lift the right crankcase half off the left half, using a soft-faced hammer to tap around the joint to initially separate the halves if necessary **(see illustration)**. **Note:** *If the halves do not separate easily, make sure all fasteners have been removed. Do not try and separate the halves by levering between the crankcase mating surfaces as they are easily damaged and will leak on reassembly.*

6 The right-hand crankcase half will come away leaving the crankshaft assembly, transmission shafts and selector drum and forks in the left-hand half – note the location

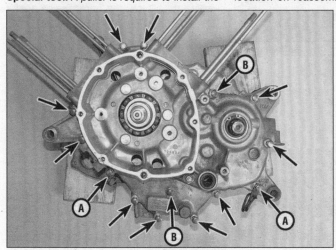

20.4 Location of the crankcase bolts, wiring clips (A) and sealing washers (B)

20.5 Lift off the right-hand crankcase half

20.6 Location of the crankcase dowels

20.7a Remove the oil strainer

20.7b Note the O-ring on the scavenge pipe

of the crankcase dowels and remove them for safekeeping if they are loose **(see illustration)**.

7 Pull out the oil strainer from the right-hand crankcase half **(see illustration)**. Pull out the oil scavenge pipe, noting the location of the O-ring **(see illustration)**. Discard the O-ring as a new one must be fitted.

8 Refer to Section 21 for inspection of the crankcases and main bearings, and Sections 22 to 25 for removal and installation of the selector drum and forks, transmission shafts and crankshaft assembly.

Reassembly

9 Remove all traces of old sealant from the crankcase mating surfaces with a suitable solvent and clean the threads of all the crankcase bolts.

10 Clean the oil scavenge pipe and oil strainer with a suitable solvent. Inspect the strainer gauze for damage and fit a new strainer if necessary **(see illustration 20.7a)**. Install the oil scavenge pipe with a new O-ring **(see illustration 20.7b)**. Ensure the scavenge pipe and strainer are pressed fully into their locations in the right-hand crankcase half **(see illustration)**.

11 Support the left-hand crankcase half securely on the work surface and ensure all the components are in place – if removed, fit the locating dowels **(see illustration 20.6)**.

12 Wipe the mating surfaces of both crankcase halves with a rag soaked in high flash-point solvent to remove all traces of oil. Apply a thin coating of suitable sealant to the mating surface of the left-hand half **(see illustrations)**.

Caution: Apply the sealant only to the shaded areas shown in the illustration.

Do not apply an excessive amount of sealant as it will ooze out when the case halves are assembled and may obstruct oil passages.

13 Carefully lower the right-hand crankcase half down onto the left-hand half, making sure the shafts and dowels all locate correctly **(see illustration)**. When you are sure everything is correctly aligned, press the halves together firmly.

Caution: The crankcase halves should fit together without being forced. If the casings are not correctly seated, remove the right-hand half and investigate the problem. Do not attempt to pull them together using the crankcase bolts as the casing will crack and be ruined.

14 Turn the crankcases over so that the left-hand side is uppermost. Install the crankcase bolts with the wiring clips and new sealing washers where appropriate – tighten the bolts finger-tight **(see illustration 20.4)**.

15 Tighten the bolts evenly and a little at a time in a criss-cross pattern to the torque setting specified at the beginning of this Chapter.

16 With all the crankcase bolts tightened, stand the crankcases upright, support the connecting rods and check that the crankshaft and transmission shafts rotate smoothly and easily – in neutral, the transmission shafts should rotate freely and independently. If there are any signs of undue stiffness, tight or rough spots, or of any other problem, the fault must be rectified before proceeding further.

17 Install the remaining components in the reverse order of removal.

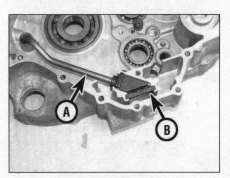

20.10 Installed position of the scavenge pipe (A) and strainer (B)

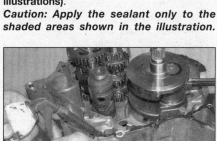

20.12a Apply a suitable sealant . . .

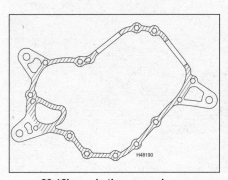

20.12b . . . in the areas shown

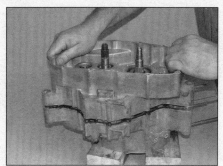

20.13 Ensure the crankcase halves are correctly aligned

21 Crankcases and main bearings

Special tool: *The crankshaft main bearings must be installed using an hydraulic press (see Step 12).*

1 After the crankcase halves have been separated (see Section 20), follow the procedures in Sections 22 to 25 for the removal of the selector drum and forks, the transmission shafts and crankshaft assembly.

21.2a Transmission output shaft oil seal (A) and retaining circlip (B)

21.2b Remove the circlip . . .

Note: *If the left-hand main bearing comes out with the crankshaft, a new bearing must be fitted on reassembly irrespective of the original bearing's apparent condition (see Step 12). To remove the bearing from the crankshaft, refer to the procedure in Section 25.*

2 Note the position of the transmission output shaft oil seal in the left-hand crankcase half **(see illustration)**. Using circlip pliers, remove the retaining circlip, then lever the seal out carefully using a flat-bladed screwdriver **(see illustrations)**. If the circlip is sprained or corroded, fit a new one on installation.

3 Similarly, remove the gearchange shaft oil seal **(see illustration)**.

4 Discard the old seals as new ones must be fitted on reassembly.

Inspection

5 If the main bearings have failed, excessive rumbling and vibration will be felt when the engine is running. Check the condition of the bearings – they should spin freely and smoothly without any rough spots (see *Tools and Workshop Tips* in the *Reference* section). Renew the bearings if there is any doubt about their condition (see Steps 10 to 12) (see **Note** above).

6 Remove all traces of old gasket from the crankcase sealing surfaces, taking care not to nick or gouge the soft aluminium if a scraper is used. Wash all the components in a suitable solvent and dry them with compressed air. Use compressed air to blow through the oil galleries in the cases.

7 Check both crankcase halves very carefully for cracks and damaged threads. Small cracks or holes in aluminium castings may be repaired with an epoxy resin adhesive as a temporary measure, or with one of the low temperature welding kits. Permanent repairs can only be effected by welding, and only a specialist in this process is in a position to advise on the economy or practical aspect of such a repair.

21.2c . . . then lever out the seal

If any damage is found that can't be repaired, renew both crankcase halves as a set.

8 Damaged threads can be reclaimed by using a thread insert of the Heli-Coil type, which is fitted after drilling and re-tapping the affected thread (see *Tools and Workshop Tips* in the *Reference* section). Most motorcycle dealers and small engineering firms offer a service of this kind. Sheared screws and studs can usually be removed with screw extractors which consist of a tapered, left thread screw of very hard steel. These are inserted into a pre-drilled hole in the broken fixing, and usually succeed in dislodging the most stubborn stud or screw (see *Tools and Workshop Tips* in the *Reference* section). If you are in any doubt about removing a sheared screw, consult a Honda dealer or automotive engineer.

9 Always wash the crankcases thoroughly after any repair work to ensure no dirt or metal swarf is trapped inside when the engine is rebuilt.

Main bearings

10 Before removing the main bearings, note which way round they are fitted. **Note:** *Before attempting to remove any of the bearings in the crankcase halves, heat the bearing*

21.3 Remove the gearchange shaft oil seal

housings with a hot air gun. Ensure all oil seals have been removed prior to heating, and that the cases have been washed to remove any residual oil. Refer to the appropriate Sections and check the condition of the transmission and selector drum bearings so that all the necessary bearings can be renewed at the same time.

 If any of the bearings are loose in their housings, or have seized and damaged their housings, have the condition of the casing assessed by a Honda dealer. A loose bearing can often be secured using a suitable bearing lock compound.

11 To remove the main bearings, heat the appropriate housing, then position the crankcase inner face down on a clean work surface and drive the bearing out from the outside using a suitably-sized socket.

 Warning: Be careful when handling the crankcases and wear protective gloves – when heated, the cases could cause severe burns.

12 Prior to installing the new bearing, check that the housing is clean and free from surface

21.12a Examine the bearing housing for damage

21.12b Install the bearing marked side uppermost

21.13 Ensure the circlip groove (arrowed) is visible

21.14 Press the new gearchange shaft oil seal into place

22.1 Installed position of the selector drum and forks

22.2 Lift out the selector forks shaft

damage **(see illustration)**. Smear the outside of the new bearing with clean oil. Note that it should be fitted with its marked side uppermost **(see illustration)**. Heat the housing again and press the bearing squarely in until it seats using an hydraulic press – ensure pressure is only applied to the bearing's outer race. Honda provides special tools (Part No. 07XMF-KGB0100 for left-hand bearing, 07XMF-KGB0200 for right-hand bearing, and installing plate Part No. 07XMF-KGB0300) for this purpose.

Reassembly

13 Locate the new transmission output shaft oil seal in position in the left-hand crankcase half, ensuring that it is the correct way round. Use a suitably-sized socket to press the seal in until the circlip groove is visible, ensuring that it enters the case squarely **(see illustration)**. Install the circlip **(see illustration 21.2b)**. Lubricate the inside of the seal with a smear of clean engine oil.

14 Install the new gearchange shaft oil seal **(see illustration)**.
15 Reassemble the crankcase halves (see Section 20).

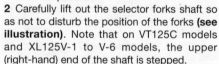

22 Selector drum and forks

Note: *To remove the selector drum and forks the engine must be removed from the frame and the crankcases separated (see Section 20).*

Removal

1 When the crankcase halves are separated the selector drum and forks remain in the left-hand crankcase half **(see illustration)**. Note how the guide pins on the forks locate in the grooves in the selector drum and note which grooves the pins locate in as an aid for

installation. The selector drum should be in the neutral position.
2 Carefully lift out the selector forks shaft so as not to disturb the position of the forks **(see illustration)**. Note that on VT125C models and XL125V-1 to V-6 models, the upper (right-hand) end of the shaft is stepped.
3 Note the position of the selector drum and lift it out **(see illustration)**.
4 Before removing the selector forks, note that each fork is marked with an identification letter – the upper (right-hand) fork is marked R, the centre fork C, and the lower (left-hand) fork L. All marks face the right-hand side of the engine. If no letters are visible, mark them yourself using paint or a marker pen.
5 Slide the upper fork out from the groove in the 4th gear pinion on the transmission output shaft **(see illustration)**.
6 Slide the centre fork out from the groove in the 3rd gear pinion on the input shaft **(see illustration)**.

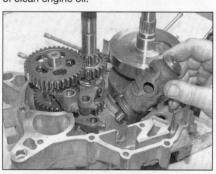

22.3 Remove the selector drum

22.5 Withdraw the upper fork (R)

22.6 Withdraw the centre fork (C)

22.7 Withdraw the lower fork (L)

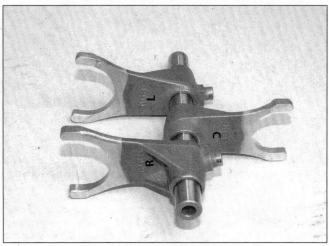

22.8 Slide the forks onto the shaft in order

22.9 Measure the fork end thickness

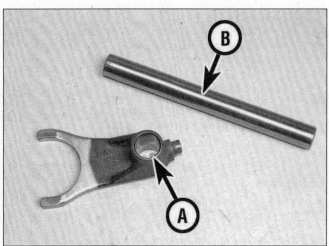

22.10 Measure the internal diameter of the fork bores (A) and the outside diameter of the shaft (B)

7 Slide the lower fork out from the groove in the 5th gear pinion on the output shaft **(see illustration)**.

8 Slide the forks back onto their shaft in the correct order and the right way round **(see illustration)**.

Inspection

9 Inspect the selector forks for any signs of wear or damage, especially around the fork ends where they engage with the grooves in the pinions. Using a micrometer, measure the ends of the forks and compare the results with the specifications at the beginning of this Chapter **(see illustration)**. Check that each fork fits correctly in its pinion groove. Check closely to see if the forks are bent. If the forks are worn or damaged in any way they must be replaced with new ones.

10 Check that the forks fit correctly on their shaft – they should be a sliding fit with no appreciable freeplay. Measure the internal diameter of the fork bores and the outside diameter of the shaft **(see illustration)**. Replace the forks and/or shaft with new ones if they are worn beyond their service limits.

11 Check that the selector fork shaft is straight by rolling it on a flat surface such as a sheet of glass. A bent shaft will cause difficulty in selecting gears and make the gearchange action heavy and should be renewed.

12 Inspect the selector drum grooves and selector fork guide pins for signs of wear or damage **(see illustration)**. If either component shows signs of wear or damage the fork(s) and drum must be renewed.

13 Check that the selector drum rotates freely in the left-hand crankcase half. Measure the diameter of the left-hand journal and compare the result with the specification **(see illustration 22.12)** – if it is worn beyond the service limit, renew the selector drum.

14 Inspect the journals in both crankcase

halves for the selector fork shaft and in the left-hand case for the selector drum – if the journals are worn or damaged, have the cases inspected by a Honda dealer or specialist repair shop.

15 Check the condition of the selector drum

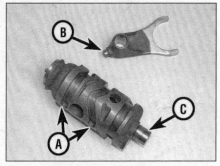

22.12 Examine the grooves (A) and guide pins (B). Note the left-hand journal (C)

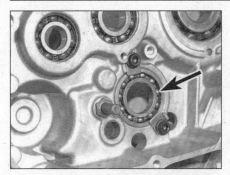

22.15 Location of the selector drum bearing

22.19 Ensure the shaft is installed fully

23.2 Lift the transmission shafts out as an assembly

bearing in the right-hand crankcase half **(see illustration)**. Only remove the bearing if it needs renewing (see *Tools and Workshop Tips* in the *Reference* section). The bearing is retained by two plates on the outside of the case – undo the screws and remove the plates. Note which way round the bearing is fitted, then heat the bearing housing with a hot air gun and press the bearing out from the other side.

16 Prior to installation, smear the outside of the new bearing with clean oil. Heat the housing again and drive the bearing in squarely until it seats using a driver or socket that bears only on the bearing's outer race. Clean the screw threads and apply a suitable non-permanent thread-locking compound. Install the retaining plates and tighten the screws to the torque setting specified at the beginning of this Chapter.

Installation

17 Lubricate the selector forks with engine oil. Starting with the lower (left-hand) fork marked L, install each fork in turn in its pinion groove, making sure they are correctly positioned **(see illustrations 22.7, 6 and 5)**.

18 Lubricate the selector drum with oil. Install the drum and locate the fork guide pins in their grooves **(see illustration 22.1)**.

19 Lubricate the selector fork shaft with molybdenum disulphide oil (a 50/50 mixture

of molybdenum disulphide grease and engine oil). With all three selector forks aligned, slide the shaft through each and into its bore in the crankcase **(see illustration)**. Ensure the shaft is fitted the correct way up (see Step 2).

20 Reassemble the crankcase halves (see Section 20).

23 Transmission shafts and bearings

Note: *To remove the transmission shafts the engine must be removed from the frame and the crankcases separated (see Section 20).*

Removal

1 When the crankcase halves are separated the transmission shafts remain in the left-hand crankcase half. Before removing the shafts, follow the procedure in Section 22 to remove the selector drum and forks.

2 Don't try to pull the shafts out individually. Note the relative positions of the input and output shafts and how they fit together, then lift them out as an assembly – hold the bottom pinions on the shafts to prevent them dropping off **(see illustration)**. If necessary, have an assistant support the left-hand crankcase half and tap the left-hand end of the output shaft with a soft-faced mallet to aid removal.

3 Lay the transmission shafts on a clean work surface **(see illustration)**.

4 Note that there is a thrust washer on the lower end of both shafts which may stick to the bearing or fall off as the shafts are removed – retrieve the washers and fit them back onto the shafts with a dab of grease.

5 If necessary, the shafts can be disassembled and the components inspected for wear or damage (see Section 24).

6 Remove the transmission output shaft oil seal from the left-hand crankcase half (see Section 21).

7 Check the condition of the transmission shaft bearings in both crankcase halves **(see illustration)**. Only remove the bearings if they need renewing (see *Tools and Workshop Tips* in the *Reference* section). If required, flush the bearings with a suitable solvent then dry them thoroughly – use low pressure compressed air if it is available. Lubricate the bearings lightly with clean engine oil, then check them as described.

8 If the bearing on one end of a shaft needs renewing, it is good practice to renew the bearing on the other end at the same time. If either of the transmission bearings in the left-hand crankcase half need renewing, take great care to avoid damaging the crankshaft assembly – to remove the crankshaft refer to Section 25.

9 The input shaft bearing in the right-hand case is retained by two plates on the inside

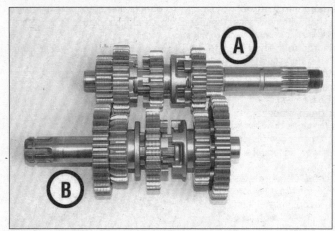

23.3 Note the relative positions of the gear pinions on the transmission input (A) and output (B) shafts

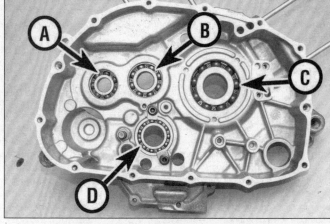

23.7 Crankcase bearings – transmission output shaft (A), input shaft (B), crankshaft main bearing (C) and selector drum bearing (D)

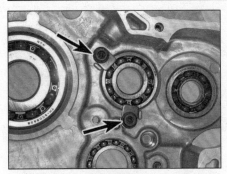

23.9 Bearing is retained by screws and plates

23.18 Support the left-hand crankcase half upright

23.20 Install the transmission shafts as an assembly

of the case – undo the screws and remove the plates **(see illustration)**.

10 To remove the input shaft bearing from the right-hand case and the output shaft bearings from the left and right-hand cases, first heat the bearing housing with a hot air gun. Note which way round the bearing is fitted, then tap the bearing out from the outside using a bearing driver or a suitable socket.

11 To remove the input shaft bearing from the left-hand case, an expanding knife-edge bearing puller with slide-hammer attachment is required (see *Tools and Workshop Tips* in the *Reference* section).

12 Prior to installation, smear the outside of the new bearing with clean oil. Heat the housing again and drive the bearing in squarely until it seats using a driver or socket that bears only on the bearing's outer race.

13 After installing a new right-hand input shaft bearing, clean the screw threads and apply a suitable non-permanent thread-locking compound. Install the retaining plates and tighten the screws to the torque setting specified at the beginning of this Chapter.

 If any of the bearings are loose in their housings, or have seized and damaged their housings, have the condition of the casing assessed by a Honda dealer. A loose bearing can often be secured using a suitable bearing lock compound.

Installation

14 If removed, install the crankshaft assembly (see Section 25).

15 If not already done, fit a new transmission output shaft oil seal (see Section 21). Lubricate the inside of the seal with engine oil.

16 Lubricate the transmission shaft bearings with engine oil.

17 Ensure the thrust washers are installed on the left-hand ends of both shafts and secure them in place with a dab of grease.

18 Stand the left-hand crankcase half securely upright on the work surface – if available, have an assistant support it **(see illustration)**.

19 Place the shafts side-by-side on the work surface and align the gear pinions **(see illustration 23.3)**.

20 Grasp the shafts assembly, align the left-hand ends of the shafts with the bearings in the left-hand casing and install the shafts **(see illustration)**.

21 Follow the procedure in Section 22 to install the selector drum and forks.

22 Reassemble the crankcase halves (see Section 20).

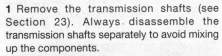

24 Transmission shaft overhaul

1 Remove the transmission shafts (see Section 23). Always disassemble the transmission shafts separately to avoid mixing up the components.

24.2a Remove the thrust washer . . .

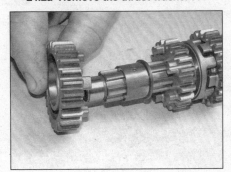

24.3 Slide off the 5th gear pinion

 When disassembling the transmission shafts, place the parts on a long rod or thread a wire through them to keep them in order and facing the proper direction.

 Warning: The gear pinions are secured by circlips – fit new circlips on reassembly, never re-use the old circlips.

Input shaft
Disassembly

2 Remove the thrust washer from the left-hand end of the shaft, then slide off the 2nd gear pinion **(see illustrations)**.

3 Slide off the 5th gear pinion, noting which way round it fits **(see illustration)**.

4 Slide off the splined 5th gear bush, noting the alignment of the oil holes in the bush and the shaft **(see illustration)**.

24.2b . . . and slide off the 2nd gear pinion

24.4 Slide off the splined bush, noting the oil holes

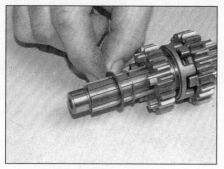

24.5a Slide off the splined washer . . .

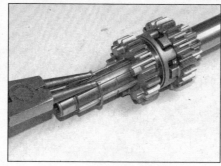

24.5b . . . and remove the circlip

24.6 Slide off the 3rd gear pinion

5 Slide off the splined washer, then remove the circlip **(see illustrations)**.
6 Slide off the 3rd gear pinion, noting which way round it fits **(see illustration)**.

7 Remove the circlip and splined washer securing the 4th gear pinion, then slide the pinion off, noting which way round it fits **(see illustrations)**.

8 Slide off the 4th gear bush **(see illustration)**. The 1st gear pinion is integral with the shaft.

Inspection

9 Wash all of the components in suitable solvent and dry them off.
10 Check the gear teeth for cracking, chipping, pitting and other obvious wear or damage **(see illustration)**. Any pinion that is damaged must be renewed. **Note:** *If a pinion on the input shaft is damaged, check the corresponding pinion on the output shaft. Transmission pinions should be renewed in matched pairs.*
11 Inspect the dogs on the gears for cracks, chips, and excessive wear especially in the form of rounded edges **(see illustration)**. Make sure mating gears engage properly. Replace the paired gears as a set if necessary.
12 Check for signs of scoring or bluing on the pinions, bushes and shaft. This could be caused by overheating due to inadequate lubrication. Check that all the oil holes and passages are clear. Replace any damaged pinions or bushes.
13 Measure the diameter of the shaft at the position of the 4th gear bush and compare the result with the Specifications at the beginning of this Chapter **(see illustration)**. Measure the inside and outside diameters of the bush, and the inside diameter of the 4th gear pinion and compare the results with the specifications

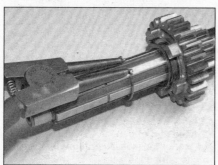

24.7a Remove the circlip . . .

24.7b . . . and the splined washer

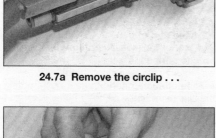

24.7c Slide off the 4th gear pinion

24.8 Slide off the 4th gear bush

24.10 Examine the gear teeth for wear and damage

24.11 Examine the dogs for wear and damage

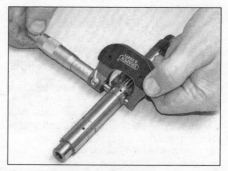

24.13a Measure the diameter of the shaft

24.13b Measure the inside . . .

24.13c . . . and outside diameters of the 4th gear bush

24.13d Measure the inside diameter of the 4th gear pinion

(see illustrations). If any components are worn beyond the service limit they should be renewed.

14 Similarly, measure the outside diameter of the 5th gear bush and the inside diameter of the 5th gear pinion and renew any component that is worn beyond the service limit.

15 The shaft is unlikely to sustain damage unless the engine has seized, placing an unusually high loading on the transmission, or the machine has covered a very high mileage. Check the surface of the shaft and the shaft splines, and renew the shaft if it has scored or picked up, or if there are any cracks. If available, check the shaft runout using V-blocks and a dial gauge and replace the shaft with a new one if it is bent.

Reassembly

16 During reassembly, apply molybdenum disulphide oil (a 50/50 mixture of molybdenum disulphide grease and engine oil) to the mating surfaces of the bushes and the selector fork groove in the 3rd gear pinion.

17 When installing the *new* circlips, do not expand their ends any further than is necessary to slide them along the shaft. Install the stamped circlips and washers so that their chamfered sides face the pinion they secure (see illustration).

18 Slide the 4th gear bush onto the shaft from the left-hand end and install it against the integral 1st gear.

19 Slide the 4th gear pinion onto the shaft with its dogs facing away from the integral 1st gear (see illustration 24.7c). Slide the splined washer onto the shaft, then fit the circlip,

making sure that it locates correctly in the groove in the shaft (see illustrations).

20 Slide on the 3rd gear pinion with the selector fork groove facing the 4th gear pinion (see illustration 24.6).

21 Fit the circlip, making sure it is locates correctly in its groove in the shaft (see illustration).

22 Slide on the splined washer and the splined bush, ensuring the oil holes align (see illustrations 24.5a and 4).

23 Install the 5th gear pinion on its bush with the dogs facing the 3rd gear pinion (see illustration).

24 Fit the 2nd gear pinion and thrust washer onto the end of the shaft (see illustrations 24.2b and a).

25 Check that all the components have been correctly installed (see illustration).

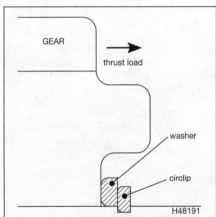

GEAR

thrust load

washer

circlip

H48191

24.17 Correct fitting of stamped circlips and washers

24.19a Slide on the splined washer

24.19b Ensure the circlip locates in the groove

24.21 Ensure the circlip locates in the groove

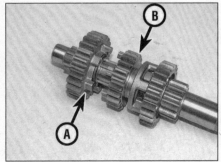

24.23 5th gear pinion dogs (A) face the 3rd gear pinion (B)

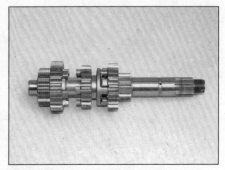

24.25 The assembled input shaft should look like this

24.26a Remove the thrust washer . . .

24.26b . . . and slide off the 2nd gear pinion

24.27a Slide off the 2nd gear bush . . .

24.27b . . . and thrust washer

24.28 Slide off the 5th gear pinion

24.29a Remove the thrust washer . . .

24.29b . . . then slide off the 1st gear pinion

24.30a Slide off the 1st gear bush . . .

24.30b . . . and thrust washer

24.31 Slide off the 4th gear pinion

24.32a Remove the circlip . . .

24.32b . . . and splined washer

24.32c Slide off the 3rd gear pinion

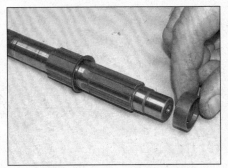

24.33a Slide off the 3rd gear bush . . .

24.33b . . . and thrust washer

Output shaft

Disassembly

26 Remove the thrust washer from the left-hand end of the shaft, then slide off the 2nd gear pinion **(see illustrations)**.

27 Slide off the 2nd gear bush and thrust washer **(see illustrations)**.

28 Slide off the 5th gear pinion, noting which way round it fits **(see illustration)**.

29 Remove the thrust washer from the right-hand end of the shaft, then slide off the 1st gear pinion **(see illustrations)**.

30 Slide off the 1st gear bush and thrust washer **(see illustrations)**.

31 Slide off the 4th gear pinion, noting which way round it fits **(see illustration)**.

32 Remove the circlip and splined washer securing the 3rd gear pinion, then slide the pinion off, noting which way round it fits **(see illustrations)**.

33 Slide off the 3rd gear bush and thrust washer **(see illustrations)**.

Inspection

34 Refer to Steps 9 to 12 above. As well as checking the gear pinion dogs for wear and damage **(see illustration 24.11)**, inspect the dog holes in the 1st and 2nd gear pinions **(see illustrations 24.29b and 26b)**.

35 Measure the diameter of the shaft at the position of the 1st gear bush and compare the result with the specification at the beginning of this Chapter **(see illustration)**. Measure the inside and outside diameters of the bush, and the inside diameter of the 1st gear pinion and

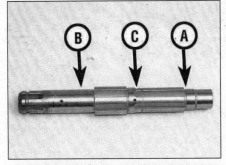

24.35 Output shaft – position of 1st gear bush (A), 2nd gear bush (B) and 3rd gear bush (C)

compare the results with the specifications **(see illustrations 24.13b, c and d)**. If any components are worn beyond the service limit they should be renewed.

36 Similarly, measure the diameter of the shaft at the position of the 2nd and 3rd gear bushes, the inside and outside diameters of the 2nd and 3rd gear bushes and the inside diameters 2nd and 3rd gear pinions. Renew any component that is worn beyond the service limit.

37 Refer to Step 15 and check the shaft for wear and damage.

Reassembly

38 During reassembly, lubricate the mating surfaces of the bushes and the selector fork grooves in the 4th and 5th gear pinions with molybdenum disulphide oil (see Step 16).

24.42 Installed position of the third (A) and fourth (B) gear pinions

Refer to Step 17 when installing the *new* circlips and washers.

39 Slide the thrust washer and 3rd gear bush onto the shaft from the right-hand end **(see illustrations 24.33b and a)**.

40 Install the 3rd gear pinion on its bush with the dogs facing the right-hand end of the shaft **(see illustration 24.32c)**.

41 Slide the splined washer onto the shaft, then fit the circlip, making sure that it locates correctly in the groove in the shaft **(see illustrations 24.32b and a)**.

42 Slide on the 4th gear pinion with the selector fork groove facing the 3rd gear pinion **(see illustration)**.

43 Slide on the thrust washer and 1st gear bush **(see illustrations 24.30b and a)**.

44 Install the 1st gear pinion on its bush with the concave side facing the 4th gear pinion **(see illustration)**.

45 Install the thrust washer and secure it with a dab of grease **(see illustration 24.29a)**.

46 Slide the 5th gear pinion onto the shaft from the left-hand end with the selector fork groove facing the 3rd gear pinion **(see illustration 24.28)**.

47 Slide on the thrust washer and 2nd gear bush **(see illustrations 24.27b and a)**.

48 Install the 2nd gear pinion on its bush with the concave side facing the 5th gear pinion **(see illustration 24.26b)**. Install the thrust washer **(see illustration 24.26a)**.

49 Check that all the components have been correctly installed **(see illustration)**.

24.44 Concave side (arrowed) faces fourth gear pinion

24.49 The assembled output shaft should look like this

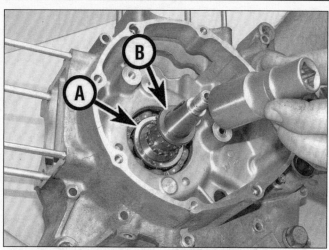

25.3 Apply pressure to inner race of main bearing (A) or outer shoulder of cam chain sprocket (B)

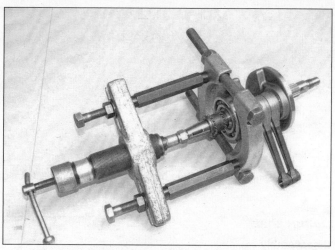

25.4a Set-up for removing the left-hand main bearing

25 Crankshaft and connecting rods

Note: *To remove the crankshaft assembly the engine must be removed from the frame and the crankcases separated. The connecting rods and cam chain sprockets are an integral part of the crankshaft assembly – individual components are not available.*
Special tools: *The left-hand crankshaft main bearing must be removed using a bearing puller (see Step 4). A puller is required for the*

25.4b Nut (arrowed) protects the end of the crankshaft

installation of the crankshaft assembly (see Step 15).

Removal

1 When the crankcase halves are separated the crankshaft assembly remains in the left-hand crankcase half. Before removing the crankshaft, follow the procedure in Sections 22 and 23 to remove the selector drum and forks and transmission shafts.
2 To avoid damaging the assembly, an hydraulic press must be used to press the crankshaft out of the crankcase. Support crankcase securely and make provision to prevent the crankshaft falling when it comes free. Heat the main bearing housing to aid removal.
3 Depending on the equipment available, apply pressure either to the inner race of the main bearing or the outer shoulder of the cam chain sprocket **(see illustration)**. *Do not* apply pressure to the end of the crankshaft.
4 If the left-hand main bearing comes out with the crankshaft, a new bearing must be fitted on reassembly. To remove the old bearing, use a puller that clamps behind the bearing as shown **(see illustration)**. Protect the end of the crankshaft by installing a suitable nut on the alternator rotor nut threads **(see illustration)**. Apply steady pressure to draw

the bearing off. Install the new bearing in the left-hand crankcase half (see Section 21).

Inspection

5 If the connecting rod (big-end) bearing has failed, there will be a pronounced knocking noise when the engine is running, particularly under load and increasing with engine speed.
6 Hold the crankshaft still and check for any radial (up and down) play in the big-end bearing by pushing and pulling the rods against the crank **(see illustration)**. If a dial gauge is available, measure the amount of radial clearance and compare the result with the service limit specified at the beginning of this Chapter.
7 Measure the connecting rod side clearance (the gap between the connecting rod big-end and the crankshaft web) with a feeler gauge and compare the result with the service limit **(see illustration)**.
8 If either clearance is greater than the service limit the big-end bearing has failed – replace the crankshaft assembly with a new one.
9 Place the crankshaft on V-blocks and check the runout using a dial gauge **(see illustration)**. Compare the reading to the

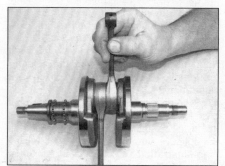

25.6 Checking for up and down (radial) play in the big-end bearing

25.7 Measuring the connecting rod side clearance

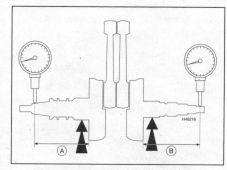

25.9 Check runout at the distance measured from the outer face of the crankshaft web

Distance (A) 83 mm, distance (B) 80 mm

25.12 Check the cam chain sprocket

25.13 Check the splines and the slot for the Woodruff key

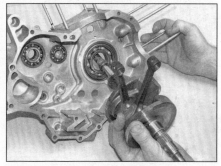

25.14 Insert the crankshaft through the main bearing

maximum specified and renew the crankshaft if the runout exceeds the limit.

10 Have the connecting rods checked for twist and bend by a Honda dealer if you are in doubt about their straightness.

11 Refer to Section 17 and check the connecting rod small-ends and piston pins for wear.

12 Check the cam chain sprocket for wear and damage **(see illustration)**. Refer to Section 19 to check the condition of the cam chains.

13 Inspect the splines for the starter clutch and the slot for the primary drive gear Woodruff key **(see illustration)**. If the splines are worn, check the corresponding splines in the centre of the starter clutch housing (see Section 9).

Installation

Note: *During this procedure, take care to avoid damaging the connecting rods.*

14 Stand the left-hand crankcase half securely upright on the work surface and insert the left-hand end of the crankshaft through the main bearing **(see illustration)**. Have an assistant support the crankshaft assembly, ensuring the left-hand (rear cylinder) connecting rod is aligned with the corresponding opening in the crankcase **(see illustration 23.18)**.

15 To install the crankshaft it must be pulled through the main bearing – Honda provides a service tool to do this (Part Nos. 07965-VM00100 and 07965-VM00200). Alternatively, a suitable

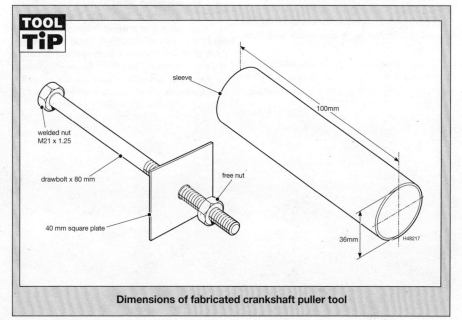

Dimensions of fabricated crankshaft puller tool

puller can be made using a steel sleeve and a drawbolt with a nut that will thread all the way onto the end of the crankshaft welded onto one end (see *Tool Tip*).

16 To assemble the puller, first fit the sleeve over the end of the crankshaft so that it bears on the inner race of the main bearing **(see illustration)**. Thread the drawbolt all the way onto the threads for the alternator rotor nut **(see illustration)**.

17 Ensure that the crankshaft is aligned exactly with the main bearing, then hold the sleeve and slowly tighten the free nut on the outer end of the drawbolt to draw the crankshaft into the bearing **(see illustration)**. Ensure that the crankshaft remains square to the bearing throughout installation.

18 Once the crankshaft is fully seated in the bearing, remove the puller. Support

25.16a Fit the sleeve over the crankshaft

25.16b Thread the drawbolt all the way onto the crankshaft threads

25.17 Draw the crankshaft into position with the puller

25.18 Ensure the crankshaft rotates freely

the connecting rods and check that the crankshaft rotates freely and easily **(see illustration)**.

19 Install the transmission shafts and selector drum and forks (Sections 23 and 22), then reassemble the crankcase halves (see Section 20).

26 Running-in procedure

1 Make sure the engine oil and coolant levels are correct (see *Pre-ride checks*). Make sure there is fuel in the tank.

2 Turn the engine kill switch to the ON position and shift the gearbox into neutral. On carburettor models, set the choke.

3 Turn the ignition ON. Start the engine and allow it to run at a moderately fast idle until it reaches operating temperature.

⚠ *Warning: If the oil pressure warning light doesn't go off, or it comes on while the engine is running, stop the engine immediately. If an engine is run without oil, even for a short period of time, severe damage will occur.*

4 Check carefully that there are no oil, coolant or fuel leaks and make sure the transmission and controls, especially the brakes, function properly before road testing the machine.

5 Treat the machine gently for the first few miles to make sure oil has circulated throughout the engine and any new parts installed have started to seat.

6 Even greater care is necessary if the cylinders have been rebored and new pistons have been fitted, or if new bearings have been fitted in the crankcase – the bike will have to be run in as when new. This means greater use of the transmission and a restraining hand on the throttle until at least 300 miles (500 km) have been covered. There's no point in keeping to any set speed limit – but don't labour the engine and gradually increase performance up to the 300 miles (500 km) mark. Experience is the best guide, since it's easy to tell when an engine is running freely.

7 Upon completion of the road test, and after the engine has cooled down completely, recheck the valve clearances (see Chapter 1) and check the engine oil and coolant levels (see *Pre-ride checks*).

Chapter 3
Cooling system

Contents

Degrees of difficulty

Easy, suitable for novice with little experience	**Fairly easy,** suitable for beginner with some experience	**Fairly difficult,** suitable for competent DIY mechanic	**Difficult,** suitable for experienced DIY mechanic	**Very difficult,** suitable for expert DIY or professional

Specifications

Coolant
Capacity
Radiator and engine .... 1.2 litres
Reservoir .... 0.4 litres
Type .... see Pre-ride checks

Coolant temperature sender
OFF to ON .... 112 to 118°C
ON to OFF .... Below 108°C

Thermostat
Opening temperature .... 81 to 84°C
Fully open .... 95°C
Valve lift .... 4.5 mm

Radiator
Cap valve opening pressure .... 16 psi (1.1 Bar)

Torque settings
Thermo-switch
VT125C .... 8 Nm
XL125V .... 18 Nm
Cooling fan switch .... 18 Nm
Fan blade nut .... 1 Nm
Fan motor screws .... 3 Nm
Fan motor shroud bolts .... 8 Nm
Water pump impeller .... 10 Nm

1 General information

The cooling system uses a water/anti-freeze coolant to carry away excess heat from the engine and maintain as constant a temperature as possible. The cylinders are surrounded by a water jacket through which the coolant is circulated by thermo-syphonic action in conjunction with a water pump. The pump is driven by the primary drive gear on the right-hand end of the crankshaft.

As it is heated, the coolant passes upwards through the engine to the thermostat, and then away from the engine to the radiator where it is cooled as it flows across the radiator core. The coolant then returns to the engine, via the pump, where the cycle is repeated.

The thermostat is fitted in the system to prevent the coolant flowing through the radiator when the engine is cold, therefore accelerating the speed at which the engine reaches normal operating temperature.

On carburettor models, a thermo-switch is located above the thermostat housing on the rear cylinder head. This is part of the high temperature warning circuit connected to the temperature indicator in the instrument cluster. Also on these models, coolant provides a source of heat for the carburettors (see Chapter 4A).

A coolant temperature sensor is located in the rear of the front cylinder on all models. On carburettor models, this sends information to the ignition control unit (ICU) and for the purpose of this manual is covered in Chapter 5. On fuel injected models, the temperature sensor (or ECT as it is known) sends information to the engine control module (ECM) as part of the engine management system – this is covered in Chapter 4B.

A fan fitted to the back of the radiator aids cooling in extreme conditions by drawing extra air through the radiator core. On carburettor models, the fan motor is controlled by a switch mounted in the right-hand side of the radiator. On fuel injected models the fan is activated by the ECM.

The complete cooling system is partially sealed and pressurised, the pressure being controlled by a valve contained in the spring-loaded radiator cap. By pressurising the coolant the boiling point is raised, preventing premature boiling in adverse conditions. The overflow hose from the system is connected to a reservoir into which excess coolant is expelled under pressure. The discharged coolant automatically returns to the radiator by the vacuum created when the engine cools.

Several of the cooling system service procedures are considered routine maintenance items and for that reason are covered in Chapter 1.

 Warning: Do not remove the pressure cap from the radiator when the engine is hot. Scalding hot coolant and steam may be blown out under pressure, which could cause serious injury. When the engine has cooled, remove the cap locking screw, then place a thick rag, like a towel, over the pressure cap; slowly rotate the cap anti-clockwise to the first stop. This procedure allows any residual pressure to escape. When the steam has stopped escaping, press down on the cap while turning it anti-clockwise and remove it.

Caution: Do not allow anti-freeze to come in contact with your skin or painted surfaces of the motorcycle. Rinse off any spills immediately with plenty of water. Anti-freeze is highly toxic if ingested. Never leave anti-freeze lying around in an open container or in puddles on the floor; children and pets are attracted by its sweet smell and may drink it. Check with the local authorities about disposing of used anti-freeze. Many communities will have collection centres which will see that anti-freeze is disposed of safely.

Caution: At all times use the specified type of anti-freeze, and always mix it with distilled water in the correct proportion. The anti-freeze contains corrosion inhibitors which are essential to avoid damage to the cooling system. A lack of these inhibitors could lead to a build-up of corrosion which would block the coolant passages, resulting in overheating and severe engine damage. Distilled water must be used as opposed to tap water to avoid a build-up of scale which would also block the passages.

2 Coolant change

 Warning: Allow the engine to cool completely before performing this maintenance operation. Also, don't allow anti-freeze to come into contact with your skin or the painted surfaces of the motorcycle. Rinse off spills immediately with plenty of water. Anti-freeze is highly toxic if ingested. Never leave anti-freeze lying around in an open container or in puddles on the floor; children and pets are attracted by its sweet smell and may drink it. Check with local authorities (councils) about disposing of anti-freeze. Many communities have collection centres which will see that anti-freeze is disposed of safely. Anti-freeze is also combustible, so don't store it near open flames.

Draining

VT125C models

1 Support the motorcycle upright on a level surface using an auxiliary stand. Remove the right-hand side panel (see Chapter 8).

2 Remove the right-hand engine cover, then remove the pressure cap from the top of the radiator (see Chapter 1, Section 14).

3 Position a suitable container beneath the water pump on the right-hand side of the engine. Unscrew the drain bolt and allow the coolant to completely drain from the system **(see illustrations)**. Retain the old sealing washer for use during flushing.

4 Release the clip securing the coolant hose to the rear cylinder and detach the hose to drain coolant from the cylinder **(see illustration)**. Reconnect the hose and tighten the clip securely.

5 Remove the coolant reservoir cap (see

2.3a Undo the drain bolt (arrowed) . . .

2.3b . . . and drain the coolant into a suitable container

2.4 Detach the hose (arrowed) from the rear cylinder

2.5 Remove the coolant reservoir cap – VT125C

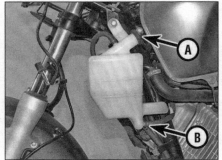

2.9 Remove the coolant reservoir cap (A) – XL125V. Note the overflow hose (B)

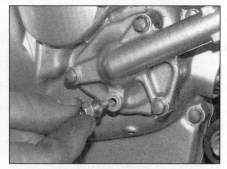

2.17 Fit the drain bolt with a new sealing washer

illustration). The reservoir is mounted on the underside of the battery holder, forward of the swingarm pivot (see Section 8). Position a suitable container beneath the reservoir, release the clip securing the overflow hose, then disconnect the hose and drain the reservoir.

XL125V models

6 Support the motorcycle upright on a level surface on an auxiliary stand. Remove the fairing (see Chapter 8).
7 Remove the radiator pressure cap (see Chapter 1, Section 14).
8 Drain the coolant from the system (see Step 3). On carburettor models, drain the coolant from the rear cylinder (see Step 4).
9 Remove the coolant reservoir cap **(see illustration)**. Position a suitable container beneath the reservoir, release the clip securing the overflow hose, then disconnect the hose and drain the reservoir.

Flushing

10 Flush the system with clean tap water by inserting a hose in the radiator filler neck. Allow the water to run through the system until it is clear and flows out cleanly. If the radiator is extremely corroded, remove it (see Section 6) and have it cleaned by a specialist. Also flush the coolant reservoir, then reconnect the overflow hose.
11 Clean the drain hole in the water pump then install the drain bolt using the old sealing washer **(see illustration 2.3a)**.

12 Fill the system to the base of the radiator filler neck with clean water mixed with a flushing compound. Make sure the flushing compound is compatible with aluminium components, and follow the manufacturer's instructions carefully. Fit the radiator cap.
13 Start the engine and allow it to reach normal operating temperature. Let it run for about ten minutes.
14 Stop the engine. Let it cool for a while, then cover the radiator cap with a heavy rag and turn it anti-clockwise to the first stop, releasing any pressure that may be present in the system. Once the hissing stops, push down on the cap and remove it completely.
15 Drain the system once again.
16 Fill the system with clean water, then fit the radiator cap and repeat Steps 13 to 15.

Refilling

17 Install the drain bolt using a new sealing washer and tighten it securely **(see illustration)**.
18 Fill the system to the base of the radiator filler neck with the correct coolant mixture (see *Pre-ride checks*) **(see illustration)**. Pour the coolant in slowly to minimise the amount of air entering the system.
19 Fill the coolant reservoir to the UPPER level line (see *Pre-ride checks*).
20 Start the engine and allow it to idle for 2 to 3 minutes. Flick the throttle twistgrip part open 3 or 4 times, so that the engine speed rises to approximately 4000 to 5000 rpm, then

stop the engine. Any air trapped in the system should bleed back to the radiator filler neck.
21 If necessary, top-up the coolant level in the radiator, then install cap and tighten the locking screw.
22 Start the engine and allow it to reach normal operating temperature, then shut it off. Let the engine cool, then check the coolant level in the reservoir and top-up if necessary. Check the system for leaks.
23 On VT125C models, install the right-hand engine cover and tighten the screws securely. Install the right-hand side panel (see Chapter 8).
24 On XL125V models, install the fairing (see Chapter 8).
25 Do not dispose of the old coolant by pouring it down the drain. Instead pour it into a heavy plastic container, cap it tightly and take it into an authorised disposal site or service station – see *Warning* at the beginning of this Section.

3 Cooling fan, fan switch and fan relay

1 If the engine is overheating and the cooling fan isn't coming on, first check the fan fuse (see Chapter 9). If the fuse has blown, check the fan circuit for a short to earth (see the *Wiring diagrams* at the end of Chapter 9). If the fuse is good, check the fan motor, then check the switch or relay (depending on model) as described below.
2 On carburettor models, if the cooling fan comes on when the ignition is turned ON and the engine is cold, check for a short to earth in the wire between the fan motor and the switch. If the wiring is good, check the switch (see Step 16).
3 On fuel injected models, if the cooling fan comes on when the ignition is turned ON, go to Step 22.

Cooling fan motor

Check

4 To test the fan motor, first remove the fuel tank (see Chapter 4A or 4B). Trace the wiring from the back of the motor and disconnect it at the connector **(see illustration)**.

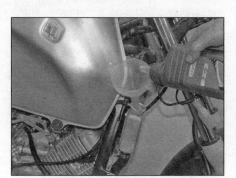

2.18 Pour the coolant in slowly

3.4 Release the catch to disconnect the connector

5 On carburettor models, also disconnect the fan switch wiring connector **(see illustration)**. Using a 12 volt battery and two jumper wires with suitable connectors, connect the battery positive (+ve) terminal to the black/blue wire terminal on the fan side of the motor wiring connector, and the battery negative (-ve) terminal to the fan switch wire terminal. Once connected the fan should operate. If not, and the wiring and connectors are all good, then the fan motor is faulty and must be renewed.

6 On fuel injected models, perform the test between the terminals of the fan motor connector. Using a 12 volt battery and two jumper wires with suitable connectors, connect the battery positive (+ve) terminal to the black/blue wire terminal on the fan side of the connector, and the battery negative (-ve) terminal to the black wire terminal. Once connected the fan should operate. If not, and the wiring and connectors are all good, then the fan motor is faulty and must be renewed.

Renewal

7 Remove the radiator (see Section 6). On carburettor models, if not already done, disconnect the fan switch wiring connector **(see illustration 3.5)**.

8 Undo the screws securing the fan assembly to the radiator **(see illustration)**. If fitted, note the location of the wiring clip secured by the lower screw. On carburettor models, note the location of the earth terminal secured by the lower screw and free the fan wiring from its clamp.

9 Unscrew the fan blade nut and remove the blade, noting how it fits. Undo the three screws securing the fan motor and separate it from the shroud.

10 Installation is the reverse of removal. Apply a suitable non-permanent thread locking compound to the fan blade nut and tighten it securely. Ensure the earth terminal connection is clean.

11 Install the radiator (see Section 6).

Fan switch – VT125C and XL125V-1 to V-6

Check

12 Carburettor models are fitted with a cooling fan switch **(see illustration 3.5)**. As the coolant temperature rises the thermo-switch completes the fan motor circuit to earth (ground) and the fan comes on (see the *Wiring diagrams* at the end of Chapter 9). No specifications are available for the switch, however the following checks will determine whether it is faulty or not.

13 Disconnect the fan switch wiring connector. Using a voltmeter, check for battery voltage at the wiring connector with the ignition ON. Turn the ignition OFF. If there is no voltage, check the wire from the switch back to the fusebox for continuity.

14 If there is voltage, check for continuity between the radiator and earth (ground). If there is no continuity, check the earth terminal secured by the fan assembly screw (see Step 8). Also check for continuity between the body of the switch and earth (ground). If there is no

continuity, remove the switch and clean the threads (see Steps 17 to 20).

15 If the tests are good the switch is faulty and must be renewed.

16 If the fan comes on when the ignition is turned ON and the engine is cold, and the wiring is good (see Step 2), disconnect the switch wiring connector and check for continuity between the switch terminal and earth (ground). There should be no continuity – if there is the switch is faulty.

Renewal

17 Drain the cooling system (see Section 2).

18 Disconnect the wiring connector from the switch. Unscrew the switch and discard the O-ring as a new one must be used.

19 Installation is the reverse of removal. Fit a new O-ring onto the switch, and take care not to over-tighten it. Ensure the wiring connector is secure.

20 Follow the procedure in Section 2 to refill the system and check the switch for leaks.

Fan relay – XL125V-7 onwards

Check

21 Fuel injected models are fitted with a cooling fan relay **(see illustration)**. As the coolant temperature rises the engine control module (ECM) activates the relay and the fan comes on (see the *Wiring Diagram* at the end of Chapter 9). The relay is located on the right-hand side of the fairing bracket – remove the fairing for access (see Chapter 8).

22 If the fan comes on when the ignition is turned ON and the engine is cold, turn the ignition OFF and remove the seat (see Chapter 8) to access the ECM. Displace the ECM and disconnect the ECM black wiring connector **(see illustration)**. Turn the ignition ON – if the fan remains off it is likely the ECM is faulty – have it checked by a Honda dealer. If the fan comes on, remove the fuel tank (see Chapter 4B), then check for a short to earth in the grey/red wire between the relay and the ECM. If the wiring is good, check the relay (see Step 25).

23 If the engine is overheating and the cooling fan isn't coming on, turn the ignition OFF and remove the seat (see Chapter 8) to access the ECM. Disconnect the ECM black wiring connector **(see illustration 3.22)**. Turn the ignition ON. Using a voltmeter, check for battery voltage between the grey/red wire terminal on the loom side of the ECM connector and earth (ground). Turn the ignition OFF. If there is no voltage, check the grey/red wire for continuity between the ECM and the relay. If the wiring is good, check the relay (see Step 25).

24 Remove the fuel tank (see Chapter 4B). Disconnect the relay wiring connector and check that the terminals are clean. Using a jumper wire, connect the blue/orange and black/blue wire terminals in the connector. Disconnect the fan motor wiring connector **(see illustration 3.4)**. Check for battery voltage between the black/blue wire terminal

3.5 Location of fan switch wiring connector

3.8 Cooling fan mounting screws

3.21 Location of the cooling fan relay

3.22 ECM mounting bolt (arrowed)

3.25a Disconnect the relay wiring connector

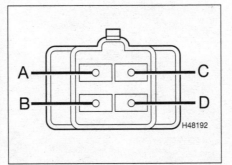

3.25b Relay terminal identification – black/blue wire terminal (A), blue/orange wire terminal (B), white/black wire terminal (C) and grey/red wire terminal (D)

on the loom side of the motor connector and earth (ground). If there is no voltage, check the blue/orange and black/blue wires for continuity (see the *Wiring diagram* at the end of Chapter 9).

25 To check the operation of the relay, displace it from its holder and disconnect the wiring connector **(see illustration)**. Using a multimeter, check for continuity between blue/orange and black/blue wire terminals on the relay **(see illustration)**. There should be no continuity. Using a 12 volt battery and two jumper wires with suitable connectors, connect the battery positive (+ve) terminal to the white/black wire terminal on the relay, and the battery negative (-ve) terminal to the grey/red wire terminal. Once connected, there should be continuity between blue/orange and black/blue terminals. If not, the relay is faulty and must be renewed.

4 Thermo-switch – VT125C and XL125V-1 to V-6

1 On VT125C models, when the ignition is turned ON, the coolant temperature warning light should come on briefly as part of a start-up system check.
2 On XL125V models, when the ignition is turned ON, the coolant temperature display should indicate the engine temperature briefly as part of a start-up system check.
3 On either machine, if the system check is

4.7 Location of the thermo switch

not as described, refer to Chapter 9 to check the instrument cluster electrics.
4 If the thermo-switch is thought to be faulty, test it as follows.

⚠️ *Warning: The engine must be completely cool before carrying out this procedure.*

5 Drain the cooling system (see Section 2).
6 Remove the left-hand cylinder head side cover (see Chapter 2, Section 11).
7 Disconnect the thermo-switch wiring connector, then unscrew the switch from the cylinder head **(see illustration)**.
8 Fill a small heatproof container with coolant and place it on a stove. Using an ohmmeter, connect the meter positive (+ve) probe to the switch terminal, and the meter negative (-ve) probe to the switch body. Suspend the switch in the coolant so that just the sensing head up to the threads is submerged, with the head a minimum of 40 mm above the bottom of the container **(see illustration)**. Also place a thermometer capable of reading temperatures up to 130°C in the coolant so that its bulb is close to the switch. **Note:** *None of the components should be allowed to touch the container directly.*
9 The meter should indicate no continuity (infinite resistance). Now heat the coolant gently – any sudden change in temperature could result in incorrect readings.

⚠️ *Warning: This must be done very carefully to avoid the risk of personal injury.*

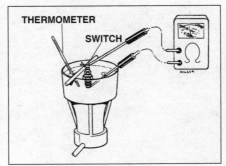

4.8 Set-up for testing the thermo switch

10 When the coolant temperature reaches between 112 to 118°C, turn the heat down and maintain that temperature for three minutes. The meter reading should indicate continuity (zero resistance).
11 Finally, turn the heat off. As the coolant temperature falls below 108°C the meter should again indicate no continuity (infinite resistance).
12 If the thermo-switch does not perform as described it is faulty and must be replaced with a new one.
13 Prior to installation, apply a suitable sealant to the threads, making sure none gets on the sensing head.
14 Install the switch and tighten it to the torque setting specified at the beginning of this chapter. Connect the wiring connector.
15 Follow the procedure in Section 2 to refill the system and check the switch for leaks.
16 Install the left-hand cylinder head side cover (see Chapter 2, Section 11).

5 Thermostat

1 The thermostat is automatic in operation and should give many years service without requiring attention. In the event of a failure, the valve will probably jam open, in which case the engine will take much longer than normal to warm up. Conversely, if the valve jams shut, the coolant will be unable to circulate and the engine will overheat. Neither condition is acceptable, and the fault must be investigated promptly.

⚠️ *Warning: The engine must be completely cool before carrying out this procedure.*

Removal

2 The thermostat housing is located on the left-hand side of the rear cylinder head **(see illustration)** – remove the fuel tank for access (see Chapter 4A or 4B).
3 Drain the coolant (see Section 2).
4 Release the clip securing the hose to the

5.2 Location of the thermostat housing

5.4 Disconnect the hose (arrowed) from the thermostat housing

5.5 Bolts (arrowed) secure thermostat housing

5.6 Thermostat should be closed at room temperature

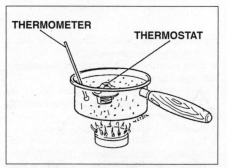

5.7 Set-up for testing the thermostat

union on the thermostat housing and detach the hose **(see illustration)**.

5 Undo the bolts securing the housing and detach it from the cylinder head **(see illustration)** – the thermostat will probably come out with the housing, otherwise withdraw it from the head.

Check

6 Examine the thermostat visually. If it remains in the open position at room temperature, it should be replaced with a new one **(see illustration)**. Check the condition of the rubber seal around the thermostat – if it is damaged or deteriorated, or there is evidence of coolant leakage, a new thermostat will have to be fitted, the seal is not available separately.

7 To check the operation of the thermostat, fill a small heatproof container with water and place it on a stove. Suspend the thermostat

in the water. Place a thermometer capable of reading temperatures up to 110°C in the water so that the bulb is close to the thermostat **(see illustration)**. **Note:** *None of the components should be allowed to touch the container directly.*

8 Heat the water gently, noting the temperature when the thermostat opens, and compare the result with the *Specifications* at the beginning of this Chapter. Continue to heat the water and check the amount the valve has opened after it has been heated at 95°C for a few minutes. Compare the result with the specification.

9 If the results obtained differ from those given, the thermostat is faulty and must be replaced with a new one.

10 In the event of the thermostat not opening at all, as an emergency measure only, it can be removed and the machine used

without it. **Note:** *Take care when starting the engine from cold as it will take much longer than usual to warm up. Ensure that a new thermostat is installed as soon as possible.*

Installation

11 Prior to installing the thermostat, smear some fresh coolant over the seal.

12 Ensure the tab on the edge of the thermostat is aligned with the cut-out in the housing, then install the assembly and tighten the housing bolts evenly **(see illustrations)**.

13 Push the hose all the way onto the union and tighten the clip securely **(see illustration 5.4)**.

14 Follow the procedure in Section 2 to refill the system.

15 Install the fuel tank (see Chapter 4A or 4B).

16 Check the thermostat housing and hose for leaks.

6 Radiator

Note: *If the radiator is being removed as part of the engine removal procedure, detach the hoses from their unions on the engine rather than on the radiator and remove the radiator with the hoses attached to it. Note the routing of the hoses.*

Removal

⚠️ *Warning: The engine must be completely cool before carrying out this procedure.*

1 On XL125V models, remove the fairing (see Chapter 8).

2 Drain the coolant (see Chapter 1). Remove the fuel tank (see Chapter 4A or 4B).

3 On XL125V models, remove the coolant reservoir (see Section 8).

4 Disconnect the fan motor wiring connector and feed the wiring back to the radiator, noting its routing **(see illustration 3.4)**.

5 Release the clip securing the overflow hose

5.12a Align tab with cut-out (arrowed)

5.12b Install the assembly . . .

5.12c . . . and tighten the bolts evenly

6.5 Disconnect the overflow hose

6.6 Disconnect the return hose from the radiator or from the thermostat housing

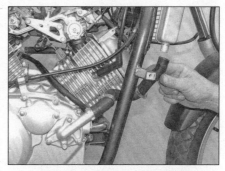

6.7 Disconnect the feed hose from the radiator or from the water pump

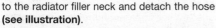
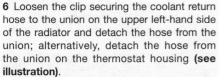

6.8a Undo the mounting bolts . . .

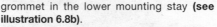

6.8b . . . and ease the radiator mounting stay off the lug (arrowed)

6.9 Note the collars (A) and grommets (B)

to the radiator filler neck and detach the hose **(see illustration)**.

6 Loosen the clip securing the coolant return hose to the union on the upper left-hand side of the radiator and detach the hose from the union; alternatively, detach the hose from the union on the thermostat housing **(see illustration)**.

7 Loosen the clip securing the coolant feed hose to the union on the lower right-hand side of the radiator and detach the hose from the union; alternatively, detach the hose from the union on the water pump **(see illustration)**.

8 Unscrew the radiator mounting bolts, then ease the radiator mounting stay off the lug on the left-hand side of the frame and remove it **(see illustrations)**.

9 Note the location of the collars and grommets in the radiator mounts **(see illustration)**. Replace the grommets with new ones if they are damaged, deformed or deteriorated. Don't forget to check the

grommet in the lower mounting stay **(see illustration 6.8b)**.

10 If required, remove the fan assembly from the back of the radiator (see Section 3).

11 Inspect the radiator for signs of damage and clear any dirt or debris that might obstruct air flow and inhibit cooling (see Chapter 1, Section 14).

Installation

12 Installation is the reverse of removal, noting the following:
● Ensure the collars and rubber grommets are in place and tighten the mounting bolts securely.
● Make sure the fan wiring is correctly connected.
● Secure the coolant hoses with the clips, using new ones if necessary.
● On XL125V models, install the coolant reservoir.
● Follow the procedure in Section 2 to refill the system and check for leaks.

Pressure cap check

13 If problems such as overheating or loss of coolant occur, check the entire system as described in Chapter 1. The radiator cap opening pressure should be checked by a Honda dealer with the special tester required to do the job. If the cap is defective, replace it with a new one.

7 Water pump

Check

1 The water pump is located on the lower right-hand side of the engine **(see illustration)**. On VT125C models, remove the right-hand engine cover for access (see Chapter 1, Section 14).

2 Check the area around the pump and below the drain hole in the crankcase cover for signs of leakage and renew the cover seal or the pump shaft seals as appropriate – refer to Chapter 1, Section 14 for further details.

Removal

3 Drain the coolant (see Section 2).

4 Loosen the clip securing the coolant feed hose to the union on the water pump cover and detach the hose from the union **(see illustration 6.7)**.

5 Release the spring clip securing the small bore hose to the pump cover and detach the hose **(see illustration)**.

7.1 Location of the water pump

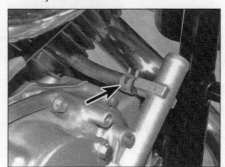

7.5 Disconnect the small bore hose

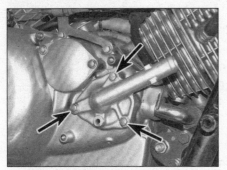

7.6a Unscrew the cover bolts . . .

7.6b . . . and remove the cover

7.8a Undo the bolt . . .

6 Unscrew the pump cover bolts and remove the cover **(see illustrations)**. Discard the cover seal as a new one must be used.
7 Wiggle the pump impeller back-and-forth and up-and-down to check for freeplay in the

pump shaft bearing. Any freeplay indicates a worn bearing and will lead to wear in the pump shaft seals. Do not disassemble the pump unless either the bearing or seals need renewing.

8 The pump housing is integral with the right-hand crankcase cover. Before removing the crankcase cover, undo the bolt securing the coolant pipe elbow and pull the elbow out from the cover, noting the location of the O-ring **(see illustrations)**. Discard the O-ring as a new one must be used.
9 Follow the procedure in Chapter 2, Section 7, to remove the crankcase cover.
10 Using circlip pliers, remove the circlip securing the pump driven gear and lift the gear off, noting how it locates over the drive pin in the pump shaft **(see illustrations)**. Withdraw the drive pin **(see illustration)**.
11 Counter-hold the inner end of the pump shaft using a spanner on the flats, then unscrew the impeller and remove the washer **(see illustrations)**. Draw the shaft out of the pump bearing **(see illustration)**.
12 Inspect the shaft and the driven gear for

7.8b . . . and pull the elbow out from the cover. Note the O-ring (arrowed)

7.10a Remove the circlip . . .

7.10b . . . and lift the gear off, noting how it locates over the drive pin (arrowed)

7.10c Remove the drive pin

7.11a Put a spanner on the shaft flats . . .

7.11b . . . and unscrew the impeller

7.11c Remove the impeller and washer (arrowed)

7.11d Draw the shaft out of the bearing

7.13 Note how the bearing is fitted

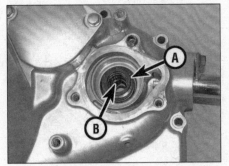

7.14 Outer water seal (A) and inner oil seal (B)

7.19 Inspect the impeller contact surface

wear and damage and renew any parts as necessary. Fit a new circlip on reassembly if the old one is sprained.

Seal renewal

Note: *Do not remove the bearing or seals unless they need to be replaced with new ones – once removed they cannot be re-used.*
13 To remove the pump bearing, an expanding knife-edge bearing puller with slide-hammer attachment is required (see *Tools and Workshop Tips* in the *Reference* section). Note which way round the bearing is fitted, then remove it **(see illustration)**.
14 Note the location of the outer water seal and inner oil seal in the pump housing **(see illustration)**. Support the crankcase cover outside down on the work surface, then drive both seals out together from the inside using a suitably-sized socket.
15 Ensure that the seal housings are clean.
16 Support the crankcase cover outside up on the work surface. Lubricate the new oil seal with a smear of multi-purpose grease and position it closed side up in the cover. Press the new seal all the way in with a suitably-sized socket that bears on the outer edge of the seal only.
17 Apply suitable sealant to the underside of the flange of the new water seal, then press it all the way in with a suitably-sized socket that bears on the flange only.
18 Turn the cover over and install the new pump bearing using a socket that bears on the outer race only.
19 Inspect the contact surface on the

underside of the pump impeller **(see illustration)**. If it is scratched or pitted, fit a new impeller.

Installation

20 Install the pump shaft from the inside of the crankcase cover **(see illustration 7.11d)**. Install the washer, then tighten the impeller finger-tight **(see illustrations 7.11c)**.
21 Counter-hold the pump shaft using a spanner on the flats, then tighten the impeller to the torque setting specified at the beginning of this Chapter **(see illustrations 7.11a and b)**.
22 Install the drive pin and the pump driven gear and secure then with the circlip – ensure the circlip fits correctly in its groove **(see illustration)**. Rotate the pump by hand to make sure it turns freely (but take into account the friction of the seals).
23 Follow the procedure in Chapter 2, Section 7, to install the crankcase cover. Refill the engine with the recommended grade and type of oil (see Chapter 1).
24 Fit a new O-ring onto the coolant pipe elbow and lubricate it with coolant, then press the elbow into the socket in the front of the crankcase cover **(see illustration 7.8b)**. Tighten the elbow bolt securely.
25 Fit a new seal into the groove in the pump cover **(see illustration)**. Lubricate the seal with coolant, then install the cover and tighten the cover bolts securely.
26 Install the coolant hoses on the pump cover unions in the reverse order of removal and secure them with the clips.

27 Follow the procedure in Section 2 to refill the system and check for leaks.

8 Coolant reservoir

VT125C

Removal

1 The coolant reservoir is located on the underside of the battery holder, forward of the swingarm pivot **(see illustration)**. Remove the rear wheel for access (see Chapter 7).
2 Release the clip securing the breather hose to the reservoir cap and disconnect the hose **(see illustration 2.5)**. Position a suitable container beneath the reservoir, release the clip securing the overflow hose, then disconnect the hose and drain the reservoir.
3 Release the trim clip securing the mounting tab on the bottom of the reservoir by pushing the centre into the body with a small punch or screwdriver, then draw the clip out **(see illustration 8.1)**. Ease the upper mounting tabs off the pegs on the underside of the battery holder and remove the reservoir.
4 Note the location of the grommets in the upper mounting tabs. Renew the grommets if they are damaged, deformed or deteriorated.

Installation

5 Installation is the reverse of removal. Before installing the trim clip, push the centre back out so that it protrudes from the top of the

7.22 Ensure the correct fitting of the circlip

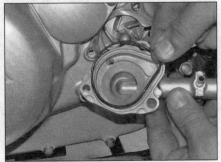

7.25 Fit a new pump cover seal

8.1 Location of the coolant reservoir – VT125C. Note the trim clip (arrowed)

8.7 Location of the coolant reservoir – XL125V

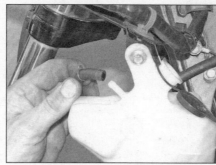

8.8a Disconnect the breather hose

8.8b Drain the coolant from the reservoir

8.9 Release the peg from the lug (arrowed)

clip. Fit the clip into its hole, then push the centre in so that it is flush with the top of the clip. Ensure the drain and breather hoses are secured by the clips.

6 On completion, refill the reservoir to the UPPER level line with the specified coolant mixture (see *Pre-ride checks*).

XL125V

Removal

7 The coolant reservoir is located on the left-hand side of the bike, forward of the fuel tank **(see illustration)**. Remove the fairing for access (see Chapter 8).

8 Release the clip securing the breather hose and disconnect the hose **(see illustration)**. Position a suitable container beneath the reservoir. Release the clip securing the overflow hose to the radiator filler neck and disconnect the hose **(see illustration 6.5)**. Drain the coolant into the container **(see illustration)**.

9 Undo the mounting bolt, release the peg on the bottom of the reservoir from the lug on the frame and lift the reservoir off **(see illustration)**.

Installation

10 Installation is the reverse of removal. Ensure the peg on the bottom of the reservoir is correctly located in the lug on the frame and tighten the mounting bolt securely. Ensure the drain and breather hoses are secured by the clips.

11 On completion, refill the reservoir to the UPPER level line with the specified coolant mixture (see *Pre-ride checks*).

9 Coolant hoses, pipes and elbows

Hoses

1 Before removing a hose, drain the coolant (see Section 2).

2 Use a screwdriver to loosen the large-bore coolant hose clips **(see illustration)**, then slide each clip back along the hose so that it is clear of the union .

3 The small-bore hoses, as used on the carburettor heater system, are secured by spring clips – release the clip by squeezing the ears together with pliers, then slide it back along the hose so that it is clear of the union **(see illustration)**.

4 Take care detaching the hoses from the unions. If a hose appears to be stuck, apply aerosol lubricant, such as WD-40, between the hose and the union, then release the hose by rotating it on the union before working it off. If all else fails, cut the hose with a sharp knife. Whilst this means fitting a new hose, it is preferable to buying a more expensive item such as a new radiator.

Caution: The radiator unions are fragile. Do not use excessive force when attempting to remove the hoses.

5 On installation, slide the clips onto the hose, then work the hose fully onto its union.

9.2 Loosen large-bore hose clips with a screwdriver

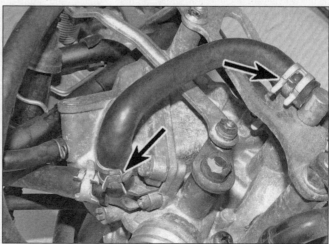

9.3 Small-bore hoses are secured by spring clips

9.8 Connection between the pump and front cylinder

9.9a Undo the elbow bolts

9.9b Note alignment of tabs with front cylinder . . .

9.9c . . . and crankcase cover

 HAYNES HiNT *If the hose is difficult to push on its union, soften it by soaking it in very hot water, or alternatively a little soapy water on the union can be used as a lubricant.*

6 Rotate the hose on its unions to settle it in position before sliding the clips into place. On the large-bore hoses, tightening the clips securely.

7 Follow the procedure in Section 2 to refill the system and check for leaks.

Pipes and elbows

8 Two coolant pipe elbows and a short section of flexible hose carry coolant from the pump into the front cylinder **(see illustration)**.

9 Undo the bolts securing the elbows, noting the alignment of the mounting tabs with the sockets in the cylinder and the crankcase cover **(see illustrations)**.

10 Pull the elbows out from the sockets, noting the location of the O-rings **(see illustration)**. Discard the O-rings as new ones must be used.

11 Refer to Chapter 1, Section 14, and check the condition of the hose. If required, loosen the hose clips and detach the elbows from the hose (see Steps 2 and 4).

12 Prior to installation, assemble the clips, hose and elbows as noted on removal (see Step 9). Do not tighten the clips at this stage.

13 Fit a new O-rings onto the elbows and lubricate them with coolant, then press the elbows into their sockets, ensuring the mounting tabs are correctly aligned **(see illustrations 9.9b and c)**. Tighten the elbow bolts securely.

14 Ensure the hose is positioned mid-way between the two elbows, then tighten the clips securely.

15 A pipe carries coolant from the front to the rear cylinder. The pipe is secured by spring clips and sealed by O-rings. If either end of the pipe is leaking, one of the cylinders will have to be removed to gain access to the O-rings (see Chapter 2, Section 16.)

9.10 Pull the elbows out from the sockets

Notes

Chapter 4A
Fuel system and exhaust – VT125C and XL125V-1 to V-6 models (carburettor engine)

Contents

Degrees of difficulty

Easy, suitable for novice with little experience	**Fairly easy,** suitable for beginner with some experience	**Fairly difficult,** suitable for competent DIY mechanic	**Difficult,** suitable for experienced DIY mechanic	**Very difficult,** suitable for expert DIY or professional

Specifications

Fuel
Grade	Unleaded. Minimum 91 RON (Research Octane Number)
Fuel tank capacity	
VT125C	
Capacity (inc. reserve)	14.0 litres
Reserve capacity	2.1 litres
XL125V-1 to XL125V-6	
Capacity (inc. reserve)	17.5 litres
Reserve capacity	2.0 litres

Carburettor
Type	CV
Size (throttle bore)	22 mm
ID number	
VT125C-X and C-Y	VPU 1A (VPU 1B Switzerland)
VT125C-1 to C-3	VPU 3A (VPU 3B Switzerland)
VT125C-4 to C-6	VPU 3C
XL125V-1 to V-3	VPU 2A
XL125V-4 to V-6	VPU 2C
Pilot screw settings	
VT125C (except Switzerland)	
Initial setting	1 3/4 turns out
Final setting	1 turn out
VT125C (Switzerland)	
Initial setting	1 1/2 turns out
Final setting	3/4 turn out
XL125V-1 to V-3	
Initial setting	1 turn out
Final setting	3/4 turn out
XL125V-4 to V-6	
Initial setting	2 3/4 turns out
Final setting	3/4 turn out

Carburettor (continued)

Float level	13.7 mm
Idle speed	1500 ± 100 rpm
Main jet	
VT125C-X and C-Y	
Front cylinder	70
Rear cylinder	75
VT125C-1 to C-6	
Front cylinder	78
Rear cylinder	78
XL125V-1 to V-3	
Front cylinder	82
Rear cylinder	88
XL125V-4 to V-6	
Front cylinder	85
Rear cylinder	92
Pilot jet	
VT125C	35
XL125V	38
Jet needle	
VT125C	
Front cylinder	B76A
Rear cylinder	B77A
XL125V-1 to V-3	
Front cylinder	C-12A
Rear cylinder	C-12B
XL125V-4 to V-6	
Front cylinder	C-12C
Rear cylinder	B76E

Torque settings

Fuel tap nut	27 Nm
Exhaust header pipe flange nuts	
VT125C	27 Nm
XL125V	18 Nm
Exhaust system clamp bolts	20 Nm
Silencer mounting nuts (VT125C)	27 Nm
Silencer mounting bolts (XL125V)	32 Nm

1 General information and precautions

General information

The fuel system consists of the fuel tank, fuel tap with fuel filter, fuel hose, two constant vacuum (CV) carburettors and the throttle and choke cables.

Opening and closing cables from the throttle twistgrip are connected to a pulley on the front cylinder's carburettor, which in turn is connected to the rear cylinder's carburettor via a link rod. The carburettor choke plungers are cable operated, connected to the choke knob on the left-hand side of the bike via a splitter. Air is drawn into the carburettors via an air filter which is housed on the right-hand side on VT125C models and underneath the fuel tank on XL125V models.

The exhaust system on VT125C models is a one-piece design with integral silencer. The exhaust system on XL125V models is a three-piece design comprising two header pipes and a silencer. A secondary air system introduces filtered air into the exhaust ports to improve exhaust gas burning and reduce emissions.

Several of the fuel system service procedures are considered routine maintenance items and for that reason are covered in Chapter 1.

Precautions

 Warning: Petrol (gasoline) is extremely flammable, so take extra precautions when you work on any part of the fuel system. Always remove the battery (see Chapter 9). Don't smoke or allow open flames or bare light bulbs near the work area, and don't work in a garage where a natural gas-type appliance is present. If you spill any fuel on your skin, rinse it off immediately with soap and water. When you perform any kind of work on the fuel system, wear safety glasses and have a fire extinguisher suitable for a class B type fire (flammable liquids) on hand.

Some residual fuel will remain in the fuel hoses and carburettors after the motorcycle has been used. Before disconnecting any fuel hose, ensure the ignition is switched OFF, and have some absorbent rag handy to catch any fuel. It is vital that no dirt or debris is allowed to enter the fuel tank or the carburettors. Any foreign matter in the fuel system components could result in damage or malfunction.

Always perform service procedures in a well-ventilated area to prevent a build-up of fumes.

Never work in a building containing a gas appliance with a pilot light, or any other form of naked flame. Ensure that there are no naked light bulbs or any sources of flame or sparks nearby.

Do not smoke (or allow anyone else to smoke) while in the vicinity of petrol (gasoline) or of components containing it. Remember the possible presence of vapour from these sources and move well clear before smoking.

Check all electrical equipment belonging to the house, garage or workshop where work is being undertaken (see the *Safety first!* section of this manual). Remember that certain electrical appliances such as drills, cutters etc, create sparks in the normal course of operation and must not be used near petrol (gasoline) or any component containing it. Again, remember the possible presence of fumes before using electrical equipment.

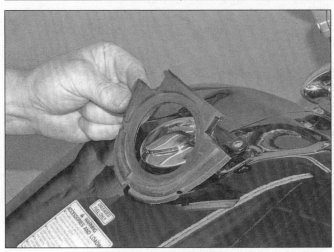

2.2 Note the location of the filler cap seal

2.3 Disconnect the fuel hose

Always mop up any spilt fuel and safely dispose of the rag used.

Any stored fuel that is drained off during servicing work must be kept in sealed containers that are suitable for holding petrol (gasoline), and clearly marked as such; the containers themselves should be kept in a safe place. Note that this last point applies equally to the fuel tank if it is removed from the machine; also remember to keep its filler cap closed at all times.

Read the *Safety first!* section of this manual carefully before starting work.

2 Fuel tank and tap

 Warning: Refer to the precautions given in Section 1 before starting work.

Note: *If the fuel tank is removed from the bike, it should not be placed in an area where sparks or open flames could ignite the fumes coming out*

of the tank. Be especially careful inside garages where a natural gas-type appliance is located, because the pilot light could cause an explosion.

Fuel tank

VT125C models

1 Remove the seat (see Chapter 8).

2 Remove the instrument cluster (see Chapter 9). Note the location of the seal around the fuel filler cap and remove it if necessary **(see illustration)**. Make sure the fuel cap is secure.

3 Make sure the fuel tap is in the OFF position. Have a rag for catching any residual fuel, then release the clip securing the fuel hose and disconnect the hose **(see illustration)**.

4 Undo the bolt and remove the collar securing the rear of the tank **(see illustration)**.

5 Draw the tank back to release the front from the mounts on the frame, then lift it off **(see illustration)**. Note the bushes on the mounts and remove them for safekeeping if required **(see illustration)**.

6 If required, remove the fuel tap (see Steps 26 to 28).

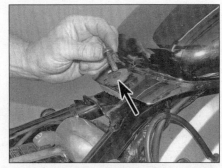

2.4 Remove the bolt and collar (arrowed)

7 Prior to installation, check the tank mounting bushes for signs of damage or deterioration and renew them if necessary **(see illustration 2.5b)**.

8 Ensure the mounting bushes are in place, then ease the tank forwards onto the mounts **(see illustration 2.5a)**.

9 Align the bracket on the rear of the tank with the frame, then install the collar and

2.5a Draw the tank back . . .

2.5b . . . off the mounts on the frame

2.14 Release the clip (arrowed) and disconnect the hose

2.15 Remove the bolt and collar

tighten the mounting bolt securely **(see illustration 2.4)**.

10 Connect the fuel hose to the tap union and secure it with the clip **(see illustration 2.3)**. Turn the tap ON and check for fuel leaks.

11 Install the remaining components in the reverse order of removal.

XL125V models

12 Remove the fairing and the seat (see Chapter 8).

13 Make sure the fuel cap is secure.

14 Make sure the fuel tap is in the OFF position. Have a rag for catching any residual fuel, then release the clip securing the fuel hose from the tap to the jointing piece and disconnect the hose **(see illustration)**.

15 Undo the bolt and remove the collar securing the rear of the tank **(see illustration)**.

16 Draw the tank back to release the front from the mounts on the frame, then lift the front up and disconnect the breather hose **(see illustrations)**.

17 Lift the tank off. Note the bushes on the mounts and remove them for safekeeping if required **(see illustration 2.5b)**.

18 If required, remove the fuel tap (see Steps 26 to 28).

19 Prior to installation, check all the tank mounting bushes for signs of damage or deterioration and renew them if necessary.

20 Ensure all mounting bushes are in place, then position the tank on the frame and connect the breather hose **(see illustration 2.16b)**.

21 Ease the tank forwards onto the mounts on the frame **(see illustration 2.16a)**.

22 Align the bracket on the rear of the tank with the frame, then install the collar and tighten the mounting bolt securely **(see illustration 2.15)**.

23 Connect the fuel hose to the jointing piece and secure it with the clip **(see illustration 2.14)**. Turn the tap ON and check for fuel leaks.

24 Install the remaining components in the reverse order of removal.

Tank repair

25 All repairs to the fuel tank should be carried out by a professional who has experience in this critical and potentially dangerous work. Even after cleaning and flushing of the fuel system, explosive fumes can remain and ignite during repair of the tank.

Fuel tap

26 To renew the tap-to-tank O-ring seal, or to clean the fuel filter, first remove the tank (see Steps 1 to 5 or 12 to 17 as appropriate). Drain any fuel into a suitable container.

27 Note the position of the tap, then unscrew the retaining nut and withdraw the tap and filter **(see illustrations)**.

2.16a Draw the tank off the mounts (arrowed) . . .

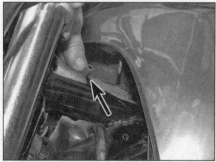

2.16b . . . and disconnect the breather hose

2.27a Note the position of the tap . . .

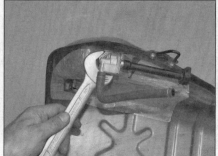

2.27b . . . then unscrew the retaining nut . . .

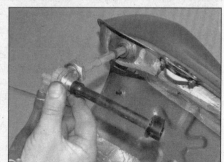

2.27c . . . and withdraw the tap and filter

2.28 Remove the O-ring

2.29 Ease the filter gauze off carefully

3.3 Loosen the clip from the left-hand side

28 Remove the O-ring as a new one must be fitted **(see illustration)**.
29 If required, ease the filter gauze off the reserve level pipe **(see illustration)**.
30 Allow the gauze to dry, then clean off any particles of dirt with a soft brush. If the gauze is damaged a new one must be fitted.
31 If the gauze is damaged and dirt particles have blocked the tap, allow the tap to dry, then blow compressed air through from the fuel hose union side with the tap in the OPEN and RES positions. If the tap remains blocked a new one must be fitted.
32 Installation is the reverse of removal. Install the filter gauze carefully to avoid damage and lubricate the new O-ring with a smear of engine oil. Position the tap as noted on removal and hold it to prevent it twisting while tightening the retaining nut. Check the tap-to-tank joint for leaks before installing the tank.

3 Air filter housing

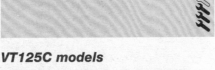

VT125C models

1 Remove the fuel tank (see Section 2).
2 If required, follow the procedure in Chapter 1 to remove the air filter cover and element.
3 Loosen the clip securing the air filter housing to the carburettor cover **(see illustration)**.
4 Undo the bolts securing the air filter housing bracket and lift the housing off **(see illustrations)**.
5 To remove the carburettor cover, follow the procedure in Section 4.
6 Installation is the reverse of removal. Make sure the air filter housing is correctly fitted onto the carburettor cover and tighten the clip securely **(see illustration 3.3)**.

XL125V models

7 Remove the fuel tank (see Section 2).
8 Follow the procedure in Chapter 1 to remove the air filter cover and element.
9 Note how the lower screws securing the filter housing are secured by locking tabs, then carefully bend back the tabs **(see illustration)**. If either of the tabs are sprained or fractured, fit a new locking piece on reassembly.
10 Undo the screws securing the filter housing to the carburettor base **(see illustration)**.
11 Release the clip securing the engine breather hose to the rear valve cover and disconnect the hose **(see illustration)**.
12 Lift the air filter housing off **(see illustration)**.

3.4a Undo the bolts . . .

3.4b . . . and remove the housing

3.9 Bend back the tabs (arrowed) . . .

3.10 . . . then undo the screws

3.11 Clip (arrowed) secures breather hose

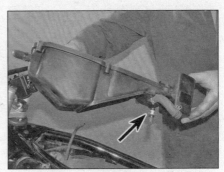

3.12 Lift housing off. Note fluid trap (arrowed)

4.4a Disconnect the breather hose

4.4b Undo the carburettor cover screws . . .

4.4c . . . and lift the cover off

13 Release the clip securing the fluid trap and wipe out any moisture.

14 Installation is the reverse of removal. Make sure the air filter housing is correctly fitted onto the carburettor base and tighten the screws securely **(see illustration 3.10)**. Don't forget to secure the lower screws with the locking tabs.

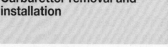

4 Carburettor removal and installation

 Warning: Refer to the precautions given in Section 1 before starting work.

Removal

1 Remove the fuel tank (see Section 2) and the air filter housing (Section 3).

2 Drain the coolant (see Chapter 3).

3 Remove the secondary air system assembly (see Section 8).

VT125C models

4 Release the clip securing the breather hose to the rear valve cover and disconnect the hose **(see illustration)**. Undo the screws securing the carburettor cover and lift it off **(see illustrations)**.

5 Disconnect the throttle cables from the throttle pulley (see Section 7).

6 Note how the screws securing the intake ducts are secured by locking tabs, then carefully bend back the tabs and undo the screws **(see illustrations)**. If any of the tabs are sprained or fractured, fit a new locking piece on reassembly.

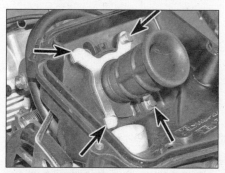

4.6a Bend back the tabs (arrowed) . . .

4.6b . . . then undo the screws

7 Note how the fork on the intake duct aligns with the peg on the carburettor base, then lift out the duct and locking piece for both carburettors **(see illustration)**.

8 Note the location of the intake tubes in the bottom of the carburettor base **(see illustration)**. Lift off the carburettor base

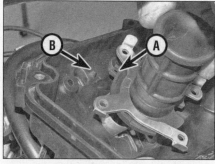

4.7 Fork (A) aligns with peg (B)

and remove the tubes, noting how the tubes locate in the carburettor intakes **(see illustrations)**.

9 Position a suitable container beneath the carburettor drain hose, then loosen the drain screws on both carburettors and drain any residual fuel **(see illustration)**. Disconnect the

4.8a Note location of the intake tubes

4.8b Remove intake tubes from the carburettor base

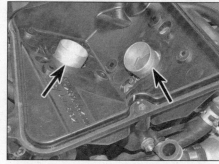

4.8c Note how the tubes locate in carburettor intakes

4.9a Front carburettor drain screw (arrowed)

4.9b Disconnect the drain hose extension

4.10a Unclip the carburettor hose . . .

4.10b . . . and coolant temperature sensor wiring

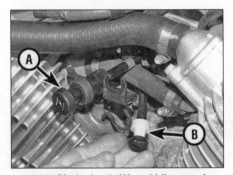

4.11 Choke knob (A) and idle speed adjuster (B)

4.12a Front cylinder's carburettor clamp screw

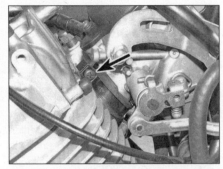

4.12b Rear cylinder's carburettor clamp screw

drain hose extension from the union on the underside of the carburettor assembly **(see illustration)**.

10 Release the carburettor hose and coolant temperature sensor wiring from their clips **(see illustrations)**.

11 Follow the procedure in Section 7 to release the choke knob from its bracket and displace the idle speed adjuster knob **(see illustration)**.

12 Fully slacken the clamp screws securing the carburettors to the intake manifolds **(see illustrations)**.

13 Ease the carburettor assembly off the cylinder heads, then release the clip securing the carburettor heater hose to the union on the rear carburettor and disconnect the hose **(see illustration)**.

Caution: Stuff clean rag into the cylinder head intakes after removing the carburettors to prevent anything from falling inside.

XL125V models

14 Disconnect the throttle cables from the throttle pulley (see Section 7).

15 Drain any residual fuel from the carburettors, then disconnect the drain hose extension (see Step 9).

16 Displace the choke and idle speed adjuster knobs (see Section 7).

17 Fully slacken the clamp screws securing the carburettors to the intake manifolds, then ease the assembly off the heads **(see illustration)**.

18 Release the clip securing the carburettor heater hose to the union on the rear

cylinder head and disconnect the hose **(see illustrations)**.

19 Note how the screws securing the intake ducts are secured by locking tabs, then

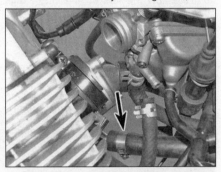

4.13 Disconnect the heater hose (arrowed)

4.17 Ease the carburettor assembly off the heads

4.18a Release the spring clip (arrowed) . . .

4.18b . . . and disconnect the heater hose

4.19 Bend back the tabs and undo the screws

4.20a Note how fork and peg (arrowed) align

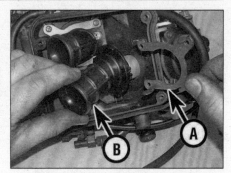

4.20b Lift out locking piece (A) and duct (B)

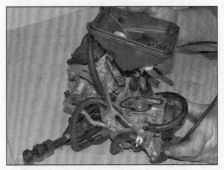

4.21a Lift off the carburettor base . . .

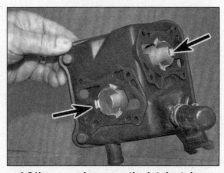

4.21b . . . and remove the intake tubes

4.22 Detach the fluid trap and wipe out any moisture

carefully bend back the tabs and undo the screws **(see illustration)**. If any of the tabs are sprained or fractured, fit a new locking piece on reassembly.

20 Note how the fork on the intake duct aligns with the peg on the carburettor base, then lift out the locking piece and duct for both carburettors **(see illustrations)**.

21 Lift off the carburettor base and remove the intake tubes, noting how they locate **(see illustrations)**.

22 Release the clip securing the fluid trap and wipe out any moisture **(see illustration)**.

Caution: Stuff clean rag into the cylinder head intake manifolds after removing the carburettors to prevent anything from falling inside.

Installation

23 Installation is the reverse of removal, noting the following.

● Check for cracks or splits in the intake manifolds and replace them with new ones if necessary **(see illustration)**.
● Make sure the intake manifold clamps are positioned correctly **(see illustration)**.
● Press the carburettors down firmly to

ensure they are fully engaged with the manifolds – a squirt of WD-40 or a smear of oil will ease entry.
● Tighten the clamp screws securely **(see illustration 4.23b)**.
● Make sure all hoses are correctly routed and secured and not trapped or kinked.
● Refer to Section 7 for installation of the throttle and choke cables. Check the operation of the cables and adjust them as necessary (see Chapter 1).
● Check idle speed and adjust as necessary (see Chapter 1).

4.23a Inspect the intake manifold for wear and damage

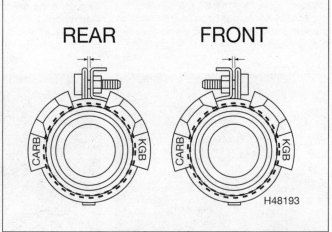

4.23b Position of upper manifold clamps. End clearance 0 to 2 mm when fully tightened

5.4 Disconnect the heater hoses from their unions

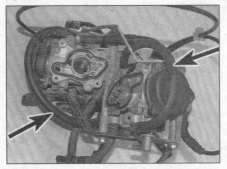

5.5 Disconnect the vent tubes from their unions

5.6 Disconnect the secondary air system vacuum hose

5 Carburettor overhaul

1 Poor engine performance, hesitation, hard starting, stalling and flooding are all signs that carburettor overhaul may be required (see *Fault Finding* in the *Reference* section).

2 Before disassembling the carburettors, make sure you have all the necessary O-rings and gaskets, some carburettor cleaner, a supply of clean rags, some means of blowing out the carburettor passages and a clean place to work.

 Warning: Refer to the precautions given in Section 1 before starting work.

Disassembly

3 Remove the carburettor assembly (see Section 4). **Note:** *Do not separate the carburettors unless absolutely necessary; each carburettor can be dismantled sufficiently for all normal cleaning and adjustments while in place on the mounting brackets. Dismantle the carburettors separately to avoid interchanging parts.*

4 Release the clips securing the heater hoses

and disconnect the hoses from their unions, noting where they fit **(see illustration)**. Undo the screws securing the heater hose unions and detach the unions.

5 Disconnect the vent tubes from their unions, noting where they fit **(see illustration)**.

6 If not already done, release the clip securing the secondary air system vacuum hose to the rear carburettor and disconnect the hose **(see illustration)**.

7 Release the clips securing the drain hoses to the float chambers and disconnect the hoses **(see illustration)**.

8 Release the choke cable splitter from the clip on the underside of the carburetor assembly **(see illustration)**. Unscrew the choke cable guides and withdraw the plunger assemblies from the carburettor bodies, noting how they fit **(see illustrations)**. Follow the procedure in Steps 21 and 22 to disassemble the plunger assemblies.

9 Release the clips securing the fuel hoses to the carburettor bodies and disconnect the hoses.

10 At this point, if required, the carburettors can be separated (see **Note** in Step 3). To do

5.7 Disconnect the drain hoses from the float chambers

5.8a Unclip the choke cable splitter

5.8b Unscrew the choke cable guides . . .

5.8c . . . and withdraw the plunger assemblies

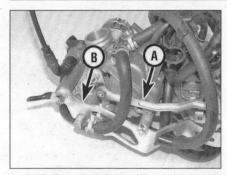

5.10 Throttle link arm (A) and joining plate (B)

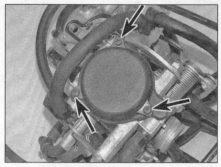

5.11a Undo the screws (arrowed) . . .

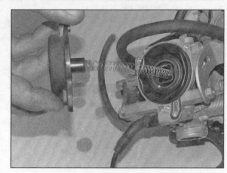

5.11b . . . and lift off the top cover

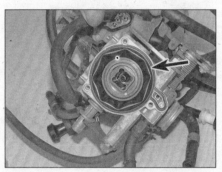

5.12a Ease the rim of the diaphragm out carefully . . .

5.12b . . . and withdraw the diaphragm/ piston assembly

this, first remove the split pin and washers securing the throttle link arm to the throttle arm on the front carburettor and disconnect the link arm **(see illustration)**. Note the location of the washers. Undo the nuts securing the left and right-hand joining plates and remove the plates, noting how they fit.

11 Working on one carburettor at a time, undo the screws securing the top cover and lift the cover off, noting the location of the spring **(see illustrations)**.

12 Carefully peel the diaphragm away from its sealing groove in the carburettor and withdraw the diaphragm/piston assembly **(see illustrations)**.

Caution: Do not use a sharp instrument to displace the diaphragm as it is easily damaged.

13 To remove the jet needle holder from inside the piston, thread a suitable screw into the top of the holder, then draw the holder out of the piston **(see illustration)**. Note that a small spring is located in the lower end of the holder – remove it for safekeeping if it is loose.

Caution: Do not push the needle holder out of the piston by pushing up on the needle.

14 Push the jet needle up from the bottom of the piston and withdraw it from the top, noting the location of the washer **(see illustration)**.

15 Undo the screws securing the float chamber to the base of the carburettor and remove it **(see illustrations)**. Remove the seal and discard it, as a new one must be used **(see illustration)**.

5.13 Draw the jet needle holder out of the piston

5.14 Remove the jet needle

5.15a Undo the screws (arrowed) . . .

5.15b . . . and remove the float chamber

5.15c Remove the float chamber seal

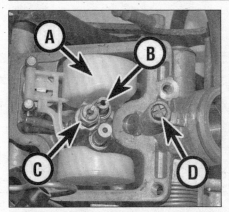

5.17a Withdraw the float pin . . .

5.17b . . . and remove the float assembly

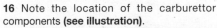

5.16 Carburettor components – float (A), pilot jet (B), main jet and jet holder (C) and pilot screw (D)

16 Note the location of the carburettor components **(see illustration)**.

17 Withdraw the float pin and remove the float assembly, noting how it fits **(see illustrations)**. Unhook the needle valve from the tab on the float, noting how it fits **(see illustration)**.

18 Unscrew the pilot jet, unscrew the main jet from the top of the jet holder, then unscrew the jet holder **(see illustration 5.16)**.

19 The pilot screw can be removed from the carburettor, but note that its setting will be disturbed. To record the pilot screw's current setting, turn the screw in until it seats lightly, counting the exact number of turns. Unscrew and remove the pilot screw along with its spring, washer and O-ring **(see illustration)**. Discard the O-ring, as a new one must be used.

20 Note the location of the choke plunger on the end of the inner cable, then compress the spring and remove the plunger, noting how it fits **(see illustration)**.

21 Slide off the spring, cable guide, elbow and boot **(see illustrations)**. Together with the choke plunger, these components comprise the choke assembly.

Cleaning

Caution: Use only a dedicated carburettor cleaner or petroleum-based solvent for carburettor cleaning, following the

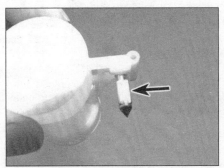

5.17c Unhook the needle valve (arrowed) from the float

5.19 Note the spring, washer and O-ring on the pilot screw

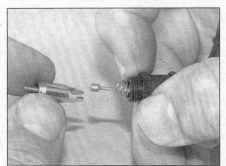

5.20 Compress the spring to remove the choke plunger

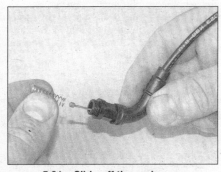

5.21a Slide off the spring . . .

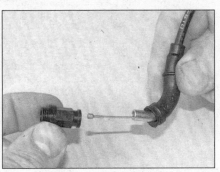

5.21b . . . cable guide . . .

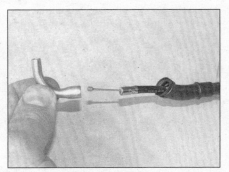

5.21c . . . elbow . . .

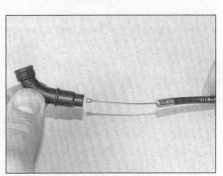

5.21d . . . and boot

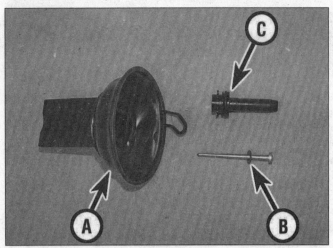

5.26 Examine the piston diaphragm (A) for damage. Note the washer (B) on the jet needle and the O-ring (C) on the jet needle holder

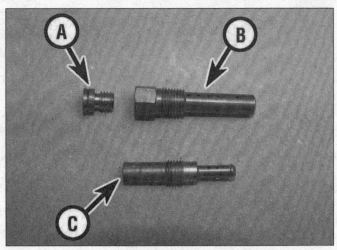

5.34 Examine the main jet (A), jet holder (B) and pilot jet (C)

manufacturer's instructions. DO NOT use caustic cleaners.

22 Squirt carburettor cleaner through all of the fuel and air passages in the carburettor body.

23 Submerge small metal components in the cleaner long enough to loosen and dissolve any varnish and other deposits. Clean inside the float chamber and the carburettor body, using a nylon-bristled brush to remove stubborn deposits. Finally, rinse all the components and dry them thoroughly.

24 Use compressed air to blow out all of the fuel and air passages, not forgetting the fuel jets.

Caution: Never clean the jets or passages with a piece of wire or a drill bit, as they will be enlarged, causing the fuel and air metering rates to be upset.

Inspection

25 Inspect the carburettor body, float chamber and top cover for cracks, distorted sealing surfaces and other damage. If any defects are found, replace the faulty component with a new one.

26 Check the piston diaphragm for splits, holes, creases and general deterioration **(see illustration)**. Holding it up to a light will help to reveal problems of this nature. Even minor defects will cause running problems – fit a new diaphragm/piston assembly.

27 Insert the piston in the carburettor

body and check that it moves up and down smoothly. Check the surface of the piston for wear. If it is worn excessively or doesn't move smoothly, replace it with a new one.

28 Check the piston spring for distortion and fatigue.

29 Inspect the jet needle for wear and pitting and ensure the needle is straight **(see illustration 5.26)**. Note that the identification marks on the needles differ front and rear (see *Specifications* at the beginning of this Chapter).

30 Discard the O-ring on the jet needle holder **(see illustration 5.26)**. Lubricate a new O-ring with a smear of engine oil and fit it carefully into the groove in the holder

31 Inspect the tip of the float needle valve **(see illustration 5.17c)**. If the tip has grooves or scratches in it, or is in any way worn, the valve must be replaced with a new one. Note that if the valve seat in the carburettor body is damaged a new carburettor will have to be fitted.

32 Check the float for damage. This will usually be apparent by the presence of fuel inside the float. If it is damaged, replace it with a new one.

33 Operate the throttle shaft to make sure the throttle butterfly valve opens and closes smoothly. If it doesn't, cleaning the throttle linkage may help. Otherwise, renew the carburettor. Do not remove the butterfly valve from the throttle shaft.

34 Inspect the jets and jet holder for pitting **(see illustration)**. Note that different size main jets are fitted front and rear (see *Specifications*).

35 Check the tapered end of the pilot screw and the spring for wear or damage **(see illustration)**. Renew the pilot screw and spring if necessary. Discard the O-ring and fit a new one.

36 Check the tapered end of the choke plunger and the spring for wear, damage or distortion **(see illustration 5.20)**. Inspect the boot for damage. Individual components are not available – fit a new choke assembly if necessary.

37 Undo the float chamber drain screw fully and renew the sealing O-ring.

38 Check the condition of the hoses and hose clips and replace them with new ones if they are damaged, deformed or deteriorated.

Reassembly and float height check

Note: *When reassembling the carburettors, be sure to use the new O-rings, seals and other parts supplied in the rebuild kit. Do not overtighten the carburettor jets and screws, as they are easily damaged.*

39 Fit the spring, washer and O-ring onto the pilot screw, then thread the screw in until it seats lightly **(see illustrations 5.35 and 5.19)**. Now, turn the screw out the number of turns previously recorded, or to the initial setting (see *Specifications*).

40 Install the jet holder, main jet and pilot jet **(see illustrations 5.34 and 5.16)**.

41 Hook the needle valve onto the float, then position the float assembly in the carburettor, making sure the needle valve locates in its seat **(see illustrations 5.17c and b)**. Install the float pin **(see illustration 5.17a)**.

42 To check the float height, hold the carburettor so the float hangs down, then tilt it back until the needle valve just touches its seat. Measure the distance between the top edge of the float and the sealing surface of the float chamber **(see illustration)**. The height

5.35 Pilot screw components

5.42 Measuring the float height

5.45 Needle holder should click into place

5.46 Install the diaphragm/piston assembly

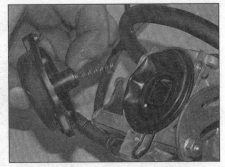

5.47 Compress and hold the spring in the top cover

should be as specified at the beginning of this Chapter. If not, replace the float assembly with a new one – it cannot be adjusted.

43 Fit a new seal onto the float chamber, making sure it is seated properly in its groove **(see illustration 5.15c)**. Fit the chamber onto the carburettor and tighten the screws securely **(see illustration 5.15b and a)**.

44 Ensure that the washer is fitted onto the jet needle, then install the needle in the piston **(see illustrations 5.26 and 5.14)**.

45 Ensure that the spring is located in the lower end of the needle holder, then thread a screw into the top of the holder as on disassembly **(see illustration 5.13)**. Align the holder with the inside of the piston, install it on top of the needle and press it down until it is felt to click into place **(see illustration)**. Remove the screw.

46 Fold the diaphragm down over the piston and fit the assembly into the carburettor, making sure the piston is aligned with the carburettor body and the needle is aligned with the jet holder **(see illustration)**. Ensure the tab on the rim of the diaphragm is aligned with the cut-out in the carburettor and press the rim of the diaphragm into its groove, making sure it is correctly seated **(see illustration 5.12a)**.

47 Compress the spring into the top cover **(see illustration)**, then install the cover and secure it with the screws **(see illustrations 5.11a)**.

48 Check that the piston moves smoothly in the carburettor body by pushing it up with your finger. Note that the piston should descend slowly and smoothly as the diaphragm draws

air into the chamber – it should not drop sharply under spring pressure.

49 If the carburettors have been separated, assemble them with the joining plates as noted on disassembly **(see illustration 5.10)**. Tighten the nuts securely. Install the link arm and washers and secure it with a new split pin.

50 Fit the fuel hoses, drain hoses and secondary air system vacuum hose and secure them with the clips.

51 Thread the choke cable guides into the carburettor bodies and tighten them carefully **(see illustrations 5.8c and b)**. Cover the joints between the cable, the elbow and the guide with the boot. Secure the cable splitter in the clip on the underside of the carburetor assembly **(see illustration 5.8a)**.

52 Install the vent tubes **(see illustration 5.5)**.

53 Install the heater hose unions and hoses and secure the hoses with the clips **(see illustrations 5.4)**.

54 Install the carburettor assembly (see Section 4).

55 If the pilot screws have been disturbed or if new pilot screws have been fitted, adjust the idle fuel/air mixture (see Section 6).

6 Idle fuel/air mixture adjustment

Special tools: *A tachometer (rev counter) that will accurately indicate a variation of 50 rpm in engine speed is necessary for this job. A special screwdriver is required to adjust the pilot screws (see Step 4).*

1 The pilot screws are located on the underside of the carburettors, between the float chambers and the intake manifolds **(see illustration)**.

2 If the engine runs extremely rough at idle or continually stalls, and if carburettor overhaul does not cure the problem, the pilot screws may require adjustment. It is worth noting at this point that unless you have the experience and tools to carry this out it is best to entrust the task to a motorcycle dealer.

3 Make sure that the valve clearances are correct and that carburettor synchronisation is within the specified tolerance (see Chapter 1).

4 Using the special screwdriver shown, turn each pilot screw clockwise until it seats lightly **(see illustrations)**, then back it out to the initial setting (see *Specifications* at the beginning of this Chapter). Warm the engine up to normal operating temperature, then adjust the idle speed to its specified setting (see Chapter 1).

5 With the engine running, turn the front carburettor pilot screw by a small amount either side of the initial setting to find the point at which the highest consistent idle speed is obtained. Next, do the same with the rear carburettor pilot screw.

6 Lightly open the throttle two or three times, then readjust the idle speed.

7 Turn the front carburettor pilot screw clockwise until the engine speed drops by 50 rpm, then back it out by the amount given as the final setting (see *Specifications*).

8 Adjust the idle speed to its specified setting (see Chapter 1).

9 Turn the rear carburettor pilot screw

6.1 Location of the rear cylinder's carburettor pilot screw

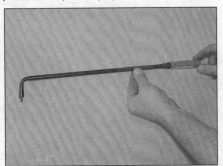

6.4a Use this special screwdriver . . .

6.4b . . . to adjust the pilot screws

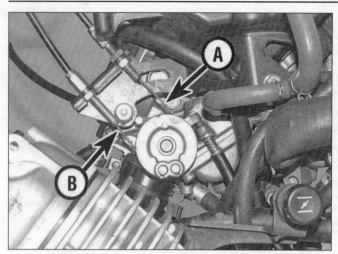

7.2 Throttle opening cable (A) and closing cable (B)

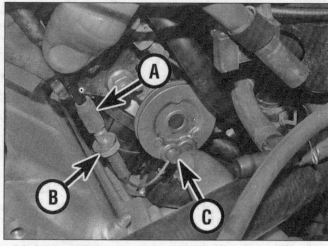

7.3 Closing cable guide (A), locknut (B) and inner cable end (C)

clockwise until the engine speed drops by 50 rpm, then back it out to the final setting (see *Specifications*).

10 Adjust the idle speed to its specified setting (see Chapter 1).

7 Throttle and choke cables

Throttle cables

VT125C models

1 Remove the fuel tank (see Section 2).

7.4 Disconnect the opening cable from the pulley

2 Note the location of the throttle opening and closing cables on the throttle pulley on the front carburettor **(see illustration)**.

3 Loosen the locknut on the closing cable guide and free the guide from the bracket, noting how it locates. Disconnect the inner cable end from the pulley **(see illustration)**.

4 Loosen the locknuts on the opening cable adjuster and free the adjuster from the bracket, noting how it locates. Disconnect the inner cable end from the pulley **(see illustration)**.

5 Loosen the adjuster locknut on the handlebar end of the opening cable and turn the adjuster all the way in **(see illustration)**.

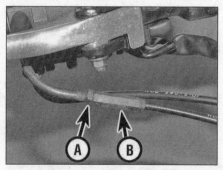

7.5 Opening cable locknut (A) and adjuster (B)

6 Undo the retaining nuts on both throttle cable elbows **(see illustration)**.

7 Undo the throttle twistgrip/switch housing screws, noting how they fit **(see illustration)**.

8 Separate the halves of the housing, noting how they align with the handlebar **(see illustration)**. Detach the inner cable ends from the pulley and draw the cables out from the housing.

9 Note the routing of the cables around the steering head and frame, then take them off.

10 Installation is the reverse of removal. Thread both cable elbows into the twistgrip/switch housing, ensuring the opening cable is fitted at the front, and tighten the retaining nuts finger-tight. Lubricate the ends of the inner cables with multi-purpose grease and fit them into the throttle pulley **(see illustration 7.8)**.

11 Assemble the housing onto the handlebar, making sure the pin in the lower half locates in the hole In the underside of the handlebar, then fit the screws with the longest one at the rear and tighten them **(see illustration 7.7)**.

12 Feed the cables through to the carburettors, making sure they are correctly routed and not kinked or bent sharply.

13 Lubricate the ends of the inner cables with multi-purpose grease. Fit the end of the opening cable onto the pulley and locate

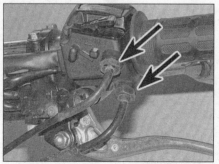

7.6 Throttle cable elbow retaining nuts

7.7 Location of throttle twistgrip housing screws

7.8 Separate the halves of the twistgrip housing

7.13 Fit the opening cable adjuster on the bracket

7.22 Release the heat shield from the brackets (arrowed)

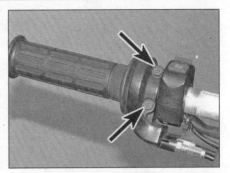

7.25a Undo the screws . . .

the cable adjuster on the bracket **(see illustration)**.

14 Fit the end of the closing cable onto the pulley, locate the cable guide on the bracket, then tighten the guide against the locknut.

15 Check that the adjuster on the handlebar end of the opening cable is turned fully in, then adjust the locknuts on the lower adjuster so the cable freeplay is as specified In Chapter 1 and tighten the locknuts.

16 Operate the throttle twistgrip to check that it opens and closes freely.

17 Tighten the retaining nuts on the throttle cable elbows **(see illustration 7.6)**.

18 Turn the handlebars back-and-forth to make sure the cables don't cause the steering to bind.

19 Install the fuel tank (see Section 2).

20 Start the engine and check that the idle speed does not rise as the handlebars are turned. If it does, the cables are routed incorrectly. Correct the problem before riding the motorcycle.

XL125V models

21 Remove the fuel tank (see Section 2).

22 Release the heat shield from the brackets on the frame and secondary air system control valve and lift the shield off **(see illustration)**.

23 Release the clip securing the hose from the front valve cover to the secondary air system control valve and displace the control valve bracket from the carburettor base (see Section 8).

24 Follow the procedure in Steps 2 to 4 to disconnect the cables from the pulley on the carburettor.

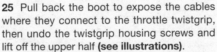

7.25b . . . and lift off the upper half of the housing

25 Pull back the boot to expose the cables where they connect to the throttle twistgrip, then undo the twistgrip housing screws and lift off the upper half **(see illustrations)**.

26 Displace the lower half of the twistgrip housing from the handlebar and disconnect the inner cable ends from the pulley **(see illustration)**.

27 Lift out the cable guide, noting how the opening (upper) cable and closing (lower) cable are routed through the guide **(see illustration)**.

28 Note the location of the opening cable adjuster and closing cable guide in the lower half of the twistgrip housing **(see illustration)**. Loosen the locknut on the adjuster then unscrew both cables from the housing.

29 Note the routing of the cables around the steering head and frame, then take them off.

30 Installation is the reverse of removal.

7.26 Disconnect the inner cable ends from the pulley

Screw the opening cable adjuster and closing cable guide into the lower half of the twistgrip housing, ensuring the opening cable is fitted above the closing cable **(see illustration 7.28)**. Tighten the opening cable adjuster locknut. Lubricate the ends of the inner cables with multi-purpose grease.

31 Install the cable guide, then connect the inner cable ends to the pulley **(see illustrations 7.27 and 7.26)**.

32 Draw the inner cables through at the lower end to remove any slack and assemble the lower half of the housing on the handlebar, making sure the pin locates in the hole on the underside of the bar **(see illustration)**.

33 Install the upper half of the housing and tighten the housing screws.

34 Feed the cables through to the carburettors, making sure they are correctly routed and not kinked or bent sharply, then

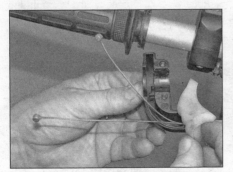

7.27 Remove the cable guide

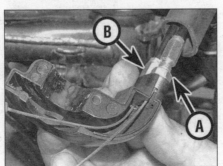

7.28 Opening cable adjuster (A) and closing cable guide (B)

7.32 Fit the lower half of the housing onto the handlebar

7.39 Unscrew the nut (arrowed) to free the choke knob

7.40 Location of the choke cable splitter

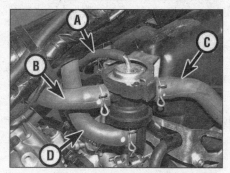

8.3 Air system hoses – VT125C. Vacuum hose (A), rear cylinder intake (B), front cylinder intake (C) and air supply hose (D)

follow the procedure in Steps 13 to 16 to connect the cables to the pulley on the carburettor.

35 Turn the handlebars back-and-forth to make sure the cables don't cause the steering to bind.

36 Install the remaining components in the reverse order of removal.

37 Start the engine and check that the idle speed does not rise as the handlebars are turned. If it does, the cables are routed incorrectly. Correct the problem before riding the motorcycle.

Choke cables

38 On VT125C models, remove the air filter housing (see Section 3) and the carburettor

cover (see Section 4). On XL125V models, remove the air filter housing (see Section 3).

39 Unscrew the nut securing the choke knob fully, then free the knob from the bracket, noting how it fits (see illustration).

40 Release the choke cable splitter from the clip on the underside of the carburetor assembly (see illustration).

41 Unscrew the choke cable guides and withdraw the plunger assemblies from the carburettors (see illustrations 5.8b and c). Carefully remove the cable assembly from the machine, noting the location of the choke plungers on the end of each inner cable.

42 Follow the procedure in Section 5 to separate the choke assemblies from the cables. The choke cables, splitter and knob

are listed as a single assembly, individual components are not available.

43 Installation is the reverse of removal. Follow the procedure in Section 5 to install the choke assemblies and secure the cable splitter in its clip.

44 Fit the choke knob in its bracket, then tighten the nut carefully – note that the nut is plastic and should only be finger-tight.

45 Operate the choke to check that it opens and closes freely. If required, adjust the friction on the knob (see Chapter 1).

46 Install the remaining components in the reverse order of removal.

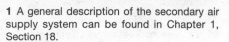

8 Secondary air system

1 A general description of the secondary air supply system can be found in Chapter 1, Section 18.

Control valve

VT125C models

2 The control valve is located behind the air filter housing – remove the fuel tank (see Section 2) and air filter housing (see Section 3) for access.

3 Note the location of the air system hoses (see illustration).

4 Pull the vacuum hose off the union on the top of the control valve, then release the clips securing the air supply and intake hoses and disconnect the hoses, either from the control valve (see illustration 8.3) or from the carburettor cover and the front and rear valve covers (see illustrations). If required, remove the cylinder head side covers for access (see Chapter 2, Section 11).

5 Unclip the control valve from the carburettor base and lift it off (see illustration).

6 If, after inspecting the system as described in Chapter 1, the control valve is thought to be faulty, test it as follows.

7 Blow into the supply hose union and ensure that air flows out through the intake hose

8.4a Air supply hose connection on carburettor cover

8.4b Front cylinder intake hose

8.4c Rear cylinder intake hose

8.5 Unclip the control valve from the bracket on the carburettor base

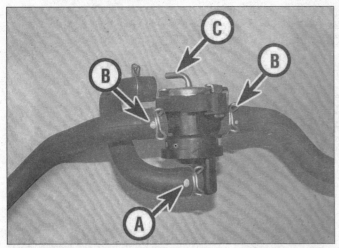

8.7 Supply hose union (A), intake hose unions (B), vacuum hose union (C)

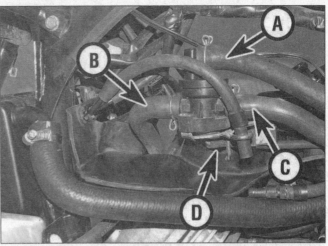

8.10 Air system hoses – XL125V. Air supply hose (A), front cylinder intake (B), rear cylinder intake (C) and vacuum hose (D)

8.11 Release the heat shield (A) and vent hose (B)

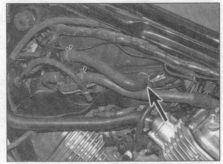

8.12 Air supply hose connection on carburettor base

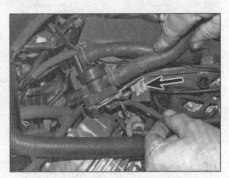

8.13 Unclip the control valve from the bracket on the carburettor base

unions **(see illustration)**. Now apply a vacuum of 280 mmHg via the vacuum hose union and repeat the check – no air should flow through the valve if it is functioning correctly. Replace the valve with a new one if it is faulty.

8 Installation is the reverse of removal.

XL125V models

9 The control valve is located on the left-hand side of the air filter housing – remove the fuel tank (see Section 2) for access.

10 Note the location of the air system hoses **(see illustration)**.

11 Release the heat shield from the bracket on the control valve and displace the vent hose **(see illustration)**.

12 Release the clips securing the air supply and intake hoses and disconnect the hoses, either from the valve **(see illustration 8.10)** or from the carburettor base **(see illustration)** and front and rear valve covers **(see illustrations 8.4b and c)** If required, remove the rear cylinder head side covers for access (see Chapter 2, Section 11).

13 Unclip the control valve from the carburettor base **(see illustration)**. Pull

the small diameter vacuum hose off the union on the bottom of the valve **(see illustration 8.10)**.

14 If, after inspecting the system as described in Chapter 1, the control valve is thought to be faulty, test it as described in Step 7.

15 Installation is the reverse of removal.

Reed valves

16 The reed valves are located in the front and rear valve covers. To inspect the valves, refer to Chapter 2, Section 11.

9   Exhaust system

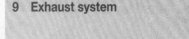

> ⚠️ **Warning: If the engine has been running the exhaust system will be very hot. Allow the system to cool before carrying out any work.**

VT125C models

1 Undo the nuts securing the front and rear header pipe flanges and pull the flanges off the exhaust studs **(see illustrations)**.

2 Undo the nuts securing the silencer to

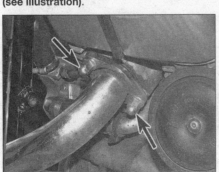

9.1a Front header pipe flange nuts

9.1b Rear header pipe flange nuts

9.2a Silencer mounting nuts

9.2b Remove the complete exhaust system

9.3 Prise out the old exhaust seals

9.4 Silencer mounting bracket bolts

9.5a Secure new seals with a dab of grease

9.5b Align flanges with exhaust studs

9.5c Fit silencer onto mounting bracket studs

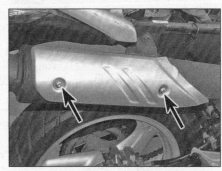

9.7 Heat shield mounting screws

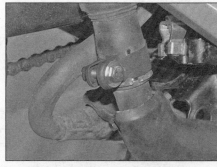

9.8 Loosen the silencer clamp bolt

9.9a Undo the mounting bolts (arrowed) . . .

9.9b . . . and lift the silencer off

9.9c Discard the old silencer front pipe seal

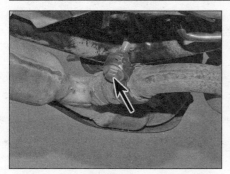

9.10 Loosen the front-to-rear exhaust clamp bolt

9.11a Front header pipe flange nuts

9.11b Ease the front exhaust pipe off

its mounting bracket, then manoeuvre the exhaust system off (see illustrations).

3 Prise the exhaust seals out from the ports and discard them as new ones must be fitted (see illustration).

4 If required, undo the bolts securing the silencer mounting bracket and remove the bracket (see illustration).

5 Installation is the reverse of removal, noting the following:

● Apply a dab of grease to the exhaust seals to hold them in place (see illustration).
● Apply a smear of copper grease to all nuts and studs to prevent them from seizing.
● Align the header pipes with the ports, install the flanges and nuts finger-tight, then fit the silencer onto its mounting bracket (see illustrations).
● Ensure the system is correctly aligned before tightening any of the fixings.
● Tighten the header pipe flange nuts first, then the silencer mounting nuts.
● Run the engine and check the system for leaks.

XL125V models

6 Remove the right-hand side panel (see Chapter 8).

7 If required, undo the screws securing the heat shield and lift it off (see illustration).

8 Loosen the silencer clamp bolt (see illustration).

 HAYNES HiNT *Exhaust system clamp bolts tend to become corroded and seized. It is advisable to spray them with WD-40 or a similar product before attempting to slacken them.*

9 Undo the bolts securing the silencer to the frame and lift the silencer off (see illustrations). Note the location of the seal inside the silencer front pipe and discard it as a new one must be fitted (see illustration).

10 Loosen the clamp bolt securing the front exhaust pipe to the rear exhaust pipe (see illustration). If required, soak the pipe joint with penetrating fluid to ease disassembly.

11 Undo the nuts securing the front header pipe flange and pull the flange off the studs (see illustration). Carefully ease the front exhaust pipe out from the front cylinder exhaust port and separate it from the rear pipe (see illustration). Note the location of the seal inside the pipe union and discard it as a new one must be fitted (see illustration).

12 Undo the nuts securing the rear header pipe flange and pull the flange off the studs (see illustration). Carefully ease the rear exhaust pipe out from the rear cylinder exhaust port and manoeuvre the pipe off the machine.

13 Prise the exhaust seals out from the ports and discard them as new ones must be fitted (see illustration 9.3).

14 Installation is the reverse of removal, noting the following:

● Apply a dab of grease to the exhaust seals to hold them in place (see illustration 9.5a).
● Apply a smear of copper grease to all nuts and bolts to prevent them from seizing.
● Leave all fasteners finger-tight until the entire system has been installed, making alignment easier.
● Install the rear header pipe first.
● Fit a new seal and the clamp onto the front header pipe, then connect it to the rear pipe (see illustrations 9.11c and 10).
● Fit a new seal and the clamp onto the silencer front pipe, then connect it to the system (see illustrations 9.9c and 8).
● Tighten the header pipe flange nuts first, then the silencer mounting bolts and finally the pipe clamp bolts.
● Run the engine and check the system for leaks.

9.11c Discard the old exhaust pipe seal

9.12 Rear header pipe flange nuts

Chapter 4B
Engine management system – XL125V-7 models onward (fuel injected engine)

Contents

Degrees of difficulty

| **Easy,** suitable for novice with little experience | | **Fairly easy,** suitable for beginner with some experience | | **Fairly difficult,** suitable for competent DIY mechanic | | **Difficult,** suitable for experienced DIY mechanic | | **Very difficult,** suitable for expert DIY or professional | |

Specifications

Fuel
Grade	Unleaded. Minimum 91 RON (Research Octane Number)

Fuel tank capacity
Capacity (inc. reserve)	17.0 litres
Reserve capacity	3.0 litres

Fuel pump
Fuel pressure, engine idling	43 psi (3.0 Bar)
Minimum fuel flow rate	56 ml every 10 seconds

Throttle body
ID number	GQV0A

Engine management system

Manifold absolute pressure (MAP) sensor
    Input voltage .... 4.75 to 5.25 V
    Output voltage at idle................................. 2.7 V
Engine coolant temperature (ECT) sensor
    Input voltage .... 4.75 to 5.25 V
    Output voltage .... 2.7 to 3.1 V at 20°C (68°F)
    Resistance
        At 20°C (68°F)..................................... 2.3 to 2.6 K-ohms
        At 80°C (176°F)................................... 0.3 to 0.4 K-ohms
        At 110°C (230°F)................................. 0.1 to 0.2 K-ohms
Throttle position sensor
    Output voltage
        Throttle fully closed............................. 0.4 to 0.6 V (approx)
        Throttle fully open.............................. 4.2 to 4.8 V (approx)
    Input voltage .... 4.75 to 5.25 V
Intake air temperature (IAT) sensor
    Output voltage .... 2.7 to 3.1 V at 30°C (86°F)
    Input voltage .... 4.75 to 5.25 V
    Resistance .... 1.0 to 4.0 K-ohms at 20°C (68°F)
Vehicle speed (VS) sensor
    Output voltage .... 0 to 5 V (pulsing signal)
Fuel injectors
    Resistance .... 10 to 12 ohms at 20°C (68°F)
Oxygen sensors
    Heater resistance .... 5 to 15 ohms at 20°C (68°F)
Idle air control valve (IACV)
    Resistance .... 99 to 121 ohms at 25°C (77°F)
    Engine idle speed .... 1500 ± 100 rpm
Crankshaft position (CKP) sensor
    Minimum peak voltage output .... 0.7 volts
Secondary air system control valve
    Resistance .... 20 to 24 ohms at 20°C (68°F)
Ignition HT coils
    Initial voltage.. Battery voltage
    Minimum primary peak voltage .... 100 volts

Torque settings

Crankshaft position (CKP) sensor bolts .... 6 Nm
Engine coolant temperature (ECT) sensor .... 23 Nm
Fuel feed hose union bolts................................... 5 Nm
Fuel pump mounting nuts .... 12 Nm
Fuel tank mounting bolt .... 12 Nm
Oxygen sensor .... 45 Nm
Exhaust header pipe flange nuts .... 17 Nm
Exhaust system clamp bolts .... 17 Nm
Silencer mounting bolts .... 20 Nm

---

1 General information and precautions

General information

The engine management system combines the operations of the fuel and ignition systems. Together they are controlled by the engine control module (ECM) which ensures that the engine is running at optimum efficiency under all riding conditions.

Fuel system

The fuel system consists of the fuel tank, an integrated fuel pump, pressure regulator, low fuel level warning sender and strainer, the fuel hose, injectors, throttle body assembly and control cables.

Fuel is pumped under pressure from the tank to the fuel injectors. The fuel pump is switched on and off by the ignition switch, via a relay. Operating pressure is maintained by the pressure regulator.

When they open, the injectors spray fuel into the throttle bodies where it mixes with air and vaporises, before entering the cylinder where it is compressed and ignited. Fuel supply varies according to the engine's needs for starting, warming-up, idling, cruising and acceleration. The timing and duration of fuel delivery is determined by the ECM using the information obtained from the various sensors it monitors (see Section 7).

The exhaust system is a three-piece design comprising two header pipes and a silencer. An oxygen sensor and a catalytic converter are located inside both header pipes. A secondary air system introduces filtered air into the exhaust ports to improve exhaust gas burning and reduce emissions.

Several of the fuel system service procedures are considered routine maintenance items and for that reason are covered in Chapter 1.

Ignition system

The ignition system consists of the crankshaft position (CKP) sensor, ignition coils and spark plugs.

The triggers on the alternator rotor, which is fitted to the left-hand end of the crankshaft, activate signals in the CKP sensor as the crankshaft rotates. The sensor sends those signals to the ECM which, in conjunction with information received from the throttle position and engine coolant temperature sensor, calculates the ignition timing and supplies the ignition coils with the power necessary to produce a spark at the plugs. There is no provision for checking or adjusting the ignition timing.

Note: *Individual engine management system components can be checked but not repaired. If system troubles occur, and the faulty component can be isolated, the only cure for the problem in most cases is to replace the part with a new one. Keep in mind that most electronic parts, once purchased, cannot be returned. To avoid unnecessary expense, make very sure the faulty component has been positively identified before buying a new part.*

Precautions

 Warning: Petrol (gasoline) is extremely flammable, so take extra precautions when you work on any part of the fuel system. Always remove the battery (see Chapter 9). Don't smoke or allow open flames or bare light bulbs near the work area, and don't work in a garage where a natural gas-type appliance is present. If you spill any fuel on your skin, rinse it off immediately with soap and water. When you perform any kind of work on the fuel system, wear safety glasses and have a fire extinguisher suitable for a class B type fire (flammable liquids) on hand.

Ensure the ignition is switched OFF before disconnecting or reconnecting any fuel injection system wiring connector. If a connector is disconnected or reconnected with the ignition switched ON, the ECM may be damaged.

Always perform service procedures in a well-ventilated area to prevent a build-up of fumes.

Never work in a building containing a gas appliance with a pilot light, or any other form of naked flame. Ensure that there are no naked light bulbs or any sources of flame or sparks nearby.

Do not smoke (or allow anyone else to smoke) while in the vicinity of petrol (gasoline) or of components containing it. Remember the possible presence of vapour from these sources and move well clear before smoking.

Check all electrical equipment belonging to the house, garage or workshop where work is being undertaken (see the *Safety first!* section of this manual). Remember that certain electrical appliances such as drills, cutters etc, create sparks in the normal course of operation and must not be used near petrol (gasoline) or any component containing it. Again, remember the possible presence of fumes before using electrical equipment.

Always mop up any spilt fuel and safely dispose of the rag used.

Any stored fuel that is drained off during servicing work must be kept in sealed containers that are suitable for holding petrol (gasoline), and clearly marked as such; the containers themselves should be kept in a safe place. Note that this last point applies equally to the fuel tank if it is removed from the machine; also remember to keep its filler cap closed at all times.

Read the *Safety first!* section of this manual carefully before starting work.

Owners of machines used in the US, particularly California, should note that their machines must comply at all times with Federal or State legislation governing the permissible levels of noise and of pollutants such as unburnt hydrocarbons, carbon monoxide etc. that can be emitted by those machines. All vehicles offered for sale must comply with legislation in force at the date of manufacture and must not subsequently be altered in any way which will affect their emission of noise or of pollutants.

In practice, this means that adjustments may not be made to any part of the fuel, ignition or exhaust systems by anyone who is not authorised or mechanically qualified to do so, or who does not have the tools, equipment and data necessary to properly carry out the task. Also if any part of these systems is to be renewed it must be renewed with only genuine Honda components or by components which are approved under the relevant legislation. The machine must never be used with any part of these systems removed, modified or damaged.

2   Fuel tank

 Warning: Refer to the precautions given in Section 1 before starting work.

Note: *If the fuel tank is removed from the bike, it should not be placed in an area where sparks or open flames could ignite the fumes coming out of the tank. Be especially careful inside garages where a natural gas-type appliance is located, because the pilot light could cause an explosion.*

Removal

1 Remove the fairing and the seat (see Chapter 8).
2 Ensure the ignition is switched OFF.
3 Make sure the fuel cap is secure.
4 Loosen the bolt securing the rear of the tank and pull the rear of the tank back and up **(see illustrations)**.

2.4a Pull the tank back . . .

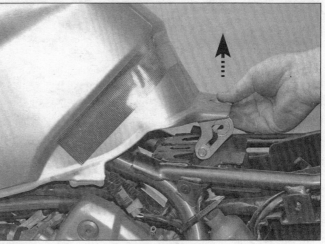

2.4b . . . and then up

2.5a Lift the front of the tank . . .

2.5b . . . as far as the restraining wire permits. Note mounting bush (arrowed)

2.5c Disconnect breather hose from the union (arrowed)

2.5d Position a wooden hammer handle across the frame . . .

2.5e . . . to support the tank

5 Note the location of the restraining wire, then lift the front of the tank as far as the wire permits and disconnect the breather hose from the union on the underside of the tank

(see illustrations). Position a suitable support (a wooden hammer handle is ideal) between the frame and the rests on the bottom edge of the tank (see illustrations).

6 Disconnect the fuel pump wiring connector (see illustration).

7 To relieve any pressure in the fuel hose, start the engine and allow it to idle until it stalls through lack of fuel. Turn the ignition OFF.

8 Note the location of the rubber security cap on the end of the hose connector (see illustration). Pull the cap out from the connector and hook it over the fuel tank union (see illustration).

9 Squeeze the tabs on the locking sleeve together to release the hose connector from the tank union (see illustrations). Note how the locking sleeve locates in the end of the connector (see illustration). **Note:** *Honda recommend that a new locking sleeve is fitted whenever the fuel hose is disconnected.*

10 Undo the bolt securing the restraining wire to the tank (see illustration 2.5b).

2.6 Disconnect the pump wiring connector

2.8a Location of the rubber security cap

2.8b Displace the security cap

2.9a Squeeze the tabs together . . .

2.9b . . . and disconnect the fuel hose

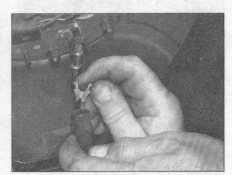

2.9c Note location of the locking sleeve

2.11 Withdraw the mounting bolt

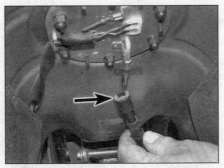

2.14 Installed position of locking sleeve

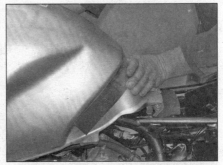

2.17 Press the rear of the tank down

11 Remove the nut and bolt securing the rear of the tank, noting the location of the washers **(see illustration)**. Lift the tank off.
12 Inspect the tank mounting bushes for signs of damage or deterioration and replace them with new ones if necessary **(see illustration 2.5b)**.

Installation

13 Support the tank on the frame and install the mounting bolt finger-tight **(see illustrations 2.10 and 2.11)**. Note that the bolt should be in the lowest position in the mounting slot **(see illustration 2.4b)**.
14 Fit a new locking sleeve in the hose connector **(see illustration 2.9c)**. Push the connector all the way onto the tank union until it clicks into place **(see illustration)**. Lock the connector in position with the security cap **(see illustration 2.8a)**. Make sure the fuel

hose is secure by pulling and pushing the connector on the union.
15 Reconnect the pump wiring connector and the breather hose **(see illustrations 2.6 and 5c)**.
16 Install the restraining wire and tighten the bolt securely **(see illustration 2.5b)**.
17 Remove the support, push the tank forwards onto the mounting bushes, then press the rear of the tank down **(see illustration)**. Note that the mounting bolt should now be in the highest position in the mounting slot **(see illustration 2.4a)**.
18 Tighten the mounting bolt to the torque setting specified at the beginning of this Chapter.
19 Turn the ignition ON and check for fuel leaks. Turn the ignition OFF.
20 Install the remaining components in the reverse order of removal.

Repair

21 All repairs to the fuel tank should be carried out by a professional who has experience in this critical and potentially dangerous work. Even after cleaning and flushing of the fuel system, explosive fumes can remain and ignite during repair of the tank.

3 Fuel pressure and delivery check

> **⚠ Warning: Refer to the precautions given in Section 1 before starting work.**

Special Tools: *A fuel pressure gauge, hose and adapter are required for the pressure check (see Step 2; in view of the cost of these items or suitable alternatives it is advisable to have this task carried out by a Honda dealer. A suitable calibrated container and length of fuel hose are required for the fuel delivery check (see Step 7).*

1 The fuel pump is located inside the fuel tank. When the ignition is switched ON, it should be possible to hear the pump run for 2 seconds until the system is up to pressure. If you can't hear anything, check the pump electrical circuit and associated components (see Section 4). If the pump appears to be good, check the fuel pressure and delivery as follows.

Fuel pressure check

2 To check the fuel pressure, a suitable gauge, gauge adapter, hoses and hose union are needed. Honda provides service tools (Part Nos. 07406-0040004, 07ZAJ-S5A0111, 07ZAJ-S5A0130, 07ZAJ-S5A0120 and 07ZAJ-S5A0150) for this purpose.
3 Follow the procedure in Section 2 to lift the front of the fuel tank and disconnect the fuel hose from the tank union. Use the service tools to connect the gauge between the fuel tank union and the fuel supply hose to the injectors **(see illustration)**.
4 Reconnect the pump wiring connector, then turn the ignition ON and start the engine. Note the fuel pressure at idle and compare the result with the specification at the beginning of this

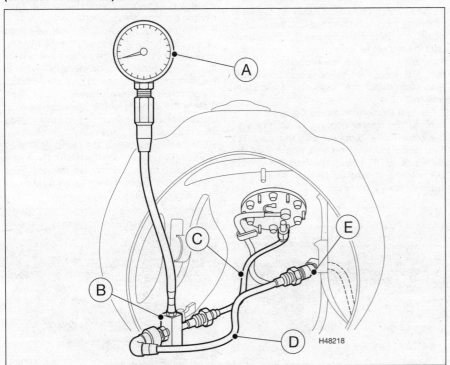

3.3 Set-up for checking the fuel pressure. Gauge (A), adapter (B), hose 0130 (C), hose 0120 (D) and hose union (E)

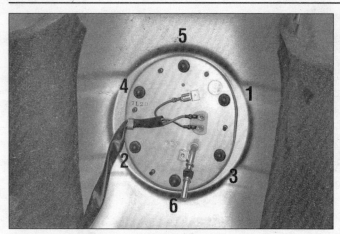

4.8a Pump base plate nuts TIGHTENING sequence

4.8b Lift the pump out carefully

Chapter. Turn the ignition OFF, disconnect the fuel pump wiring connector, then follow the procedure in Section 2 relieve any pressure in the fuel hoses and service equipment before removing the equipment.

5 If the pressure is too high, either the pump or pressure regulator is faulty. Individual components are not available – a new pump assembly will have to be fitted (see Section 4).

6 If the pressure is too low, first check for a leak between the fuel hoses and the injectors. If there is no leakage, ensure the tank breather hose and union are clear. Check the fuel delivery (see Steps 7 to 9). Finally check the pump and fuel strainer (see Section 4).

Fuel delivery check

7 Follow the procedure in Section 2 to lift the front of the fuel tank and disconnect the fuel hose from the tank union. Connect a length of suitable hose to the tank union and place the open end of the hose in a calibrated container capable for holding approximately 2 litres of fuel. **Note:** *The fuel pressure check hose Part No. 07ZAJ-S5A0130 is ideal for this purpose.*

8 Turn the ignition ON – the pump should operate for 2 seconds. Repeat the procedure five times (total delivery time 10 seconds).

9 Measure the amount of fuel that has flowed into the container and compare it to the amount specified at the beginning of this

Chapter. If the flow rate is below the minimum, first check the battery condition (see Chapter 9). If the battery is good, either the fuel strainer is blocked or the pump is defective and must be replaced with a new one (see Section 4).

4 Fuel pump and relay

> ⚠️ *Warning: Refer to the precautions given in Section 1 before starting work.*

Fuel pump

Voltage check

1 The fuel pump is located inside the fuel tank. When the ignition is switched ON, it should be possible to hear the pump run for 2 seconds until the system is up to pressure. If you can't hear anything, follow the procedure in Section 2 to access the pump wiring connector, then disconnect the connector **(see illustration 2.6)**.

2 Using a multimeter set to the volts scale, connect the meter positive (+ve) probe to the brown wire terminal and the negative (-ve) probe to the green wire terminal on the loom side of the connector. Turn the ignition ON – there should be battery voltage for approximately 2 seconds.

3 If there is battery voltage it is likely the pump is faulty – have it checked by a Honda dealer.

4 If there is no voltage, first check the pump fuse (see Chapter 9), then inspect the wiring for damage (see *Wiring Diagrams* at the end of Chapter 9).

5 If the fuse and wiring are good, check the fuel pump relay (see Steps 21 to 29), the tip-over (TO) sensor and engine stop relay (see Section 12).

6 If all the components are good it is likely the ECM is faulty – have it checked by a Honda dealer.

Removal

7 The fuel pump is located inside the fuel tank. If required, drain any fuel from the tank using a commercially available pump, then remove the tank (see Section 2).

8 Turn the tank upside down and rest it on some clean rag to protect the paintwork. Note which way round the pump base plate is fitted, then undo the mounting nuts evenly in the reverse of the tightening sequence and lift the pump out **(see illustrations)**.

9 Note the location of the pump cover, then unclip it from the pump and remove it **(see illustrations)**.

10 Note the location of the pump seal, then release the pegs on the seal from the pump base plate and remove the seal **(see illustrations)**. Discard the seal as a new one must be fitted.

4.9a Release the tabs (arrowed) . . .

4.9b . . . and remove the pump cover

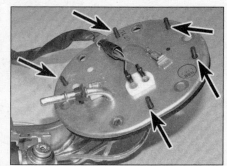

4.10a Release the pegs (arrowed) . . .

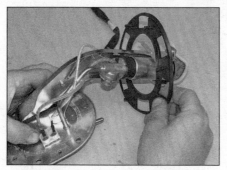

4.10b ... and remove the seal

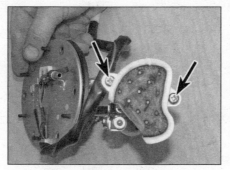

4.11a Undo the screws ...

4.11b ... and remove the retaining plate and collar

11 Note the location of the fuel strainer – if required, undo the screws securing the strainer retaining plate and collar and lift them off **(see illustrations)**.

12 Note how the strainer is secured on the end of the pump, then twist the strainer clockwise to release it from the pump **(see illustration)**.

13 Allow the strainer to dry, then clean any sediment off the gauze with a soft brush or low pressure compressed air. The strainer is an integral part of the pump – if the gauze is damaged, or if there is sediment inside the strainer, a new pump will have to be fitted.

14 Make sure the wiring terminals on the pump body and base plate are secure.

Installation

15 Fit the strainer onto the end of the pump and twist it anti-clockwise to hold it in place **(see illustration 4.12)**. Install the collar and retaining plate and tighten the screws securely **(see illustrations 4.11b and a)**.

16 Ensure the base plate and tank surfaces are clean and dry, then fit the new seal ensuring the mounting holes align **(see illustration)**. Pull the pegs on the seal through the holes in the base plate **(see illustration 4.10a)**.

17 Install the pump cover and secure it as noted on removal **(see illustrations 4.9b and a)**.

18 Lubricate the pump seal with a smear of engine oil, then install the pump, ensuring it is the correct way round **(see illustration 4.8b)**.

19 Tighten the mounting nuts finger-tight, then tighten them evenly and a little at a time in the sequence shown to the torque setting specified at the beginning of this Chapter **(see illustration 4.8a)**.

20 Install the fuel tank (see Section 2).

Fuel pump relay

21 The fuel pump relay is located on the right-hand side of the fairing bracket **(see illustration)**. Remove the fairing for access (see Chapter 8).

22 Turn the ignition ON – the relay should be heard to click.

23 If the relay clicks but the pump does not operate, check the relay continuity as follows.

24 Ensure the ignition is OFF, then unclip the relay from its bracket and disconnect the wiring connector **(see illustrations 12.14a and b)**.

25 Using a multimeter, check for continuity between terminals A and B on the relay **(see illustration)**. There should be no continuity. Now use jumper wires to connect the positive (+ve) terminal of a fully charged 12 volt battery to relay terminal D and the negative (-ve) battery terminal to relay terminal C. There should now be continuity between terminals A and B. If the relay fails either of the checks it is faulty and must be replaced with a new one.

26 If the relay is good, use an insulated jumper wire to connect the white/black and brown wire terminals on the loom side of the relay connector. Disconnect the fuel pump wiring connector (see Section 2), then connect the meter positive (+ve) probe to the brown wire terminal on the loom side of the pump connector and the negative (-ve) probe to earth (ground). Turn the ignition ON and check for battery voltage. Turn the ignition OFF.

27 If there is no battery voltage, check for

continuity in the white/black wire between the pump relay and the engine stop relay, and in the brown wire between the pump relay and the pump. No continuity indicates a fault in the wire.

28 If there is battery voltage, follow the procedure in Section 9, Step 6, to access the ECM multi-pin wiring connectors. Disconnect the black ECM connector, then connect the meter positive (+ve) probe to the brown/black wire terminal on the loom side of the connector and the negative (-ve) probe to earth (ground). Turn the ignition ON and check for battery voltage. Turn the ignition OFF.

29 If there is no battery voltage, check for continuity in the white/black wire between the pump relay and the engine stop relay, and in the brown/black wire between the pump relay and the ECM (see *Wiring Diagrams* at the end of Chapter 9). No continuity indicates a fault in the wire.

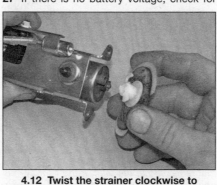

4.12 Twist the strainer clockwise to release it

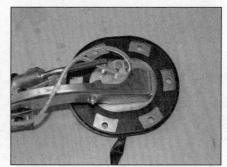

4.16 Align the seal with the base plate

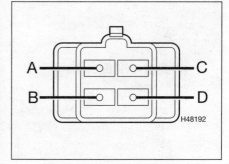

4.21 Location of engine stop relay (A) and fuel pump relay (B)

```
A —          — C

B —          — D
                    H48192
```

4.25 Fuel pump relay terminals

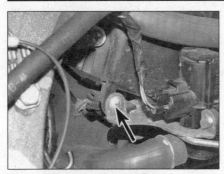

5.5a Screw secures secondary air system control valve bracket

5.5b Disconnect the air supply hose

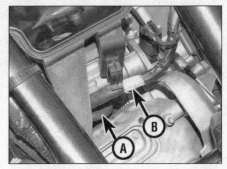

5.6 Release the fuel hose (A) and throttle body sub loom (B)

5 Air filter housing

1 Remove the fuel tank (see Section 2).
2 Follow the procedure in Chapter 1 to remove the air filter cover and element.
3 Disconnect the MAP sensor wiring connector and vacuum hose (see illustration 9.5).
4 Disconnect the IAT sensor wiring connector (see illustration 9.31).
5 Undo the screw securing the secondary air system control valve bracket to the filter housing (see illustration). Release the clip securing the control valve air supply hose to the housing and disconnect the hose (see illustration).
6 Release the fuel hose and throttle body sub loom from the clips on the rear of the housing (see illustration).
7 Undo the screws securing the intake ducts and lift the ducts out (see illustrations).
8 Ease the housing off the throttle bodies, release the clip securing the engine breather hose to the front of the housing and disconnect the hose (see illustration).
9 Lift the housing off, noting the location of the O-rings on the underside (see illustrations). Inspect the O-rings for signs of damage or deterioration and replace them with new ones if necessary.
10 Installation is the reverse of removal. Make sure the air filter housing is correctly fitted onto the throttle bodies and tighten the

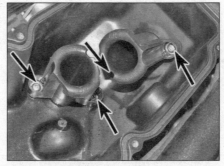

5.7a Undo the screws . . .

intake duct screws securely. Ensure all hoses and wiring connectors are secure.

6 Low fuel level sender

Check

1 The low fuel level warning light in the instrument cluster should come on briefly when the ignition is switched ON, then go out – this serves as a check that the sender circuit is working correctly. If the warning light comes on and stays on, or does not come on, carry out the checks as follows. Note: In use, the low fuel level warning light will come on when there are approximately 3.0 litres of fuel remaining in the tank. If the light comes on when the tank is full it is likely the sender is faulty.

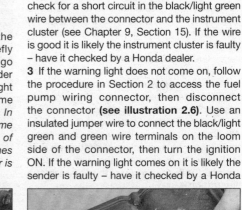

5.7b . . . and remove the intake ducts

2 If the warning light comes on and stays on, follow the procedure in Section 2 to access the fuel pump wiring connector, then disconnect the connector (see illustration 2.6). Turn the ignition ON – if the warning light stays off it is likely the sender is faulty – have it checked by a Honda dealer. If the warning light comes on, check for a short circuit in the black/light green wire between the connector and the instrument cluster (see Chapter 9, Section 15). If the wire is good it is likely the instrument cluster is faulty – have it checked by a Honda dealer.
3 If the warning light does not come on, follow the procedure in Section 2 to access the fuel pump wiring connector, then disconnect the connector (see illustration 2.6). Use an insulated jumper wire to connect the black/light green and green wire terminals on the loom side of the connector, then turn the ignition ON. If the warning light comes on it is likely the sender is faulty – have it checked by a Honda

5.8 Disconnect the engine breather hose

5.9a Lift the housing off . . .

5.9b . . . and remove the O-rings

7.7a Location of ECM. Note mounting bolt (arrowed)

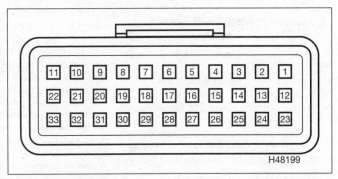

7.7b ECM wiring connector (loom side) terminal numbering.
Black connector terminal numbers are prefixed A, grey connector
terminal numbers are prefixed B

dealer. If the warning light stays off, check for continuity in the black/light green wire between the connector and the instrument cluster (see Chapter 9, Section 15). No continuity indicates a fault in the wire. If there is continuity it is likely the instrument cluster is faulty – have it checked by a Honda dealer.

Removal and installation

4 The low fuel level warning sender is an integral part of the fuel pump assembly. If the sender is faulty a new fuel pump will have to be fitted, individual components are not available.
5 Refer to Section 4 for removal and installation of the fuel pump.

7 Engine management system operation

1 The engine management system consists of the fuel system and the ignition circuit, controlled and co-ordinated by the engine control module (ECM). An overview of the engine management system can be found in Section 1.
2 To ensure optimum engine efficiency, the ECM monitors signals from the following components:
● Manifold absolute pressure (MAP) sensor
● Engine coolant temperature (ECT) sensor
● Throttle position (TP) sensor
● Intake air temperature (IAT) sensor
● Vehicle speed (VS) sensor
● Oxygen sensors
● Idle air control valve (IACV)
● Crankshaft position (CKP) sensor
● Tip-over (TO) sensor
3 The FI warning light in the instrument cluster should come on briefly when the ignition is switched ON, then go out – this serves as a check that the engine management system circuit is working correctly. If the warning light does not come on, or comes on and stays on, carry out the checks in Steps 7 to 11 below.
4 In the event of an abnormality in any of the components or sensor signals, the FI warning light comes on and the ECM determines whether the engine can still be run safely. If it can, a back-up mode substitutes the sensor signal with a fixed signal, restricting

performance but allowing the bike to be ridden home or to a dealer. If the fault is serious, the fuel and ignition systems will be shut down and the engine will not run.
5 Once a fault has been indicated by the FI warning light, the fault code should be accessed from the system and appropriate checks undertaken (see Section 9).
6 The system incorporates two safety circuits. The sidestand switch, clutch switch and neutral switch circuit which prevent or stop the engine running if the transmission is in gear whilst the side stand is down, and prevents the engine from starting if the transmission is in gear unless the side stand is up and the clutch lever is pulled in (see Chapter 9 for component test details). The second is the tip-over sensor circuit, which automatically switches off the fuel pump and cuts power to the ignition and injection circuits if the motorcycle falls over (see Section 12).

FI warning light check

7 If the light does not come on, ensure the ignition is switched OFF, then remove the seat (see Chapter 8). Locate the ECM at the rear of the underseat area (see illustration). Undo the bolt securing the ECM, draw it out and disconnect the black multi-pin connector. Using an insulated jumper wire, connect the white/blue wire terminal A20 (see illustration) on the loom side of the connector to earth (ground). Turn the ignition ON.
8 If the FI warning light comes on it is likely the ECM is faulty – have it checked by a

Honda dealer. If the light does not come on, check for continuity between the white/blue wire terminal and the instrument cluster. If there is continuity it is likely the instrument cluster is faulty – have it checked by a Honda dealer.
9 If, when the ignition is switched ON, the FI warning light comes on and stays on, ensure the ignition is switched OFF, then follow the procedure in Step 7 to disconnect the ECM black multi-pin connector. Turn the ignition ON – the warning light should turn off.
10 If the warning light comes on, check for a short circuit in the white/blue wire between terminal A20 (see illustration 7.7b) and the instrument cluster. If the wire is good it is likely the instrument cluster is faulty – have it checked by a Honda dealer.
11 If the warning light turns off, ensure the ignition is switched OFF, then disconnect the ECM grey multi-pin connector. Check for continuity between the brown wire terminal B19 on the loom side of the connector (see illustration 7.7b) and earth (ground). If there is continuity, check for a short circuit in the brown wire between terminal B19 and the data link connector (DLC). The DLC is located inside the boot for the rear light assembly wiring connectors on the right-hand side under the rear light assembly cover – remove the rear light assembly for access (see Chapter 9). Unclip the DLC cap to access the brown wire terminal (see illustrations). If there is no continuity, it is likely the ECM is faulty – have it checked by a Honda dealer.

7.11a Pull the DLC out from the wiring boot . . .

7.11b . . . and unclip the cap

8 Engine management system fault diagnosis

1 There are two ways to access the system fault codes:
● Using the Honda Diagnostic System (HDS) pocket tester – fault codes are displayed as a hyphenated number. The digits in front of the hyphen indicate the faulty component, those behind the hyphen indicate a specific failure symptom.
● Using Honda's inexpensive Service Check Short (SCS) connector or an insulated auxiliary wire (see Step 4) – fault codes are displayed by the FI warning light as a series of flashes.
2 Both units connect to the data link connector (DLC) at the rear of the bike (see illustrations 7.11a and b).
3 For the purpose of this manual the SCS connector has been used to access the fault codes (see illustration 8.4).
4 The DLC is located inside the boot for the rear light assembly wiring connectors on the right-hand side under the rear light assembly cover – remove the rear light assembly for access (see Chapter 9). Unclip the DLC cap to access the brown wire terminal (see illustrations 7.11a and b). Ensure the ignition is switched OFF, then unclip the DLC cap and install the SCS connector (see illustration) or link the auxiliary wire across the brown and green wires inside the DLC.
5 Turn the ignition ON and the FI light should start to flash, denoting the fault code(s) as follows.
6 The FI light emits short (0.5 second) and long (1.3 second) flashes – the short flashes represent the units and the long flashes represent the tens. For example, fault code 7 is represented as seven short flashes; fault code 21 is represented as two long flashes and one short flash.
7 If there is more than one fault code, the codes are displayed in numerical order, lowest to highest.
8 Note the fault codes and keep the SCS connector connected until you have finished reading the fault code(s). Turn the ignition OFF and disconnect the SCS connector.

8.4 SCS connector installed on the DLC

9 Compare the codes with the fault code table to identify the faulty component, then refer to Section 9 for checking procedures.
10 To delete the fault code from the system memory once the fault has been corrected, install the SCS connector (see Step 4) and turn the ignition ON. Disconnect the SCS link wire, then as soon as the FI light comes on, reconnect the link wire. The FI light should go off and then start flashing to denote the code has been erased. Turn the ignition OFF.

Code	Faulty component – ECM response	Possible causes
1	Manifold absolute pressure (MAP) sensor – engine will run in fail-safe mode	Faulty wiring or wiring connector Faulty, damaged or improperly installed sensor
2	Manifold absolute pressure (MAP) sensor – engine will run	Faulty vacuum hose or hose connection Faulty, damaged or improperly installed sensor
7	Engine coolant temperature (ECT) sensor – engine hard to start when cold, temperature signal fixed at 90°C, cooling fan comes on	Faulty wiring or wiring connector Faulty, damaged or improperly installed sensor
8	Throttle position (TP) sensor – engine will run in fail-safe mode, poor acceleration	Faulty wiring or wiring connector Faulty, damaged or improperly installed sensor Faulty ECM
9	Intake air temperature (IAT) sensor – engine will run, temperature signal fixed at 30°C	Faulty wiring or wiring connector Faulty, damaged or improperly installed sensor
11	Vehicle speed (VS) sensor – engine will run	Faulty wiring or wiring connector Faulty damaged or improperly installed speed sensor Faulty ECM
12	Rear cylinder fuel injector – engine will not run, fuel and ignition systems turned OFF	Faulty wiring or wiring connector Faulty or damaged fuel injector Faulty ECM
13	Front cylinder fuel injector – engine will not run, fuel and ignition systems turned OFF	Faulty wiring or wiring connector Faulty or damaged fuel injector Faulty ECM
21	Rear cylinder oxygen sensor – engine will run	Faulty wiring or wiring connector Faulty, damaged or improperly installed sensor Faulty ECM
22	Front cylinder oxygen sensor – engine will run	Faulty wiring or wiring connector Faulty, damaged or improperly installed sensor Faulty ECM
23	Rear cylinder oxygen sensor heater – engine will run	Faulty wiring or wiring connector Faulty, damaged or improperly installed sensor Faulty ECM
24	Front cylinder oxygen sensor heater – engine will run	Faulty wiring or wiring connector Faulty, damaged or improperly installed sensor Faulty ECM
29	Idle air control valve (IACV) – engine will run	Faulty wiring or wiring connector Faulty, damaged or improperly installed valve
33	ECM fault code memory malfunction – engine will run	Faulty ECM – will not retain self diagnosis information

9.3 Back-probing an ECM connector terminal with a needle probe

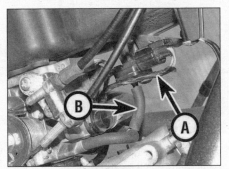

9.5 Location of the MAP sensor (A). Note vacuum hose (B)

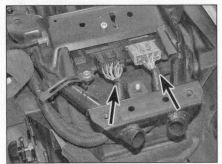

9.6a Access to ECM connectors with rear light assembly cover removed

9 Engine management system components

Caution: Ensure the ignition is switched OFF before disconnecting/reconnecting any engine management system wiring connectors. If a connector is disconnected/ reconnected with the ignition switched ON the engine control module (ECM) could be damaged.

1 If a fault is indicated on any of the system components, first check the wiring and connectors between the appropriate component and the engine control module (ECM) – see *Wiring Diagram* at the end of Chapter 9. A continuity test (see Chapter 9, Section 2) of all wires will locate a break or short in any circuit. Inspect the terminals inside the wiring connectors and ensure that they are not loose or corroded. Spray the inside of the connectors with a proprietary electrical terminal cleaner before reconnection. Where appropriate, remove the sensor and check the sensor head and clean it if it is dirty – an accumulation of dirt could affect the signal it transmits. Recheck the FI warning light to see if the fault has been cleared before proceeding.

2 It is possible to undertake some checks on system components using a multimeter (see Chapter 9, Section 2) and comparing the results with the specifications at the beginning of this Chapter. **Note:** *Different meters may give slightly different results to those specified*

even though the component being tested is not faulty – do not consign a component to the bin before having it double-checked. If the appropriate equipment is not available, the checks should be undertaken by a Honda dealer.

3 Honda provides a test harness and pin box (Part No. 070MZ-MCA0100) for checking circuits to-and-from the ECM. If this is not available, you will need needle probes for your multimeter to enable you to back-probe the ECM connector terminals with the connectors connected **(see illustration)**. For the purpose of this manual checks are described by back-probing the connector terminals – if the service equipment is available, connect the meter probes to the designated terminals on the pin box.

4 If, after a thorough check, the source of a fault has not been identified, it is possible that the ECM itself is faulty. No test specifications are available for the ECM. In order to determine conclusively that the unit is defective, it should be substituted for a known good one (see Steps 81 to 84). If the problem is then rectified, the original unit is confirmed faulty.

Manifold absolute pressure (MAP) sensor

Fault code 1

5 The MAP sensor is located on the underside of the air filter housing **(see illustration)**. Remove the fuel tank for access (see Section 2).

6 To check the sensor output voltage,

either displace the ECM (see Section 7, Step 7) or remove the rear light assembly cover (see Chapter 9) to access the rear of the ECM multi-pin wiring connectors **(see illustrations)**.

7 Back-probe the light green/yellow wire terminal B9 on the grey connector with the meter positive (+ve) probe and the green/ orange wire terminal A18 on the black connector with the meter negative (-ve) probe. Turn the ignition ON and check the output voltage. Turn the ignition OFF. A result within the range 1.9 to 2.5 volts indicates loose or poor ECM connector contacts.

8 If the result is above 5 volts, disconnect the MAP sensor wiring connector **(see illustration)**. Connect the meter positive (+ve) probe to the light green/yellow wire terminal and the negative (-ve) probe to the green/ orange wire terminal on the loom side of the connector. Turn the ignition ON and check the voltage, then turn the ignition OFF. A result within the range 4.75 to 5.25 volts indicates a faulty MAP sensor. If there is no voltage, inspect the wiring for damage.

9 If no voltage is recorded in the output voltage check, test the input voltage at the MAP sensor wiring connector. Connect the meter positive (+ve) probe to the yellow/red wire terminal on the loom side of the connector and the negative (-ve) probe to earth (ground). Turn the ignition ON and check the voltage, then turn the ignition OFF.

10 If the result is within the range specified at the beginning of this Chapter, check for continuity between the light green/yellow

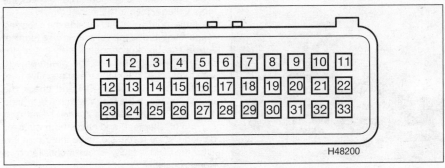

9.6b ECM terminal numbering. Black connector terminal numbers are prefixed A, grey connector terminal numbers are prefixed B

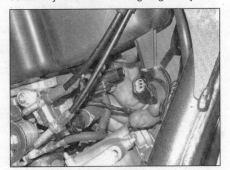

9.8 Disconnect the MAP sensor wiring connector

wire terminal and earth (ground). Continuity indicates a short circuit in the light green/yellow wire. No continuity indicates a faulty MAP sensor.

11 If no voltage is recorded, check for continuity in the yellow/red wire between the MAP sensor connector and terminal A9 on the black ECM connector. If there is continuity it is likely the ECM is faulty – have it checked by a Honda dealer. No continuity indicates a fault in the yellow/red wire.

Fault code 2

12 First inspect the MAP sensor wiring connector contacts and ensure that the connector is secure, then check to see if the fault has been cleared. If not, inspect the vacuum hose and hose connections and renew the hose if necessary **(see illustration 9.5)**.

13 If the fault persists, follow the procedure in Steps 6 and 7 to check the MAP sensor output voltage.

14 If the result is outside the range 2.7 to 3.1 volts the MAP sensor is faulty. If the result is within the specified range, start the engine and check that the voltage remains at the standard output voltage at idle speed (see *Specifications* at the beginning of this Chapter). If the voltage drops it is likely the ECM is faulty – have it checked by a Honda dealer.

Removal and installation

15 To remove the MAP sensor, first remove the air filter housing (see Section 5). Undo the screw securing the sensor and lift it off **(see illustration)**. On installation, ensure the

vacuum hose is a tight fit on the sensor union and that the wiring connector terminals are clean.

Engine coolant temperature (ECT) sensor

16 The ECT sensor is located on the rear of the front cylinder **(see illustration)**.

17 To check the sensor output voltage, either displace the ECM (see Section 7, Step 7) or remove the rear light assembly to access the rear of the ECM multi-pin wiring connectors **(see illustration 9.6a and b)**.

18 Back-probe the pink/white wire terminal B13 on the grey connector with the meter positive (+ve) probe and the green/orange wire terminal A18 on the black connector with the meter negative (-ve) probe. Turn the ignition ON and check the output voltage. Turn the ignition OFF. A result within the range specified at the beginning of this Chapter indicates loose or poor ECM connector contacts.

19 If the result is outside the specified range, disconnect the ECT sensor wiring connector **(see illustration)**. Connect the meter positive (+ve) probe to the pink/white wire terminal and the negative (-ve) probe to the green/orange wire terminal on the loom side of the connector. Turn the ignition ON and check the input voltage, then turn the ignition OFF.

20 If the input voltage is within the specified range, check the resistance between the pink/white and green/orange wire terminals on the sensor. A result within the range specified at the beginning of this Chapter indicates a faulty ECM – have it checked by a Honda dealer. If the result is outside the specified range the

ECT sensor is faulty. **Note:** *If the sensor is working correctly, the resistance should drop as the engine warms up. A check for sensor performance is described in Section 13.*

21 If the input voltage is outside the specified range, check for continuity in the pink/white wire between the ECT sensor connector and terminal B13 on the grey ECM connector, and in the green/orange wire between the ECT sensor connector and terminal A18 on the black ECM connector. No continuity indicates a fault in the wire.

22 If there is continuity, disconnect both ECM wiring connectors, then check for continuity between the pink/white wire terminal B13 on the loom side of the ECT sensor connector and earth (ground). If there is continuity, check for a short circuit in the pink/white wire. If there is no continuity it is likely the ECM is faulty – have it checked by a Honda dealer.

Removal and installation

23 Follow the procedure in Section 13.

Throttle position (TP) sensor

24 The TP sensor is located on the front left-hand side of the throttle body assembly **(see illustration)**. Remove the air filter housing for access (see Section 5).

25 To check the sensor output voltage, either displace the ECM (see Section 7, Step 7) or remove the rear light assembly to access the rear of the ECM multi-pin wiring connectors **(see illustration 9.6a and b)**.

26 Back-probe the red/yellow wire terminal B31 on the grey connector with the meter positive (+ve) probe and the green/orange wire terminal A18 on the black connector with the meter negative (-ve) probe. Turn the ignition ON and check the output voltage with the throttle fully closed and with the throttle fully open. Turn the ignition OFF. A result within the ranges specified at the beginning of this Chapter indicates loose or poor ECM connector contacts. **Note:** *A minor variance in the figures is acceptable for this test.*

27 If the result is not as specified, disconnect the TP sensor wiring connector **(see illustration 9.24)**. Connect the meter positive (+ve) probe to the yellow/red wire terminal and the negative (-ve) probe to the green/orange wire terminal on the loom side of the connector. Turn the ignition ON and check the input voltage, then turn the ignition OFF.

28 If the input voltage is outside the specified range, back-probe the yellow/red wire terminal A9 on the black connector with the meter positive (+ve) probe and the green/orange wire terminal A18 with the meter negative (-ve) probe. Turn the ignition ON and check the output voltage. If the result is within the range 4.75 to 5.25 volts, refer to *Wiring Diagrams* at the end of Chapter 9 and check both wires for damage. If the result is outside that range it is likely the ECM is faulty – have it checked by a Honda dealer.

29 If the input voltage is within the specified range, check for continuity in the red/yellow

9.16 Location of the ECT sensor

9.15 Screw (arrowed) secures MAP sensor

9.19 Disconnect the ECT sensor wiring connector

9.24 Location of the TP sensor

wire between the TP sensor connector and terminal B13 on the grey ECM connector. No continuity indicates a fault in the wire.

30 If there is continuity, disconnect both ECM wiring connectors, then check for continuity between the red/yellow wire terminal on the loom side of the TP sensor connector and earth (ground). If there is continuity, check for a short circuit in the red/yellow wire. If there is no continuity it is likely the TP sensor is faulty – have it checked by a Honda dealer. **Note:** *The TP sensor is supplied as an integral part of the throttle body assembly and should not be removed.*

Intake air temperature (IAT) sensor

31 The IAT sensor is located on the front left-hand side of the air filter housing **(see illustration)**. Remove the fuel tank for access (see Section 2).

32 To check the sensor output voltage, either displace the ECM (see Section 7, Step 7) or remove the rear light assembly to access the rear of the ECM multi-pin wiring connectors **(see illustration 9.6a and b)**.

33 Back-probe the grey/blue wire terminal B29 on the grey connector with the meter positive (+ve) probe and the green/orange wire terminal A18 on the black connector with the meter negative (-ve) probe. Turn the ignition ON and check the output voltage. Turn the ignition OFF. A result within the range specified at the beginning of this Chapter indicates loose or poor ECM connector contacts.

34 If the result is not as specified, disconnect the IAT sensor wiring connector **(see illustration)**. Connect the meter positive (+ve)

probe to the grey/blue wire terminal and the negative (-ve) probe to the green/orange wire terminal on the loom side of the connector. Turn the ignition ON and check the input voltage, then turn the ignition OFF.

35 If the input voltage is within the specified range, check the resistance between the sensor terminals. A result within the range specified at the beginning of this Chapter indicates a faulty ECM – have it checked by a Honda dealer. If the result is outside the specified range the IAT sensor is faulty.

36 If the input voltage is outside the specified range, check for continuity in the grey/blue wire between the IAT sensor connector and terminal B29 on the grey ECM connector, and in the green/orange wire between the IAT sensor connector and terminal A18 on the black ECM connector. No continuity indicates a fault in the wire.

37 If there is continuity, disconnect both ECM wiring connectors, then check for continuity between the grey/blue wire terminal on the loom side of the IAT sensor connector and earth (ground). If there is continuity, check for a short circuit in the grey/blue wire. If there is no continuity it is likely the ECM is faulty – have it checked by a Honda dealer.

Removal and installation

38 To remove the IAT sensor, first remove the air filter element and note the location of the sensor probe **(see illustration)**. Undo the screws securing the sensor and remove it from the air filter housing. On installation, check that the wiring connector terminals are clean.

Vehicle speed (VS) sensor

39 The VS sensor is located on the rear left-hand side of the crankcase **(see illustration)**. The sensor wiring connector is located inside the wiring boot forward of the battery **(see illustration)**. Remove the left-hand side panel for access (see Chapter 8).

40 If the speedometer isn't working, follow the procedure for checking the speedometer and VS sensor in Chapter 9.

41 If the speedometer is working, either displace the ECM (see Section 7, Step 7) or remove the rear light assembly to access the rear of the ECM multi-pin wiring connectors **(see illustration 9.6a and b)**.

42 Using an auxiliary stand, support the bike with the rear wheel off the ground.

43 Back-probe the pink/green wire terminal B28 on the grey connector with the meter positive (+ve) probe and connect the negative (-ve) probe to earth (ground). Turn the ignition ON, rotate the rear wheel slowly by hand and check the output voltage. Turn the ignition OFF.

44 If the result is as specified at the beginning of this Chapter, delete the fault code from the system memory (see Section 8), then test ride the machine for ten to fifteen minutes or until it reaches normal operating temperature. Follow the procedure in Section 8 to check the system for the fault code. If no code is present check for loose or poor ECM connector contacts. If the code has reoccurred it is likely the ECM is faulty – have it checked by a Honda dealer.

45 If the result is not as specified, disconnect the sensor wiring connector **(see illustration)**. Check for continuity between the pink/green

9.31 Location of the IAT sensor

9.34 Disconnect the IAT sensor wiring connector

9.38 Location of the IAT sensor probe inside air filter housing

9.39a Location of the VS sensor

9.39b Sensor connector is inside wiring boot

9.45 Disconnect the VS sensor wiring connector

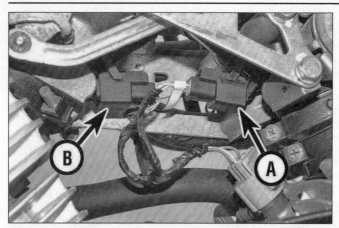

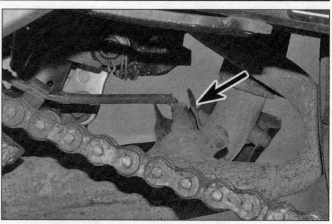

9.47 Fuel injector wiring connectors – front (A) and rear (B)

9.53a Location of the rear cylinder oxygen sensor

wire terminal on the loom side of the connector and terminal B28 on the grey ECM connector. No continuity indicates a fault in the wire.

46 If there is continuity, disconnect both ECM wiring connectors. Disconnect the instrument cluster wiring connector (see Chapter 9). Check for continuity between the pink/green wire terminal on the loom side of the sensor connector and earth (ground). If there is continuity, check for a short circuit in the pink/green wire. If there is no continuity the VS sensor is faulty – refer to Chapter 9 for the removal and installation procedure.

Rear cylinder fuel injector

47 The individual fuel injector wiring connectors are located on the underside of the throttle body assembly (see illustration).

48 To check the injector input voltage, first disconnect the wiring connector. Connect the meter (+ve) probe to the white/black wire terminal on the loom side of the connector and the negative (-ve) probe to earth (ground). Turn the ignition ON and check for battery voltage. Turn the ignition OFF. No voltage indicates a fault in the white/black wire.

49 If the input voltage is good, check the resistance between the injector terminals. If the result is not as specified at the beginning of this Chapter the injector is faulty. Follow the procedure in Section 17 for removal and installation. If the result is within the specified range, either displace the ECM (see Section 7, Step 7) or remove the rear light assembly to

access the rear of the ECM multi-pin wiring connectors (see illustration 9.6a and b).

50 To check the injector signal wire, back-probe the pink/yellow wire terminal A17 on the black connector and check for continuity in the wire between the ECM and the pink/yellow wire terminal on the loom side of the injector connector. No continuity indicates a fault in the wire.

51 If there is continuity, disconnect both ECM wiring connectors, then check for continuity between the pink/yellow wire terminal on the loom side of the injector connector and earth (ground). If there is continuity, check for a short circuit in the pink/yellow wire. If there is no continuity it is likely the ECM is faulty – have it checked by a Honda dealer.

Front cylinder fuel injector

52 Follow the procedure in Steps 47 to 51. Note that to test the injector signal wire, back-probe the pink/blue wire terminal A6 on the ECM black connector and check for continuity in the wire between the ECM and the pink/blue wire terminal on the loom side of the injector connector.

Rear cylinder oxygen sensor

53 The rear cylinder oxygen sensor is located in the exhaust system below the rear of the engine unit (see illustration). The oxygen sensor wiring connector is located above the rear cylinder valve cover (see illustration) – remove the seat for access (see Chapter 8).

54 Either displace the ECM (see Section 7, Step 7) or remove the rear light assembly to access the rear of the ECM multi-pin wiring connectors (see illustration 9.6a and b). Disconnect the sensor wiring connector.

55 Back-probe the green/orange wire terminal A18 on the black connector and check for continuity in the wire between the ECM and the green/orange wire terminal on the loom side of the sensor connector. No continuity indicates a fault in the wire.

56 Back-probe the white/orange wire terminal B20 on the grey connector and check for continuity in the wire between the ECM and the white/orange wire terminal on the loom side of the sensor connector. No continuity indicates a fault in the wire.

57 If there is continuity in both tests, disconnect both ECM wiring connectors, then check for continuity between the white/orange wire terminal on the loom side of the sensor connector and earth (ground). If there is continuity, check for a short circuit in the white/orange wire. If there is no continuity it is likely that either the oxygen sensor or the ECM is faulty – have them checked by a Honda dealer. **Note:** *For removal and installation follow the procedure in Section 19.*

Front cylinder oxygen sensor

58 The front cylinder oxygen sensor is located in the exhaust system below the front of the engine unit (see illustration). The oxygen

9.53b Location of the rear oxygen sensor wiring connector

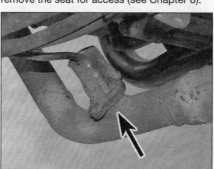

9.58a Location of the front cylinder oxygen sensor

9.58b Location of the front oxygen sensor wiring connector

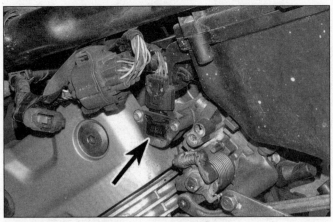

9.73 Location of the IACV

9.74 Disconnect the IACV wiring connector

sensor wiring connector is located on the front left-hand side of the frame **(see illustration)** – remove the fairing for access (see Chapter 8).

59 Either displace the ECM (see Section 7, Step 7) or remove the rear light assembly to access the rear of the ECM multi-pin wiring connectors **(see illustration 9.6a and b)**. Disconnect the sensor wiring connector.

60 Back-probe the green/orange wire terminal A18 on the black connector and check for continuity in the wire between the ECM and the green/orange wire terminal on the loom side of the sensor connector. No continuity indicates a fault in the wire.

61 Back-probe the pink/black wire terminal B30 on the grey connector and check for continuity in the wire between the ECM and the pink/black wire terminal on the loom side of the sensor connector. No continuity indicates a fault in the wire.

62 If there is continuity in both tests, disconnect both ECM wiring connectors, then check for continuity between the pink/black wire terminal on the loom side of the sensor connector and earth (ground). If there is continuity, check for a short circuit in the pink/black wire. If there is no continuity it is likely that either the oxygen sensor or the ECM is faulty – have them checked by a Honda dealer. **Note:** *For removal and installation follow the procedure in Section 19.*

Rear cylinder oxygen sensor heater

63 Note the location of the rear cylinder oxygen sensor and sensor wiring connector (see Step 53).

64 Disconnect the wiring connector and check the resistance between the two white wire terminals on the sensor side of the connector. If the result is not within the range specified at the beginning of this Chapter the sensor is faulty. Follow the procedure in Section 19 for removal and installation

65 If the result is within the specified range, connect the meter (+ve) probe to the white/black wire terminal on the loom side of the connector and the negative (-ve) probe to earth (ground). Turn the ignition ON and check

for battery voltage. Turn the ignition OFF. No voltage indicates a fault in the white/black wire.

66 If the input voltage is good, either displace the ECM (see Section 7, Step 7) or remove the rear light assembly to access the rear of the ECM multi-pin wiring connectors **(see illustration 9.6a and b)**.

67 Back-probe the black/green wire terminal B2 on the grey connector and check for continuity in the wire between the ECM and the black/green wire terminal on the loom side of the sensor connector. No continuity indicates a fault in the wire.

68 If there is continuity, disconnect both ECM wiring connectors, then check for continuity between the black/green wire terminal on the loom side of the sensor connector and earth (ground). If there is continuity, check for a short circuit in the black/green wire. If there is no continuity it is likely the ECM is faulty – have it checked by a Honda dealer.

Front cylinder oxygen sensor heater

69 Note the location of the front cylinder oxygen sensor and sensor wiring connector (see Step 58).

70 Follow the procedure in Steps 64 and 65 to check the heater resistance and input voltage. If the results are good, either displace the ECM (see Section 7, Step 7) or remove the rear light assembly to access the rear of the ECM multi-pin wiring connectors **(see illustration 9.6a and b)**.

71 Back-probe the light blue/white wire terminal B6 on the grey connector and check for continuity in the wire between the ECM and the light blue/white wire terminal on the loom side of the sensor connector. No continuity indicates a fault in the wire.

72 If there is continuity, disconnect both ECM wiring connectors, then check for continuity between the light blue/white wire terminal on the loom side of the sensor connector and earth (ground). If there is continuity, check for a short circuit in the light blue/white wire. If there is no continuity it is likely the ECM is faulty – have it checked by a Honda dealer.

Idle air control valve (IACV)

73 The IACV is located on the rear right-hand side of the throttle body assembly **(see illustration)**. Remove the fuel tank for access (see Section 2).

74 Disconnect the wiring connector and check for continuity between each of the four wire terminals on the loom side of the connector and earth (ground) **(see illustration)**. If any of the checks indicates continuity, check for a short circuit in the appropriate wire.

75 If the wiring is good, either displace the ECM (see Section 7, Step 7) or remove the rear light assembly to access the rear of the ECM multi-pin wiring connectors **(see illustration 9.6a and b)**.

76 Back-probe the following wire terminals on the ECM's black connector and check for continuity in the wires between the ECM and the corresponding wire terminals on the loom side of the IACV connector – yellow/violet wire terminal A19; violet/white wire terminal A27; violet wire terminal A16; violet /yellow wire terminal A29. No continuity indicates a fault in the wire.

77 If all the wiring is good, check the resistance between the following pairs of wire terminals on the IACV – yellow/violet and violet/yellow; violet and violet/white. If the results are not within the range specified at the beginning of this Chapter the IACV is faulty

78 If the results are within the specified range, check for continuity between the following pairs of wire terminals on the IACV – violet/yellow and violet; yellow/violet and violet/white. If there is no continuity it is likely the ECM is faulty – have it checked by a Honda dealer. If there is continuity the IACV is faulty.

Removal and installation

79 Follow the procedure in Section 11.

ECM

80 If a fault develops with the ECM or with the FI warning light, refer to the test procedures in Section 7.

Removal and installation

81 Remove the seat (see Chapter 8).

82 Locate the ECM at the rear of the

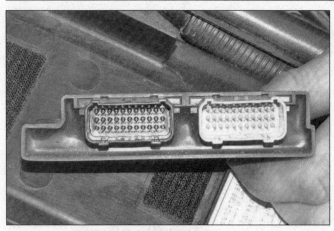

9.83a Inspect the ECM terminals . . .

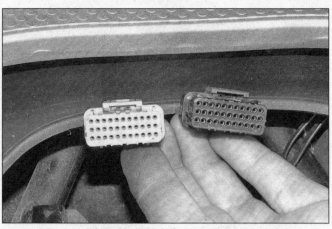

9.83b . . . and inside the wiring connectors for damage

underseat area (see illustration 7.7a). Ensure the ignition is OFF, then undo the bolt securing the ECM, draw it out and disconnect the grey and black multi-pin connectors.

83 Inspect the terminals on the ECM and inside the wiring connectors for damage and corrosion (see illustrations).

84 On installation, align the connectors carefully, then press them into place ensuring they are secure.

10 Crankshaft position sensor

Caution: Ensure the ignition is switched OFF before disconnecting/reconnecting any engine management system wiring connectors. If a connector is disconnected/reconnected with the ignition switched ON the engine control module (ECM) could be damaged.

Special tools: *A multimeter and peak voltage adapter are required for this procedure (see Step 2).*

1 The crankshaft position (CKP) sensor is part of the ignition system (see Section 1).

Check

2 To test the sensor a multimeter with a minimum input resistance of 10 M ohms is

required in conjunction with a peak voltage adapter. Honda provides a peak voltage adapter (Part No. 07HGJ-0020100 for this purpose). If the appropriate equipment is not available, the checks should be undertaken by a Honda dealer.

3 Either displace the ECM (see Section 7, Step 7) or remove the rear light assembly, to access the ECM multi-pin wiring connectors. Disconnect both wiring connectors. Connect the peak voltage adapter positive (+ve) probe to the white/yellow wire terminal (A32) on the loom side of the black ECM connector, and the negative (-ve) probe to the yellow wire terminal (B22) on the loom side of the grey ECM connector.

4 Check that the transmission is in neutral, then turn the ignition ON, crank the engine on the starter motor and note the sensor peak voltage. Turn the ignition OFF. **Note:** *The machine's battery must be fully charged to perform this test successfully.*

5 Compare the result with the specification at the beginning of this Chapter. If the result is below the specified minimum, repeat the test at the CKP wiring connector as follows.

6 The CKP sensor is located inside the alternator cover on the left-hand side of the engine unit. Remove the left-hand side panel (see Chapter 8) and the front sprocket cover (see Chapter 7). Trace the CKP sensor wiring from the back of the alternator cover to the

boot to the rear of the fusebox and disconnect the wiring connector (see illustrations).

7 Connect the peak voltage adapter positive (+ve) probe to the white/yellow wire terminal on the sensor side of the connector, and the negative (-ve) probe to the yellow wire terminal on the sensor side of the connector. Repeat the procedure in Step 4.

8 If the result in the second test is as specified, inspect the wiring and connections between the wiring connector and the ECM for damage. If the result is again below the specified minimum, either the test equipment is not suitable for the task or the CKP is faulty – have it checked by a Honda dealer.

Removal and installation

9 The CKP sensor and wiring are integral parts of the alternator stator assembly. If the sensor is faulty a new stator assembly will have to be fitted, individual components are not available.

10 Remove the left-hand side panel (see Chapter 8) and the front sprocket cover (see Chapter 7). Trace the CKP sensor wiring from the back of the alternator cover to the boot to the rear of the fusebox and disconnect the wiring connector (see illustrations 10.6a and b). Release the wiring from any clips or ties, then follow the procedure in Chapter 9 to remove the alternator stator.

11 Installation is the reverse of removal.

11 Idle air control valve

1 The idle air control valve (IACV) is located on the rear right-hand side of the throttle body assembly (see illustration 9.73). The valve eliminates the need for manual idle speed adjustment. An electrical fault with the IACV should be indicated by the FI warning light (see Section 8). However, if the engine idle speed is outside the specification shown at the beginning of this Chapter the valve may be worn or there may be carbon deposits inside the IACV passage in the throttle body.

10.6a Trace the wiring from the alternator cover . . .

10.6b . . . and disconnect the CKP sensor connector

11.4a Undo the screws . . .

11.4b . . . and remove the plate

11.5 Withdraw the valve from the slide bore

2 Ensure that the spark plugs and air filter element are in good condition (see Chapter 1). Check the throttle cable freeplay (see Chapter 1). Ensure there are no air leaks between the air filter housing, throttle bodies and intake manifolds (see Section 16).

3 If not already done, remove the fuel tank (see Section 2).

4 Undo the screws securing the IACV and remove the plate **(see illustrations)**.

5 Withdraw the valve from the slide bore in the throttle body cover **(see illustration)**. Turn the ignition ON and check that the valve slide rotates. Turn the ignition OFF. If the slide does not rotate the IACV is faulty and must be renewed.

6 Disconnect the wiring connector. Clean any carbon deposits off the slide carefully with a suitable solvent and ensure there are no carbon deposits inside the slide bore. Inspect the slide and bore for wear and replace them with new ones if necessary – the bore is part of the throttle body cover (see Section 16).

7 Prior to installation, rotate the slide clockwise until it is seated. Align the slot in the slide with the pin inside the slide bore and install the IACV **(see illustrations)**. Install the plate and tighten the screws securely **(see illustrations 11.4b and a)**.

8 Ensure that the terminals inside both sides of the connector are clean and reconnect the connector **(see illustration 9.74)**.

9 If required, follow the procedure in Section 16 to remove the throttle body cover and inspect the IACV passage in the throttle body.

12 Tip-over sensor and engine stop relay

Tip-over (TO) sensor

1 If the machine falls over while the ignition is switched ON, the TO sensor cuts power to the fuel pump, ignition coils and fuel injectors.

2 The TO sensor is located on the front of the fairing bracket **(see illustration)**. Remove the fairing for access (see Chapter 8).

Check

3 Undo the screws securing the sensor and hold it upright **(see illustration)**. Turn

11.7a Align the slot in the slide . . .

the ignition ON – the engine stop relay **(see illustration 4.21)** should be heard to click, indicating that the circuit is closed.

4 Now tilt the sensor 60 to 70° to the right **(see illustration)** – the engine stop relay should be heard to click, indicating that the circuit is open. Turn the ignition OFF.

12.2 Location of TO sensor

12.4 Tilt the sensor to the right

11.7b . . . with the pin inside the slide bore

5 Repeat the test in Steps 3 and 4, this time tilting the sensor to the left. Turn the ignition OFF.

6 If the TO sensor appears to be faulty (the engine stop relay does not perform as described) check the sensor wiring as follows.

7 Trace the sensor wiring to the connector and disconnect it **(see illustration)**. Using a

12.3 Hold the sensor upright

12.7 Disconnect the TO sensor wiring connector

12.14a Unclip the relay . . .

12.14b . . . and disconnect the wiring connector

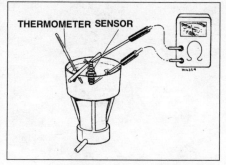

13.4 Set-up for testing the ECT sensor

multimeter, connect the positive (+ve) probe to the black wire terminal on the loom side of the connector and the negative (-ve) probe to the green wire terminal. Turn the ignition ON and check for battery voltage. Turn the ignition OFF.

8 If there is no battery voltage, inspect the green and black wires for damage.

9 If there is battery voltage, connect the meter positive (+ve) probe to the red/orange wire terminal on the loom side of the connector and the negative (-ve) probe to the green wire terminal. Turn the ignition ON and check for battery voltage. Turn the ignition OFF. If there is no battery voltage, inspect the red/orange wire for damage.

10 If the sensor wiring is good the TO sensor is faulty and must be replaced with a new one.

Engine stop relay

11 The engine stop relay is located on the right-hand side of the fairing bracket **(see illustration 4.21)**. Remove the fairing for access (see Chapter 8).

12 Turn the ignition ON – the relay should be heard to click.

13 If the relay does not click, go to Step 19. If the relay clicks but the fuel pump does not operate, check the relay continuity as follows.

14 Ensure the ignition is OFF, then unclip the relay from its bracket and disconnect the wiring connector **(see illustrations)**.

15 Using a multimeter, check for continuity between terminals A and B on the relay **(see illustration 4.25)**. There should be no continuity. Now use jumper wires to connect the positive (+ve) terminal of a fully charged 12 volt battery to relay terminal D and the negative (-ve) battery terminal to relay terminal C. There should now be continuity between terminals A and B. If the relay fails either of the checks it is faulty and must be replaced with a new one.

16 If the relay is good, use an insulated jumper wire to connect the white/black and black wire terminals on the loom side of the relay connector. Either displace the ECM (see Section 7, Step 7) or remove the rear light assembly to access the ECM multi-pin wiring connectors. Disconnect the black ECM connector, then connect the meter positive

(+ve) probe to the white/black wire terminal on the loom side of the connector and the negative (-ve) probe to earth (ground). Turn the ignition ON and check for battery voltage. Turn the ignition OFF.

17 If there is no battery voltage, check for continuity in the black wire between the engine stop relay and the fuse box, and in the white/black wire between the relay and the ECM (see *Wiring Diagram* at the end of Chapter 9). No continuity indicates a fault in the wire.

18 If the relay and the wiring are good it is likely the ECM is faulty – have it checked by a Honda dealer.

19 Ensure the ignition is OFF. Disconnect the TO sensor wiring connector (see Step 7). Using a multimeter, connect the positive (+ve) probe to the red/orange wire terminal on the loom side of the connector and the negative (-ve) probe to earth (ground). Turn the ignition ON and check for battery voltage. Turn the ignition OFF.

20 If there is no battery voltage, check for continuity in the black/white wire between the engine stop relay and the engine stop switch, and in the red/orange wire between the relay and the TO sensor (see *Wiring Diagram* at the end of Chapter 9). No continuity indicates a fault in the wire.

21 If the wiring is good, check the operation of the relay (see Step 15).

13 Engine coolant temperature sensor

1 The engine coolant temperature (ECT) sensor is located on the rear of the front cylinder **(see illustration 9.16)**. An electrical fault with the ECT sensor should be indicated by the FI warning light (see Section 8). To ensure that the sensor resistance changes with engine temperature, check it as follows.

Check

2 Follow the procedure in Steps 7 and 8 to remove the ECT sensor from the cylinder.

3 Fill a small heatproof container with coolant and place it on a stove.

4 Using a multimeter set to the K-ohms scale,

connect the meter probes to the green/orange and pink/white wire terminals on the sensor. Using some wire or other support, suspend the sensor in the coolant so that just the sensing portion and the threads are submerged **(see illustration)**. The tip of the sensor should be approximately 40 mm from the bottom of the container. Place a thermometer capable of reading temperatures up to 120°C in the coolant so that its bulb is close to the sensor tip. **Note:** *None of the components should be allowed to touch the container directly.*

5 Allow the temperature of the coolant to stabilise at 20°C and note the meter reading, then slowly heat the coolant. As the temperature rises, the sensor resistance should fall. Check that the specified resistance is obtained at the correct temperature (see *Specifications* at the beginning of this Chapter.)

> ⚠ **Warning: This must be done very carefully to avoid the risk of personal injury.**

6 If the readings obtained are different, or are obtained at different temperatures, the sensor is faulty and must be renewed.

Removal and installation

7 To remove the ECT sensor, first drain the coolant (see Chapter 3).

8 Disconnect the ECT sensor wiring connector **(see illustration 9.19)**. Unscrew the sensor and discard the sealing washer as a new one must be fitted.

9 On installation, fit a new sealing washer and tighten the sensor to the torque setting specified at the beginning of this Chapter. Check that the wiring connector terminals are clean.

10 Refill the cooling system (see Chapter 3).

14 Secondary air system (SAS)

1 A general description of the secondary air supply system can be found in Chapter 1, Section 18.

Control valve

2 The secondary air system control valve is located on the left-hand side of the air filter

14.2 Location of the control valve

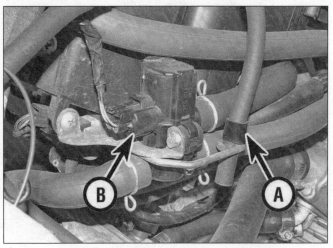

14.3 Vent hose (A) and wiring connector (B)

housing **(see illustration)**. Remove the fuel tank for access (see Section 2).

Removal

3 Displace the vent hose from the control valve bracket and disconnect the wiring connector **(see illustration)**.
4 Note the location of the air system hoses, then release the clips securing the hoses and disconnect them from the valve unions **(see illustration)**.
5 Undo the screw securing the control valve bracket to the air filter housing and lift the valve off.

Check

6 Using a multimeter set to the ohms scale, measure the resistance between the control valve terminals and compare the result with the specification at the beginning of this Chapter. If the result is not as specified the control valve is faulty.
7 To check the operation of the valve, blow

into the air supply union and ensure air flows out the intake unions **(see illustration)**. Now connect the positive (+ve) terminal of a 12 volt battery to the black/white wire terminal on the valve and the negative (-ve) battery terminal to the orange/black wire terminal on the valve. Blow into the supply union – air should not flow out the intake unions.
8 If the control valve does not perform as described it should be renewed.
9 If the control valve is good, either displace the ECM (see Section 7, Step 7) or remove the rear light assembly to access the ECM multi-pin wiring connectors. Disconnect the black ECM connector, then check for continuity in the orange/black wire between the control valve connector and terminal A22 in the ECM connector (see *Wiring Diagram* at the end of Chapter 9).

Installation

10 Installation is the reverse of removal.

Reed valves

11 The reed valves are located in the front and rear valve covers. To inspect the valves, refer to Chapter 2, Section 11.

15 Ignition coils

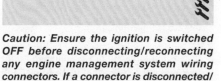

Caution: Ensure the ignition is switched OFF before disconnecting/reconnecting any engine management system wiring connectors. If a connector is disconnected/ reconnected with the ignition switched ON the engine control module (ECM) could be damaged.
Special tools: *A multimeter and peak voltage adapter are required for this procedure (see Step 3).*
1 The front cylinder ignition coil is located inside the frame behind the steering head

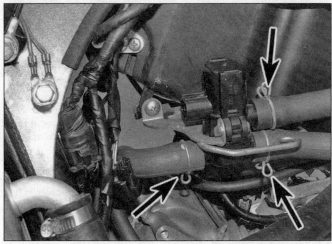

14.4 Disconnect the hoses from the valve unions

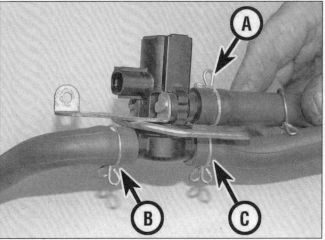

14.7 Air supply union (A), front cylinder intake union (B) and rear cylinder intake union (C)

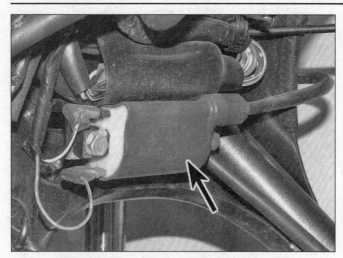

15.1a Location of the front cylinder ignition coil

15.1b Location of the rear cylinder ignition coil

(see illustration). Remove the fuel tank (see Section 2) and the air filter housing (see Section 5) for access. The rear cylinder ignition coil is located inside the frame behind the rear cylinder head (see illustration). Remove the seat and the side panels for access (see Chapter 8).

2 Ensure that the spark plugs and spark plug caps are in good condition (see Chapter 1).

Check

3 To test the ignition coils a multimeter with a minimum input resistance of 10 M ohms is required in conjunction with a peak voltage adapter. Honda provides a peak voltage adapter (Part No. 07HGJ-0020100 for this purpose). If the appropriate equipment is not available, the checks should be undertaken by a Honda dealer.

4 Pull the caps off the spark plugs, connect known good plugs to the caps and earth the plugs against the cylinder heads.

5 To test the front cylinder coil, back probe the blue/yellow wire terminal on the coil with the peak voltage adapter positive (+ve) probe and connect the negative (-ve) probe to earth (ground). Turn the ignition ON and check the initial voltage – see Specifications

15.14 Disconnect the coil primary wire connectors

at the beginning of this Chapter. If there is no initial voltage, turn the ignition OFF and check for continuity in the white/black wire between the coil and the engine stop relay (see Wiring Diagram at the end of Chapter 9).

6 If there is initial voltage, check that the transmission is in neutral, then turn the ignition ON, crank the engine on the starter motor and note the coil peak voltage. Turn the ignition OFF. **Note:** *The machine's battery must be fully charged to perform this test successfully.* Compare the result with the specification at the beginning of this Chapter.

7 If the initial voltage reading drops while the engine is being cranked, follow the procedure in Section 7, Step 7, to access the ECM multi-pin wiring connectors. Disconnect the black ECM connector and check for continuity in the white/black wire between the coil and the ECM connector terminal A4 (see illustration 7.7b). Check for continuity between the green/pink wire terminal A23 in the black ECM connector and earth (ground). Disconnect the grey ECM connector and check for continuity between the green wire terminal B4 in the connector and earth (ground). Check for continuity in the blue/yellow wire between the coil and the black ECM connector terminal A3. Check the operation and associated wiring of the sidestand switch and neutral switch (see Chapter 9). Check the CKP sensor (see Section 10). If no faults can be found it is likely the ECM is faulty – have it checked by a Honda dealer.

8 If no peak voltage is recorded, check the CKP sensor. If the CKP sensor is good it is likely the ECM is faulty – have it checked by a Honda dealer.

9 If the peak voltage is lower than the specified minimum it is likely the ECM is faulty – have it checked by a Honda dealer.

10 If the peak voltage is good but there is no spark across the plug electrodes, the ignition coil is faulty.

11 To test the rear cylinder coil, back probe

the yellow/blue wire terminal on the coil with the peak voltage adapter positive (+ve) probe and connect the negative (-ve) probe to earth (ground). Follow the procedures in Steps 5 to 10 to test the coil. Note that the test for continuity between the coil and the ECM is in the yellow/blue wire from the coil to the black ECM connector terminal A12.

Removal and installation

12 To remove the front cylinder ignition coil, first remove the fuel tank (see Section 2) and the air filter housing (see Section 5).

13 Ensure the ignition is OFF.

14 Disconnect the cap from the front cylinder spark plug (see Chapter 1). Disconnect the coil primary wire connectors, noting how they fit (see illustration).

15 Undo the bolts securing the coil and lift it off, noting the routing of the HT lead.

16 Installation is the reverse of removal.

17 To remove the rear cylinder ignition coil, first remove the seat and the side panels (see Chapter 8). The remainder of the procedure is the same as for the front cylinder ignition coil (see Steps 13 to 16).

16 Throttle bodies

Warning: Refer to the precautions given in Section 1 before starting work.

Removal

1 Remove the fuel tank (see Section 2) and the air filter housing (see Section 5).

2 Disconnect the throttle cables from the throttle pulley (see Section 18).

3 Displace the throttle body assembly sub-loom wiring connector from its bracket on the right-hand side of the frame (see

16.3a Displace the sub-loom wiring connector

16.3b Release the tabs . . .

16.3c . . . and pull the connector apart

illustration). Release the tabs securing the two halves of the connector and pull the connector apart (see illustrations).

4 Disconnect the ECT sensor wiring connector (see illustration).

5 Loosen the upper clamp screws securing the throttle body assembly to the intake manifolds (see illustrations).

6 Ease the throttle body assembly off the intake manifolds (see illustration).
Caution: Stuff clean rag into the cylinder head intake manifolds after removing the throttle body assembly to prevent anything from falling inside.

7 If required, disconnect the TP sensor wiring connector (see illustration 9.24), the IACV wiring connector (see illustration 9.73),

and the fuel injector wiring connectors (see illustration 9.47). Unclip the wiring sub-loom wiring from the left-hand joining plate and remove the sub-loom, noting how it fits (see illustration).

8 To disconnect the fuel hose from the 'Y' union, squeeze the tabs on the locking sleeve together to release the hose connector from the union (see illustration). Note how the locking sleeve locates in the end of the union (see Section 2, Step 9). Note: Honda recommend that a new locking sleeve is fitted whenever the fuel hose is disconnected.

Inspection

Caution: The throttle body assembly must be treated as a complete unit. Do not

loosen any nuts/bolts/screws other than as directed here or in Section 17 as they are pre-set at the factory to ensure correct operation. The only components on the assembly which may be removed are the throttle body cover and fuel injectors.

9 Clean the assembly with suitable solvent using a nylon-bristled brush to remove stubborn deposits.
Caution: Use only a dedicated carburettor/ injector cleaner or petroleum-based solvent, following the manufacturer's instructions. DO NOT use caustic cleaners.

10 Inspect the throttle bodies for cracks or any other damage which may result in air leaks.

11 Check that the throttle pulleys move smoothly and freely in the bodies (see

16.4 Disconnect the ECT sensor wiring connector

16.5a Front cylinder upper clamp screw

16.5b Rear cylinder upper clamp screw

16.6 Ease the assembly off the intake manifolds

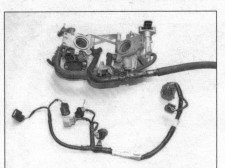

16.7 Throttle bodies wiring sub-loom

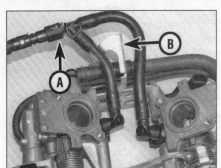

16.8 Disconnect fuel hose at 'Y' union (A). Note the support bracket (B)

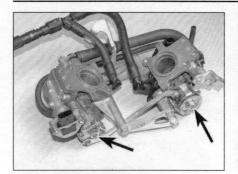

16.11 Check the operation of the throttle pulleys

16.12 Remove the throttle body cover and seal

16.13 Ensure the air passages are carbon-free

16.17 Examine the intake manifolds and clamps

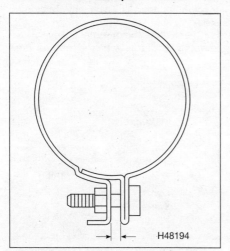

16.18 Position of upper manifold clamps. End clearance 2 to 4 mm when fully tightened

illustration). Inspect the valve shafts and throttle bodies for wear. Check the condition of the valve shaft springs.

12 If, on inspection, there are carbon deposits inside the IACV slide bore (see Section 11), undo the screws securing the throttle body cover and lift the cover off **(see illustration)**. Discard the cover seal as a new one must be fitted.

13 Clean out any carbon deposits with a suitable solvent, ensuring no dirt falls into the air passages in the throttle body **(see illustration)**.

14 Ensure the new cover seal is correctly fitted in the groove in the cover, then install the cover.

15 If required, remove the fuel injectors (see Section 17).

16 Inspect the sub-loom wiring and wiring connectors for damage **(see illustration 16.7)**. If any damage is found a new sub-loom will have to be fitted.

17 Note the location of the clamps on the intake manifolds – if they are corroded or damaged they must be renewed **(see illustration)**. If the manifolds are hardened or split new ones should be fitted (see Chapter 2, Section 15).

Installation

18 Installation is the reverse of removal, noting the following:
● If removed, install the wiring sub-loom and secure it to the left-hand joining plate (see Step 7).
● Make sure the intake manifold clamps are positioned correctly **(see illustration)**.
● Press the throttle bodies down firmly to ensure they are fully engaged with the intake manifolds – a squirt of WD-40 or a smear of oil will ease entry.
● Tighten the clamp screws securely.

● Make sure all hoses and wires are correctly routed and secured and not trapped or kinked.
● Refer to Section 18 for installation of the throttle cables. Check the operation of the cables and adjust them as necessary (see Chapter 1).

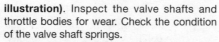

17 Fuel injectors

> ⚠ *Warning: Refer to the precautions given in Section 1 before starting work.*

1 The front and rear cylinder fuel injectors are located between the throttle bodies (see Section 16). A fault with either injector should be indicated by the FI warning light (see Section 8). Follow the procedure in Section 9 to test the injectors.

Removal

2 Remove the throttle body assembly (see Section 16).

3 If not already done, disconnect the fuel hose from the 'Y' union, then release the rear injector fuel feed hose from the support bracket **(see illustration 16.8)**.

4 Working on one injector at a time, undo the bolts securing the fuel feed hose union **(see illustration)**. Carefully lift the hose union off the injector, noting how the tabs locate either side of the injector wiring connector **(see illustration)**.

5 Note the alignment of the injector with the throttle body, then ease the injector out **(see illustration)**.

6 Note the location of the upper O-ring and

17.4a Bolts secure fuel union

17.4b Note location of tabs (arrowed)

17.5 Remove the fuel injector

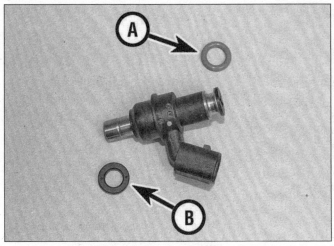

17.6 Upper O-ring (A) and lower seal (B)

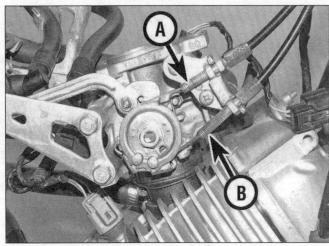

18.2 Throttle opening cable (A) and closing cable (B)

lower seal on the injector and discard them as new ones must be fitted **(see illustration)**.

7 Inspect the end of the fuel injector for accumulations of carbon and signs of damage. Check that the terminals in the wiring connector are clean.

8 Modern fuels contain detergents which should keep the injectors clean and free of gum or varnish from fuel residue. If an injector is suspected of being blocked, clean it through with injector cleaner. If the injector is clean but its performance is suspect, take it to a Honda dealer for assessment.

Installation

Note: *Apply a smear of engine oil to the new seals and O-rings before reassembly.*

9 Installation is the reverse of removal, noting the following:

● Install the new seals and O-rings onto the injectors carefully.
● Ensure the injectors are correctly aligned with the throttle bodies before installation.
● Ensure the fuel hose unions are correctly aligned with the injectors before installation.
● Tighten the fuel hose union bolts to the specified torque.

18 Throttle cables

 Warning: Refer to the precautions given in Section 1 before proceeding.

Removal

1 Remove the fuel tank (see Section 2).

2 Note the location of the throttle opening and closing cables on the throttle pulley on the front throttle body **(see illustration)**.

3 Loosen the locknuts on the opening cable adjuster and free the adjuster from the bracket, noting how it locates **(see illustration)**. Disconnect the inner cable end from the pulley **(see illustration)**.

4 Loosen the locknut on the closing cable guide and free the guide from the bracket, noting how it locates **(see illustration)**. Disconnect the inner cable end from the pulley.

5 Follow the procedure in Chapter 4A, Section 7, to disconnect the upper ends of the cables from the throttle twistgrip (see Steps 25 to 28).

6 Note the routing of the cables around the steering head and frame, then take them off.

Installation

7 Follow the procedure in Chapter 4A, Section 7, Steps 30 to 33 to connect the upper ends

18.3a Free the cable adjuster from the bracket

18.4 Free the cable guide from the bracket

of the cables to the twistgrip pulley.

8 Feed the cables through to the throttle bodies, making sure they are correctly routed and not kinked or bent sharply **(see illustration)**.

9 Lubricate the ends of the inner cables with multi-purpose grease. Fit the end of the closing cable onto the pulley, locate the cable guide on the bracket, then tighten the guide against the locknut **(see illustration 18.4)**.

10 Fit the end of the opening cable onto the pulley and locate the cable adjuster on the bracket **(see illustrations 18.3b and a)**.

11 Check that the adjuster on the handlebar end of the opening cable is turned fully in, then

18.3b Disconnect the cable end from the pulley

18.8 Feed the cables through to the throttle bodies

19.3a Front cylinder oxygen sensor (A). Note wiring tie (B)

adjust the locknuts on the lower adjuster so the cable freeplay is as specified In Chapter 1 and tighten the locknuts.

12 Operate the throttle twistgrip to check that it opens and closes freely.

13 Turn the handlebars back-and-forth to make sure the cables don't cause the steering to bind.

14 Install the remaining components in the reverse order of removal.

15 Start the engine and check that the idle speed does not rise as the handlebars are turned. If it does, the cables are routed incorrectly. Correct the problem before riding the motorcycle.

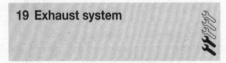

19 Exhaust system

> **Warning: If the engine has been running the exhaust system will be very hot. Allow the system to cool before carrying out any work.**

1 The procedure for removal and installation of the exhaust system is the same as for XL125V models in Chapter 4A, Section 9, noting the following.

2 Before removing the exhaust pipes remove the fairing, the seat and both side panels (see Chapter 8).

3 Note the location of the front and rear oxygen sensors and the sensor wiring connectors **(see illustrations 9.58a and b, 9.53a and b)**.

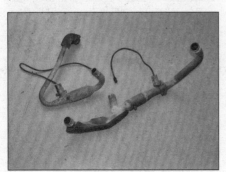

19.4 Front and rear sections of the exhaust system

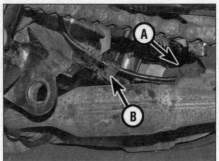

19.3b Rear cylinder oxygen sensor (A). Note wiring clip (B)

Disconnect the wiring connectors, release the wiring from any clips or ties and feed it back to the sensors **(see illustrations)**. Note the routing of the wiring – the wiring for the rear sensor passes through the guide above the swingarm pivot.

4 When removing the pipes, take care not to damage the sensor wiring **(see illustration)**. Note also that catalytic converters are incorporated in both exhaust pipes. The catalytic converters are FRAGILE – do not strike or drop the exhaust system during servicing.

5 If required, undo the bolts securing the sensor covers and remove the covers, then unscrew the sensors using one of the commercially available ring spanners or deep sockets **(see illustrations)**. Take care not to damage the exhaust pipe. DO NOT apply oil or grease to the sensor threads on installation. If available, use the deep socket and tighten the sensor to the torque setting specified at the beginning of this Chapter.

6 Tighten the header pipe flange nuts, the silencer mounting bolts and the clamp bolts to the torque settings specified at the beginning of this Chapter.

7 Once the exhaust system has been installed, secure the sensor wiring as noted on removal.

8 Install the remaining components in the reverse order of removal.

9 Run the engine and check the system for leaks.

19.5a Bolts (arrowed) secure sensor cover

20 Catalytic converter

General information

1 A catalytic converter is incorporated in the exhaust system to minimise the level of exhaust pollutants released into the atmosphere.

2 The catalytic converter consists of a heat tube impregnated with a catalyst material, over which the hot exhaust gases pass. The catalyst speeds up the oxidation of harmful carbon monoxide, unburned hydrocarbons and soot, effectively reducing the quantity of harmful products released into the atmosphere via the exhaust gases.

3 The catalytic converter is of the closed-loop type, providing feedback to ECM.

Precautions

4 The catalytic converter is a reliable and simple device which needs no maintenance in itself, but there are some facts of which an owner should be aware if the converter is to function properly for its full service life.

● DO NOT use leaded or lead replacement petrol (gasoline) – the additives will coat the precious metals, reducing their converting efficiency and will eventually destroy the catalytic converter.

● Always keep the ignition and fuel systems well-maintained in accordance with the manufacturer's schedule – if the fuel/air mixture is suspected of being incorrect have it checked on an exhaust gas analyser.

● If the engine develops a misfire, do not ride the bike at all (or at least as little as possible) until the fault is cured.

● DO NOT use fuel or engine oil additives – these may contain substances harmful to the catalytic converter.

● DO NOT continue to use the bike if the engine burns oil to the extent of leaving a visible trail of blue smoke.

● Remember that the catalytic converter Is FRAGILE – do not strike or drop the exhaust system during servicing.

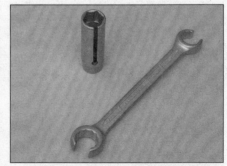

19.5b Slotted deep socket and special spanner for use on oxygen sensor

Chapter 5
Ignition system –
VT125C and XL125V-1 to V-6 models

Contents

Degrees of difficulty

Easy, suitable for novice with little experience	**Fairly easy,** suitable for beginner with some experience	**Fairly difficult,** suitable for competent DIY mechanic 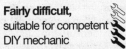	**Difficult,** suitable for experienced DIY mechanic	**Very difficult,** suitable for expert DIY or professional

Specifications

General information

Spark plug . . . . see Chapter 1

Coolant temperature sensor

Resistance at 20°C (68°F) . . . . 2.0 to 3.0 K-ohms

Resistance at 80°C (176°F) . . . . 0.2 to 0.4 K-ohms

Ignition pulse generator

Minimum peak voltage . . . . 0.7 volts

Ignition coils

Initial voltage . . . . Battery voltage

Minimum primary peak voltage . . . . 100 volts

Torque wrench settings

Coolant temperature sensor . . . . 23 Nm

Ignition pulse generator bolts . . . . 5 Nm

1 General information

All models are fitted with a fully transistorised electronic ignition system. The system consists of the pulse generator, ignition control unit (ICU), ignition coils and spark plugs.

The triggers on the alternator rotor, which is fitted to the left-hand end of the crankshaft, activate signals in the pulse generator as the crankshaft rotates. The pulse generator sends those signals to the ICU which, in conjunction with information received from the coolant temperature sensor, calculates the ignition timing and supplies the ignition coils with the power necessary to produce a spark at the plugs. The ICU incorporates an electronic advance system. There is no provision for checking or adjusting the ignition timing.

The system incorporates a safety interlock circuit which will cut the ignition if the sidestand is extended whilst the engine is running and in gear, or if a gear is selected whilst the engine is running and the sidestand is extended. It also prevents the engine from being started if the engine is in gear unless the clutch lever is pulled in (see Chapter 9 for component test details).

Because of their nature, the individual ignition system components can be checked but not repaired. If ignition system troubles occur, and the faulty component can be isolated, the only cure for the problem is to replace the part with a new one. Keep in mind that most electrical parts, once purchased, cannot be returned. To avoid unnecessary expense, make very sure the faulty component has been positively identified before buying a replacement part.

2 Ignition system check

> **Warning: The energy levels in electronic systems can be very high. On no account should the ignition be switched on whilst a plug or plug cap is being held. Shocks from the HT circuit can be most unpleasant. Secondly, it is vital that the engine is not turned over or run with a plug cap removed, and that the plug is soundly earthed (grounded) when the system is checked for sparking. The ignition system components can be seriously damaged if the HT circuit becomes isolated.**

1 As no means of adjustment is available, any failure of the system can be traced to failure of a system component or a simple wiring fault. Of the two possibilities, the latter is by far the most likely. In the event of failure, check the system in a logical fashion, as described below.

2 Working on one cylinder at a time, pull the cap off the spark plug **(see illustration)**. Fit a spare spark plug into the cap and lay the plug against the cylinder head with the threads contacting it. If necessary, hold the spark plug with an insulated tool.

> **Warning: Do not remove the spark plug from the engine to perform this check – atomised fuel being pumped out of the open spark plug hole could ignite, causing severe injury! Make sure the plug is securely held against the engine – if it is not earthed when the engine is turned over, the ignition control unit could be damaged.**

3 Check that the transmission is in neutral, then turn the ignition switch ON, and turn the engine over on the starter motor. If the system is in good condition a regular, fat blue spark should be evident at the plug electrodes. If the spark appears thin or yellowish, or is

non-existent, further investigation will be necessary.

4 The ignition system must be able to produce a spark which is capable of jumping a particular size gap – Honda do not give a specification, but a healthy system should produce a spark capable of jumping at least 6 mm. Simple ignition spark gap testing tools are commercially available – follow the manufacturer's instructions, and check each spark plug **(see illustration)**.

5 If the test results are good the entire ignition system can be considered good. If the spark appears thin or yellowish, or is non-existent, further investigation is necessary.

6 Ignition faults can be divided into two categories, namely those where the ignition system has failed completely, and those which are due to a partial failure. The likely faults are listed below, starting with the most probable source of failure. Work through the list systematically, referring to the subsequent sections for full details of the necessary checks and tests, and to the *Wiring Diagrams* at the end of Chapter 9. Before checking the following items ensure that the battery is fully charged and that all fuses are in good condition.

● Loose, corroded or damaged wiring connections, broken or shorted wiring between any of the component parts of the ignition system (see Chapter 9).
● Faulty HT lead or spark plug cap, faulty spark plug, dirty, worn or corroded plug electrodes, or incorrect gap between electrodes.
● Faulty ignition switch (see Chapter 9).
● Faulty neutral, clutch or sidestand switch, or safety circuit diode (see Chapter 9).
● Faulty ignition HT coil.
● Faulty ignition pulse generator.
● Faulty coolant temperature sensor.
● Faulty ICU.

7 If the above checks don't reveal the cause of the problem, have the ignition system tested by a Honda dealer.

2.2 Pull the cap off the spark plug

2.4 Using a spark gap testing tool

3.1a Location of the front cylinder ignition coil

3.1b Location of the rear cylinder ignition coil – VT125C

3.1c Location of the rear cylinder ignition coil – XL125V

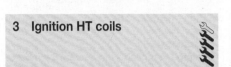

3 Ignition HT coils

Caution: Ensure the ignition is switched OFF before disconnecting/reconnecting any ignition system wiring connectors. If a connector is disconnected/reconnected with the ignition switched ON the ignition control unit (ICU) could be damaged.
Special tools: *A multimeter and peak voltage adapter are required for this procedure (see Step 3).*

1 The front cylinder ignition coil is located inside the frame behind the steering head **(see illustration)**. Remove the fuel tank and the air filter housing (see Chapter 4A) for access. On VT125C models, the rear cylinder ignition coil is located above the coolant reservoir **(see illustration)**. Remove the right-hand side panel for access (see Chapter 8). On XL125V models, the rear ignition coil is located inside the frame behind the rear cylinder head **(see illustration)**. Remove the seat and the side panels for access (see Chapter 8).
2 Ensure that the spark plugs, spark plug caps and HT leads are in good condition (see Chapter 1).

Check

3 To test the ignition coils a multimeter with a minimum input resistance of 10 M-ohms is required in conjunction with a peak voltage adapter. Honda provides a peak voltage adapter (Part No. 07HGJ-0020100) for this purpose. If the appropriate equipment is not available, the checks should be undertaken by a Honda dealer.
4 Pull the caps off the spark plugs, connect known good plugs to the caps and earth the plugs against the cylinder heads.
5 To test the front cylinder coil, back probe the blue/yellow wire terminal on the coil with the peak voltage adapter positive (+ve) probe and connect the negative (-ve) probe to earth (ground). Turn the ignition ON and check that battery voltage is shown. If there is no initial voltage, turn the ignition OFF and check for continuity in the black/white wire between the coil(s) and the engine stop switch (see *Wiring Diagrams* at the end of Chapter 9).
6 If there is initial (battery) voltage, check

that the transmission is in neutral, then turn the ignition ON, crank the engine on the starter motor and note the coil peak voltage. Turn the ignition OFF. **Note:** *The machine's battery must be fully charged to perform this test successfully.* Compare the result with the specification at the beginning of this Chapter.
7 When testing the front cylinder coil, if no peak voltage is recorded, follow the procedure in Section 6 to access the ICU and disconnect the multi-pin wiring connector **(see illustration 6.6b)**. Check for continuity in the blue/yellow wire between the coil and the ICU connector.
8 Test the rear cylinder initial voltage as described in Step 5, noting that the yellow/blue wire must be back-probed. If no peak voltage is recorded, follow the procedure in Section 6 to access the ICU and disconnect the multi-pin wiring connector **(see illustration 6.6b)**. Check for continuity in the yellow/blue wire between the coil and the ICU connector.
9 Check for continuity between the green wire terminal in the ICU connector and earth (ground). Check the operation and associated wiring of the sidestand switch and neutral switch (see Chapter 9). Check the ignition pulse generator (see Section 4). If no faults can be found it is likely the ICU is faulty – have it checked by a Honda dealer.
10 If the peak voltage is lower than the specified minimum, check the operation and associated wiring of the sidestand switch and neutral switch (see Chapter 9). If no faults can be found it is likely the ICU is faulty – have it checked by a Honda dealer.

3.13 Location of rear cylinder coil primary wire connectors – VT125C

11 If the peak voltage is good but there is no spark across the plug electrodes, the ignition coil is faulty.

Removal and installation – VT125C

12 On VT125C models, follow the procedure in Chapter 4B, Section 15, to remove the front cylinder ignition coil.
13 To remove the rear cylinder coil, first remove right-hand side panel (see Chapter 8). Disconnect the cap from the spark plug (see Chapter 1). Disconnect the coil primary wire connectors, noting how they fit **(see illustration)**. Undo the bolts securing the coil and lift it off, noting the routing of the HT cable.
14 Installation is the reverse of removal.

Removal and installation – XL125V

15 On XL125V models, follow the procedure in Chapter 4B, Section 15.

4 Ignition pulse generator

Caution: Ensure the ignition is switched OFF before disconnecting/reconnecting any ignition system wiring connectors. If a connector is disconnected/reconnected with the ignition switched ON the ignition control unit (ICU) could be damaged.
Special tools: *A multimeter and peak voltage adapter are required for this procedure (see Step 1).*

Check

1 To test the ignition pulse generator a multimeter with a minimum input resistance of 10 M-ohms is required in conjunction with a peak voltage adapter. Honda provides a peak voltage adapter (Part No. 07HGJ-0020100 for this purpose. If the appropriate equipment is not available, the checks should be undertaken by a Honda dealer.
2 Follow the procedure in Section 6 to access the ICU and disconnect the multi-pin wiring connector **(see illustration 6.6b)**. Connect the peak voltage adapter probes to the white/

4.5a Trace the wiring to the boot . . .

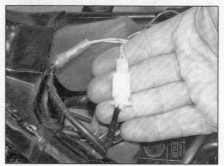

4.5b . . . and disconnect the 2-pin connector

5.1 Location of the coolant temperature sensor

yellow and yellow wire terminals on the loom side of the multi-pin connector.

3 Check that the transmission is in neutral, then turn the ignition ON, crank the engine on the starter motor and note the pulse generator peak voltage. Turn the ignition OFF. **Note:** *The machine's battery must be fully charged to perform this test successfully.*

4 Compare the result with the specification at the beginning of this Chapter. If the result is below the specified minimum, repeat the test at the pulse generator wiring connector as follows.

5 The ignition pulse generator is located inside the alternator cover on the left-hand side of the engine unit. On VT125C models, remove the seat and the left-hand side panel (see Chapter 8) and the front sprocket cover (see Chapter 7). On XL125V models remove the left-hand side panel (see Chapter 8) and the front sprocket cover (see Chapter 7). Trace the pulse generator wiring from the back of the alternator cover to the wiring boot and disconnect the 2-pin wiring connector **(see illustrations)**.

6 Connect the peak voltage adapter probes to the white/yellow and yellow wire terminals on the pulse generator side of the connector and repeat the procedure in Step 3.

7 If the result in the second test is as specified, inspect the wiring and connections between the wiring connector and the ICU for damage. If the result is again below the specified minimum, either the test equipment is not suitable for the task or the ignition pulse generator is faulty – have it checked by a Honda dealer.

Removal and installation

8 The ignition pulse generator is located inside the alternator cover on the left-hand side of the engine unit. Follow the procedure in Step 5 to identify the wiring from the ignition pulse generator and disconnect it at the connector. Release the wiring from any clips or ties and feed it back to the alternator cover.

9 Follow the procedure in Chapter 9 to remove the alternator cover.

10 Undo the bolts securing the ignition pulse generator and the wiring clamp, displace the wiring grommet from the cover and lift the pulse generator and wiring sub-loom out.

11 Installation is the reverse of removal. Clean the threads of the ignition pulse generator mounting bolts and apply a suitable non-permanent thread-locking compound, then tighten the bolts to the torque setting specified at the beginning of this Chapter. Don't forget to clean the old sealant off the grommets for the alternator and ignition pulse generator wiring and apply fresh sealant.

5 Coolant temperature sensor

1 The coolant temperature sensor is located on the rear of the front cylinder **(see illustration)**.

Check

2 If the sensor is thought to be faulty, first check the sensor wiring as follows.

3 Release the wire clip securing the sensor connector and disconnect it **(see illustrations)**.

4 Follow the procedure in Section 6 to access the ICU and disconnect the multi-pin wiring connector **(see illustration 6.6b)**.

5 Check for continuity in the green/orange and pink/white wires between the appropriate terminals in the ECT and ICU connectors.

6 If the wiring is good, check that the sensor resistance changes with engine temperature as follows.

7 Follow the procedure in Steps 12 and 13 to remove the sensor from the cylinder.

8 Fill a small heatproof container with coolant and place it on a stove.

9 Using a multimeter set to the K-ohms scale, connect the meter probes to the terminals on the sensor. Using some wire or other support, suspend the sensor in the coolant so that just the sensing portion and the threads are submerged **(see illustration)**. The tip of the sensor should be approximately 40 mm from the bottom of the container. Place a thermometer capable of reading temperatures up to 100°C in the coolant so that its bulb is close to the sensor tip. **Note:** *None of the components should be allowed to touch the container directly.*

10 Allow the temperature of the coolant to stabilise at 20°C and note the meter reading, then slowly heat the coolant. As the temperature rises, the sensor resistance should fall. Check that the specified resistance is obtained at 80°C (see *Specifications* at the beginning of this Chapter).

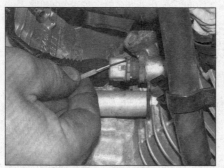

5.3a Release the wire clip . . .

5.3b . . . and disconnect the connector

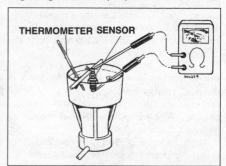

5.9 Set-up for testing the coolant temperature sensor

6.6a Release the rubber band

6.6b Disconnect the ICU multi-pin connector

6.7 Examine the ICU and connector terminals

 Warning: This must be done very carefully to avoid the risk of personal injury.

11 If the readings obtained are different, or are obtained at different temperatures, the sensor is faulty and must be renewed.

Removal and installation

12 To remove the sensor, first drain the coolant (see Chapter 3).

13 Disconnect the sensor wiring connector **(see illustration 5.3a and b)**. Unscrew the sensor and discard the sealing washer as a new one must be fitted.

14 On installation, fit a new sealing washer and tighten the sensor to the torque setting specified at the beginning of this Chapter. Check that the wiring connector terminals are clean.

15 Refill the cooling system (see Chapter 3).

6 Ignition control unit

1 If the tests shown in the preceding Sections have failed to isolate the cause

of an ignition fault, it is possible that the ignition control unit (ICU) itself is faulty. No specifications are available for the ICU – the only way to determine whether it is faulty is to substitute it with a known good one. Otherwise, take the unit to a Honda dealer for assessment.

2 Before condemning the ICU make sure the wiring connector terminals are clean and check the wiring between the ICU and the system components for continuity (see *Wiring Diagrams* at the end of Chapter 9).

Removal and installation

3 Make sure the ignition is OFF.

VT125C models

4 Remove the seat (see Chapter 8).

5 Displace the wiring loom boot to access the ICU **(see illustration 4.5a)**.

6 Release the rubber band securing the ICU to the front of the battery housing, lift the ICU out and disconnect the multi-pin wiring connector **(see illustrations)**.

7 Inspect the terminals on the ICU and inside the wiring connector for damage and corrosion **(see illustration)**.

8 On installation, align the connector carefully, then press it into place ensuring it is secure.

9 Slide the ICU into position and secure it with the rubber band.

10 Reposition the wiring loom boot, ensuring none of the wires have become disconnected or are kinked or trapped, then install the seat (see Chapter 8).

XL125V models

11 Remove the seat and the left-hand side panel (see Chapter 8).

12 Undo the bolt securing the battery bracket and remove the bracket – note the location of the ICU **(see illustrations)**.

13 Draw the ICU out from its holder and disconnect the multi-pin wiring connector **(see illustration)**.

14 Inspect the terminals on the ICU and inside the wiring connector for damage and corrosion **(see illustration 6.7)**.

15 On installation, align the connector carefully, then press it into place ensuring it is secure.

16 Slide the ICU into position, then install the battery bracket and tighten the retaining bolt securely.

6.12a Undo the bolt and remove the battery bracket

6.12b Location of the ICU

6.13 Lift out the ICU and disconnect the connector

Notes

Chapter 6
Frame and suspension

Contents

Degrees of difficulty

Easy, suitable for novice with little experience 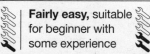	**Fairly easy,** suitable for beginner with some experience	**Fairly difficult,** suitable for competent DIY mechanic	**Difficult,** suitable for experienced DIY mechanic	**Very difficult,** suitable for expert DIY or professional

Specifications

Front forks

Fork oil type	Honda fork oil
Fork oil capacity	
VT125C	317 ± 2.5 cc
XL125V	346 ± 2.5 cc
Fork oil level*	
VT125C	125 mm
XL125V	117 mm
Fork spring free length	
VT125C	
Standard	463.7 mm
Service limit	459.1 mm
XL125V	
Standard	470.6 mm
Service limit	461.0 mm
Fork tube runout limit	0.2 mm

*Oil level is measured from the top of the tube with the fork spring removed and the leg fully compressed.

Torque settings

Footrest bracket bolts . . . . 27 Nm
Fork damper bolt . . . . 20 Nm
Fork top bolt. . . . . 22 Nm
Fork yoke clamp bolts
    Top yoke bolts . . . . 27 Nm
    Bottom yoke bolts . . . . 34 Nm
Front brake master cylinder clamp bolts (XL125V) . . . . 12 Nm
Handlebar clamp bolts (XL125V) . . . . 24 Nm
Handlebar mounting nuts (VT125C). . . . . 39 Nm
Shock absorber bolts
    VT125C
        Top bolt. . . . . 26 Nm
        Bottom bolt. . . . . 42 Nm
    XL125V
        Top and bottom bolts . . . . 44 Nm
Sidestand pivot bolt . . . . 10 Nm
Sidestand pivot bolt nut . . . . 10 Nm
Steering head bearing adjuster
    Initial setting . . . . 34 Nm
    Final setting . . . . 15 Nm
Steering stem nut. . . . . 103 Nm
Swingarm pivot bolt nut . . . . 88 Nm

1 General information

All models have a tubular steel cradle frame with a box-section steel swingarm.

Front suspension is by a pair of conventional, non-adjustable, oil-damped telescopic forks.

On VT125C models the rear swingarm is supported by twin shock absorbers. On XL125V models the swingarm is supported by a single shock absorber. The rear suspension on both models is adjustable for spring preload.

2 Frame inspection and repair

1 The frame should not require attention unless accident damage has occurred. In most cases, fitting a new frame is the only satisfactory remedy for such damage. Frame specialists have the jigs and other equipment necessary for straightening a frame to the required standard of accuracy, but even then there is no simple way of assessing to what extent it may have been over-stressed.

2 After a high mileage, the frame should be examined closely for signs of cracking or splitting at the welded joints. Loose engine mounting bolts can cause ovaling or fracturing of the mounting points. Minor damage can often be repaired by specialised welding, depending on the extent and nature of the damage.

3 Remember that a frame that is out of alignment will cause handling problems. If, as the result of an accident, misalignment is suspected, it will be necessary to strip the machine completely so the frame can be thoroughly checked.

3 Footrests, brake pedal and gearchange lever

VT125C

Footrests

1 To remove a rider's footrest, first straighten and remove the split pin on the bottom of the footrest pivot pin and remove the washer (see illustration). Discard the split pin as a new one must be used.

2 Withdraw the pivot pin and lift off the footrest, noting the location of the return spring (see illustrations).

3 If required undo the bolts on the underside and remove the end plate, then draw the rubber off the peg. All components are available individually.

4 To remove the footrest brackets, follow the procedure in Steps 8 to 10 (right-hand side) and 18 and 19 (left-hand side).

5 To remove a passenger's footrest, first remove the split pin and washer (see Step 1).

6 Withdraw the pivot pin and lift off the footrest. Note that the passenger footrest is held in the up or down position by compressing the footrest rubber. If required, draw the washer and rubber off the peg. All components are available individually.

7 Installation is the reverse of removal. Apply a small amount of multi-purpose grease to the pivot pin. Use new split pins on the pivot pins, and bend the ends as shown (see illustration 3.1).

3.1 Remove the split pin and washer

3.2a Withdraw the pivot pin

3.2b Note location of the return spring

3.8 Make alignment marks as necessary

3.9a Remove the pinch bolt . . .

3.9b . . . and ease the arm off the shaft

3.10a Undo the footrest bracket bolts . . .

3.10b . . . and lift the brake pedal assembly off

3.11 Location of the pedal stop bolt

Brake pedal assembly

8 Note the alignment between the rear brake linkage arm and the pivot shaft – if no marks are visible, make your own (see illustration).

9 Undo the linkage arm pinch bolt and ease the arm off the shaft (see illustrations). To remove the pivot shaft and rear brake rod assembly, if required, follow the procedure in Section 12.

10 Undo the footrest bracket bolts and lift the brake pedal assembly off (see illustrations).

11 Note the location of the pedal stop bolt on the reverse of the bracket (see illustration). If required, use the stop bolt to adjust the position of the brake pedal. Ensure the stop bolt locknut is tightened securely.

12 If required, remove the nut and washer securing the brake pedal and lift it off the footrest bracket (see illustration).

13 The brake rod is secured at both ends by a clevis pin – remove the split pin and withdraw the clevis pin to separate the pedal, rod and linkage arm (see illustration).

14 Installation is the reverse of removal. Apply a small amount of multi-purpose grease to the clevis pins and brake pedal pivot. Use new split pins on the clevis pins, and bend the ends as shown (see illustration 3.13). Align the linkage arm with the pivot shaft (see illustration 3.8) then tighten the pinch bolt securely. Check the brake pedal freeplay (see Chapter 1).

Gearchange lever assembly

15 Remove the front sprocket cover (see Chapter 7).

16 Note the alignment between the gearchange linkage arm and the gearchange

3.12 Brake pedal is secured by nut and washer

3.13 Brake rod is secured by split pin and clevis pin

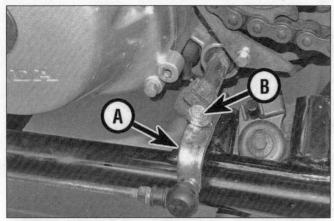

3.16 Note alignment between linkage arm (A) and gearchange shaft (B)

3.17 Remove the linkage arm pinch bolt

3.18a Undo the nut and washer . . .

shaft – if no marks are visible, make your own **(see illustration)**.

17 Undo the linkage arm pinch bolt and ease the arm off the shaft **(see illustration)**.

18 Remove the nut and washer securing the gearchange lever and lift the assembly off **(see illustrations)**.

19 If required, undo the footrest bracket bolts and remove the bracket **(see illustration)**.

20 If required, loosen the locknuts on both ends of the linkage rod and unscrew the rod from the unions on the gearchange lever and linkage arm **(see illustration)**.

21 Installation is the reverse of removal. Apply a small amount of multi-purpose grease to the gearchange lever pivot. If removed, ensure the linkage rod is screwed securely into the unions at both ends before tightening the locknuts.

22 Align the linkage arm with the gearchange shaft **(see illustration 3.16)** then tighten the pinch bolt securely.

XL125V

Footrests

23 To remove a rider's footrest, first note the location of the return spring **(see illustration)**. Straighten and remove the split pin on the bottom of the footrest pivot pin and remove the washer **(see illustration)**. Discard the split pin as a new one must be used.

24 Withdraw the pivot pin and lift off the footrest **(see illustration)**.

3.18b . . . and lift the gearchange assembly off

3.19 Undo the footrest bracket bolts

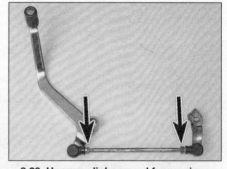

3.20 Unscrew linkage rod from unions (arrowed)

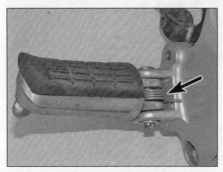

3.23a Note location of the return spring

3.23b Remove the split pin and washer

3.24 Withdraw the pivot pin to free the footrest

3.30 Undo the lower mounting bolt and lift the bracket off

3.31 Brake light switch spring (A) and pedal return spring (B)

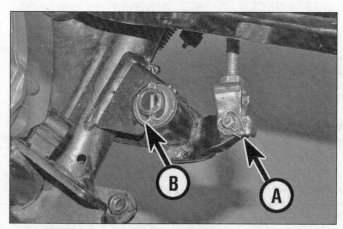

3.32a Clevis pin (A) connects pedal to brake pushrod. Split pin (B) secures brake pedal

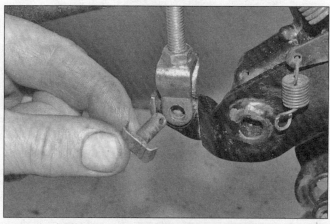

3.32b Note how the head of the clevis pin fits

25 If required undo the bolts on the underside and remove the rubber. All components are available individually.

26 To remove a passenger's footrest, first remove the split pin and washer (see Step 23).

27 Withdraw the pivot pin and lift off the footrest. Note that the passenger footrest is held in the up or down position by compressing the footrest rubber. If required, draw the washer and rubber off the peg. All components are available individually.

28 Installation is the reverse of removal. Apply a small amount of multi-purpose grease to the pivot pin. Use new split pins on the pivot pins **(see illustration 3.23b)**, and bend the ends as shown in illustration 3.1.

29 To remove the footrest brackets, follow the procedure in Steps 30 (right-hand side) and 38 to 42 (left-hand side).

Brake pedal

30 Undo the swingarm pivot bolt nut (see Section 12) then undo the lower mounting bolt and lift the footrest bracket off **(see illustration)**.

31 Disconnect the brake light switch and pedal return springs from the pedal **(see illustration)**.

32 Straighten and remove the split pin on the clevis pin connecting the brake pedal to the master cylinder pushrod **(see illustration)**. Discard the split pin as a new one must be used. Withdraw the clevis pin, noting how it fits **(see illustration)**.

33 Straighten and remove the split pin securing the brake pedal **(see illustration 3.32a)**. Discard the split pin as a new one must be used. Remove the washer and seal from the back of the pedal pivot pin, then remove the pedal. Note the location of the seal on the front of the pivot pin.

34 Installation is the reverse of removal. Ensure the pivot pin seals are in good condition and renew them if necessary. Apply a small amount of multi-purpose grease to the pivot pin. Don't forget to install the washer and secure the pivot with a new split pin **(see illustration 3.32a)**.

35 Apply a small amount of multi-purpose grease to the clevis pin then reconnect the brake pedal to the master cylinder pushrod **(see illustration 3.32b)**. Secure the clevis pin with a new split pin, then bend the ends of the split pins as shown **(see illustration 3.32a)**.

36 Reconnect the brake light switch and pedal return springs **(see illustration 3.31)**.

37 Install the footrest bracket and tighten the mounting bolt securely, then tighten the swingarm pivot bolt nut to the torque setting specified at the beginning of this Chapter.

Gearchange lever assembly

38 Remove the front sprocket cover (see Chapter 7).

39 Note the alignment between the gearchange linkage arm and the gearchange shaft – if no marks are visible, make your own **(see illustration)**.

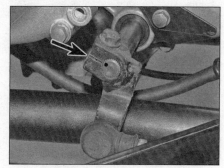

3.39 Make alignment marks as necessary

3.41 Undo the lower mounting bolt

3.42 Withdraw the pivot bolt and lift off the footrest bracket

3.43 Gearchange lever pivot bolt (arrowed)

3.44 Unscrew linkage rod from unions (arrowed)

40 Undo the linkage arm pinch bolt and ease the arm off the shaft.

41 Undo the footrest bracket lower mounting bolt **(see illustration)**.

42 Ensure the swingarm is supported, then undo the swingarm pivot bolt nut (see Section 12), withdraw the pivot bolt and lift the footrest bracket off **(see illustration)**.

43 Undo the lever pivot bolt and remove the lever assembly **(see illustration)**. Note the

location of the washer and seal between the lever and the footrest bracket. Withdraw the pivot bolt from the lever, noting the location of the seal between the pivot bolt and the lever.

44 If required, loosen the locknuts on both ends of the linkage rod and unscrew the rod from the unions on the gearchange lever and linkage arm **(see illustration)**.

45 Installation is the reverse of removal. Ensure the pivot bolt seals are in good condition and renew them if necessary. Apply a small amount of multi-purpose grease to the pivot bolt. Don't forget to install the washer and tighten the pivot bolt securely. If removed, ensure the linkage rod is screwed securely into the unions at both ends before tightening the locknuts.

46 Install the footrest bracket and tighten the mounting bolt securely, then tighten the swingarm pivot bolt to the torque setting specified at the beginning of this Chapter.

47 Align the linkage arm with the gearchange shaft **(see illustration 3.39)** then tighten the pinch bolt securely.

4 Stand

Sidestand

1 The side stand pivots on a bracket on the frame. Springs between the bracket and the stand ensure that it is held in the retracted or extended position.

2 To remove the sidestand, support the bike using the centrestand (if fitted) or an auxiliary stand. Ease the lower end of the springs off the lug on the stand, then remove the springs, noting how they fit **(see illustration)**.

3 On VT125C models, remove the front sprocket cover for access (see Chapter 7, Section 20).

4 On all models, undo the bolt securing the sidestand switch and displace the switch, noting how it fits. The switch is located either on the top of the stand pivot, or on the underside of the stand pivot **(see illustrations)**.

5 Unscrew the pivot bolt locknut, then unscrew the pivot bolt and remove the stand **(see illustration)**.

6 Inspect the stand carefully for wear and damage. Clean the stand bracket and pivot bolt and inspect them for wear – fit a new bolt if necessary.

7 Prior to installation, lubricate the bracket and pivot bolt with multi-purpose grease. Fit the stand onto the bracket and install the pivot bolt. Tighten the bolt securely, then install and tighten the locknut. Check that the stand pivots freely around the bolt.

8 Install the sidestand switch ensuring the peg on the switch locates in the hole on the stand. Tighten the switch bolt securely. Check the operation of the switch (see Chapter 1).

9 Hook the upper ends of the springs over the

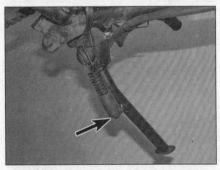

4.2 Release the lower end of the springs first

4.4a Location of sidestand switch – VT125C

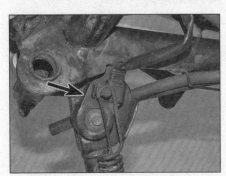

4.4b Location of sidestand switch – XL125V

4.5 Location of sidestand pivot bolt locknut

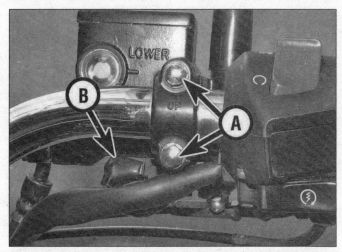

5.4 Front brake master cylinder clamp bolts (A) and light switch connectors (B)

5.7 Clutch switch wiring connectors

lug on the stand bracket, then pull the springs down carefully and hook them over the lug on the stand. It is essential that the springs are in good condition and are capable of holding the stand up when not in use – an accident is almost certain to occur if the stand extends while the machine is in motion.

Centrestand (optional equipment on XL125V-1 to V-3)

10 The centrestand pivots on a tube held between two brackets on the underside of the frame. Springs between the frame and the stand ensure that it is held in the retracted or extended position. When the stand is retracted the springs should hold a rubber cushion on the stand firmly against the underside of the frame.

11 To remove the centrestand, support the bike on its sidestand. Ease the lower end of the springs off the lug on the stand, then remove the springs, noting how they fit.

12 Straighten and remove the split pin securing the pivot tube – discard the split pin as a new one must be used.

13 Withdraw the pivot tube and remove the stand.

14 Inspect the stand carefully for wear and damage. Clean off all old grease and corrosion. Inspect the pivot tube for wear and ensure the rubber cushion on the stand is in good condition. Renew any components as necessary.

15 Prior to installation, lubricate the stand brackets on the frame and the pivot tube with multi-purpose grease. Fit the stand between the mounting brackets and slide in the retaining bolt, then secure the stand with a new split pin. Check that the stand pivots freely.

16 Install the springs. It is essential that the springs are in good condition and are capable of holding the stand up when not in use. A broken or weak spring is an obvious safety hazard.

5 Handlebars and levers

Handlebars

Note: *If required, the handlebars can be displaced without removing the switch housings, clutch lever or the front brake master cylinder.*

VT125C

1 Support the machine securely in an upright position.

2 If required, remove the fuel tank to avoid damaging its paintwork (see Chapter 4A).

3 Remove the mirrors (see Chapter 8).

4 Undo the front brake master cylinder clamp bolts and remove the back of the clamp **(see illustration)**. Disconnect the wiring connectors for the front brake light switch.

5 Secure the master cylinder assembly clear of the handlebar and ensure no strain is placed on the brake hose. Keep the fluid reservoir upright to prevent air entering the system.

6 Follow the procedure in Chapter 4A to detach the throttle cables from the twistgrip pulley, then slide the twistgrip off the handlebar. Position the switch/twistgrip housing away from the handlebar.

5.8 Clutch lever clamp bolts

7 Disconnect the wiring connectors for the clutch switch **(see illustration)**.

8 Undo the clutch lever clamp bolts and remove the back of the clamp **(see illustration)**. Secure the lever assembly clear of the handlebar.

9 Follow the procedure in Chapter 9 to separate the two halves of the left-hand switch housing and position them away from the handlebar. Note the location of the spacer inside the housing.

10 Pull the left-hand grip off the handlebar. **Note:** *The grip will probably be stuck in place – it may be necessary to slit the grip with a sharp knife in order to remove it. Slide the switch housing spacer off the handlebar.*

11 Undo the nuts securing the handlebars on the underside of the fork top yoke **(see illustration)**. Lift the handlebars off.

12 Installation is the reverse of removal, noting the following:

● Tighten the handlebar nuts to the torque setting specified at the beginning of this Chapter.

● Don't forget to install the spacer for the left-hand switch housing before fitting the handlebar grip.

● If a new left-hand grip is being fitted, secure it with a suitable adhesive.

5.11 Undo handlebar nuts on both sides

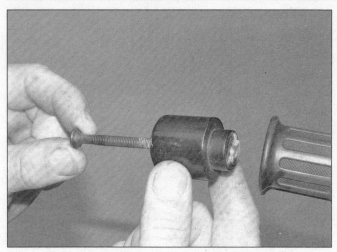

5.16 Remove the bar end-weights

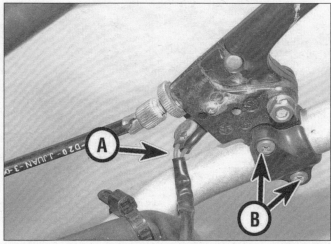

5.21 Clutch switch wiring connectors (A). Note the clamp screws (B)

● Follow the procedure in Chapter 9 to install the left-hand switch housing.
● Follow the procedure in Chapter 4A to install the right-hand switch/twistgrip housing.
● Ensure the backs of the clutch lever and front brake master cylinder clamps are installed with the UP mark facing up, and align the clamp joint with the punch mark on the top of the handlebar **(see illustration 5.4)**. Tighten the top clamp bolt first.
● Check the operation of the front brake light switch and clutch switch before riding the motorcycle.

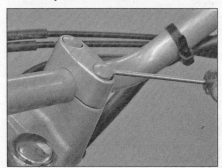

5.25a Prise out the plugs

XL125V

13 Support the machine securely in an upright position.
14 Remove the fairing (see Chapter 8). If required, remove the fuel tank to avoid damaging its paintwork (see Chapter 4A or 4B).
15 Remove the mirrors (see Chapter 8).
16 Undo the screws retaining the left and right-hand bar-end weights and draw the weight assemblies out from the ends of the handlebar, noting how they fit **(see illustration)**.
17 Undo the front brake master cylinder clamp bolts and remove the back of the clamp **(see illustration 5.4)**. Disconnect the wiring connectors for the front brake light switch.
18 Secure the master cylinder assembly clear of the handlebar and ensure no strain is placed on the brake hose. Keep the fluid reservoir upright to prevent air entering the system.
19 Follow the procedure in Chapter 4A to detach the throttle cables from the twistgrip pulley. Slide the twistgrip off the handlebar.
20 Follow the procedure in Chapter 9 to separate the two halves of the right-hand switch housing and position them away from the handlebar.
21 Follow the procedure in Chapter 9 to

separate the two halves of the left-hand switch housing and position them away from the handlebar. Disconnect the wiring connectors for the clutch switch **(see illustration)**.
22 Undo the clutch lever clamp bolts or clamp screws as fitted, and remove the back of the clamp **(see illustration 5.21)**. Secure the lever assembly clear of the handlebar.
23 Pull the left-hand grip off the handlebar. **Note:** *The grip will probably be stuck in place – it may be necessary to slit the grip with a sharp knife in order to remove it.*
24 Release any ties securing the wiring to the handlebars
25 Prise out the plugs in the tops of the handlebar clamp bolts **(see illustration)**. Loosen the clamp bolts, then support the handlebars and remove the clamps **(see illustration)**. Lift the handlebars off.
26 Installation is the reverse of removal, noting the following:
● Align the punch mark on the handlebars with the mating surface of the left-hand bracket **(see illustration)**.
● Install the handlebar clamps with the punch marks at the front **(see illustration)**.
● Tighten the clamp bolts to the torque setting specified at the beginning of this Chapter.

5.25b Remove the handlebar clamps

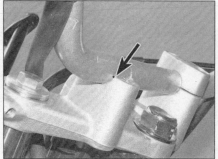

5.26a Align punch mark with mating surface of bracket

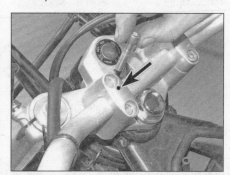

5.26b Handlebar clamp with punch mark at front

5.26c Align clamp joint with punch mark

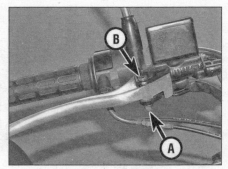

5.27 Locknut (A) and lever pivot (B)

5.29 Unscrew the clutch lever pivot locknut

- If a new left-hand grip is being fitted, secure it with a suitable adhesive.
- Follow the procedure in Chapter 9 to install the left and right-hand switch housings.
- On XL125V-1 to V-6 models, ensure the back of the clutch lever clamp is installed with the UP mark facing up, and align the clamp joint with the punch mark on the top of the handlebar (see illustration 5.8). Tighten the top clamp bolt first.
- On XL125V-7 models onward, align the clutch lever clamp joint with the punch mark on the back of the handlebar. Tighten the front clamp screw first.
- Follow the procedure in Chapter 4A to connect the throttle cables from the twistgrip pulley.
- Connect the front brake light switch wiring connectors.
- Ensure the back of the front brake master cylinder clamp is installed with the UP mark facing up, and align the clamp joint with the punch mark on the top of the handlebar (see illustration). Tighten the top clamp bolt first, then tighten the lower bolt to the torque setting specified at the beginning of this Chapter.
- Check the operation of the front brake light switch and clutch switch before riding the motorcycle.

Levers

27 To remove the front brake lever, first undo the lever pivot locknut, then unscrew the pivot and remove the lever (see illustration).
28 To remove the clutch lever, first follow the procedure in Chapter 2, Section 8, to disconnect the cable from the lever.
29 Undo the locknut on the underside of the lever (see illustration), then unscrew the pivot and remove the lever.
30 Installation is the reverse of removal, noting the following.

- Apply silicone grease to the contact area between the front brake master cylinder pushrod tip and the brake lever.
- Apply multi-purpose grease to the pivot shafts and the contact areas between the levers and their brackets.
- Tighten the pivots securely first, then tighten the locknuts. Check the operation of the levers.
- Adjust clutch cable freeplay (see Chapter 1).

6 Fork removal and installation

Removal

1 On XL125V models, remove the fairing (see Chapter 8).
2 On all models, remove the front wheel and secure the brake caliper to the machine so that it is clear of the front forks (see Chapter 7). On XL125V-1 to V-6 models (except Type IIG German market models) note how the speed sensor wiring is secured to the left-hand fork outer tube and the front mudguard and release it from the clips (see illustration).
3 Remove the front mudguard (see Chapter 8).
4 Note the routing of the cables, hose and wiring around the fork legs.
5 Working on one fork leg at a time, loosen the fork clamp bolt in the top yoke (see illustrations). If the fork is to be disassembled, or if the fork oil is being changed, loosen the fork top bolt now (see illustration). Note the alignment between the top of the fork inner tube and the top surface of the yoke.

6.2 Release the speed sensor wiring from the clips

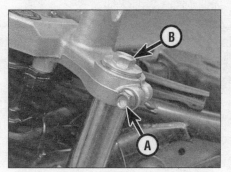

6.5a Fork clamp bolt – VT125C

6.5b Fork clamp bolt (A) and fork top bolt (B) – XL125V

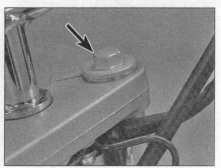

6.5c Fork top bolt – VT125C

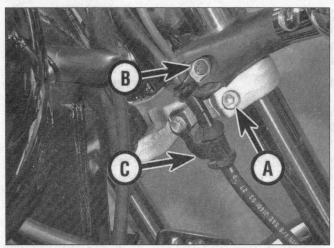

6.6a Bottom yoke clamp bolt (A), turn signal stem pinch bolt (B) and brake hose guide (C) – VT125C

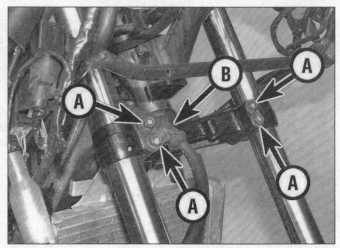

6.6b Bottom yoke clamp bolts (A) and brake hose guide (B) – XL125V

6 Loosen the fork clamp bolt(s) in the bottom yoke and, on VT125C models, loosen the turn signal stem pinch bolt (see illustrations).

7 Remove the fork by twisting it and pulling it down (see illustration).

HAYNES HiNT If the fork legs are seized in the yokes, spray the area with penetrating oil and allow time for it to soak in before trying again.

Installation

8 Remove all traces of corrosion from the fork inner tube and the yokes. Make sure you install the fork legs the correct way round – the right-hand fork outer tube has the lugs to carry the brake caliper.

9 Slide the fork leg up through the bottom yoke and into the top yoke, making sure all cables, hoses and wiring are routed on the correct side of the tube. Make sure the top of the fork inner tube is correctly aligned with the top surface of the yoke (see illustrations 6.5b and c) then tighten the clamp bolt(s) in the bottom yoke to the torque setting specified at the beginning of this Chapter (see illustrations 6.6a and b).

10 If the fork leg has been dismantled or if the fork oil was changed, tighten the top bolt to the specified torque setting (see illustrations 6.5b and c).

11 Tighten the clamp bolt in the top yoke to the specified torque setting (see illustrations 6.5a and b).

12 On VT125C models, tighten the turn signal stem pinch bolt (see illustration 6.6a).

13 Install the remaining components in the reverse order of removal.

14 Check the operation of the front forks and brake before riding the motorcycle.

7 Fork oil change

1 After a high mileage the fork oil will deteriorate and its damping and lubrication qualities will be impaired. Always change the oil in both fork legs.

2 Follow the procedure in Section 6 to remove the fork legs, ensuring the top bolts are loosened while the legs are still clamped in the bottom yoke.

3 Working on one fork leg at a time, support the leg in an upright position and unscrew the top bolt (see illustration). Note: *The bolt is under pressure from the fork spring so use a ratchet tool that does not need to be removed from the bolt as you unscrew it. Maintain some downward pressure on the bolt, particularly as you come to the end of the threads.*

6.7 Removing the fork leg

7.3 Unscrew the fork top bolt

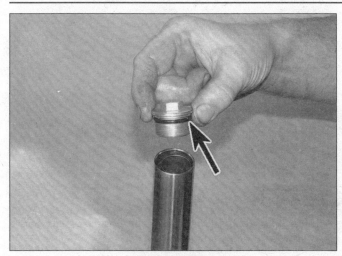

7.4 Note location of the O-ring

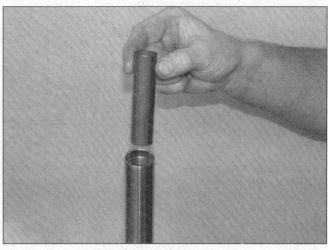

7.5a Remove the spacer . . .

4 Note the location of the O-ring on the top bolt and discard it as a new one must be fitted **(see illustration)**.

5 Compress the fork inner tube down into the outer tube and remove the spacer, the spring seat and spring **(see illustrations)**. Note which way up the spring is fitted. Wipe any excess oil off the spring.

6 Invert the fork leg over a suitable container and pump the fork to expel as much oil as possible **(see illustration)**. Support the fork upside down in the container and allow it to drain for a few minutes. If the oil contains metal particles inspect the internal components for wear (see Section 8).

7 Hold the fork leg upright and slowly pour in the specified quantity of the correct grade of fork oil (see Specifications at the beginning of this Chapter). Pump the fork up-and-down several times to expel any trapped air, then compress the inner tube fully and measure the oil level to the top of the tube **(see illustration)**. Add or subtract oil until it is at the level specified at the beginning of this Chapter.

8 Pull the inner tube up and install the spring with its closer-wound coils at the bottom **(see illustration 7.5c)**.

9 Install the spring seat and the spacer **(see illustration 7.5b and a)**.

10 Fit a new O-ring into the groove in the top bolt and lubricate it with a smear of fork oil, then thread the bolt into the fork tube, compressing the spring as you do. Keep downward pressure on the spring and ensure the bolt is not cross-threaded **(see illustration 7.3)**. The bolt can be tightened fully to the specified torque setting once the leg has been installed and is securely held in the bottom yoke (see Section 6).

7.5b . . . the spring seat . . .

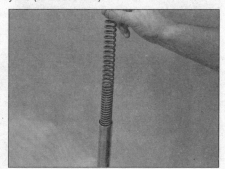

7.5c . . . and spring

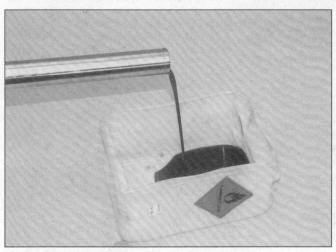

7.6 Pump out as much oil as possible

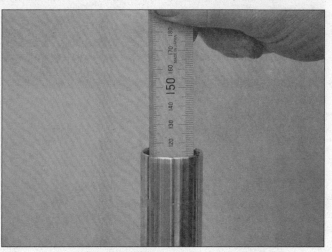

7.7 Measure the oil level to the top of the tube

8 Fork overhaul

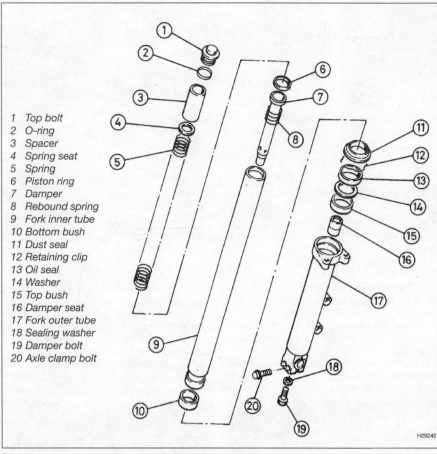

1 Top bolt
2 O-ring
3 Spacer
4 Spring seat
5 Spring
6 Piston ring
7 Damper
8 Rebound spring
9 Fork inner tube
10 Bottom bush
11 Dust seal
12 Retaining clip
13 Oil seal
14 Washer
15 Top bush
16 Damper seat
17 Fork outer tube
18 Sealing washer
19 Damper bolt
20 Axle clamp bolt

8.2 Front fork components

Disassembly

1 Follow the procedure in Section 6 to remove the fork legs, ensuring the top bolts are loosened while the legs are still clamped in the bottom yoke.

2 Always dismantle the fork legs separately to avoid interchanging parts. Store all components in separate, clearly marked containers **(see illustration)**.

3 Start by loosening the damper bolt in the underside of the outer tube **(see illustration)**. To prevent the damper from turning inside the leg, hold the fork leg upside-down and compress it so that the spring exerts maximum pressure on the damper. If the bolt will not loosen, or the damper turns inside the leg, try again once the spring has been removed (see Step 5). Alternatively, use an air-wrench if available.

4 Follow the procedure in Section 7 to unscrew the top bolt and remove the spacer, the spring seat and spring, then drain the oil out of the fork leg.

5 Remove the previously loosed damper bolt and its sealing washer **(see illustration)**. Discard the sealing washer as a new one must be used. If the damper bolt was not loosed earlier, insert a length of wood doweling, tapered on the end to engage the head of the damper, into the fork leg. Press the leg down onto the doweling and undo the bolt.

6 Tip the damper and rebound spring out of the fork leg **(see illustration)**.

7 Carefully prise out the dust seal from the top of the outer tube **(see illustration)**. Discard the seal as a new one must be used.

8 Remove the oil seal retaining clip, taking care not to scratch the surface of the inner tube **(see illustration)**.

9 To separate the inner tube from the outer tube it is necessary to displace the top bush and oil seal **(see illustration 8.2)**. The bottom bush will not pass through the top bush, and this can be used to good effect. Compress the fork leg fully, then pull the tubes sharply apart so that the bottom bush strikes the top

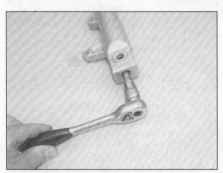

8.3 Loosen the damper bolt

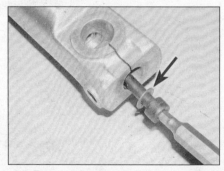

8.5 Remove the damper bolt and sealing washer

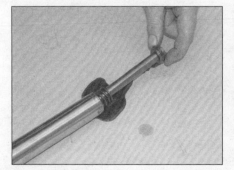

8.6 Tip out the damper and rebound spring

8.7 Prise out the dust seal

8.8 Remove the oil seal retaining clip

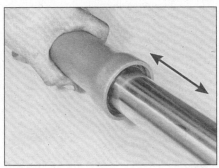

8.9 Pull the fork tubes apart to drive out the top bush

8.10 Slide off the oil seal (A), washer (B) and top bush (C). Note location of bottom bush (D)

8.11 Tip out the damper seat

bush. Repeat this operation until the top bush and seal are tapped out of the outer tube and the two tubes can be separated **(see illustration)**.

10 Slide the oil seal, washer and top bush off the inner tube, noting which way up the seal is fitted **(see illustration)**. Discard the seal as a new one must be used.

Caution: Do not remove the bottom bush from the tube unless it is to be renewed.

11 Tip the damper seat out of the outer tube, noting which way up it fits **(see illustration)**.

Inspection

12 Clean all parts in solvent and blow them dry with compressed air, if available. Check the inner tube for score marks, scratches, flaking of the chrome finish and excessive or abnormal wear. Look for dents in the tube and replace the tube in both forks if any are found. Check the fork seal seat for nicks, gouges and scratches. If damage is evident, leaks will occur. Also check the oil seal washer for damage or distortion and renew it if necessary.

13 Check the inner tube for runout using V-blocks and a dial gauge, or have it done by a Honda dealer. If the amount of runout exceeds the service limit specified, the tube should be renewed.

 Warning: If the tube is bent or exceeds the runout limit, it should not be straightened; replace it with a new one.

14 Check the spring for cracks and other damage. Measure the spring free length and

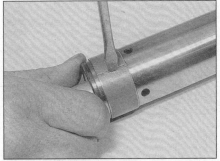

8.15 Prise the bush apart and slide it off

compare the result to the specification at the beginning of this Chapter. If either fork spring is defective or has sagged below the service limit, replace both springs with new ones. Never renew only one spring. Also check the rebound spring.

15 Examine the working surfaces of the two bushes; if worn or scuffed they must be renewed. To remove the bottom bush from the fork leg, prise it apart at the slit using a flat-bladed screwdriver and slide it off **(see illustration)**. Make sure the new bush seats properly.

16 Check the damper and its piston ring for damage and wear, and renew them if necessary **(see illustration)**. Do not remove the ring from the piston unless it requires renewal

Reassembly

17 If removed, install the new piston ring into the groove in the damper, then slide

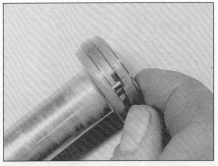

8.16 Examine the damper and piston ring

the rebound spring onto the damper **(see illustration)**. Insert the damper into the top of the inner tube and slide it down so that it projects fully from the bottom of the tube, then install the damper seat **(see illustration)**.

18 Lubricate the inner tube and bottom bush with fork oil, then insert the assembly into the outer tube.

19 Clean the threads of the damper bolt and apply a few drops of a suitable non-permanent thread-locking compound. Fit a new sealing washer to the damper bolt, then install the bolt into the bottom of the outer tube and tighten it to the torque setting specified at the beginning of this Chapter. If the damper rotates inside the tube, hold it with spring pressure or a wooden dowel as on disassembly (see Steps 3 and 5).

20 Compress the fork leg fully, then oil the top bush and slide it down the inner tube **(see illustration)**. Press the bush squarely into

8.17a Slide the rebound spring onto the damper

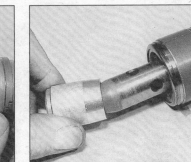

8.17b Install the damper seat

8.20a Install the top bush . . .

8.20b . . . and the washer

8.21a Install the oil seal . . .

8.21b . . . and secure it with the clip

8.22 Press the dust seal into place

its recess in the outer tube, then install the washer **(see illustration)**. If necessary, use a pin punch to tap the washer and bush down until the bush is seated.

21 Lubricate the inside of the new oil seal with fork oil and slide it down the inner tube with its markings facing upwards **(see illustration)**. Press the seal into the outer tube until the retaining clip groove is visible above the seal, then fit the retaining clip **(see illustration)**. If required, Honda provides a service tool (Part Nos. 07747-0010100 and 07945-4150400)

for installing the oil seals. Alternatively, use a piece of tubing slightly larger in diameter than the inner tube and slightly smaller in diameter than the bush recess in the outer tube. Take care not to scratch the fork inner tube during this operation; if the fork inner tube is pushed fully into the outer tube any accidental scratching will be confined to the area above the oil seal.

22 Lubricate the inside of the new dust seal then slide it down the inner tube and press it into position **(see illustration)**.

23 Follow the procedure in Section 7 to fill the fork with the specified quantity of oil, then install the spring, spring seat, spacer and top bolt.

24 Follow the procedure in Section 6 to install the fork legs.

9 Steering stem

Removal

Special tool: *A peg spanner is described in Step 15 for tightening the bearing adjuster nut*

to the specified torque setting. Note, however, that the procedure can be accomplished without the tool.

1 Follow the procedure in Section 6 to remove the front fork legs.

2 Undo the bolt(s) securing the front brake hose guide to the bottom yoke **(see illustration 6.6a or b)**.

3 Remove the fuel tank (see Chapter 4A or 4B) and remove or displace the handlebars (see Section 5).

4 On VT125C models, displace the turn signal assemblies from the bottom fork yoke, then undo the nut securing the headlight and displace the headlight (see Chapter 9). Undo the bolts securing the cable guide to the underside of the top yoke **(see illustration)**.

5 On XL125V models, if the top yoke is being removed from the bike rather than just being displaced, trace the wiring from the ignition switch on the underside of the yoke, free it from the wiring boot and disconnect it at the connector **(see illustration)**. Feed the wiring through to the yoke, noting its routing.

6 Unscrew the steering stem nut and remove

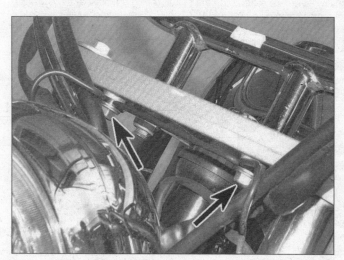

9.4 Location of cable guide bolts

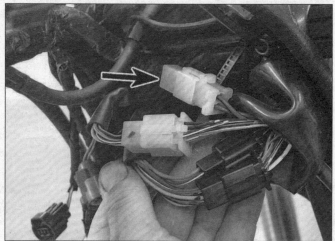

9.5 Disconnect the ignition switch wiring connector

the washer **(see illustration)**. Lift the top yoke up off the steering stem **(see illustration)**.

7 Support the bottom yoke and unscrew the bearing adjuster using a C-spanner if required **(see illustrations)**.

8 Lift off the adjuster and cover and the bearing upper inner race **(see illustrations)**.

9 Lower the steering stem out of the steering head **(see illustration)**.

10 The steering head bearings are caged ball bearings – the lower caged bearing will remain on the steering stem and the upper bearing will be in the upper outer race on the steering head. Remove all traces of old grease from the bearings and races using a suitable solvent, then check them for wear or damage as described in Section 10.

Installation

11 Apply a liberal quantity of lithium-based multi-purpose grease (with NLGI 2) to the bearing races in the frame and on the steering stem. Work the grease well into both the upper and lower bearing cages and install the lower bearing on the steering stem.

12 Lubricate the threads of the bearing adjuster with engine oil.

13 Lift the steering stem up through the steering head and install the upper bearing **(see illustration)**.

14 Install the upper inner race, pressing it firmly into the bearing, then thread the adjuster and cover onto the stem and tighten it finger-tight **(see illustrations 9.8b and a)**.

15 If the Honda service tool (Part No. 07916-3710101) or a suitable peg spanner

9.6a Remove the steering stem nut and washer . . .

9.6b . . . and lift off the top yoke

9.7a Unscrew the bearing adjuster . . .

9.7b . . . using a C-spanner if required

and a torque wrench are available, tighten the adjuster to the initial torque setting specified at the beginning of this Chapter **(see illustrations)**. Turn the steering stem through its full lock at least five times to

settle the bearings, then slacken the adjuster completely. Tighten the adjuster to the final torque setting, then turn it 45° anti-clockwise.

16 If the special tools are not available, a peg spanner can be made by cutting castellations

9.8a Remove the adjuster and cover . . .

9.8b . . . and the bearing upper inner race

9.9 Lower the steering stem out

9.13 Install the upper bearing

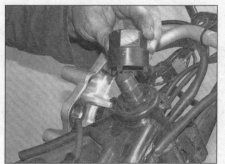

9.15a Using a peg spanner . . .

9.15b . . . and torque wrench

9.16 A peg spanner can be made by cutting castellations into an old socket

into an old socket **(see illustration)**. Alternatively, tighten the adjuster using a C-spanner so that bearing play is eliminated but the steering is able to move freely from lock-to-lock, then slacken the nut so that it is loose. Now tighten it lightly – the nut must be literally on the point of being loose.
Caution: Take great care not to apply excessive pressure because this will cause premature failure of the bearings.
17 Fit the top yoke onto the steering stem **(see illustration 9.6b)**. Fit the steering stem nut with its washer and tighten it finger-tight **(see illustration 9.6a)**. Temporarily install one of the fork legs to align the top and bottom yokes, and secure it by tightening the bottom yoke clamp bolt(s) only (see Section 6). Now tighten the steering stem nut to the torque setting specified at the beginning of the Chapter **(see illustration)**.
18 Install the remaining components in the reverse of the removal.

10.4b . . . the lower inner race and bearing . . .

10.4d . . . and the lower outer race

9.17 Tightening the steering stem nut to the specified torque

19 Recheck the steering head bearing adjustment as described in Chapter 1.

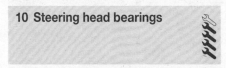

10 Steering head bearings

Note: *Do not attempt to remove the outer races from the steering head or the lower inner race from the steering stem unless they are to be renewed.*

Inspection

1 Remove the steering stem (see Section 9).
2 Remove the upper caged bearing from the upper outer race on the steering head and lift the lower caged bearing off the steering stem, noting how they fit.
3 Remove all traces of old grease from the bearings and races using a suitable solvent,

10.4c . . . the upper outer race . . .

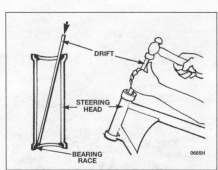

10.6 Drive the bearing outer races out with a brass drift as shown

10.4a Examine the upper inner race and bearing . . .

then inspect them for wear or damage.
4 The inner and outer races should be polished and free from indentations **(see illustrations)**. The bearing balls should be polished and free from signs of wear, pitting or discoloration. Examine the bearing ball retainer cage for cracks or splits.
5 If there are any signs of wear on any of the bearing components, both upper and lower bearing assemblies must be renewed as a set. **Note:** *Once the outer races in the steering head and the lower bearing inner race have been removed they should be discarded – do not reuse them.*

Renewal

6 The outer races are an interference fit in the steering head – tap them from position using a suitable drift located on the exposed inner lip of the race **(see illustration)**. Tap firmly and evenly around each race to ensure that it is driven out squarely. Curve the end of the drift slightly to improve access if necessary.
7 Alternatively, remove the outer races using a bearing puller with slide-hammer attachment (see *Tools and Workshop Tips* in the *Reference* section).
8 Install the new outer races using a drawbolt arrangement **(see illustration)**. Ensure the

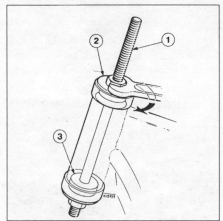

10.8 Drawbolt arrangement for fitting steering head bearing outer races

1 Long bolt or threaded bar
2 Thick washer
3 Guide for lower outer race

HAYNES HiNT *Installation of new outer races is easier if the races are left overnight in the freezer. This causes them to contract slightly making them a looser fit. Alternatively, use a freeze spray.*

drawbolt washer rests only on the outer edge of the race and does not contact the bearing surface. Ensure both races are drawn all the way into their seats.

9 To remove the lower inner race from the steering stem, use two screwdrivers placed on opposite sides to work it free, using blocks of wood to improve leverage and protect the yoke, or tap under it using a cold chisel **(see illustrations)**. If you use a cold chisel, fit the steering stem nut to protect the threads on the end of the stem. If the race is firmly in place it will be necessary to use a puller **(see illustration)**, or split the race using an angle grinder – be very careful not to gouge the steering stem

10 Remove the dust seal from the bottom of the stem and replace it with a new one. Note the location of the washer underneath the seal.

11 Fit the new lower inner race onto the steering stem. Tap the new race into position using a length of tubing with an internal diameter slightly larger than the steering stem **(see illustration)**. Ensure that the drift rests only on the inner edge of the race and does not contact the bearing surface.

12 Install the steering stem (see Section 9).

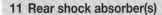

11 Rear shock absorber(s)

⚠ *Warning: Do not attempt to disassemble the shock absorber(s) – no individual components are available. Improper disassembly could result in serious injury.*

VT125C

Removal

1 Support the machine securely in an upright position. Position a support under the rear wheel so that it does not drop when the shock absorbers are removed, but also making sure that the weight of the machine is off the rear suspension so that the shocks are not compressed.

2 Unscrew the upper shock absorber mounting bolt and washer **(see illustration)**.

3 Unscrew the lower shock absorber mounting bolt, pull the shock towards the rear of the bike so that it is free of the lower mounting bracket, and then pull it off the upper mounting bracket **(see illustrations)**.

Inspection

4 Inspect the shock absorbers for obvious physical damage and oil leakage. Check the springs for looseness, cracks or signs of

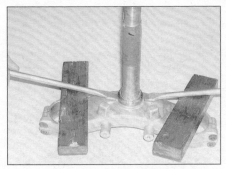

10.9a Removing the lower inner race using screwdrivers

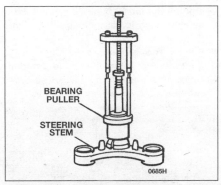

10.9c Set-up for removing the lower race with a puller

fatigue, and inspect the damper rods for signs of wear, corrosion or pitting **(see illustration)**. If either shock absorber is in any way faulty, renew both shocks as a pair.

11.2 Unscrew the upper shock mounting bolt and washer

11.3b Pull the shock off the upper bracket

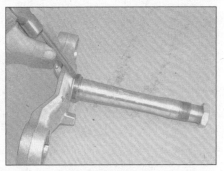

10.9b Removing the lower inner race with a cold chisel

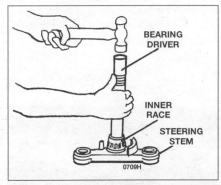

10.11 Set-up for installing the lower inner race

5 Ensure that the spring pre-load adjusters are clean and free from corrosion. Using the C-spanner from the bike's toolkit, check that the adjusters move freely.

11.3a Unscrew the lower shock mounting bolt

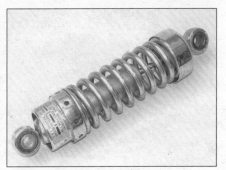

11.4 Examine the shock for damage and corrosion

11.10 Remove the lower shock mounting bolt

11.11a Remove the trim clip . . .

11.11b . . . by unscrewing the centre

6 Inspect the bushes in the upper and lower shock absorber mounts for wear or damage and renew them if necessary.

Installation

7 Installation is the reverse of removal, noting the following:

11.12a Counter-hold the bolt . . .

11.12c Withdraw the bolt . . .

* Tighten the mounting bolts to the torque settings specified at the beginning of this Chapter.
* Follow the procedure in Chapter 1, Section 8, to adjust the spring pre-load. **Note:** *Always ensure both shock absorber pre-load adjusters are adjusted equally.*

11.12b . . . and undo the nut

11.12d . . . and lift the shock out

XL125V

Removal

8 Remove the seat and the side panels (see Chapter 8).

9 Remove the rear wheel (see Chapter 7).

10 Unscrew the nut and withdraw the bolt securing the bottom of the shock absorber to the swingarm **(see illustration)**.

11 To access the bolt securing the top of the shock absorber, unscrew the centre of the trim clip securing the cover to the left-hand side of the frame, pull out the trim clip and displace the cover **(see illustrations)**.

12 Counter-hold the bolt on the left-hand side and undo the nut securing the top of the shock **(see illustrations)**. Support the shock, then withdraw the bolt and lift the shock out **(see illustrations)**.

Inspection

13 Inspect the shock absorber for obvious physical damage and oil leakage. Check the spring for looseness, cracks or signs of fatigue **(see illustration)**.

14 Ensure that the spring pre-load adjuster is clean and free from corrosion. Using the C-spanner from the bike's toolkit, check that the adjuster moves freely.

15 Inspect the bush in the upper shock mount for wear or damage **(see illustration)**. If required, replace the bush with a new one.

16 Withdraw the sleéve from the lower shock mount and inspect the needle bearing **(see illustration)**. If required, prise out the bearing seals and remove all traces of old

11.13 Examine the shock for damage and corrosion

11.15 Check the bush in the upper shock mount

11.16a Inspect the needle bearing in the lower shock mount

11.16b Prise out the bearing seals

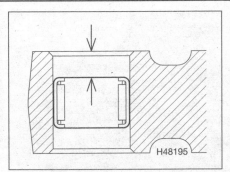

11.17 Rear shock absorber needle bearing installed depth 7.8 to 8.2 mm

12.1 Withdraw the chain adjusters from the swingarm

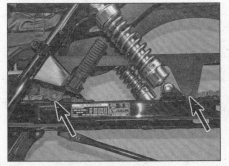

12.2a Undo the bolts . . .

12.2b . . . release the clip . . .

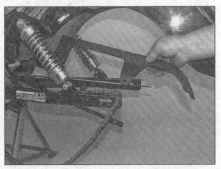

12.2c . . . and remove the chainguard

grease from the bearing **(see illustration)**. Discard the seals as new ones must be used.

17 If the bearing sleeve or the needle rollers are worn, corroded or pitted, a new bearing must be fitted. Drive or press out the old bearing (see *Tools and Workshop Tips* in the *Reference* section). Ensure the bearing housing is clean, then lubricate the housing with a smear of grease and press the new bearing in to the depth shown **(see illustration)**.

18 Lubricate the bearing and sleeve with lithium-based grease.

19 Lubricate the new seals with a smear of grease and press them into place.

Installation

20 Installation is the reverse of removal, noting the following:

● Apply multi-purpose grease to the shock absorber bolts.

● Tighten the bolts to the torque setting specified at the beginning of this Chapter.

● Follow the procedure in Chapter 1, Section 8, to adjust the spring pre-load.

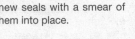

12 Swingarm

VT125C

Removal

1 Remove the rear wheel (see Chapter 7). Note the location of the chain adjusters and remove them for safekeeping **(see illustration)**.

2 Undo the bolts securing the chainguard, unclip the chainguard from the swingarm and lift it off **(see illustrations)**.

3 Remove the shock absorbers (see Section 11).

4 Disconnect the rear brake rod return spring from the lug on the swingarm **(see illustration)**.

5 At this point, if required, check the swingarm bearings as follows. Grasp the rear of the swingarm with one hand and place your other hand at the junction of the swingarm and the frame. Try to move the rear of the swingarm from side-to-side. Any wear (play) in the bearings should be felt as movement between the swingarm and the frame at the front. If there is any play the swingarm will be felt to move forward and backward at the front (not from side-to-side). Next, move the swingarm up and down through its full travel **(see illustration)**. It should move freely, without any binding or rough spots.

6 Undo the nut on the right-hand end of the swingarm pivot bolt, then support the swingarm and withdraw the bolt and lift the swingarm out **(see illustrations)**.

12.4 Unhook the return spring

12.5 Checking for play in the swingarm bearings

12.6a Undo the nut . . .

12.6b ... and withdraw the pivot bolt

12.7a Press the pivot shaft ...

12.7b ... out from the frame ...

12.7c ... and disconnect the brake light switch spring

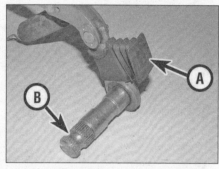

12.7d Examine the shaft stop (A), splines (B) ...

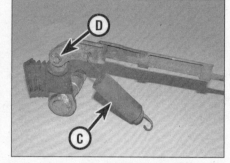

12.7e ... and return spring (C). Note pivot pin (D)

7 If required, disconnect the rear brake linkage arm from the pivot shaft (see Section 3). Press the pivot shaft out from the frame, disconnect the brake light switch spring and remove the brake rod and pivot shaft assembly (see illustrations). Clean all traces of old grease

from the pivot shaft and remove any corrosion with wire wool. Examine the shaft stop, the splines on the end of the shaft and the return spring and renew any parts that are worn or damaged (see illustration). To separate the rod from the pivot shaft, straighten and

remove the split pin, then pull out the pivot pin (see illustration). Use a new split pin on reassembly.

Inspection

8 Thoroughly clean the swingarm, removing all traces of dirt, corrosion and grease.

9 If required, undo the screws securing the drive chain slider and lift it off, noting how it fits (see illustrations).

10 If required, straighten and remove the split pin, then undo the nut on the shouldered bolt securing the rear brake torque arm to the underside of the swingarm. Remove the plain washer and the spring washer, then withdraw the bolt and remove the torque arm, noting how it locates between the two halves of its mounting bracket. Discard the split pin as a new one must be used.

11 Temporarily install the swingarm pivot bolt, the chain adjusters and the rear axle. Lay the swingarm on the work surface and support it so that the pivot bolt is level (check this with a spirit level), then check the level of the axle. If the axle is not level, the swingarm is out of true and must be renewed.

12 Check the pivot bolt for straightness by rolling it on a flat surface such as a piece of plate glass (first wipe off all old grease and remove any corrosion using wire wool). If the equipment is available, place the bolt in V-blocks and measure the runout using a dial gauge. If the bolt is bent or the runout excessive, or if it shows signs of wear, it must be renewed.

13 Pull the seals off both sides of the bearing housings and withdraw the bearing sleeves (see illustrations).

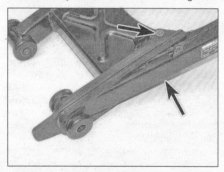

12.9a Screws secure top and bottom of chain slider

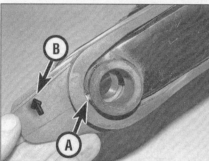

12.9b Note mounting lug (A) and wear limit arrow (B)

12.13a Pull off the seals ...

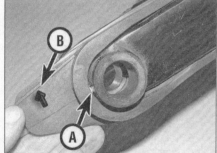

12.13b ... and withdraw the bearing sleeves

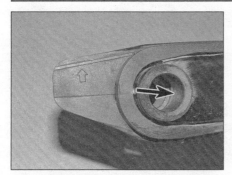

12.14 Examine the bushes (arrowed) for wear

12.23 Position swingarm between top and bottom runs of the chain

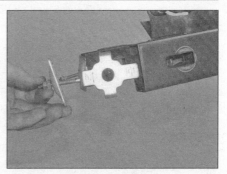

12.26 Withdraw the chain adjusters from the swingarm

14 Remove all traces of old grease from the bearing sleeves and the bushes inside the swingarm pivots and examine them for wear **(see illustration)**. If any components are worn, renew the sleeves and bushes as a set.

15 The bushes are an interference fit in the swingarm pivots – tap them from position using a suitable drift located on the exposed inner lip of the bush. Tap firmly and evenly around each bush to ensure that it is driven out squarely. Curve the end of the drift slightly to improve access if necessary.

16 Alternatively, remove the bushes using a bearing puller with slide-hammer attachment (see *Tools and Workshop Tips* in the *Reference* section).

17 Install the new bushes using a drawbolt arrangement **(see illustration 10.8)**. Install the bushes in pairs, ensuring both bushes are drawn all the way into their seats.

18 Examine the chain adjusters for wear and damage – they should be a sliding fit inside the ends of the swingarm **(see illustration 12.1)**. Ensure the threads, adjuster nuts and locknuts are in good condition

Installation

19 If removed, install the chain slider ensuring the directional arrow is pointing UP **(see illustrations 12.9b and a)**.

20 If removed, install the rear brake torque arm, locating the end of the arm between the two halves of its mounting bracket. Apply a smear of grease to the shouldered bolt, then fit the bolt from the inside of the bracket. Fit the spring washer, plain washer and nut on the outside of the bracket and tighten the nut securely. Secure the nut with a new split pin.

21 Lubricate the swingarm bushes and bearing sleeves with lithium-based grease and install the bushes **(see illustration 12.13b)**.

22 Apply a smear of grease to the inside of the seals and install them on the bearing housings **(see illustration 12.13a)**.

23 Apply a smear of grease to the pivot bolt. Position the swingarm in the frame

12.27a Undo the bolt . . .

between the pivot bolt lugs and install the pivot bolt from the left-hand side – if the drive chain is in place on the front sprocket, don't forget to position the swingarm between the top and bottom runs of the chain as it is manoeuvred into the frame **(see illustration)**.

24 Counter-hold the pivot bolt and tighten the pivot bolt nut to the torque setting specified at the beginning of this Chapter.

25 Install the remaining components in the reverse order of removal.

XL125V

Removal

26 Remove the rear wheel (see Chapter 7). Note the location of the chain adjusters

12.28a Prise off the covers . . .

12.27b . . . and displace the rear brake caliper

and remove them for safekeeping **(see illustration)**.

27 Undo the bolt securing the brake hose guide to the swingarm, then displace the rear brake caliper assembly and secure it clear of the swingarm **(see illustrations)**.

28 Prise off the swingarm pivot bolt covers, then undo the swingarm pivot bolt nut **(see illustrations)**.

29 Undo the right-hand footrest bracket lower mounting bolt and lift the bracket off **(see illustration 3.30)**.

30 Remove the shock absorber (see Section 11).

31 Undo the left-hand footrest bracket lower mounting bolt **(see illustration 3.41)**.

32 Ensure the swingarm is supported, then withdraw the pivot bolt and remove the footrest bracket **(see illustration 3.42)**.

12.28b . . . and undo the pivot bolt nut

12.33 Lift out the swingarm

12.35a Screws secure top and bottom of chain slider

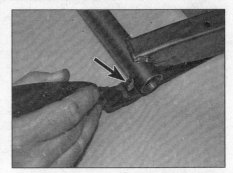

12.35b Note mounting lug (arrowed)

33 Lift the swingarm out **(see illustration)**.

Inspection

34 Thoroughly clean the swingarm, removing all traces of dirt, corrosion and grease.

35 If required, undo the screws securing the drive chain slider, noting the location of the collars, and lift the slider off, noting how it fits **(see illustrations)**.

36 Temporarily install the chain adjusters and the rear axle. Lay the swingarm on the work surface and support it so that the pivot bolt tube is level (check this with a spirit level), then check the level of the axle. If the axle is not level, the swingarm is out of true and must be renewed.

12.38a Pull off the seals . . .

12.39 Examine the bearings (arrowed) for wear

37 Check the pivot bolt for straightness (see Step 12).

38 Pull the seals off both ends of the pivot bolt tube and withdraw the bearing sleeve **(see illustrations)**.

39 Remove all traces of old grease from the bearing sleeve and the needle bearings in both ends of the tube and examine them for wear **(see illustration)**. If any components are worn renew the sleeve and bearings as a set.

40 Refer to *Tools and Workshop Tips* in the *Reference* section and remove the bearings using a bearing puller with slide-hammer attachment.

41 Ensure the bearing housings are clean, then lubricate them with a smear of grease.

12.38b . . . and withdraw the bearing sleeve

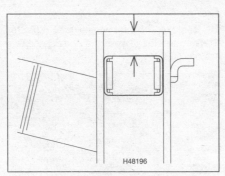

12.41 Swingarm needle bearing installed depth 7.5 mm

Install the new bearings using a drawbolt arrangement **(see illustration 10.8)**. Install the bearings one at a time, using a suitably-sized socket that bears on the outer edge of the bearing cage. Ensure the bearings are drawn in squarely to the depth shown **(see illustration)**.

42 Examine the chain adjusters for wear and damage – they should be a sliding fit inside the ends of the swingarm. Ensure the threads, adjuster nuts and locknuts are in good condition **(see illustration 12.26)**.

Installation

43 If removed, install the chain slider **(see illustrations 12.35b and a)**.

44 Lubricate the needle bearings and sleeve with lithium-based grease and install the sleeve **(see illustration 12.39 and 38b)**.

45 Apply a smear of grease to the inside of the seals and install them on the ends of the tube **(see illustration 12.38a)**.

46 Apply a smear of grease to the pivot bolt. Support the swingarm in the frame between the pivot bolt lugs. If the drive chain is in place on the front sprocket, don't forget to position the swingarm between the top and bottom runs of the chain as it is manoeuvred into the frame.

47 Assemble the left-hand footrest bracket on the pivot bolt, then slide the pivot bolt through the frame and swingarm pivot tube **(see illustration 3.42)**. Ensure the pivot bolt is pressed all the way through the right-hand frame lug.

48 Install the shock absorber (see Section 11).

49 Fit the rear brake caliper assembly onto the swingarm and secure the brake hose guide **(see illustrations 12.27b and a)**.

50 Install the right-hand footrest bracket and secure it with the lower mounting bolt **(see illustration 3.30)**.

51 Counter-hold the pivot bolt and tighten the pivot bolt nut to the torque setting specified at the beginning of this Chapter. Install the pivot bolt covers.

52 Install the remaining components in the reverse order of removal.

Chapter 7
Brakes, wheels and final drive

Contents Section

Degrees of difficulty

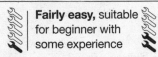

Easy, suitable for novice with little experience	**Fairly easy,** suitable for beginner with some experience	**Fairly difficult,** suitable for competent DIY mechanic	**Difficult,** suitable for experienced DIY mechanic	**Very difficult,** suitable for expert DIY or professional

Specifications

Front brake

Brake fluid type	DOT 4
Caliper bore ID	
Standard.	25.400 to 25.450 mm
Service limit	25.460 mm
Caliper piston OD	
Standard.	25.318 to 25.368 mm
Service limit	25.310 mm
Disc thickness	
Standard.	3.8 to 4.2 mm
Service limit	3.5 mm
Disc maximum runout	0.1 mm
Master cylinder bore ID	
Standard.	11.000 to 11.043 mm
Service limit	11.055 mm
Master cylinder piston OD	
Standard.	10.957 to 10.984 mm
Service limit	10.945 mm

Rear brake – VT125C

Brake drum ID	
Standard	130.00 to 130.30 mm
Service limit	131.00 mm
Brake pedal freeplay	see Chapter 1

Rear brake – XL125V

Brake fluid type	DOT 4
Caliper bore ID	
Standard	32.030 to 32.080 mm
Service limit	32.090 mm
Caliper piston OD	
Standard	31.948 to 31.998 mm
Service limit	31.94 mm
Disc thickness	
Standard	3.8 to 4.2 mm
Service limit	3.5 mm
Disc maximum runout	0.1 mm
Master cylinder bore ID	
Standard	12.700 to 12.743 mm
Service limit	12.755 mm
Master cylinder piston OD	
Standard	12.657 to 12.684 mm
Service limit	12.644 mm
Pushrod clevis position (see text)	
XL125V-1 to V6	67.5 mm
XL125V-7 onwards	100.0 mm

Wheels – VT125C

Maximum wheel runout (front and rear)	
Axial (side-to-side)	2.0 mm
Radial (out-of-round)	2.0 mm
Maximum axle runout (front and rear)	0.2 mm

Wheels – XL125V

Maximum wheel runout (front and rear)	
Axial (side-to-side)	1.0 mm
Radial (out-of-round)	1.0 mm
Maximum axle runout (front and rear)	0.2 mm

Tyres

Tyre pressures	see *Pre-ride checks*
Tyre sizes	
VT125C	
Front	100/90-17 MC (56P)
Rear	130/90-15 MC (66P)
XL125V	
Front	100/90-18 MC (56P)
Rear	130/80-17 MC (65P)

Final drive – VT125C

Drive chain slack and lubricant	see Chapter 1
Drive chain type	
DID	DID520DM
RK	RK520 KZ6
Length	112 links
Drive chain stretch limit over 41-pin length	647.7 mm max
Sprocket sizes	
Front (engine) sprocket	14T
Rear (wheel) sprocket	41T

Final drive – XL125V

Drive chain slack and lubricant	see Chapter 1
Drive chain type	
DID	DID520V6
RK	RK520 SMOZ2
Regina	135 ORNV2
Length	110 links

Final drive – XL125V (continued)

Soft link
  Pin projection from side plate
    DID . . . . 1.15 to 1.55 mm
    RK . . . . 1.20 to 1.40 mm
    Regina. . . . . not applicable
  Diameter of staked pin ends
    DID . . . . 5.40 to 5.46 mm
    RK . . . . 5.50 to 5.80 mm
    Regina. . . . . not applicable
Sprocket sizes
  Front (engine) sprocket. 14T
  Rear (wheel) sprocket. 44T

Torque settings

Brake disc bolts . . . . 42 Nm
Brake hose banjo bolts. . . . . 34 Nm
Front sprocket retainer plate bolts . . . . 12 Nm
Front axle
  VT125C. . . . . 62 Nm
  XL125V . . . . 66 Nm
Front axle clamp bolt . . . . 22 Nm
Front brake caliper mounting bolts . . . . 30 Nm
Front brake pad retaining pin . . . . 18 Nm
Rear axle nut . . . . 88 Nm
Rear brake arm pinch bolt – VT125C . . . . 10 Nm
Rear brake pad retaining pin – XL125V . . . . 17 Nm
Rear sprocket nuts . . . . 64 Nm

1 General information

All models have a single hydraulically operated front disc brake. The sliding-type caliper contains two pistons.

VT125C models have a single leading shoe drum rear brake. XL125V models have a single hydraulically operated rear disc brake with a single piston sliding caliper.

VT125C models have wire-spoked wheels with inner tubes fitted inside the tyres. XL125V models are fitted with cast alloy wheels designed for tubeless tyres only.

The drive to the rear wheel is by chain and sprockets on all models.

Caution: Disc brake components rarely require disassembly. Do not disassemble components unless absolutely necessary. If an hydraulic brake hose is loosened or disconnected, the union sealing washers must be renewed and the system bled upon reassembly. Do not use solvents on internal brake components. Solvents will cause the seals to swell and distort. Use only clean DOT 4 brake fluid for cleaning. Use care when working with brake fluid as it can injure your eyes and it will damage painted surfaces and plastic parts.

2 Front brake pads

⚠ *Warning: The dust created by the brake system is harmful to your health. Never blow it out with compressed air and don't inhale any of it. An approved filtering mask should be worn when working on the brakes.*

Removal

1 Unscrew the plugs and loosen the pad retaining pins **(see illustrations)**.
2 Unscrew the caliper bracket mounting bolts

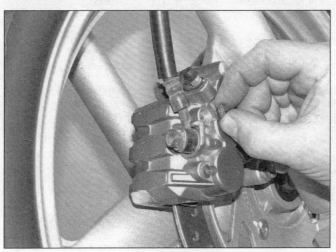

2.1a Unscrew the plugs . . .

2.1b . . . and loosen the pad retaining pins

2.2a Unscrew the mounting bolts . . .

2.2b . . . and slide the caliper assembly off

2.2c Pad wear indicators

2.3a Remove the pad pins . . .

2.3b . . . and lift out the pads

2.4 Location of the pad spring

and slide the caliper assembly off the disc **(see illustrations)**. Note the location of the pad wear indicators **(see illustration)**.

3 Unscrew and remove the pad pins, then remove the pads, noting how they fit **(see illustrations)**. Note the location of the pad shim on the back of the inner pad **Note:** *Do not operate the brake lever while the pads are out of the caliper.*

4 Note the location of the pad spring inside the caliper **(see illustration)**.

5 Inspect the surface of each pad for contamination and check that the friction material has not worn beyond its service limit (see Chapter 1) – if necessary, measure the thickness of the friction material. If either pad is worn down to, or beyond, the service limit, is fouled with oil or grease, or heavily scored or damaged, fit a set of new pads. **Note:** *It is not possible to degrease the friction material;*

if the pads are contaminated in any way they must be replaced with new ones.

6 Check that each pad has worn evenly at each end, and that each has the same amount of wear as the other. If uneven wear is noticed, one of the pistons is probably sticking in the caliper, or the caliper is seized on its slider pins – in either case the caliper must be overhauled (see Section 3).

7 If the pads are in good condition clean them carefully, using a fine wire brush which is completely free of oil and grease to remove all traces of road dirt and corrosion. Using a pointed instrument, dig out any embedded particles of foreign matter. If required, spray with a dedicated brake cleaner to remove any dust.

8 Check the condition of the brake disc (see Section 4).

9 Remove all traces of corrosion from the pad

pins and check them for wear and damage. Renew the pins if necessary.

10 If required, clean the pad spring and the inside of the brake caliper **(see illustration 2.4)**.

11 Clean around the exposed section of each piston to remove any dirt that could cause the internal seals to be damaged. If new pads are being fitted, push the pistons all the way back into the caliper to create room for them. If the old pads are still serviceable push the pistons in a little way.

12 To push the pistons back use finger pressure, a piece of wood and a pair of grips, or place the old pads back in the caliper and use a metal bar or a screwdriver inserted between them **(see illustrations)**. Alternatively, use a commercially available piston-pushing tool **(see illustration)**. **Note:** *Due to the increased friction material thickness of new pads, it may*

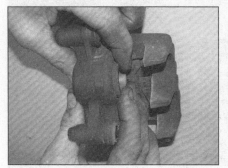

2.12a Push the pistons back using your fingers . . .

2.12b . . . some grips and a piece of wood . . .

2.12c . . . or a piston-pushing tool

2.16 Installed position of the outer pad

2.17 Locate curved end of inner pad over the post

3.1 Free the brake hose guide

be necessary to remove the master cylinder reservoir cover and siphon out some fluid (see Section 11)

13 If either piston appears seized, the caliper will have to be overhauled (see Section 3).

Installation

14 Make sure the pad spring is correctly located in the caliper (see illustration 2.4).

15 Make sure the pad shim is securely clipped to the back of the inner brake pad. Smear the backs of the pads with copper-based grease, making sure that none gets on the front or sides of the pads.

16 Fit the outer pad into the caliper, making sure its lower end locates correctly against the caliper bracket (see illustration).

17 Fit the inner pad, locating its curved end over the post on the caliper bracket (see illustration). Press the pads against the spring so the holes for the pad pins align, then insert the pins and tighten them finger-tight (see illustration 2.3a).

18 Slide the caliper onto the disc making sure the pads locate correctly on each side with the friction material facing the disc.

19 Clean the threads of the mounting bolts and apply a suitable non-permanent thread-locking compound. Install the bolts and tighten them to the torque setting specified at the beginning of this Chapter.

20 Tighten the pad pins to the specified torque setting and install the plugs (see illustrations 2.1b and a).

21 Operate the brake lever several times to bring the pads into contact with the disc.

22 Check the fluid level in the master cylinder reservoir and top-up if necessary (see Pre-ride checks).

23 Check the operation of the brake before riding the motorcycle.

3 Front brake caliper

Warning: *If a caliper is in need of an overhaul all old brake fluid should be flushed from the system. Also, the dust created by the brake system may contain asbestos, which is harmful to your health. Never blow it out with compressed air and do not inhale any of it. An approved filtering mask should be worn when working on the brakes. Overhaul of the brake caliper must be done in a spotlessly clean work area to avoid contamination and possible failure of the brake hydraulic system components. Do not, under any circumstances, use petroleum-based solvents to clean brake parts. Use clean DOT 4 brake fluid, dedicated brake cleaner or denatured alcohol only. To prevent damage from spilled brake fluid, always cover paintwork when working on the braking system.*

Removal

Special tool: *A source of compressed air may be required to ease the pistons out from the brake caliper (see Step 10).*

Note: *If the caliper is being overhauled (usually due to sticking pistons or fluid leaks) read through the entire procedure first and make sure that you have obtained all the new parts required, including some new DOT 4 brake fluid.*

1 If required, undo the right-hand front mudguard mounting bolts and free the brake hose guide (see illustration).

2 If the caliper assembly is just being displaced from the front forks, unscrew the mounting bolts and slide it off the disc (see illustrations 2.2a and b). Secure the caliper to the bike with a cable-tie to avoid straining the brake hose. **Note:** *Do not operate the brake lever while the caliper is off the disc.*

3 If the caliper is being completely removed or overhauled, follow the procedure in Section 11 and drain the brake fluid.

4 Unscrew the brake hose banjo bolt and detach the banjo union, noting its alignment with the caliper (see illustrations). Wrap a small plastic bag around the banjo union and secure the hose in an upright position to minimise fluid loss. Discard the sealing washers, as new ones must be fitted on reassembly.

5 Follow the procedure in Section 2 to remove the caliper assembly, then remove the brake pads.

Overhaul

6 Slide the caliper off the bracket (see illustration).

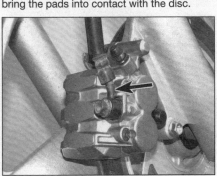

3.4a Note alignment of banjo union (arrowed) with caliper

3.4b Unscrew banjo bolt, noting sealing washers

3.6 Slide the caliper off the bracket

3.7 Remove the pad spring

3.9 Examine slider pin boots (arrowed)

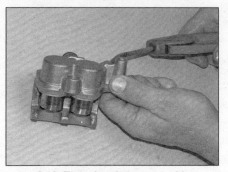

3.10 Ease the pistons out with compressed air

7 Remove the pad spring, noting how it fits **(see illustration)** then clean the exterior of the caliper and bracket with denatured alcohol or brake system cleaner. Have some clean rag ready to catch any spilled brake fluid.

8 Clean off all traces of corrosion and hardened grease from the slider pins on the bracket and make sure the lower slider pin is tight.

9 Examine the boots in the caliper and renew them if they are damaged, deformed or deteriorated **(see illustration)**.

10 Hold the caliper pistons-down on the workbench on a cushion of clean rag, then apply low pressure compressed air into the fluid inlet to ease the pistons out **(see illustration)**. Make sure both pistons are

displaced at the same time. Mark each piston head and caliper bore with a felt marker to ensure that the pistons can be matched to their original bores on reassembly.

11 If one piston sticks in its bore, block the free piston with a piece of wood, then try to ease the other piston out as before **(see illustration)**. Do not try to remove a piston by levering it out or by using pliers or other grips. If the piston has completely seized you will have to replace the caliper with a new one.

12 Remove the (outer) dust seal and the (inner) piston seal from each piston bore using a soft wooden or plastic tool to avoid scratching the bore **(see illustration)**. Discard the seals as new ones must be fitted.

13 Clean the pistons and bores with fresh brake fluid and blow compressed air through the fluid galleries in the caliper to ensure they are clear (make sure the air is filtered and unlubricated).

Caution: Do not, under any circumstances, use a petroleum-based solvent to clean brake parts.

14 Inspect each caliper bore and piston for signs of corrosion, nicks and burrs and loss of plating. If surface defects are present, the pistons and/or the caliper assembly must be replaced with new ones. If the necessary measuring equipment is available, compare the dimensions of the caliper bores and pistons to those specified at the beginning of this Chapter, and obtain new pistons or a new caliper if necessary.

15 Lubricate the new piston seals with fresh brake fluid and install them in their grooves in the caliper bores **(see illustrations)**.

16 Lubricate the new dust seals with silicone grease and install them in their grooves in the caliper bores.

17 Lubricate the pistons with clean brake fluid and install them closed-end first into the caliper bores. Using your thumbs, push the pistons all the way in, making sure they enter the bores squarely and taking care not to displace the seals **(see illustration)**.

18 Install the pad spring, then apply a smear of silicone-based grease to the slider pins

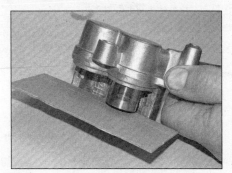

3.11 Block free piston as shown

3.12 Remove piston seals carefully

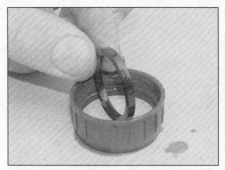

3.15a Lubricate piston seals with brake fluid . . .

3.15b . . . and install them in their grooves

3.17 Push the pistons all the way in

3.18a Installed position of pad spring

3.18b Apply silicone grease to the slider pins

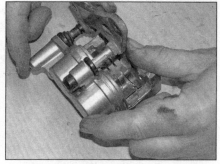

3.18c Slide the caliper onto the bracket

and slide the caliper onto the bracket **(see illustrations)**.

Installation

19 If the caliper has not been overhauled, ease the brake pads apart so that they will fit either side of the disc **(see illustration)**, then install the caliper assembly (see Section 2, Steps 19 to 24).

20 If the caliper has been overhauled, install the brake pads, then install the caliper assembly (see Section 2, Steps 16 to 21).

21 Connect the brake hose to the caliper – locate the banjo union between the lugs on the caliper and use new sealing washers on both sides of the union **(see illustrations 3.4b and a)**. Tighten the banjo bolt to the torque setting specified at the beginning of this Chapter.

22 If displaced, secure the brake hose with the mudguard mounting bolts **(see illustration 3.1)**.

23 Top up the master cylinder reservoir with DOT 4 brake fluid and bleed the system as described in Section 11. Check that there are no fluid leaks.

24 Check the operation of the brake before riding the motorcycle.

4 Front brake disc

Inspection

1 Inspect the surface of the disc for score marks and other damage **(see illustration)**. Light scratches are normal after use and won't affect brake operation, but deep grooves and heavy score marks will reduce braking efficiency and accelerate pad wear. If the disc is badly grooved it must be replaced with a new one.

2 The disc must not be machined or allowed to wear down to a thickness less than the service limit as listed in this Chapter's *Specifications*. The minimum thickness is also stamped on the disc **(see illustration)**. Measure the thickness of the disc with a micrometer and replace it with a new one if necessary **(see illustration)**.

3 To check if the disc is warped, position the bike on an auxiliary stand with the front wheel raised off the ground. Mount a dial gauge to the fork leg, with the gauge plunger touching the surface of the disc about 10 mm from the outer edge **(see illustration)**. Rotate the wheel and watch the gauge needle, comparing the

3.19 Ease the brake pads apart

4.1 Deep grooves and heavy score marks will reduce braking efficiency

4.2a Minimum thickness – VT125C

4.2b Minimum thickness – XL125V

4.2c Measure disc thickness with a micrometer

4.3 Checking disc runout

4.5 Front brake disc retaining bolts

5.4a Note alignment of banjo union (arrowed) with master cylinder

reading with the limit listed in *Specifications* at the beginning of this Chapter. If the runout is greater than the service limit, check the wheel bearings for play (see Chapter 1). If the bearings are worn, install new ones (see Section 17) and repeat this check. If the disc runout is still excessive, a new disc will have to be fitted.

Removal

4 Remove the wheel (see Section 15).
5 If you are not replacing the disc with a new one, mark the relationship of the disc to the wheel, so it can be installed in the same position. Unscrew the disc retaining bolts, loosening them evenly and a little at a time in a criss-cross pattern to avoid distorting the disc, then remove the disc **(see illustration)**.

Installation

6 Before installing the disc, make sure there is no dirt or corrosion where it seats on the hub. If the disc does not sit flat when it is bolted down, it will appear to be warped when checked or when the front brake is applied.
7 Install the disc on the wheel with its marked side facing out, aligning the previously applied matchmarks (if you're reinstalling the original disc).

8 Clean the threads of the disc mounting bolts, then apply a suitable non-permanent thread locking compound. Install the bolts and tighten them evenly and a little at a time in a criss-cross pattern to the torque setting specified at the beginning of this Chapter. Clean the disc using acetone or brake system cleaner. If a new disc has been installed remove any protective coating from its working surfaces. **Note:** *Always fit new brake pads when installing a new disc.*
9 Install the front wheel (see Section 15).
10 Operate the brake lever several times to bring the pads into contact with the disc.
11 Check the operation of the brake before riding the motorcycle.

5 Front brake master cylinder

⚠️ *Warning: If the brake master cylinder is in need of an overhaul all old brake fluid should be flushed from the system. Overhaul must be done in a spotlessly clean work area to avoid contamination and possible failure of the brake hydraulic system components.*

Do not, under any circumstances, use petroleum-based solvents to clean brake parts; use clean DOT 4 brake fluid, dedicated brake cleaner or denatured alcohol only. To prevent damage from spilled brake fluid, always cover paintwork when working on the braking system.

Removal

Note: *If the master cylinder is being overhauled (usually due to sticking or poor action, or fluid leaks) read through the entire procedure first and make sure that you have obtained all the new parts required, including some new DOT 4 brake fluid.*

1 If the master cylinder is just being displaced from the handlebars, follow the procedure in Chapter 6, Section 5. Note that it is not necessary to remove the fuel tank or, on XL125V models, the fairing, unless access to other components is required. On VT125C models, remove the right-hand mirror.
2 If the master cylinder is being completely removed or overhauled, follow the procedure in Section 11 and siphon out the brake fluid. Temporarily install the diaphragm, diaphragm plate and cover.
3 On VT125C models, remove the right-hand mirror (see Chapter 8).
4 Unscrew the brake hose banjo bolt and detach the banjo union, noting its alignment with the master cylinder **(see illustrations)**. Wrap a small plastic bag around the banjo union and secure the hose in an upright position to minimise fluid loss. Discard the sealing washers, as new ones must be fitted on reassembly.
5 Undo the master cylinder clamp bolts and remove the back of the clamp **(see illustration)**. Lift the master cylinder off the handlebar and disconnect the wiring connectors for the front brake light switch.
6 Remove the reservoir cover, diaphragm plate and diaphragm and wipe any remaining

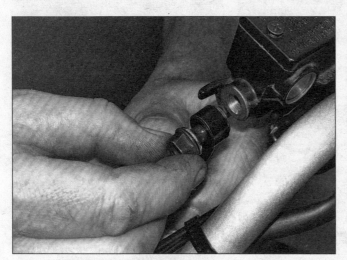

5.4b Unscrew banjo bolt, noting sealing washers

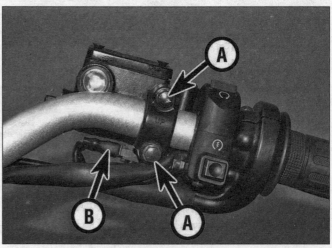

5.5 Master cylinder clamp bolts (A). Note brake light switch connectors (B)

5.7 Screw (arrowed) secures brake light switch

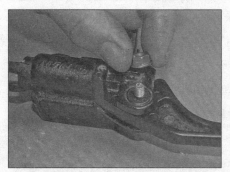

5.8a Undo pivot bolt locknut . . .

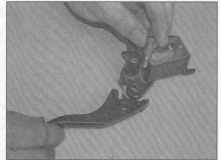

5.8b . . . then unscrew pivot bolt and remove lever

5.9 Remove the rubber boot

5.10a Note location of the circlip . . .

5.10b . . . then remove it . . .

brake fluid out of the reservoir with a clean rag.

7 If required, undo the screw securing the brake light switch to the bottom of the master cylinder and remove the switch **(see illustration)**.

8 Undo the brake lever pivot bolt locknut, then unscrew the pivot bolt and remove the lever **(see illustrations)**.

Overhaul

9 Remove the rubber boot from the master cylinder **(see illustration)**.

10 Note the location of the circlip securing the master cylinder piston **(see illustration)**.

Depress the piston and use circlip pliers to remove the circlip, then remove the plain washer **(see illustrations)**.

11 Draw out the piston assembly and the spring, noting how they fit **(see illustration)**. If the piston is difficult to remove, apply low pressure compressed air to the brake fluid outlet. Lay the parts out in the proper order to prevent confusion during reassembly.

12 Clean the inside of the master cylinder and reservoir with fresh brake fluid. If compressed air is available, blow it through the fluid galleries to ensure they are clear (make sure the air is filtered and unlubricated).

Caution: Do not, under any circumstances, use a petroleum-based solvent to clean brake parts.

13 Check the master cylinder bore for corrosion, scratches, nicks and score marks. If the necessary measuring equipment is available, compare the dimensions of the piston and bore to those given in the Specifications at the beginning of this Chapter. If damage or wear is evident, the master cylinder must be replaced with a new one. If the master cylinder is in poor condition, then the caliper should be checked as well.

14 The dust boot, circlip, washer, piston and

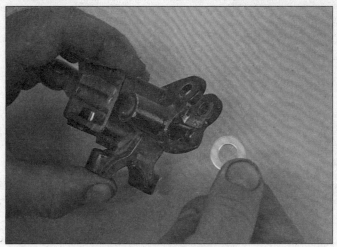

5.10c . . . and the plain washer

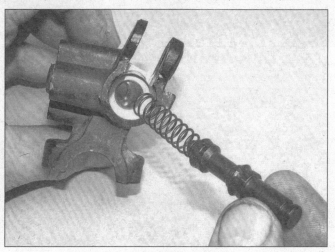

5.11 Draw out the piston assembly and spring

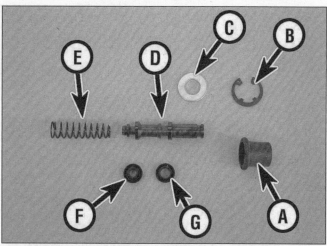

5.14 Master cylinder rebuild kit – dust boot (A), circlip (B), washer (C), piston (D), spring (E), primary seal (F) and secondary seal (G)

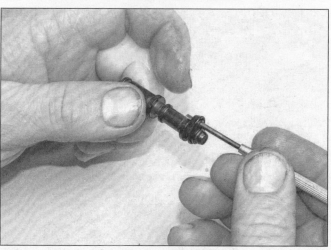

5.15a Ease the secondary seal into its groove . . .

its seals, and the spring, are all included in the master cylinder rebuild kit **(see illustration)**. Use all of the new parts, regardless of the apparent condition of the old ones.

15 If the seals are not fitted to the piston, first lubricate them with fresh brake fluid. Ease the thinner secondary seal into its groove in the middle of the piston, narrow end first **(see illustrations)**. Now ease the thicker primary seal into its groove in the inner end of the piston, narrow end first **(see illustrations)**. **Note:** *When the piston is inserted into the master cylinder, the wider ends of the seals should go in first.*

16 Lubricate the master cylinder bore and the piston assembly with brake fluid, then fit the narrow end of the spring onto the piston **(see illustration)**.

17 Carefully slide the assembly into the master cylinder **(see illustration 5.11)**.

18 Push the piston all the way in, compressing the spring, then fit the washer and secure it with the new circlip, making sure it locates properly in its groove **(see illustrations 5.10c, b and a)**.

19 Smear the inside of the rubber boot with silicone grease, fit it over the end of the piston and press the wide rim into the master cylinder against the circlip using a suitably-

sized socket. The outer rim of the boot should locate in the groove in the outer end of the piston **(see illustration)**.

20 Inspect the fluid reservoir diaphragm and fit a new one if it is damaged or deteriorated.

Installation

21 If the master cylinder has just been displaced from the handlebars, follow the procedure in Steps 24 and 25.

22 If the master cylinder has been completely removed or overhauled, install the brake lever and secure it with the pivot bolt, then tighten the pivot bolt locknut securely **(see illustrations 5.8b and a)**.

23 If removed, fit the brake light switch onto the bottom of the master cylinder and tighten the screw securely **(see illustration 5.7)**.

24 Connect the brake light switch wiring connectors **(see illustration 5.5)**.

25 Align the master cylinder clamp joint with the punch mark on the top of the handlebar (see Chapter 6, Section 5), then fit the back of the clamp with its UP mark facing up **(see illustration 5.5)**. Tighten the upper clamp bolt to the torque setting specified at the beginning of this Chapter, followed by the lower bolt so that any gap is at the bottom of the clamp joint. On VT125C models, install the right-hand mirror.

5.15b . . . in the middle of the piston

5.15c Ease the primary seal into its groove

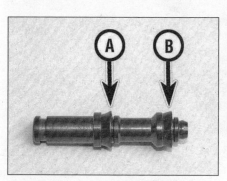

5.15d Installed positions of the secondary (A) and primary (B) seals

5.16 Fit the spring onto the piston

5.19 Ensure rim of the boot (arrowed) locates in groove in piston

26 Connect the brake hose to the master cylinder, using new sealing washers on both sides of the banjo union **(see illustration 5.4b and a)**. Align the hose as noted on removal, then tighten the banjo bolt to the specified torque setting.

27 Fill the fluid reservoir with new DOT 4 brake fluid (see *Pre-ride checks*) and bleed the system as described in Section 11. Check that there are no fluid leaks.

28 Check the operation of the brake before riding the motorcycle.

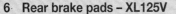

6 Rear brake pads – XL125V

⚠️ *Warning: The dust created by the brake system is harmful to your health. Never blow it out with compressed air and don't inhale any of it. An approved filtering mask should be worn when working on the brakes.*

Removal

1 Push the caliper against the disc to force the piston into the caliper – this creates clearance for removing the pads and room for fitting new ones if necessary. **Note:** *Due to the increased friction material thickness of new pads, it may be necessary to remove the master cylinder reservoir cover and siphon out some fluid (see Section 11).*

2 If the piston appears seized, the caliper will have to be overhauled (see Section 7).

3 Unscrew the pad pin plug, then unscrew the pad retaining pin **(see illustrations)**.

4 Remove the brake pads, noting how they fit **(see illustrations)**. **Note:** *Do not operate the brake pedal while the pads are out of the caliper.*

5 Note the location of the pad spring inside the caliper **(see illustration)**.

6 Inspect the surface of each pad for contamination and check that the friction material has not worn beyond its service limit (see Chapter 1) – if necessary, measure the thickness of the friction material. If either pad is worn down to, or beyond, the service limit, is fouled with oil or grease, or heavily

6.3a Remove the plug . . .

6.3b . . . and unscrew the pad retaining pin

6.4a Remove the outer . . .

6.4b . . . and inner brake pads

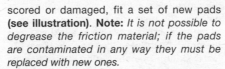

scored or damaged, fit a set of new pads **(see illustration)**. **Note:** *It is not possible to degrease the friction material; if the pads are contaminated in any way they must be replaced with new ones.*

7 Check that each pad has worn evenly, and that each has the same amount of wear as the other. If uneven wear is noticed, the piston is probably sticking in the caliper, or the caliper is seized on its slider pins – in either case the caliper must be overhauled (see Section 7).

8 If the pads are in good condition clean them carefully, using a fine wire brush which is completely free of oil and grease to remove all traces of road dirt and corrosion. Using a pointed instrument, dig out any embedded particles of foreign matter. If required, spray with a dedicated brake cleaner to remove any dust.

9 Check the condition of the brake disc (see Section 8).

10 Remove all traces of corrosion from the pad pin and check it for wear and damage. Renew the pin if necessary.

11 Clean the pad spring and the inside of the brake caliper **(see illustration 6.5)**.

Installation

12 Make sure the pad spring is correctly located in the caliper.

13 Smear the backs of the pads with copper-based grease, making sure that none gets on the front or sides of the pads.

14 Fit the inner pad, ensuring the friction material is facing the disc, and locate its curved end over the post on the caliper bracket **(see illustration)**.

15 Fit the outer pad **(see illustration 6.4a)**, then press both pads against the spring so

6.5 Note location of the pad spring

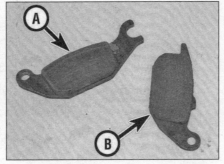

6.6 Examine the inner (A) and outer (B) pad for wear

6.14 Installed position of inner pad on caliper bracket post (arrowed)

6.15 Hold pads against the spring to install pin

the holes for the pad pin align and insert the pin **(see illustration)**.

16 Tighten the pad pin to the torque setting specified at the beginning of this Chapter, then install the plug **(see illustration 6.3a)**.

17 Operate the brake pedal several times to bring the pads into contact with the disc.

18 Check the fluid level in the master cylinder reservoir and top-up if necessary (see *Pre-ride checks*).

19 Check the operation of the brake before riding the motorcycle.

7 Rear brake caliper – XL125V

⚠️ *Warning: If the caliper is in need of overhaul all old brake fluid should be flushed from the*

system. Also, the dust created by the brake system may contain asbestos, which is harmful to your health. Never blow it out with compressed air and do not inhale any of it. An approved filtering mask should be worn when working on the brakes. Overhaul must be done in a spotlessly clean work area to avoid contamination and possible failure of the brake hydraulic system components. Do not, under any circumstances, use petroleum-based solvents to clean brake parts; use clean DOT 4 brake fluid, dedicated brake cleaner or denatured alcohol only, as described. To prevent damage from spilled brake fluid, always cover paintwork when working on the braking system.

Removal

Special tool: *A source of compressed air may be required to ease the piston out from the brake caliper (see Step 10).*

Note: *If the caliper is being overhauled (usually due to a sticking piston or fluid leaks) read through the entire procedure first and make sure that you have obtained all the new parts required, including some new DOT 4 brake fluid.*

1 If the caliper assembly is just being displaced from the swingarm, remove the rear wheel (see Section 16). Undo the bolt securing the brake hose guide to the swingarm, then displace the caliper assembly and secure it to the bike with a cable-tie to avoid straining the brake hose (see Chapter 6, Section 12).

Note: *Do not operate the brake pedal while the caliper is off the disc.*

2 If the caliper is being completely removed or overhauled, follow the procedure in Section 11 and drain the brake fluid.

3 Remove the brake pads (see Section 6).

4 Unscrew the brake hose banjo bolt and detach the banjo union, noting its alignment with the caliper **(see illustration)**. Wrap a small plastic bag around the banjo union and secure the hose in an upright position to minimise fluid loss. Discard the sealing washers, as new ones must be fitted on reassembly.

5 Remove the rear wheel (see Section 16). Remove the rear brake caliper assembly from the swingarm, noting how it locates **(see illustration)**.

Overhaul

6 Slide the caliper off the bracket **(see illustration)**.

7 Remove the pad spring, noting how it fits **(see illustration)**, then clean the exterior of the caliper and bracket with denatured alcohol or brake system cleaner. Have some clean rag ready to catch any spilled brake fluid.

8 Clean off all traces of corrosion and hardened grease from the slider pins on the bracket and make sure the rear slider pin is tight.

9 Examine the boots in the caliper and renew them if they are damaged, deformed or deteriorated **(see illustration)**.

10 Hold the caliper piston-down on the workbench on a cushion of clean rag, then apply low pressure compressed air into the fluid inlet to ease the piston out **(see illustration)**.

7.4 Unscrew the brake hose banjo bolt

7.5 Note location of brake caliper bracket

7.6 Slide the caliper off the bracket

7.7 Remove the pad spring

7.9 Examine slider pin boots (arrowed)

7.10 Ease the piston out with compressed air

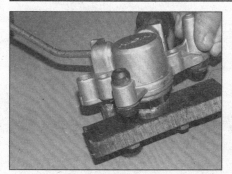

7.11 Block the open side of the caliper with a piece of wood

7.12 Remove piston seals carefully

7.15a Lubricate the new piston seal with brake fluid . . .

7.15b . . . and install it in its groove

7.17 Push the piston all the way in

7.22 Fit new sealing washers on the banjo union

11 If the piston sticks in its bore, block the open side of the caliper with a piece of wood, then increase the air pressure and try to ease the piston out as before **(see illustration)**. Do not try to remove a piston by levering it out or by using pliers or other grips. If the piston has completely seized you will have to replace the caliper with a new one.

12 Remove the (outer) dust seal and the (inner) piston seal from the piston bore using a soft wooden or plastic tool to avoid scratching the bore **(see illustration)**. Discard the seals as new ones must be fitted.

13 Clean the piston and bore with fresh brake fluid and blow compressed through the fluid galleries in the caliper to ensure they are clear (make sure the air is filtered and unlubricated).

Caution: Do not, under any circumstances, use a petroleum-based solvent to clean brake parts.

14 Inspect the caliper bore and piston for signs of corrosion, nicks and burrs and loss of plating. If surface defects are present, the piston and/or the caliper assembly must be replaced with new ones. If the necessary measuring equipment is available, compare the dimensions of the caliper bore and piston to those specified at the beginning of this Chapter, and obtain a new piston or a new caliper if necessary.

15 Lubricate the new piston seal with fresh brake fluid and fit it into its groove in the caliper bore **(see illustrations)**.

16 Lubricate the new dust seal with silicone grease and fit it into the outer groove in the caliper bore.

17 Lubricate the piston with clean brake fluid

and fit it, closed-end first, into the caliper bore. Using your thumbs, push the piston all the way in, making sure it enters the bore squarely and taking care not to displace the seals **(see illustration)**.

18 Install the pad spring, then apply a smear of silicone-based grease to the slider pins and slide the caliper onto the bracket **(see illustrations 7.7 and 7.6)**.

Installation

19 If the caliper has not been overhauled, fit the caliper assembly onto the swingarm and secure the brake hose guide (see Chapter 6, Section 12). Install the rear wheel (see Section 16).

20 If the caliper has been overhauled, fit the caliper assembly onto the swingarm **(see illustration 7.5)**, then install the rear wheel (see Section 16).

21 Install the brake pads (see Section 6).

22 Connect the brake hose to the caliper –

8.3 Rear brake disc retaining bolts

locate the banjo union between the lugs on the caliper and use new sealing washers on both sides of the union **(see illustration)**. Tighten the banjo bolt to the torque setting specified at the beginning of this Chapter.

23 Top up the master cylinder reservoir with DOT 4 brake fluid and bleed the system as described in Section 11. Check that there are no fluid leaks.

24 Check the operation of the brake before riding the motorcycle.

8 Rear brake disc – XL125V

Inspection

1 Refer to Section 4 of this Chapter, noting that the dial gauge should be attached to the swingarm.

Removal

2 Remove the rear wheel (see Section 16).

Caution: Don't lay the wheel down and allow it to rest on the disc or sprocket – they could become warped. Set the wheel on wood blocks so the wheel rim supports the weight of the wheel.

3 If you are not replacing the disc with a new one, mark the relationship of the disc to the wheel so it can be installed in the same position. Unscrew the disc retaining bolts, loosening them evenly and a little at a time in a criss-cross pattern to avoid distorting the disc, then remove the disc **(see illustration)**.

Installation

4 Before installing the disc, make sure there is no dirt or corrosion where It seats on the hub. If the disc does not sit flat when it is bolted down, it will appear to be warped when checked or when the rear brake is used.

5 Install the disc on the wheel with its marked side facing out, aligning the previously applied matchmarks (if you're reinstalling the original disc).

6 Clean the threads of the disc mounting bolts, then apply a suitable non-permanent thread locking compound. Install the bolts and tighten them evenly and a little at a time in a criss-cross pattern to the torque setting specified at the beginning of this Chapter. Clean the disc using acetone or brake system cleaner. If a new disc has been installed, remove any protective coating from its working surfaces. Always fit new brake pads with a new disc.

7 Install the rear wheel (see Section 16).

8 Operate the brake pedal several times to bring the pads into contact with the disc.

9 Check the operation of the brake before riding the motorcycle.

9 Rear brake master cylinder – XL125V

⚠️ **Warning:** *If the brake master cylinder is in need of an overhaul all old brake fluid should be flushed from the system. Overhaul must be done in a spotlessly clean work area to avoid contamination and possible failure of the brake hydraulic system components. Do not, under any circumstances, use petroleum-based solvents to clean brake parts; use clean DOT 4 brake fluid, dedicated brake cleaner or denatured alcohol only, as described. To prevent damage from spilled brake fluid, always cover paintwork when working on the braking system.*

Removal

Note: *If the master cylinder is being overhauled (usually due to sticking or poor action, or fluid leaks) read through the entire procedure first and make sure that you have obtained all the new parts required, including some new DOT 4 brake fluid and a roll pin for the pushrod (see Step 14).*

9.7b Remove the circlip securing the hose union

9.5 Undo the brake hose banjo bolt and detach the banjo union

9.6b . . . and remove the master cylinder

9.8a Displace the boot . . .

1 If the master cylinder is just being displaced it may not be necessary to disconnect the hydraulic hoses. The extent of disassembly will depend upon the job being undertaken. If either of the hoses need to be disconnected, first drain the brake fluid to avoid spillage, otherwise follow Steps 2, 3 and 6.

2 Remove the seat and the right-hand side panel (see Chapter 8).

3 Remove the right-hand footrest bracket and disconnect the brake pedal from the master cylinder pushrod (see Chapter 6, Section 3).

4 Follow the procedure in Section 11 and empty the brake fluid from the reservoir. Temporarily install the diaphragm, diaphragm plate and cover and secure the reservoir to its bracket.

5 Undo the brake hose banjo bolt and detach the banjo union, noting its alignment with the master cylinder **(see illustration)**. Wrap a small plastic bag around the banjo union and secure the hose in an upright position to minimise

9.6a Undo the mounting bolts . . .

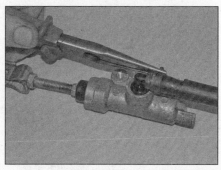

9.7a Disconnect the reservoir hose

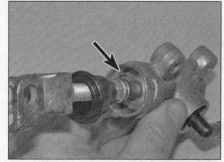

9.8b . . . to access the circlip

fluid loss. Discard the sealing washers, as new ones must be fitted on reassembly.

6 Undo the bolts securing the master cylinder to the frame, then remove the master cylinder and reservoir assembly **(see illustrations)**.

Overhaul

7 Release the clip securing the reservoir hose to the union on the master cylinder and detach the hose **(see illustration)**. Inspect the hose for cracks or splits and replace it with a new one if necessary. If the clips are corroded or have weakened, fit new ones. If required, use circlip pliers to remove the circlip securing the hose union and detach it from the master cylinder **(see illustration)**. Discard the O-ring as a new one must be used.

8 Displace the rubber boot from the base of the master cylinder, noting how it locates, to access the circlip securing the pushrod assembly **(see illustrations)**. Depress the

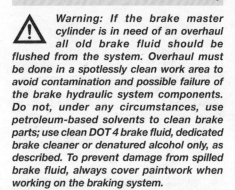

9.8c Remove the circlip . . .

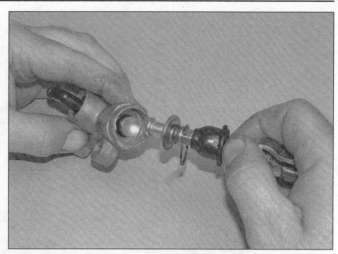

9.8d . . . and ease out the pushrod

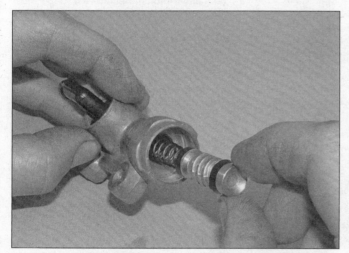

9.9 Withdraw the piston assembly and spring

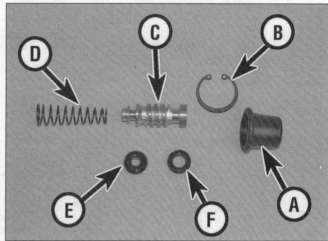

9.12 Master cylinder rebuild kit – dust boot (A), circlip (B), piston (C), spring (D), primary seal (E) and secondary seal (F)

pushrod and use circlip pliers to remove the circlip, then ease out the pushrod (see illustrations).

9 Draw out the piston assembly and the spring, noting how they fit (see illustration). If the piston is difficult to remove, apply low pressure compressed air to the brake fluid outlet. Lay the parts out in the proper order to prevent confusion during reassembly.

10 Clean the inside of the master cylinder and reservoir with fresh brake fluid. If compressed air is available, blow it through the fluid galleries to ensure they are clear (make sure the air is filtered and unlubricated).

Caution: Do not, under any circumstances, use a petroleum-based solvent to clean brake parts.

11 Check the master cylinder bore for corrosion, scratches, nicks and score marks. If the necessary measuring equipment is available, compare the dimensions of the piston and bore to those given in the Specifications at the beginning of this Chapter. If damage or wear is evident, the master cylinder must be replaced with a new one. If

the master cylinder is in poor condition, then the caliper should be checked as well.

12 The dust boot, circlip, piston and its seals, and the spring are all included in the master cylinder rebuild kit (see illustration). Use all of the new parts, regardless of the apparent condition of the old ones.

13 If the seals are not fitted to the piston, first lubricate them with fresh brake fluid. Ease the

thinner secondary seal into its groove in the outer end of the piston, wide end first (see illustration). Now ease the thicker primary seal into its groove in the inner end of the piston, narrow end first (see illustration). *Note: When the piston is inserted into the master cylinder, the wider ends of the seals should go in first.*

14 Note the location of the roll pin in the lower

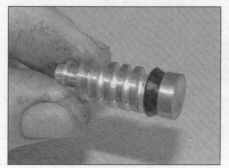

9.13a Ease the secondary seal into its groove

9.13b Ease the primary seal into its groove

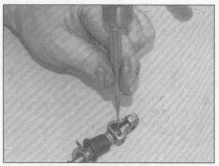

9.14 Remove the roll pin with a pin punch

9.15a Thread off the clevis . . .

9.15b . . . and locknut

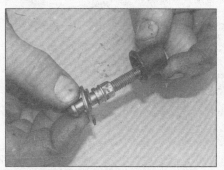

9.15c Remove the boot . . .

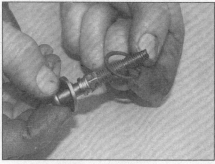

9.15d . . . and circlip

9.16 Fit a new roll pin in the pushrod

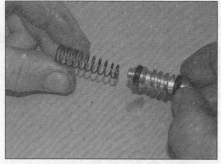

9.17 Fit the spring onto the piston

end of the pushrod, then drive it out using a suitable pin punch **(see illustrations)**.

15 Loosen the locknut above the clevis on the pushrod, then thread off the clevis and locknut **(see illustrations)**. Remove the rubber boot and the circlip **(see illustrations)**.

16 Lubricate the inside of the new rubber boot with silicone grease, then fit the new circlip and boot onto the pushrod followed by the locknut and clevis – the clevis can be locked in the correct position once the piston and pushrod have been installed in the master cylinder (see Step 21). Drive a new roll pin into the end of the pushrod **(see illustration)**.

17 Lubricate the master cylinder bore and the piston assembly with brake fluid, then fit the narrow end of the spring onto the piston **(see illustration)**.

18 Carefully slide the assembly into the master cylinder **(see illustration 9.9)**.

19 Smear some silicone grease onto the rounded end of the pushrod and locate it against the end of the piston **(see illustration 9.8d)**. Push the piston in with the pushrod until the washer on the pushrod is beyond the circlip groove inside the master cylinder, then install the circlip **(see illustrations 9.8c and b)**.

20 Press the wide rim of the boot into place in the end of the master cylinder and fit the lower end into the groove in the pushrod **(see illustrations)**.

9.20a Press the wide rim into the master cylinder

9.20b Locate the lower end on the pushrod

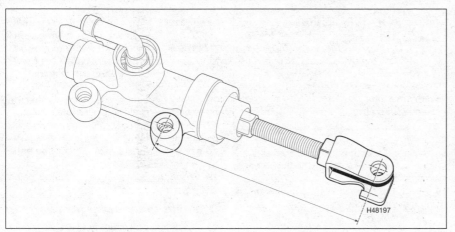

9.21 Measured distance between clevis and mounting hole should be as specified

21 Refer to the specification at the beginning of this Chapter and position the clevis at the measured distance between the centre of the lower mounting bolt hole and the centre of the clevis eye as shown **(see illustration)**. Tighten the locknut securely.

22 If removed, fit a new fluid reservoir hose union O-ring into the master cylinder, then press the union in and secure it with the circlip **(see illustration 9.7b)**.

23 Connect the reservoir hose to the union on the master cylinder and secure it with the clip **(see illustration 9.7a)**. Check that the hose is secured with a clip at the reservoir end as well.

24 Inspect the fluid reservoir diaphragm and fit a new one if it is damaged or deteriorated.

Installation

25 Locate the master cylinder on the inside of the frame bracket, then fit the mounting bolts and tighten them securely **(see illustration 9.6a)**.

26 Temporarily secure the fluid reservoir to its bracket **(see illustration)**. If the master cylinder and reservoir assembly has just been displaced, tighten the reservoir mounting bolt securely, then go to Step 29.

27 Connect the brake hose to the master cylinder, locating the banjo union against the outer face of the lug on the master cylinder **(see illustration 9.5)**. Use new sealing washers on both sides of the banjo union and tighten the banjo bolt to the torque setting specified at the beginning of this Chapter.

28 Fill the fluid reservoir with new DOT 4 brake fluid (see *Pre-ride checks*) and bleed the system as described in Section 11. Check that there are no fluid leaks.

29 Connect the brake pedal to the master cylinder pushrod and install the right-hand footrest bracket (see Chapter 6, Section 3).

30 Install the remaining components in the revere order of removal.

31 Check the operation of the brake before riding the motorcycle.

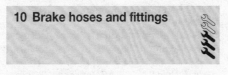

10 Brake hoses and fittings

Inspection

1 Brake hose condition should be checked regularly and the hoses replaced with new ones if they show signs of hardening, cracking or abrasion.

2 Twist and flex the hoses while looking for cracks, bulges and seeping hydraulic fluid. Check extra carefully around the areas where the hoses connect with the banjo unions, as these are common areas for hose failure.

3 Inspect the banjo unions connected to

9.26 Temporarily secure the fluid reservoir

the brake hoses. If the unions are rusted, scratched or cracked, fit new hoses.

Removal and installation

4 The brake hoses have banjo unions on both ends. Cover the surrounding area with plenty of rags and unscrew the banjo bolt at both ends of the hose, noting the alignment of the union with the master cylinder or brake caliper **(see illustrations 5.4a and 3.4a)**. Free the hose from any clips or guides and remove it, noting its routing. Discard the sealing washers. **Note:** *Do not operate the brake lever or pedal while a brake hose is disconnected.*

5 Position the new hose, making sure it isn't twisted or otherwise strained, and ensure that it is correctly routed through any clips or guides and is clear of all moving components.

6 Check that the unions align correctly, then install the banjo bolts, using new sealing washers on both sides of the unions **(see illustrations 5.4b and 3.4b)**. Tighten the banjo bolts to the torque setting specified at the beginning of this Chapter.

7 Flush the old brake fluid from the system, refill with new DOT 4 brake fluid and bleed the air from the system (see Section 11).

8 Check the operation of the brakes before riding the motorcycle.

11 Brake system bleeding and fluid change

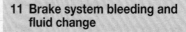

Bleeding

1 Bleeding the brakes is simply the process of removing air from the brake fluid reservoir, master cylinder, the hose and the brake caliper. Bleeding is necessary whenever a brake system connection is loosened, after a component or hose is replaced with a new one, or when the master cylinder or caliper is overhauled. Leaks in the system may also allow air to enter, but leaking brake fluid will reveal their presence and warn you of the need for repair.

2 To bleed the brakes, you will need some new DOT 4 brake fluid, a length of clear flexible hose, a small container partially filled with clean brake fluid, some rags, a spanner to fit the brake caliper bleed valve, and help from an assistant **(see illustrations)**. Bleeding kits

11.2a Set-up for bleeding the front brake

11.2b Set-up for bleeding the rear brake

that include the hose, a one-way valve and a container are available and greatly simplify the task.

3 Cover painted components to prevent damage in the event that brake fluid is spilled.

4 Refer to *Pre-ride checks* and remove the reservoir cover, diaphragm plate and diaphragm and slowly pump the brake lever (front brake) or pedal (rear brake) a few times, until no air bubbles can be seen floating up from the holes in the bottom of the reservoir. This bleeds the air from the master cylinder end of the line. Temporarily refit the reservoir cover.

5 Pull the dust cap off the bleed valve. If using a ring spanner fit it onto the valve **(see illustration 11.2a or b)**. Attach one end of the hose to the bleed valve and, unless you're using a one-man kit, submerge the other end in the clean brake fluid in the container.

 To avoid damaging the bleed valve during the procedure, loosen it and then tighten it temporarily with a ring spanner before attaching the hose. With the hose attached, the valve can then be opened and closed either with an open-ended spanner, or by leaving the ring spanner located on the valve and fitting the hose above it.

6 Check the fluid level in the reservoir. Do not allow the fluid level to drop below the lower mark during the procedure.

7 Slowly pump the brake lever or pedal three or four times and hold it in (front) or down (rear) while opening the bleed valve. When the valve is opened, brake fluid will flow out of the caliper into the clear tubing, and the lever will move toward the handlebar, or the pedal will move down. If there is air in the system there will be air bubbles in the brake fluid coming out of the caliper.

8 Tighten the bleed valve, then release the brake lever or pedal gradually. Repeat the process until no air bubbles are visible in the brake fluid leaving the caliper, and the lever or pedal is firm when applied, topping the reservoir up when necessary. On completion, disconnect the hose, then tighten the bleed valve and install the dust cap.

 If it is not possible to produce a firm feel to the lever or pedal, the fluid may be aerated. Let the brake fluid in the system stabilise for a few hours and then repeat the procedure when the tiny bubbles in the system have settled out.

9 Top-up the reservoir, then install the diaphragm, diaphragm plate, and cover. Wipe up any spilled brake fluid. Check the entire system for fluid leaks.

10 Check the operation of the brakes before riding the motorcycle.

Fluid change

11 Changing the brake fluid is a similar process to bleeding the brakes and requires the same materials (see Step 2) plus a suitable syringe for siphoning the fluid out of the front brake master cylinder reservoir. Also ensure that the container is large enough to take all the old fluid when it is flushed out of the system.

12 Follow Steps 3 and 5, then, if working on the front brake, remove the reservoir cover, diaphragm plate and diaphragm and siphon the old fluid out of the reservoir. If working on the rear brake, displace the reservoir, remove the reservoir cover, diaphragm plate and diaphragm and empty the old fluid into the container.

13 Wipe the reservoir clean, then fill it with new brake fluid.

14 Slowly pump the brake lever or pedal three or four times and hold it in (front) or down (rear) while opening the caliper bleed valve. When the valve is opened, brake fluid will flow out of the caliper into the clear tubing, and the lever will move toward the handlebar, or the pedal will move down.

15 Tighten the bleed valve, then release the brake lever or pedal gradually. Keep the reservoir topped-up with new fluid to above the LOWER level at all times or air may enter the system and greatly increase the length of the task. Repeat the process until new fluid can be seen emerging from the caliper bleed valve.

 Old brake fluid is invariably much darker in colour than new fluid, making it easy to see when all old fluid has been expelled from the system.

16 Disconnect the hose, then tighten the bleed valve securely and install the dust cap.

17 Top-up the reservoir, then install the diaphragm, diaphragm plate, and cover. Wipe up any spilled brake fluid. Check the entire system for fluid leaks.

18 Check the operation of the brakes before riding the motorcycle.

Draining the system for overhaul

19 Follow the procedure in Steps 11 and 12, then connect the syringe to the caliper bleed valve using a length of hose. Open the bleed valve and draw the fluid out from the brake hose and caliper. **Note:** *After draining a small amount of brake fluid will remain in the system. Take care when disconnecting the brake hoses to avoid spilling fluid onto painted surfaces.*

12 Rear drum brake – VT125C

Removal

1 Before you start, check the position of the rear brake wear indicator (see Chapter 1, Section 3).

2 Remove the rear wheel (see Section 16).

3 Lift off the brake plate. Mark the brake shoes to aid reassembly – if they are not going to be renewed they must be installed in their original positions **(see illustration)**. Note the position of the brake springs and mark the end of the brake cam to aid reassembly. Ensure the springs hold the shoes together firmly otherwise they should be renewed (see Step 9).

4 Fold the shoes toward each other to release the spring tension and lift the shoes and springs off as an assembly **(see illustration)**.

Inspection

5 Check the brake linings for wear, damage

12.3 Installed position of the rear brake shoes

12.4 Remove the shoes and springs as an assembly

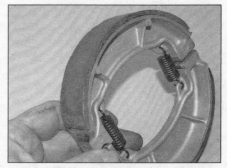

12.5 Examine the linings for wear and damage

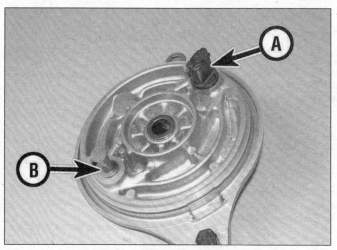

12.10 Brake cam (A) and pivot post (B)

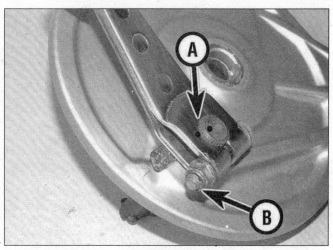

12.11 Brake arm/cam shaft alignment marks (A). Pinch bolt (B)

and signs of contamination **(see illustration)**. Note that it is not possible to degrease the friction material – if the linings are contaminated in any way, new brake shoes must be fitted.

6 If the wear indicator shows that the linings are worn down to the service limit (see Step 1), renew the shoes as a pair.

7 Check the ends of the shoes where they contact the brake cam and pivot post. Renew the shoes if there's visible wear.

8 If the linings are in good condition, clean them carefully using a fine wire brush which is completely free of oil and grease, to remove all traces of dirt and corrosion. Using a pointed instrument, dig out any embedded particles of foreign matter.

9 Examine the springs – if they are sprained and do not hold the shoes together tightly when in place, discard them and fit a new pair.

10 Clean all old grease from the brake cam and pivot post and check them for wear and damage **(see illustration)**. If the pivot post is worn or loose, a new backplate will have to be fitted.

11 To renew the brake cam, first note the alignment between the marks on the brake arm and the outer end of the cam shaft, then remove the brake arm pinch bolt and pull the arm off the shaft **(see illustration)**.

12 Note how the wear indicator locates on

the shaft, them pull the cam shaft out of the backplate. Note the location of the seal.

13 Lubricate the brake cam shaft with lithium-based grease and install it in the backplate, then fit the seal, the wear indicator and brake arm. Check the alignment of the components **(see illustration 12.11)**. Tighten the brake arm pinch bolt to the torque setting specified at the beginning of this Chapter.

14 Inspect the inside of the brake drum for wear or damage and measure the inside diameter of the drum at several points with a Vernier caliper **(see illustration)**. If the measurements are uneven (indicating that the drum is out-of-round) or if there deep scratches in the surface, have the drum skimmed by a brake specialist. If the wear or damage cannot be corrected within the service limit specified at the beginning of this Chapter, the hub must be renewed.

12.14 Measure the inside diameter of the brake drum in several positions

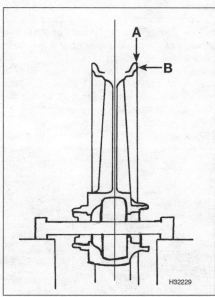

13.3 Check the wheel for radial (out-of-round) runout (A) and axial (side-to-side) runout (B)

Installation

15 Apply a smear of lithium-based grease to the pivot post and the faces of the brake cam.

Caution: Do not apply too much grease otherwise there is a risk of it contaminating the brake drum and linings.

16 Assemble the brake shoes and springs, position the shoes in a V on the brake plate, then fold the them down into position **(see illustration 12.4)**. Make sure the ends of the shoes fit correctly on the pivot post and cam **(see illustration 12.3)**.

17 Check the operation of the brake arm.

18 Install the brake plate, then install the rear wheel (see Section 16).

19 Check and adjust the brake pedal freeplay (see Chapter 1).

13 Wheel inspection and repair

1 In order to carry out a proper inspection of the wheels, it is necessary to support the bike upright so that the wheel being inspected is raised off the ground. Position the motorcycle on an auxiliary stand.

2 Clean the wheels thoroughly to remove mud and dirt that may interfere with the inspection procedure or mask defects. Make a general check of the wheels (see Chapter 1) and tyres (see *Pre-ride checks*).

3 Attach a dial gauge to the fork or the swingarm and position its tip against the side of the wheel rim. Spin the wheel slowly and check the axial (side-to-side) runout of the rim **(see illustration)**.

4 In order to accurately check radial (out of round) runout with the dial gauge, remove the wheel from the machine, and the tyre from the wheel. With the axle clamped in a vice and the dial gauge positioned on the top of the rim, the wheel can be rotated to check the runout **(see illustration 13.3)**.

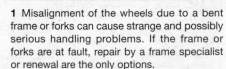

14.6 Wheel alignment check using string

5 An easier, though slightly less accurate, method is to attach a stiff wire pointer to the fork or the swingarm and position the end a fraction of an inch from the wheel rim where the wheel and tyre join. If the wheel is true, the distance from the pointer to the rim will be constant as the wheel is rotated. **Note:** *If wheel runout is excessive, check the wheel bearings very carefully before renewing the wheel.*

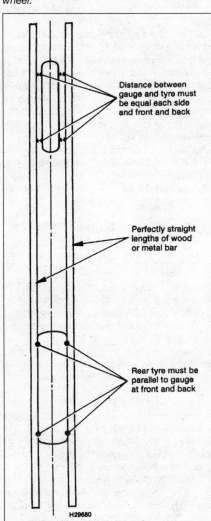

14.8 Wheel alignment check using a straight-edge

6 The spoked wheels on VT125C models can be rebuilt or the spokes adjusted to correct poor runout, but this is a job for a wheel building specialist.

14 Wheel alignment check

1 Misalignment of the wheels due to a bent frame or forks can cause strange and possibly serious handling problems. If the frame or forks are at fault, repair by a frame specialist or renewal are the only options.
2 To check wheel alignment you will need an assistant, a length of string or a perfectly straight piece of wood and a ruler. A plumb bob or spirit level for checking that the wheels are vertical will also be required.
3 In order to make a proper check of the wheels it is necessary to support the bike in an upright position, using an auxiliary stand.
4 First ensure that the chain adjuster markings coincide on each side of the swingarm (see Chapter 1, Section 1). Next, measure the width of both tyres at their widest points. Subtract the smaller measurement from the larger measurement, then divide the difference by two. The result is the amount of offset that should exist between the front and rear tyres on both sides of the machine.
5 If a string is used, have your assistant hold one end of it about halfway between the floor and the rear axle, with the string touching the back edge of the rear tyre sidewall.
6 Run the other end of the string forward and pull it tight so that it is roughly parallel to the

15.3a Front axle clamp bolt – VT125C

floor **(see illustration)**. Slowly bring the string into contact with the front edge of the rear tyre sidewall, then turn the front wheel until it is parallel with the string. Measure the distance from the front tyre sidewall to the string.
7 Repeat the procedure on the other side of the motorcycle. The distance from the front tyre sidewall to the string should be equal on both sides.
8 As previously mentioned, a perfectly straight length of wood or metal bar may be substituted for the string **(see illustration)**.
9 If the distance between the string and tyre is greater on one side, or if the rear wheel appears to be out of alignment, have your machine checked by a Honda dealer or frame specialist.
10 If the front-to-back alignment is correct, the wheels still may be out of alignment vertically.
11 Using a plumb bob or spirit level, check the rear wheel to make sure it is vertical. To do this, hold the string of the plumb bob against the tyre upper sidewall and allow the weight to settle just off the floor. If the string touches both the upper and lower tyre sidewalls and is perfectly straight, the wheel is vertical. If it is not, adjust the stand until it is.
12 Once the rear wheel is vertical, check the front wheel in the same manner. If both wheels are not perfectly vertical, the frame and/or major suspension components are bent.

15 Front wheel

Removal

1 Position the motorcycle on an auxiliary stand so that the front wheel is off the ground. Always make sure the motorcycle is securely supported.
2 If required, displace the front brake caliper (see Section 3). Secure the caliper with a cable-tie so that no strain is placed on the hydraulic hose. There is no need to disconnect the hose from the caliper. **Note:** *Do not operate the front brake lever while the caliper is off the disc.*
3 Loosen the front axle clamp bolt **(see illustrations)**.

15.3b Front axle clamp bolt – XL125V

Labels in figure 14.6:
Fix string here
String held taut
Hold string so that these distances are equal
Check for contact here
H29679

Labels in figure 14.8:
Distance between gauge and tyre must be equal each side and front and back
Perfectly straight lengths of wood or metal bar
Rear tyre must be parallel to gauge at front and back
H29680

4 Unscrew the axle, then support the wheel and withdraw the axle from the left-hand side **(see illustration)**. On XL125V-1 to V-6 models (except type IIG German market models) note how the tab on the speed sensor locates between the lugs on the lower end of the left-hand front fork outer tube **(see illustration)**.

5 Lower the wheel and draw it forwards **(see illustration)**.

6 On XL125V-1 to V-6 models, lift off the speed sensor noting how it locates on the drive tabs in the hub **(see illustration)**.

7 On all other models, remove the shouldered spacer from the left-hand side of the hub, noting how it fits **(see illustration)**.

8 On all models, remove the top hat spacer from the right-hand side of the hub **(see illustration)**.

Caution: Don't lay the wheel down and allow it to rest on the disc – it could become warped. Set the wheel on wood blocks so the disc doesn't support the weight of the wheel.

9 Clean all old grease off the axle, spacers, bearing seals and the speed sensor.

10 Check the axle is straight by rolling it on a flat surface such as a piece of plate glass (first remove any corrosion using wire wool). If the equipment is available, place the axle in V-blocks and measure the runout using a dial gauge. If the axle is bent or the runout exceeds the limit specified, replace it with a new one.

11 Check the condition of the wheel bearings and seals (see Section 17).

Installation

12 Apply a smear of grease to the inside of the bearing seals then install the spacers (see Steps 7 and 8) – fit the narrow end of the left-hand spacer into the seal **(see illustration)**. The wide rim of the right-hand spacer fits against the fork leg.

13 Manoeuvre the wheel into position between the forks, making sure the brake disc is on the right-hand side. If the brake caliper is in place ensure there is sufficient room between the brake pads to accept the brake disc – ease the pads apart

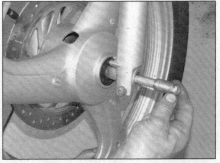
15.4a Withdraw the axle from the left-hand side

15.5 Withdraw the wheel forwards

with a clean, flat-bladed screwdriver if necessary.

14 On XL125V-1 to V-6 models, fit the speed sensor onto the tabs in the hub **(see illustration 15.6)**.

15 Lubricate the axle with a smear of grease, then lift the wheel into position and slide the axle through from the left-hand side **(see illustration 15.4a)**. On XL125V-1 to V-6 models, ensure the speed sensor is correctly installed **(see illustration 15.4b)**.

16 Tighten the axle to the torque setting specified at the beginning of this Chapter.

17 If displaced, install the brake caliper (see Section 3). Operate the brake lever to bring the pads into contact with the disc.

18 Take the machine off the stand. While standing alongside the bike, apply the front brake and push on the handlebars to

15.4b Note location of tab

15.6 Lift off the speed sensor. Note drive tabs (arrowed)

compress the forks several times to seat the axle. Tighten the front axle clamp bolt to the specified torque **(see illustration 15.3a or b)**.

16 Rear wheel

VT125C

Removal

1 Position the motorcycle on an auxiliary stand so that the rear wheel is off the ground. Always make sure the motorcycle is securely supported.

2 Straighten and remove the split pin, then undo the nut securing the rear brake torque

15.7 Remove the left-hand axle spacer

15.8 Remove the right-hand axle spacer

15.12 Fit narrow end of left-hand spacer into seal

16.2a Remove the split pin . . .

16.2b . . . and undo the nut

16.2c Remove the plain washer and the rubber washer . . .

arm to the brake plate **(see illustrations)**. Discard the split pin as a new one must be used. Remove the plain washer and the rubber washer, then disconnect the torque arm from the brake plate **(see illustrations)**.

16.2d . . . then detach the torque arm

16.3b Note location of the brake arm trunnion

16.6 Remove the right-hand axle spacer

3 Unscrew the rear brake adjuster nut and disconnect the brake rod from the brake arm **(see illustration)**. Note the location of the brake arm trunnion and the brake rod spring and remove them for safekeeping **(see illustration)**.

16.3a Unscrew the rear brake adjuster nut

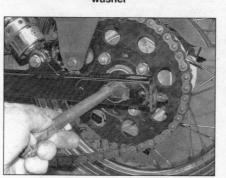

16.5 Unscrew the axle nut and remove the washer

16.7a Withdraw the axle . . .

4 Loosen the rear axle nut, then loosen the locknut on the left and right-hand chain adjusters and turn both adjuster nuts to create some slack in the chain (see Chapter 1).
5 Unscrew the axle nut and remove the washer **(see illustration)**.
6 Support the wheel and partially withdraw the axle from the left-hand side so that the right-hand spacer can be removed – note which way round the spacer fits **(see illustration)**.
7 Withdraw the axle, lower the wheel to the ground and remove the left-hand spacer, noting how it fits **(see illustrations)**. Disengage the chain from the sprocket and remove the wheel from the swingarm. Keep the wheel upright – if you need to lay it down, first lift the brake plate off the brake drum.
Caution: Don't lay the wheel down and allow it to rest on the sprocket – it could become warped. Set the wheel on wood blocks so the sprocket doesn't support the weight of the wheel.
8 Clean all old grease off the axle, spacers and bearing seals. If required, remove the sprocket coupling (see Section 21).
9 Check the axle is straight by rolling it on a flat surface such as a piece of plate glass (first remove any corrosion using wire wool). If the equipment is available, place the axle in V-blocks and measure the runout using a dial gauge. If the axle is bent or the runout exceeds the limit specified, replace it with a new one.
10 Check the condition of the wheel bearings and seals (see Section 17).

16.7b . . . and remove the left-hand spacer

16.13 Fit the chain onto the sprocket

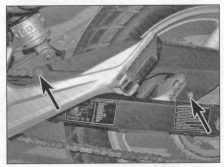

16.21a Undo the bolts . . .

16.21b . . . then unclip the rear edge (arrowed) . . .

Installation

11 Ensure both chain adjusters are correctly installed in the ends of the swingarm.

12 If removed, install the sprocket coupling and apply a smear of grease to the inside of the coupling bearing seal. Ensure the brake plate is correctly installed on the brake drum.

13 Manoeuvre the wheel into position between the ends of the swingarm with the sprocket on the left-hand side, and engage the drive chain with the sprocket **(see illustration)**. Install the left-hand spacer **(see illustration 16.7b)**.

14 Lubricate the axle with a smear of grease, then lift the wheel into position and insert the axle from the left-hand side **(see illustration 16.7a)**. Install the right-hand spacer between the brake plate and the swingarm with the shouldered end against the swingarm, then push the axle all the way through.

15 Check that everything is correctly aligned, then fit the washer and tighten the axle nut finger-tight **(see illustration 16.5)**.

16 Fit the torque arm onto the shouldered bolt on the brake plate, then install the rubber washer and plain washer and tighten the nut securely **(see illustrations 16.2d, c, and b)**. Secure the nut with a new split pin and bend the ends as shown **(see illustration 16.2a)**.

17 Install the brake rod spring and brake arm trunnion, then connect the rod to the brake arm and thread on the adjuster nut **(see illustrations 16.3b and a)**.

18 Check and adjust the drive chain slack (see Chapter 1, Section 1).

19 Check and adjust the brake pedal freeplay (see Chapter 1, Section 3).

XL125V

Removal

20 Position the motorcycle on an auxiliary stand so that the rear wheel is off the ground. Always make sure the motorcycle is securely supported.

21 Undo the bolts securing the chainguard, then unclip the rear edge from the swingarm and lift it off **(see illustrations)**.

22 Loosen the rear axle nut, then loosen the locknut on the left and right-hand chain adjusters and turn both adjuster nuts to create some slack in the chain (see Chapter 1).

23 Unscrew the axle nut and remove the washer **(see illustration)**.

24 Support the wheel and withdraw the axle from the left-hand side **(see illustration)**.

25 Lower the wheel to the ground, disengage the chain from the sprocket and remove the wheel from the swingarm **(see illustration)**. Take care not to dislodge the rear brake caliper assembly from the lug on the swingarm – if necessary secure it with a cable-tie **(see illustration 7.5)**.

26 Remove the left and right-hand spacers, noting how they fit **(see illustrations 16.32 and 17.25)**.

Caution: Do not lay the wheel down and allow it to rest on the disc or the sprocket – they could become warped. Set the wheel on wood blocks so the disc or the sprocket doesn't support the weight of the wheel. Do not operate the brake pedal with the wheel removed.

16.21c . . . and lift the chainguard off

16.24 Withdraw the axle

27 Clean all old grease off the axle, spacers and bearing seals. If required, remove the sprocket coupling (see Section 21).

28 Check the axle is straight by rolling it on a flat surface such as a piece of plate glass (first remove any corrosion using wire wool). If the equipment is available, place the axle in V-blocks and measure the runout using a dial gauge. If the axle is bent or the runout exceeds the limit specified, replace it with a new one.

29 Check the condition of the wheel bearings and seals (see Section 17).

Installation

30 Ensure both chain adjusters are correctly installed in the ends of the swingarm.

31 If removed, install the sprocket coupling. Apply a smear of grease to the inside of the coupling bearing seal and install the spacer **(see illustration 17.25)**.

16.23 Unscrew the axle nut and remove the washer

16.25 Lift the chain off the sprocket

16.32 Install the right-hand axle spacer

16.33 Slide the brake disc between the pads

32 Apply a smear of grease to the inside of the right-hand bearing seal and install the spacer **(see illustration)**.

33 Manoeuvre the wheel into position between the ends of the swingarm. Ensure there is sufficient room between the brake pads to accept the brake disc – ease the pads apart with a clean, flat-bladed screwdriver if necessary **(see illustration)**. Engage the drive chain with the sprocket **(see illustration 16.25)**.

34 Lubricate the axle with a smear of grease, then lift the wheel into position and insert the axle from the left-hand side **(see illustration 16.24)**. Check that everything is correctly aligned, then push the axle all the way through.

35 Fit the washer and tighten the axle nut finger-tight **(see illustration 16.23)**.

36 Check and adjust the drive chain slack (see Chapter 1, Section 1).

37 Operate the brake pedal to bring the pads into contact with the disc.

38 Check the operation of the rear brake before riding the motorcycle.

17 Wheel bearings

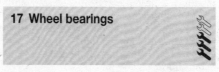

Caution: Don't lay the wheel down and allow it to rest on the disc – it could become warped. Set the wheel on wood blocks so the wheel rim supports the weight of the wheel, or keep the wheel upright. Don't operate the brake lever/pedal with the wheel removed.

Note: *Always renew the wheel bearings in pairs, never individually. Never reuse bearings once they have been removed.*

Front wheel bearings

1 Remove the wheel (see Section 15).

2 Lever out the bearing seal from each side of the hub using a flat-bladed screwdriver or a seal hook **(see illustration)**. Take care not to damage the hub. Discard the seals as new ones must be fitted on reassembly.

3 On XL125V-1 to V-6 models, remove the speedometer drive plate from the left-hand side, if applicable **(see illustration)**.

4 Inspect the bearings – check that the inner race turns smoothly, quietly and freely and that the outer race is a tight fit in the hub.

5 If the bearings are worn, remove them using a metal rod (preferably a brass punch) inserted through the centre of the opposite bearing and locating it on the inner race, pushing the bearing spacer aside to expose it **(see illustration)**. Curve the end of the rod to obtain better purchase if necessary. Strike the rod with a hammer, working evenly around the bearing, to drive it from the hub **(see illustration)**. Remove the spacer which fits between the bearings.

6 Turn the wheel over and remove the other bearing using the same procedure.

7 Thoroughly clean the hub area of the wheel with a suitable solvent and inspect the bearing seats for scoring and wear. If the seats are damaged, consult a Honda dealer before reassembling the wheel.

8 The new bearings can be installed in the hub using a drawbolt arrangement (see *Tools and Workshop Tips* in the *Reference* section) or by using a bearing driver or suitable socket. Ensure that the drawbolt washer or driver (as applicable) bears only on the bearing's outer race and does not contact the bearing housing.

9 Install the left-hand bearing first, with the sealed side facing outwards **(see illustration)**. Ensure the bearing is fitted squarely and all the way into its seat.

10 Turn the wheel over. Lubricate the bearing spacer with a smear of grease, then install the spacer. Install the right-hand bearing, sealed side facing outwards, driving it in until it is fully seated.

11 Lubricate the right-hand bearing seal with a smear of grease and press it into the hub

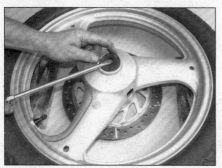

17.2 Lever out the bearing seals

17.3 Remove the speedometer drive plate (where fitted)

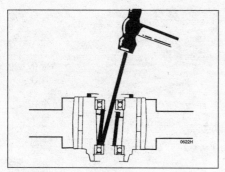

17.5a Position the rod as shown . . .

17.5b . . . to drive out the wheel bearings

17.9 Installed position of the sealed wheel bearing

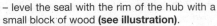

17.11 Installed position of the right-hand bearing seal

17.17 Lever out the right-hand bearing seal – XL125V

17.24 Installed position of the right-hand bearing seal – XL125V

– level the seal with the rim of the hub with a small block of wood **(see illustration)**.

12 Turn the wheel over.

13 On XL125V-1 to V-6 models, install the speedometer drive plate (see Step 3).

14 Lubricate the left-hand bearing seal with a smear of grease and press it into the hub – level the seal with the rim of the hub with a small block of wood.

15 Clean the brake disc using acetone or brake system cleaner, then install the front wheel (see Section 15).

Rear wheel bearings

16 Remove the wheel (see Section 16) and lift the sprocket coupling out of the hub (see Section 21).

17 On XL125V models, lever out the bearing seal from the right-hand side of the hub using a flat-bladed screwdriver or a seal hook **(see illustration)**. Take care not to damage the hub. Discard the seal as a new one should be fitted on reassembly.

18 Inspect the bearings in both sides of the hub – check that the inner race turns smoothly, quietly and freely and that the outer race is a tight fit in the hub.

19 If the bearings are worn, follow the procedure in Steps 5 and 6 to drive out the bearings and remove the spacer.

20 Thoroughly clean the hub area of the wheel with a suitable solvent and inspect the bearing seats for scoring and wear. If the seats are damaged, consult a Honda dealer before reassembling the wheel.

21 The new bearings can be installed in the hub using a drawbolt arrangement or by using a bearing driver or suitable socket (see Step 8).

22 Install the left-hand bearing first, with the sealed side facing outwards. Ensure the bearing is fitted squarely and all the way into its seat.

23 Turn the wheel over. Lubricate the bearing spacer with a smear of grease, then install the spacer. Install the right-hand bearing, sealed side facing outwards, driving it in until it is fully seated.

24 On XL125V models, lubricate the new right-hand bearing seal with a smear of grease and press it into the hub – level the seal with

the rim of the hub with a small block of wood **(see illustration)**.

Sprocket coupling bearing

25 If not already done, remove the outer spacer from the coupling bearing seal **(see illustration)**.

26 Remove the spacer from inside the coupling bearing if it is loose **(see illustration)**.

27 Lever out the bearing seal on the outside of the coupling using a flat-bladed screwdriver or a seal hook **(see illustration 17.17)**. Take care not to damage the seal housing. Discard the seal as a new one should be fitted on reassembly.

28 Inspect the bearing – check that the

inner races turn smoothly, quietly and freely, and that the outer race is a tight fit in the coupling.

29 If the bearing is worn, first drive out the inner spacer, if not already removed **(see illustration)**. Support the coupling sprocket side down and drive out the old bearing with a suitably-sized socket **(see illustration)**.

30 Thoroughly clean the bearing seat with a suitable solvent and inspect it for scoring and wear. If the seat is damaged, consult a Honda dealer before reassembling the wheel.

31 Lay the new bearing sealed (or marked) side down on the work surface, then press the inner spacer into the new bearing until it seats.

32 Use a bearing driver or suitable socket to

17.25 Remove the outer axle spacer

17.26 Remove the inner coupling bearing spacer

17.29a Drive out the spacer from the outside

17.29b Drive out the bearing from the inside

17.32 Install the bearing/spacer assembly from the outside

17.35 Renew the hub O-ring if required

install the bearing/spacer assembly into the coupling, sprocket side up **(see illustration)**. Ensure that the driver bears only on the bearing's outer race. Ensure the bearing is fitted squarely and all the way onto its seat.

33 Lubricate the new seal with a smear of grease, then press it into the coupling. Level the seal with the rim of the coupling with a small block of wood.

34 Check the sprocket coupling/rubber dampers (see Section 21).

35 Check the condition of the hub O-ring – if it is damaged or flattened, remove it and fit a new one **(see illustration)**. Ensure the O-ring is correctly located in its groove and lubricate it with a smear of grease.

36 Install the sprocket coupling (see Section 21) then install the rear wheel (see Section 16).

18 Tyres

General information

1 The tyres fitted to the wire spoked wheels on VT125C models have inner tubes. The wheels fitted to XL125V models are designed to take tubeless tyres only.

2 Tyre sizes are given in *Bike spec* at the beginning of this manual. They are also listed in the Owner's Handbook and on the tyre information label on the swingarm.

3 Refer to the *Pre-ride checks* listed at the beginning of this manual for tyre maintenance.

Fitting new tyres

4 When selecting new tyres, refer to the tyre information in the Owner's Handbook. Ensure that front and rear tyre types are compatible, the correct size and correct speed rating **(see illustration)**. If necessary seek advice from a Honda dealer or tyre fitting specialist.

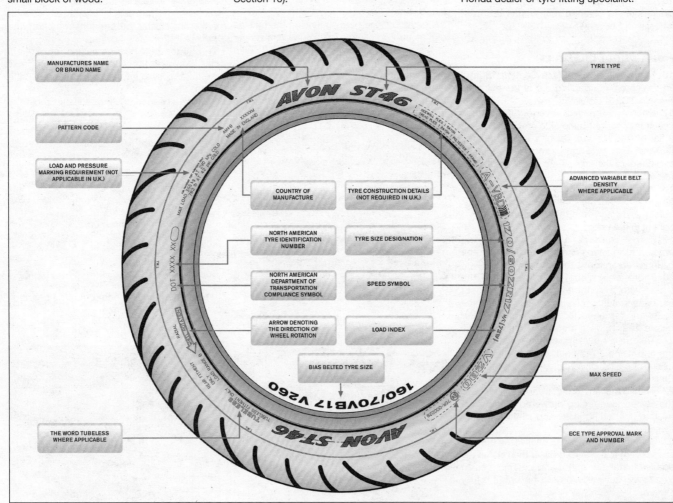

18.4 Common tyre sidewall markings

5 It is recommended that tyres are fitted by a motorcycle tyre specialist rather than attempted in the home workshop. This is particularly relevant in the case of tubeless tyres because the force required to break the seal between the wheel rim and tyre bead is substantial, and is usually beyond the capabilities of an individual working with normal tyre levers. Additionally, the specialist will be able to balance the wheels after tyre fitting and renew the tyre valve.

6 Note that punctured tubeless tyres can in some cases be repaired. Repairs must be carried out by a motorcycle tyre fitting specialist. Honda advise that a repaired tyre should not be used at speeds above 50 mph (80 kmh) for the first 24 hours, and not above 75 mph (120 kmh) thereafter.

19 Drive chain

Cleaning

1 Refer to Chapter 1, Section 1, for details of routine cleaning with the chain installed on the sprockets.

2 If the chain is extremely dirty remove it from the motorcycle and soak it in paraffin (kerosene) for approximately five or six minutes, then clean it using a soft brush.
Caution: Don't use gasoline (petrol), solvent or other cleaning fluids which might damage its internal sealing properties. Don't use high-pressure water. Remove the chain, wipe it off, then blow dry it with compressed air immediately. The entire process shouldn't take longer than ten minutes – if it does, the O-rings in the chain rollers could be damaged.

Removal and installation

3 The original equipment chain specified for the machines covered in this manual is of the staked soft link type sealed with O-rings, although a split link type chain may be found on certain VT125C models. Examine the chain to establish the type fitted and follow the appropriate procedure described below.
Note: *If the chain is to be reused, clean it as*

19.8 Note location of chain over sprocket and swingarm

described and wipe all old grease and dirt off the sprockets, swingarm chain slider and front sprocket cover. If the chain is to be renewed, fit new front and rear sprockets as described in Section 20.

4 Remove the front sprocket cover (see Section 20).

5 Remove the chainguard – on VT125C models, refer to the procedure in Chapter 6, Section 12; on XL125V models, refer to the procedure in Section 16 of this Chapter.

Staked soft link chain

Special tool: *The original equipment chain fitted to most of the machines covered in this manual has a staked-type joining link which can be disassembled using either Honda service tool, Part No. 07HMH-MR10103, or one of several commercially-available drive chain cutting/staking tools. Such chains can be identified by the joining link side plate's identification marks (and usually its different colour), as well as by the staked ends of the link's two pins which look as if they have been deeply centre-punched, instead of peened over as with all the other pins.*

6 Locate the joining link in a suitable position to work on by rotating the back wheel.

7 Slacken the drive chain (see Chapter 1).

8 Split the chain at the joining link using the chain breaker, carefully following the manufacturer's operating instructions (see also Section 8 in *Tools and Workshop Tips* in the *Reference* section). Draw the chain off the front sprocket, noting how it fits around the swingarm, and lift it off **(see illustration)**.

9 On installation, fit the chain around the front

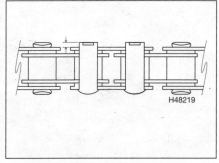

19.11 Measure pin projection above sideplate

and rear sprockets, leaving the two ends in a convenient position to work on.

10 Refer to Section 8 in *Tools and Workshop Tips* in the *Reference* section. Install the new joining link from the inside with the four O-rings correctly located between the link plates. DO NOT re-use old joining link components.

11 Install the new side plate with its identification marks facing outward. Measure the amount that the joining link pins project from the side plate and check they are within the measurements specified at the beginning of this Chapter **(see illustration)**.

12 Stake the new link using the drive chain cutting/staking tool, carefully following the instructions of both the chain manufacturer and the tool manufacturer. Ensure the chain is staked correctly by measuring the diameter of the staked ends in two directions and check that they are evenly staked and within the measurements specified at the beginning of this Chapter **(see illustration)**.

13 After staking, check the joining link and staking for any signs of cracking **(see illustration)**. If there is any evidence of cracking, the joining link, O-rings and side plate must be renewed.

14 Adjust and lubricate the chain following the procedures described in Chapter 1.

15 Install the remaining components in the reverse order of removal.

Split link chain

16 Rotate the rear wheel to position the split link on the rear sprocket **(see illustration)**. Note which way round the clip is fitted (closed end facing direction of travel).

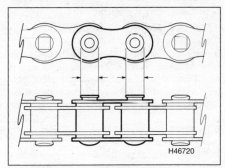

19.12 Check the diameter of the staked pin ends

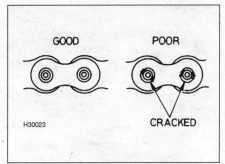

19.13 Check staking for any signs of cracking

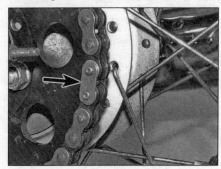

19.16 Position split link (arrowed) on the rear sprocket

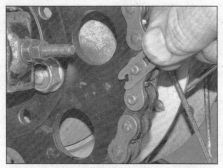

19.17 Slide the clip off – don't lever it

19.18 Lift off the side plate

19.19 Withdraw the joining link

19.22 Use pliers to install the clip

17 Using pliers, slide the open end of the clip up over the lower pin, then lift the clip off the upper pin **(see illustration)**. **Do not** try to lever the clip off as it will be sprained.

18 Lift off the side plate **(see illustration)**.

19 Support the lower run of the chain and withdraw the joining link **(see illustration)**.

20 Draw the chain off the front sprocket, noting how it fits around the swingarm, and lift it off **(see illustration 19.8)**.

21 Honda provide a stretch limit for the split link type chain (see Specifications). Anchor one end of the chain and pull on the other end so that it is taut. Using a ruler, measure a 40-link section of chain, i.e. from the first pin to the 41st pin and compare the distance measured with the maxium limit. Check the chain in several different places and if it has stretched beyond the limit, renew it.

22 Installation is the reverse of removal, noting the following:

● If a new chain is being fitted, loosen the rear axle and chain adjusters to allow for a shorter chain (see Chapter 1).

● Fit the chain over the front sprocket and swingarm and join the two ends on the rear sprocket **(see illustration 19.19)**.

● Install the rear link and then the front link.

● Fit the clip over the upper pin, then use pliers to slide the open end into place on the lower pin **(see illustration)**.

● The installed clip should look like this – closed end facing direction of travel **(see illustration 19.16)**.

● Adjust and lubricate the chain following the procedures described in Chapter 1.

● Install the remaining components in the reverse order of removal.

20 Sprockets

Check

1 Unscrew the bolts securing the front sprocket cover and remove it **(see illustrations)**.

2 Remove the chainguard – on VT125C models, refer to the procedure in Chapter 6, Section 12; on XL125V models, refer to the procedure in Section 16 of this Chapter.

3 Check the wear pattern on both sprockets (see Chapter 1, Section 1). If the sprocket teeth are worn excessively, replace the chain and both sprockets as a set – worn sprockets can ruin a new drive chain and vice versa.

Removal and installation

Front sprocket

4 Remove the front sprocket cover (see Step 1).

5 Remove the drive chain (see Section 19). Alternatively, if only the front sprocket is being removed, slacken the chain (see Chapter 1) – the sprocket can then be pulled off the transmission output shaft with the chain *in situ*.

6 Unscrew the sprocket retainer plate bolts **(see illustration)**.

7 Turn the sprocket retainer plate to unlock it from the splines on the output shaft, then slide it off the shaft **(see illustration)**.

8 Slide the sprocket off the shaft **(see**

20.1a Undo the bolts . . .

20.1b . . . and remove the front sprocket cover

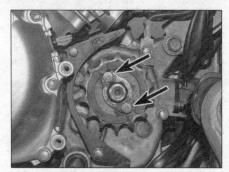

20.6 Unscrew the retainer plate bolts

20.7 Remove the retainer plate as described

20.8 Draw the front sprocket off

20.11a Sprocket mounting nuts – VT125C

20.11b Sprocket mounting nuts – XL125V

illustration). Note which way round the sprocket is fitted.

9 Installation is the reverse of removal, noting the following:

● Ensure the marked side of the sprocket faces out.
● Ensure the retainer plate is correctly installed.
● Clean the threads of the retainer plate bolts and apply a suitable non-permanent thread-locking compound.
● Tighten the retainer plate bolts to the specified torque setting.

Rear sprocket

10 Remove the rear wheel (see Section 16). Support the wheel on wooden blocks with the sprocket uppermost.

11 Unscrew the nuts securing the sprocket to the sprocket coupling **(see illustrations)**.

12 Lift off the sprocket, noting which way round it fits. Check the condition of the sprocket studs and replace them all with new ones if any are damaged. Make sure the studs are tight.

13 Before installing the sprocket, make sure there is no dirt or corrosion where it seats on the hub. Fit the sprocket with the marked side facing out, then install the nuts and tighten them evenly and in a criss-cross sequence to the torque setting specified at the beginning of this Chapter.

14 Install the rear wheel (see Section 16).

21 Rear sprocket coupling dampers

1 Remove the rear wheel (see Section 16). Grasp the sprocket and feel for play between the sprocket coupling and the wheel hub by attempting to twist the sprocket in each direction **(see illustration)**. Any play indicates worn rubber damper segments.
Caution: Do not lay the wheel down on the

disc as it could become warped. Lay the wheel on wooden blocks so that the disc is off the ground.

2 Lift the sprocket coupling out from the wheel hub leaving the rubber dampers in position **(see illustration)**. Note the spacer inside the coupling and remove it if it is loose **(see illustration 17.26)**.

3 Examine the coupling vanes for cracks or any obvious signs of damage **(see illustration)**.

4 Lift the rubber damper segments from the wheel and check them for cracks, hardening

and general deterioration **(see illustration)**. Renew them as a set if necessary.

5 Check the condition of the hub O-ring – if it is damaged or flattened, replace it with a new one (see Section 17, Step 35).

6 To check and renew the sprocket coupling bearing see Section 17.

7 Installation is the reverse of removal. Lubricate the hub O-ring with a smear of grease. Make sure the spacer is correctly installed in the coupling **(see illustration 17.26)**. Align the vanes with the dampers and press the coupling in firmly.

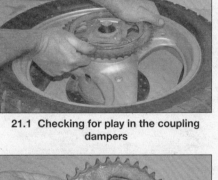

21.1 Checking for play in the coupling dampers

21.2 Lift out the sprocket coupling

21.3 Examine the coupling vanes for damage

21.4 Examine the damper segments

Notes

Chapter 8
Bodywork

Contents

Degrees of difficulty

Easy, suitable for novice with little experience		**Fairly easy,** suitable for beginner with some experience	**Fairly difficult,** suitable for competent DIY mechanic	**Difficult,** suitable for experienced DIY mechanic	**Very difficult,** suitable for expert DIY or professional

1 General information

This Chapter covers the procedures necessary to remove and install the bodywork. Since many service and repair operations on these motorcycles require the removal of the body panels, the procedures are grouped here and referred to from other Chapters.

In the case of damage to the bodywork, it is usually necessary to remove the broken component and replace it with a new (or used) one. The material that the body panels are composed of doesn't lend itself to conventional repair techniques. Note that there are however some companies that specialize in 'plastic welding' and there are a number of DIY bodywork repair kits now available for motorcycles.

When attempting to remove any body panel, first study it closely, noting any fasteners and associated fittings, to be sure of returning everything to its correct place on installation. In some cases the aid of an assistant will be required when removing panels, to help avoid the risk of damage to paintwork. Once the evident fasteners have been removed, try to withdraw the panel as described but DO NOT FORCE IT – if it will not release, check that all fasteners have been removed and try again.

When installing a body panel, first study it closely, noting any fasteners and associated fittings removed with it, to be sure of returning everything to its correct place. Check that all fasteners are in good condition, including the rubber mounts; replace any faulty fasteners with new ones before the panel is reassembled. Check also that all mounting brackets are straight and repair them or replace them with new ones if necessary before attempting to install the panel.

Tighten the fasteners securely, but be careful not to overtighten any of them or the panel may break (not always immediately) due to the uneven stress.

Trim clips

Some body panels are secured with trim clips **(see illustration)**. To release a clip, unscrew the centre, then prise the clip out. On installation, ensure the holes in the body panels are aligned. Insert the clip with the centre pulled out, then press the centre in to secure the clip. If a clip is sprained or broken it should be replaced with a new one.

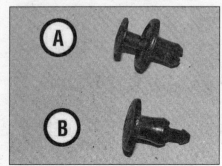

1.1 Trim clips – unscrew the centre to release (A), push the centre in to secure (B)

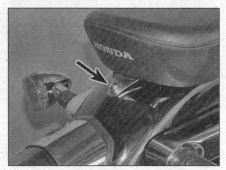

2.1a Undo the bolt at the back . . .

2.1b . . . and on both sides of the rider's seat

2.2 Draw the seat assembly back and off

2 Seat

VT125C

1 Undo the bolt at the back of the passenger's seat unit and the bolts on both sides of the rider's seat **(see illustrations)**.

2 Lift the back of the seat assembly and draw it back to disengage the tab from under the rear of the fuel tank **(see illustration)**.

3 If required, undo the nuts securing the passenger's seat to the rider's seat and separate the seats **(see illustration)**.

4 On installation, make sure the tab at the front of the rider's seat is fitted under the rear of the fuel tank **(see illustration)**. Tighten the mounting bolts securely.

XL125V

5 Insert the ignition key into the seat lock located behind the left-hand side panel and release the seat catch **(see illustration)**.

6 Lift the back of the seat and draw it back to disengage the tabs on the underside from the brackets on the frame and the rear edge of the fuel tank **(see illustration)**.

7 On installation, slide the seat forwards to engage the tabs, then push down on the back of the seat to engage the latch.

3 Side panels

VT125C

1 To remove the left-hand side panel, use a suitably-sized coin to undo the screw on the lower rear edge of the panel **(see illustration)**. Carefully pull the top edge away from the frame to release the peg from the grommet, then lift the bottom edge off the tab on the frame **(see illustration)**.

2 To remove the right-hand side panel, carefully pull the top and rear edges

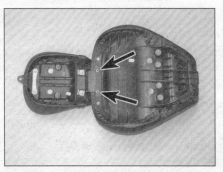

2.3 Undo nuts to separate seats

2.4 Tab (arrowed) locates under rear of fuel tank

2.5 Release the seat catch

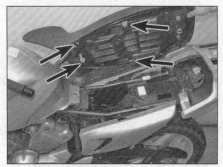

2.6 Draw the seat back to release tabs (arrowed)

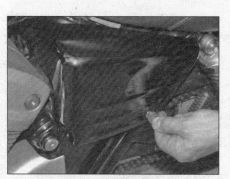

3.1a Undo the screw as described

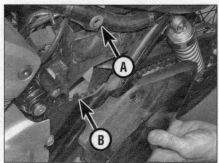

3.1b Location of grommet (A) and tab on frame (B)

3.2 Release the pegs from the grommets

3.6 Undo the screw (arrowed) . . .

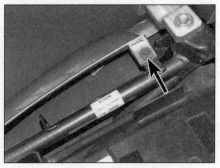

3.7 . . . and the bolt

away from the frame to release the pegs from the grommets, then lift the bottom edge off the tab on the frame **(see illustration)**.

3 On installation, ensure the bottom edge of the panel is fitted correctly over the tab, then press the peg(s) firmly into the grommet. If required, lubricate the grommet with WD-40 or similar.

4 Tighten the fixing screw to secure the left-hand panel.

XL125V

5 Remove the seat (see Section 2).
6 Undo the screw on the lower front edge of the panel **(see illustration)**.
7 Undo the bolt on the upper rear of the panel **(see illustration)**.
8 Carefully pull the panel away from the frame to release the peg from the grommet **(see illustration)**.
9 On installation, align the upper mounting **(see illustration 3.7)** then press the peg firmly

into the grommet. If required, lubricate the grommet with WD-40 or similar.
10 Install the mounting bolt and screw, then tighten them both securely.

4   Mirrors

VT125C

1 Lift the rubber boot off the mirror bracket, counter-hold the mounting adapter on the handlebar bracket and slacken the locknut **(see illustration)**.
2 Unscrew the mirror stem from the adapter **(see illustration)**.
3 If required, unscrew the adapter from the front brake master cylinder or clutch lever bracket, as applicable.
4 Installation is the reverse of removal. Set the position of the mirror as required, then tighten the locknut to secure it.

XL125V-1 to V-6

5 Lift the rubber boot off the mirror bracket **(see illustration)**.

3.8 Release the peg from the grommet (arrowed)

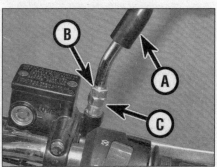

4.1 Rubber boot (A), locknut (B) and mounting adapter (C)

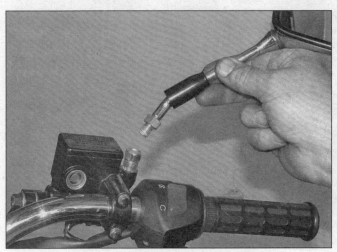

4.2 Unscrew mirror stem from the adapter

4.5 Lift the rubber boot . . .

4.6 . . . and unscrew the mounting adapter

4.8a Undo the mounting bolts . . .

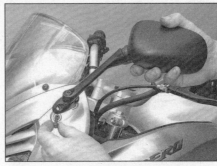

4.8b . . . and lift the mirror assembly off

5.1a Windshield screws, left-hand side –
XL125V-1 to V-6 models

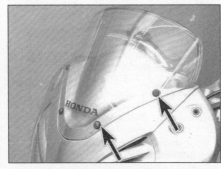

5.1b Windshield screws, left-hand side –
XL125V-7 models onward

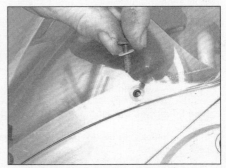

5.1c Note location of plastic washers

6 Unscrew the mounting adapter and remove the mirror **(see illustration)**.

7 On installation, screw the mounting adapter into the bracket, set the position of the mirror as required, then tighten the adapter to secure it.

XL125V-7 onward

8 Undo the mounting bolts and lift the mirror off **(see illustrations)**.

9 Installation is the reverse of removal.

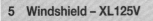

5 Windshield – XL125V

1 Undo the screws securing the windshield, noting the location of the plastic washers, and lift it off **(see illustrations)**.

2 Inspect the wellnuts in the fairing – if they are loose, new ones must be fitted. Apply a smear of grease to the screw threads on installation.

6 Fairing panels – XL125V

Inner fairing panels

1 On XL125V-1 to V-6 models, release

the trim clips securing the bridging panel, draw the panel forwards and lift it out **(see illustrations)**.

2 On XL125V-7 models onward, undo the bolts securing the panel to the underside on

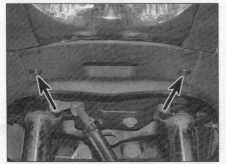

6.1a Release the trim clips . . .

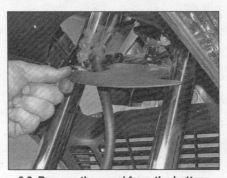

6.2 Remove the panel from the bottom yoke

the front fork bottom yoke and lift the panel out **(see illustration)**.

3 Release the trim clips securing the main centre panel – there are three down both sides along the inner edge **(see illustration)**.

6.1b . . . and remove the bridging panel

6.3 Release the trim clips on both sides

6.4 Undo the lower mounting screws

6.5a Inner fairing panel – XL125V-1 to V-6 models

6.5b Inner fairing panel – XL125V-7 models onward

4 Undo the lower mounting screws – there is one on each side **(see illustration)**.
5 Ease the inner fairing panel out **(see illustrations)**.
6 On XL125V-1 to V-6 models, undo the bolts securing the panel to the underside on the front fork bottom yoke and lift the panel out **(see illustration)**.
7 Installation is the reverse of removal. Make sure the inner panels engage correctly with the sides of the main fairing. Install the trim clips as described in Section 1.

Cockpit trim panel

8 On XL125V-1 to V-6 models, release the trim clips securing the panel and lift it out **(see illustrations)**.
9 On XL125V-7 models onward, undo the screws securing the front edge of the panel **(see illustration)**. Release the trim clips securing the edges of the panel to the main fairing – there are three down both sides **(see illustration)**. Ease the panel out to release the pegs on the underside of the instrument cluster from the grommets on the fairing bracket and disconnect the instrument cluster wiring connector **(see illustrations)**. Manoeuvre the trim panel and instrument cluster assembly out.
10 Installation is the reverse of removal. On XL125V-7 models onward, ensure the instrument cluster wiring connector is secure. Install the trim clips as described in Section 1.

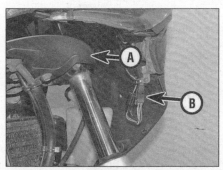

6.6 Remove the panel (A) from the bottom yoke. Note wiring connectors (B)

6.8a Release the trim clips . . .

6.8b . . . and lift the panel out

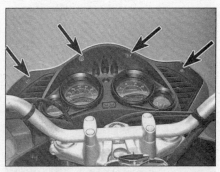

6.9a Undo the screws . . .

6.9b . . . and the trim clips

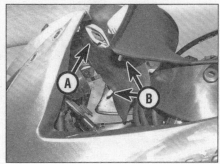

6.9c Wiring connector (A). Pegs (B) . . .

6.9d . . . locate in grommets (arrowed)

6.13 Undo the bolts (arrowed)

6.14 Right-hand turn signal wiring connector

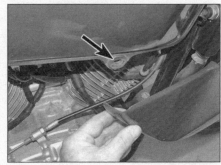

6.15 Peg on fairing locates in grommet

Fairing

XL125V-1 to V-6 models

11 Remove the inner fairing panels and the cockpit trim panel.

12 Remove the instrument cluster (see Chapter 9, Section 15).

13 Undo the bolts securing the fairing panel to the fairing bracket **(see illustration)**.

14 Locate the wiring connectors for the headlight assembly and left-hand front turn signal and disconnect them **(see illustration 6.6)**. Locate the wiring connector for the right-hand front turn signal and disconnect it **(see illustration)**. Free the loom side of all wiring from any clips or ties on the fairing.

15 Working on the left and right-hand sides of the bike, undo the screw securing the top edge of the fairing to the fuel tank, then ease the peg securing the fairing out from the grommet on the lower edge of the fuel tank **(see illustration)**.

16 Draw the fairing forwards and off the bike **(see illustration)**.

17 Follow the procedures in Chapter 9 to remove the headlight unit and turn signals.

18 Installation is the reverse of removal. Ensure all wiring connectors are secure and test the operation of the headlight, turn signals and instrument cluster before riding the motorcycle.

XL125V-7 models onward

19 Remove the mirrors (see Section 4).

20 Remove the inner fairing panel and the cockpit trim panel.

21 Working on the left and right-hand sides of the bike, undo the screw securing the top edge of the fairing to the fuel tank, then ease the peg securing the fairing out from the grommet on the lower edge of the fuel tank **(see illustrations)**.

22 Draw the fairing forwards and disconnect the wiring connectors for the headlight assembly and left-hand front turn signal **(see illustration)**. Disconnect the wiring connector for the right-hand front turn signal **(see illustration)**.

23 Lift the fairing off the bike **(see illustration)**.

24 Follow the procedures in Chapter 9 to remove the headlight unit and turn signals.

25 Installation is the reverse of removal. Ensure all wiring connectors are secure and test the operation of the headlight, turn signals and instrument cluster before riding the motorcycle.

6.16 Draw the fairing off

6.21a Undo the screw (arrowed) . . .

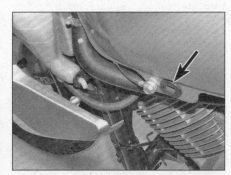

6.21b . . . and release the peg from the grommet

6.22a Headlight and left-hand turn signal wiring connectors

6.22b Right-hand turn signal wiring connector

6.23 Draw the fairing off

7.1a Unscrew the bolts

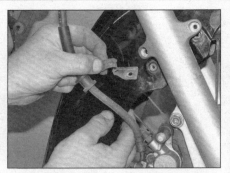

7.1b Note location of brake hose guide

7.2 Draw the mudguard forwards

7 Front mudguard

VT125C

1 Unscrew the bolts on both sides securing the mudguard to the front forks – note the location of the guide on the right-hand side for the brake hose **(see illustrations)**.
2 Draw the mudguard forwards and remove it **(see illustration)**.
3 Note the location of the brace on the underside of the mudguard – if required, ease the collars on the brace out from the mounting bolt holes and remove it **(see illustration)**.
4 Installation is the reverse of removal.

Don't forget to secure the brake hose on the right-hand side.

XL125V

5 On XL125V-1 to V-6 models (except Type IIG German models), ease the speed sensor wiring guide out from the left-hand side of the mudguard (see Chapter 6, Section 6).
6 Note the location of the brake hose guide on the right-hand side, then unscrew the bolts on both sides securing the mudguard to the front forks and displace the guide **(see illustration)**.
7 Draw the mudguard forwards and remove it **(see illustration)**.
8 Note the location of the brace on the underside of the mudguard – if required, ease the collars on the brace out from the

mounting bolt holes and remove it **(see illustration)**.
9 Installation is the reverse of removal. Don't forget to secure the speedometer wiring, where fitted. Don't forget to secure the brake hose on the right-hand side.

8 Rear carrier

1 Remove the seat (see Section 2).
2 Unscrew the bolts securing the carrier **(see illustration)**.
3 Note the location of the washers and top-hat spacers on the bolts **(see illustration)**. On XL125V-1 to V-6 models the spacers are fitted underneath the carrier, on XL125V-7 models

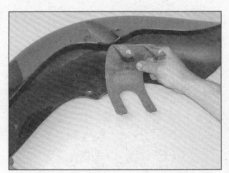

7.3 Note location of mudguard brace

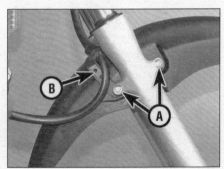

7.6 Unscrew bolts (A) noting location of brake hose guide (B)

7.7 Draw the mudguard forwards

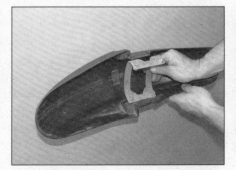

7.8 Note location of mudguard brace

8.2 Carrier mounting bolts

8.3 Note location of washers and top-hat spacers

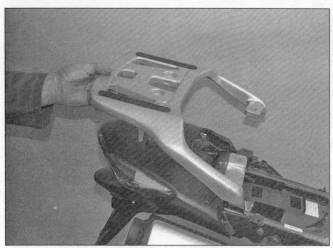

8.4 Lift the carrier off

9.3 Disconnect the tail light wiring connectors

onward the rear spacers are fitted into the top of the carrier.

4 Lift off the carrier **(see illustration)**.

5 Installation is the reverse of removal.

9 Rear mudguard

VT125C

1 Remove the seat (see Section 2).

2 Remove the right-hand side panel (see Section 3).

3 Displace the wiring boot, then refer to *Wiring Diagrams* at the end of Chapter 9 and disconnect the tail light wiring connectors **(see illustration)**. Release the wiring from any clips or ties.

4 Loosen the bolts securing the mudguard, then support the mudguard and withdraw the bolts **(see illustration)**. Note the location of the countersunk washers **(see illustration)**.

5 Displace the chrome frame covers and allow them to hang from the rear turn signal

stems, then draw the mudguard backwards to disengage the bracket at the front from the frame and lift it off **(see illustrations)**.

6 Note the location of the sub-frame and tail light support bracket on the underside of the mudguard and the routing of the tail light wiring **(see illustration)**.

7 Note how the rear turn signal wiring is clipped to the inside of the frame **(see illustration)**. To remove the chromed frame covers, first remove the turn signal assemblies (see Chapter 9), then lift the covers off.

8 Follow the procedure in Chapter 9 to

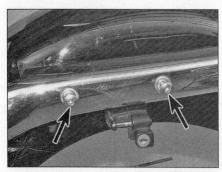

9.4a Loosen bolts on both sides

9.4b Note location of counter-sunk washers

9.5a Displace the chrome covers

9.5b Disengage bracket (arrowed) from frame . . .

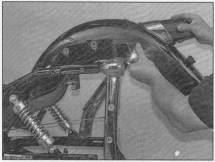

9.5c . . . and draw the mudguard off

9.6 Tail light wiring (A) and support bracket (B)

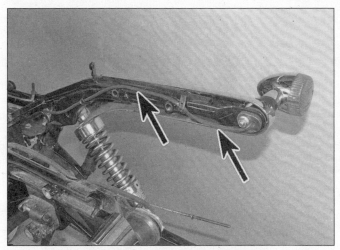

9.7 Location of turn signal wiring

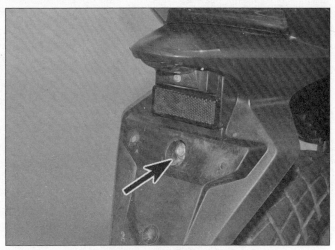

9.13a Undo the bolt (arrowed)

9.13b Release wiring boot from the clip

9.14 Disconnect the wiring connectors

separate the tail light unit from the mudguard.
9 Installation is the reverse of removal. Ensure
the bracket at the front of the mudguard
locates correctly on the frame **(see illustration
9.5b)**. Install the washers on the bolts and
tighten the bolts securely **(see illustration
9.4a)**. Ensure all wiring connectors are secure
and test the operation of the tail light and
brake light before riding the motorcycle.

XL125V

10 Remove the seat (see Section 2).
11 Remove the side panels (see Section 3).
12 Remove the rear carrier (see Section 8).
13 Undo the bolt securing the rear of the
mudguard/tail light unit assembly, then lift the
assembly up and release the wiring boot from
the clip on the frame **(see illustrations)**.

14 Disconnect the wiring connectors for the
tail light unit, turn signals and licence plate
light **(see illustration)**.
15 Follow the procedure in Chapter 9 to
separate the tail light unit from the mudguard.
16 Installation is the reverse of removal.
Ensure all wiring connectors are secure and
test the operation of the tail light, brake light
and turn signals before riding the motorcycle.

Chapter 9
Electrical system

Contents

Degrees of difficulty

| **Easy,** suitable for novice with little experience | 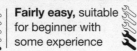 | **Fairly easy,** suitable for beginner with some experience | | **Fairly difficult,** suitable for competent DIY mechanic | | **Difficult,** suitable for experienced DIY mechanic | | **Very difficult,** suitable for expert DIY or professional | |

Specifications

Battery

Capacity	12 V, 6 Ah
Voltage	
Fully-charged	13.0 to 13.2 V
Uncharged	below 12.3 V
Charging rate	
Normal	0.6 A for 5 to 10 hrs
Quick	3.0 A for 1 hr (max)

Charging system

Alternator stator coil resistance	0.1 to 0.5 ohms
Alternator output	260 W @ 5000 rpm
Current leakage	
VT125C	0.1 mA (max)
XL125V-1 to V-6	1.0 mA (max)
XL125V-7 onwards	0.2 mA (max)
Regulated voltage output	13.2 to 15.5 V @ 5000 rpm

Starter motor

Brush length	
Standard	10 to 10.5 mm
Service limit (min)	3.5 mm

Tachometer
Input voltage . . . . 10.5 V minimum

Fuses
Main fuse . . . . 30 A
Circuit fuses . . . . 10 A

Bulbs
Headlight
  VT125C . . . . 60/55 W
  XL125V . . . . 35/35 W x 2
Sidelight
  VT125C . . . . 4 W
  XL125V . . . . 5 W
Brake/tail light . . . . 21/5 W
Licence plate light . . . . 5 W
Turn signal lights
  VT125C and XL125V-7 onwards . . . . 21 W x 4
  XL125V-1 to V-6 . . . . 10 W x 4
Instrument light
  VT125C and XL125V-1 to V-6 . . . . 1.7 W
  XL125V-7 onwards . . . . LED
Warning lights
  VT125C
    Turn signal . . . . 3.4 W x 2
    High beam . . . . 3.4 W
    Neutral indicator . . . . 3.5 W
    Temperature indicator . . . . 3.0 W
  XL125V-1 to V-6
    Turn signal . . . . 2.0 W x 2
    High beam . . . . 1.2 W
    Neutral indicator . . . . 2.0 W
    Temperature indicator . . . . 1.7 W
  XL125V-7 onwards . . . . LED

Torque settings
Alternator rotor nut . . . . 64 Nm
Alternator stator bolts . . . . 12 Nm
Alternator stator wiring clamp bolts . . . . 5 Nm
CKP sensor/ignition pulse generator bolts 5Nm
Neutral switch . . . . 12 Nm
Starter motor housing bolts . . . . 5 Nm
Starter motor terminal nut . . . . 12 Nm

1 General information

All models covered in this manual have a 12 volt electrical system charged by a three-phase alternator with a separate regulator/rectifier.

The regulator maintains the charging system output within the specified range to prevent overcharging, and the rectifier converts the ac (alternating current) output of the alternator to dc (direct current) to power the lights and other components and to charge the battery. The alternator rotor is mounted on the left-hand end of the crankshaft.

The starter motor is mounted on the lower front of the crankcase. The starting system includes the motor, the battery, the relay and the various wires and switches. Some of the switches are part of a safety circuit which prevents the engine from being started initially if the sidestand is down or the engine is in gear. The system will also cut the engine should the sidestand extend while the bike is being ridden – see Chapter 1 for checks on the system.

Note: *Keep in mind that electrical parts, once purchased, often cannot be returned. To avoid unnecessary expense, make very sure the faulty component has been positively identified before buying a replacement part.*

2 Electrical system fault finding

1 A typical electrical circuit consists of an electrical component, the switches, relays, etc, related to that component and the wiring and connectors that link the component to the battery and the frame.

2 Before tackling any troublesome electrical circuit, first study the wiring diagram thoroughly to get a complete picture of what makes up that individual circuit. Trouble spots, for instance, can often be narrowed down by noting if other components related to that circuit are operating properly or not. If several components or circuits fail at one time, chances are the fault lies either in the fuse or in the common earth (ground) connection, as several circuits are often routed through the same fuse and earth (ground) connections.

3 Electrical problems often stem from simple causes, such as loose or corroded connections or a blown fuse. Prior to any electrical fault finding, always visually check the condition of the fuse, wires and connections in the problem circuit. Intermittent failures can be especially frustrating, since you can't always duplicate

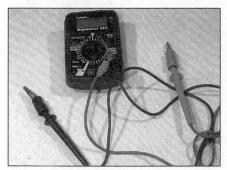

2.4a A digital multimeter can be used for all electrical tests

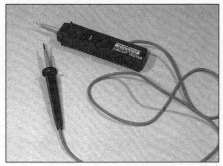

2.4b A battery powered continuity tester

2.4c A simple test light can be used for voltage checks

the failure when it's convenient to test. In such situations, a good practice is to clean all connections in the affected circuit, whether or not they appear to be good. All of the connections and wires should also be wiggled to check for looseness which can cause intermittent failure.

4 A multimeter will enable a full range of electrical tests to be made. If you donít have a multimeter it is highly advisable to obtain one – they are not expensive and will enable a full range of electrical tests to be made. Go for a modern digital one with LCD display as they are easier to use. A continuity tester and/ or test light are useful for certain electrical checks as an alternative, though are limited in their usefulness compared to a multimeter **(see illustrations)**.

Continuity checks

5 The term continuity describes the uninterrupted flow of electricity through an electrical circuit. Continuity can be checked with a multimeter set either to its continuity function (a beep is emitted when continuity is found), or to the resistance (ohms / Ω) function, or with a dedicated continuity tester. Both instruments are powered by an internal battery, therefore the checks are made with the ignition OFF. As a safety precaution, always disconnect the battery negative (–) lead before making continuity checks, particularly if ignition switch checks are being made.

6 If using a multimeter, select the continuity function if it has one, or the resistance (ohms)

function. Touch the meter probes together and check that a beep is emitted or the meter reads zero, which indicates continuity. If there is no continuity there will be no beep or the meter will show infinite resistance. After using the meter, always switch it OFF to conserve its battery.

7 A continuity tester can be used in the same way – its light should come on or it should beep to indicate continuity in the switch ON position, but should be off or silent in the OFF position.

8 Note that the polarity of the test probes doesnít matter for continuity checks, although care should be taken to follow specific test procedures if a diode or solid-state component is being checked.

Switch continuity checks

9 If a switch is at fault, trace its wiring to the wiring connectors. Separate the connectors and inspect them for security and condition. A build-up of dirt or corrosion here will most likely be the cause of the problem – clean up and apply a water dispersant such as WD40, or alternatively use a dedicated contact cleaner and protection spray.

10 If using a multimeter, select the continuity function if it has one, or the resistance (ohms/ Ω) function, and connect its probes to the terminals in the connector **(see illustration)**. Simple ON/ OFF type switches, such as brake light switches, only have two wires whereas combination switches, like the handlebar switches, have many wires. Study the wiring diagram to ensure that you are connecting to the correct pair of wires. Continuity should be indicated with the switch ON and no continuity with it OFF.

Wiring continuity checks

11 Many electrical faults are caused by damaged wiring, often due to incorrect routing or chaffing on frame components. Loose, wet or corroded wire connectors can also be the cause of electrical problems.

12 A continuity check can be made on a single length of wire by disconnecting it at each end and connecting the meter or continuity tester probes to each end of the wire **(see illustration)**. Continuity (low or no resistance – zero ohms) should be indicated if the wire is good. If no continuity (high resistance) is shown, suspect a broken wire.

13 To check for continuity to earth in any earth wire connect one probe of your meter or tester to the earth wire terminal in the connector and the other to the frame, engine, or battery earth (–) terminal. Continuity (low or no resistance – zero ohms) should be indicated if the wire is good. If no continuity (high resistance) is shown, suspect a broken wire or corroded or loose earth point (see below).

Voltage checks

14 A voltage check can determine whether power is reaching a component. Use a multimeter set to the dc voltage scale, or a test light. The test light is the cheaper component, but the meter has the advantage of being able to give a voltage reading.

15 Connect the meter or test light in parallel, i.e. across the load **(see illustration)**.

16 First identify the relevant wiring circuit by referring to the wiring diagram at the end of this manual. If other electrical components

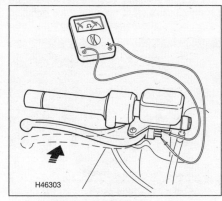

H46303

2.10 Testing a brake light switch for continuity

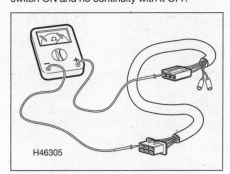

H46305

2.12 Testing for continuity in a wiring loom

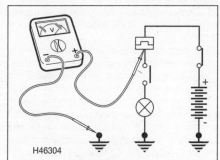

H46304

2.15 Connect the multimeter in parallel, or across the load, as shown

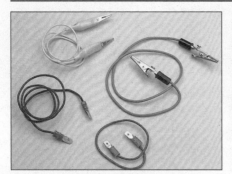

2.23 A selection of jumper wires for making earth (ground) checks

3.2a Unscrew the negative (–) terminal first . .

3.2b . . . and disconnect the lead from the battery

share the same power supply, take note whether they are working correctly – this is useful information in deciding where to start checking the circuit.

17 If using a meter, check first that the meter leads are plugged into the correct terminals on the meter (red to positive (+), black to negative (–). Set the meter to the dc volts function, where necessary at a range suitable for the battery voltage – 0 to 20 volts dc. Connect the meter red probe (+) to the power supply wire and the black probe to a good metal earth (ground) on the motorcycleís frame or directly to the battery negative terminal. Battery voltage should be shown on the meter with the ignition switch, and if necessary any other relevant switch, ON.

18 If using a test light, connect its positive (+) probe to the power supply terminal and its negative (–) probe to a good earth (ground) on the motorcycleís frame. With the switch, and if necessary any other relevant switch, ON, the test light should illuminate.

19 If no voltage is indicated, work back towards the switch continuing to check for voltage. When you reach a point where there is voltage, you know the problem lies between that point and your last check point.

Earth (ground) checks

20 Earth connections are made either directly to the engine (such as the oil pressure switch and starter motor which only have a positive feed) or to the engine or frame via the earth circuit of the appropriate wiring system (see *Wiring Diagrams* at the end of this Chapter).

21 Corrosion is a common cause of a poor earth connection, as is a loose earth terminal fastener.

22 If total or multiple component failure is experienced, check the security of the main earth lead from the negative (–) terminal of the battery, the earth leads bolted to the engine (at the front of the crankcase and the rear of the cylinder head), and the main earth point(s) on the frame. If corroded, dismantle the connection and clean all surfaces back to bare metal. Remake the connection and prevent further corrosion from forming by smearing battery terminal grease over the connection.

23 To check the earth of a component, use an

insulated jumper wire to temporarily bypass its earth connection **(see illustration)** – connect one end of the jumper wire to the earth terminal or metal body of the component and the other end to the motorcycleís frame. If the circuit works with the jumper wire installed, the earth circuit is faulty.

24 To check an earth wire first check for corroded or loose connections, then check the wiring for continuity (Steps 16 and 17) between each connector in the circuit in turn, and then to its earth point, to locate the break.

3 Battery

Caution: Be extremely careful when handling or working around the battery. The electrolyte is very caustic and an explosive gas (hydrogen) is given off when the battery is charging. Always disconnect the battery negative (–) lead first, and reconnect it last.

Removal and installation

1 Make sure the ignition is switched OFF. Remove the seat and, on XL125V models, the left-hand side panel (see Chapter 8).

2 Unscrew the negative (–) terminal bolt first and disconnect the lead from the battery **(see illustrations)**. Lift up the red insulating cover to access the positive (+) terminal, then

3.3 Unhook the battery strap – VT125C

unscrew the bolt and disconnect the lead.

3 On VT125C models, unhook the battery strap then lift the battery out **(see illustration)**.

4 On XL125V models, undo the bolt securing the battery bracket and remove the bracket, then lift the battery out **(see illustration)**.

5 Prior to installation, ensure the battery terminals and lead ends are clean (see Step 9). Fit the battery into its holder and reconnect the leads, connecting the positive (+) terminal first.

> **HAYNES HINT** *Battery corrosion can be kept to a minimum by applying a layer of battery terminal grease or petroleum jelly (Vaseline) to the terminals after the leads have been connected. DO NOT use a mineral based grease.*

6 Secure the battery with its strap or bracket, then install the side panel and/or seat as applicable.

Inspection

7 The battery fitted to all models covered in this manual is of the maintenance-free (sealed) type – however, the following checks should still be performed.

8 Check the condition of the battery by measuring the voltage at the terminals. Connect the voltmeter positive (+) probe to the battery positive (+) terminal, and the negative (–) probe to the negative (–) terminal **(see**

3.4 Undo the bolt and remove the battery bracket – XL125V

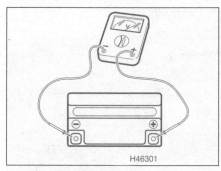

3.8 Checking the battery voltage

3.15 Ensure the charging rate is safe

illustration). When fully-charged there should be 13.0 to 13.2 volts present. If the voltage falls below 12.3 volts remove the battery and recharge it (see Steps 13 to 19).

9 Check the battery terminals and leads are tight and free of corrosion. If corrosion is evident, remove the battery and clean the terminals and lead ends with a wire brush, knife or wire wool.

10 Keep the battery case clean to prevent current leakage, which can discharge the battery over a period of time (especially when it sits unused). If necessary, wash the outside of the case with a solution of baking soda and water. Rinse the battery thoroughly, then dry it.

11 Look for cracks in the case and replace the battery with a new one if any are found. If acid has been spilled on the frame or battery holder, neutralise it with a baking soda and water solution, dry it thoroughly, then touch up any damaged paint.

12 If the motorcycle sits unused for long periods of time, disconnect the leads from the battery terminals, negative (–) terminal first. Check the battery condition regularly and charge the battery once every month.

Charging

13 Ensure the battery charger is suitable for charging a 12 volt battery.

14 Remove the battery (see Steps 1 to 4). Before switching the charger ON, connect it to the battery, making sure that the positive (+) lead on the charger is connected to the positive (+) terminal on the battery, and the negative (–) lead is connected to the negative (–) terminal.

15 Honda recommends that the battery is charged at a rate of 0.6 amps for 5 to 10 hours. Exceeding this figure can cause the battery to overheat, buckling the plates and rendering it useless. Few owners will have access to an expensive current controlled charger, so if a normal domestic charger is used, check that after a possible initial peak, the charge rate falls to a safe level **(see illustration)**. Note: *In emergencies the battery can be charged at a maximum rate of 3.0 amps for a period of 1 hour. However, this is not recommended and the low amp charge is by far the safer method of charging the battery.*

16 If the battery becomes hot during charging **STOP**. Further charging will cause damage

17 After charging, allow the battery to stand for 30 minutes, then measure its terminal voltage (see Step 8). If the voltage is below 13.0 volts, charge the battery again and repeat the voltage measuring process. If the voltage is still low, the battery is failing and should be replaced with a new one.

18 Install the battery (see Steps 5 and 6).
19 If the recharged battery discharges rapidly when left disconnected, it is likely that an internal short caused by physical damage or sulphation has occurred. A new battery will be required. A good battery will tend to lose its charge at approximately 1% per day.

4 Fuses

1 The electrical systems are protected by fuses. If a fuse blows, be sure to check the appropriate wiring circuit very carefully for evidence of a short-circuit (see *Wiring Diagrams* at the end of this Chapter). Look for bare wires and chafed, melted or burned insulation, or a damaged switch. If the fuse is renewed before the cause is located, the new fuse will blow immediately.

2 Occasionally a fuse will blow or cause an open-circuit for no obvious reason. Corrosion of the fuse and fusebox terminals may occur and cause poor electrical contact. If this happens, remove the corrosion with a knife or wire wool, then spray the terminals with electrical contact cleaner.

Check and renewal

3 The main fuse is integral with the starter relay. On VT125C models, the starter relay is located behind the rear cylinder head – remove the left-hand side panel (see Chapter 8) for access **(see illustration)**. A spare main fuse is located in an adjacent holder. On XL125V models, the starter relay is located behind the left-hand side panel – remove the seat and left-hand side panel (see Chapter 8) for access **(see illustration)**. A spare main fuse is located in a holder taped to the wiring loom.

4 To check the main fuse, first disconnect the battery negative lead (see Section 3). Displace

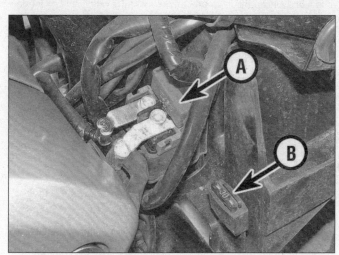

4.3a Location of main fuse (A). Note spare fuse (B) – VT125C

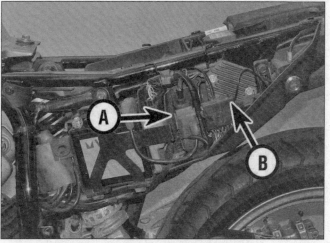

4.3b Location of main fuse (A). Note fusebox (B) – XL125V

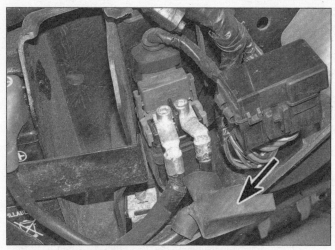

4.4a Displace the terminal cover (arrowed) . . .

4.4b . . . then unclip the relay wiring connector

4.5 Location of fusebox – VT125C

4.6 Unclip the fusebox lid. Note spare fuse (arrowed)

the relay terminal cover, then unclip the relay wiring connector **(see illustrations)**.

5 The circuit fuses are housed in the fusebox. On VT125C models, the fusebox is located above the coolant reservoir – remove the right-hand side panel (see Chapter 8) for access **(see illustration)**. On XL125V models, the fusebox is located behind the left-hand side panel – remove the seat and left-hand

side panel (see Chapter 8) for access **(see illustration 4.3b)**.

6 To check any of the circuit fuses, unclip the fusebox lid – fuse locations are detailed on a label inside the lid **(see illustration)**.

7 The fuses should be removed and checked visually **(see illustration)**. If you can't pull the fuse out with your fingertips, use a pair of long-nose pliers.

8 A blown fuse is easily identified by a break in the element **(see illustration)**. Each fuse is clearly marked with its rating and must only be replaced by a fuse of the correct rating. A spare main fuse is located adjacent to the starter relay. A spare circuit fuse is located in the fusebox **(see illustrations 4.6)**.

9 If a spare fuse is used, always replace it with a new one so that a spare of each rating is carried on the bike at all times.

⚠ *Warning: Never put in a fuse of a higher rating or bridge the terminals with any other substitute, however temporary it may be. Serious damage may be done to the circuit, or a fire may start.*

4.7 Pull out the fuse for a visual check

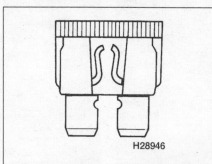

4.8 A blown fuse can be identified by a break in its element

H28946

5 Lighting system check

Note: *On VT125C-X to C-21 models and XL125V-1 to V-3 models, the lighting is switched ON and OFF by a handlebar mounted*

switch. On all other models covered in this manual the lighting is controlled by the ignition switch – on these machines the headlight will go OFF temporarily when the starter button is pressed.

1 The battery provides power for operation of the lights. If none of the lights work, always check battery voltage before proceeding. Low battery voltage indicates either a faulty battery or a defective charging system. Refer to Section 3 for battery checks and Section 26 for charging system tests. Also, check the condition of the fuses (see Section 4) – if there is more than one problem at the same time, it is likely to be a fault relating to a multi-function component, such as one of the fuses governing more than one circuit, or the ignition switch.

2 When checking for a blown filament in a bulb, it is advisable to back up a visual check with a continuity test of the filament as it is not always apparent that a bulb has blown. When testing for continuity, remember that on single terminal bulbs it is the metal body of the bulb that is the earth (ground).

Headlight

3 VT125C models have one twin filament bulb. XL125V models have two twin filament bulbs.

4 If one headlight beam fails to work, first check the bulb (see Section 6). If both headlight beams fail to work, first check the fuse (see Section 4), and then the bulb(s) (see Section 6). If they are good, the problem lies in the wiring or connectors, or one of the switches in the lighting circuit.

5 Disconnect the headlight bulb wiring connector (see Section 6) and check for battery voltage on the supply side of the connector – connect the negative probe of a multimeter to the green wire (earth) terminal, and the positive probe to the blue wire terminal for the high beam or the white wire terminal for the low beam. Donít forget to select either high or low beam as appropriate at the dimmer switch.

6 Turn the ignition and/or lighting switch ON – if no voltage is indicated, check for continuity between the green wire terminal and earth (ground). If there is no continuity, check the earth (ground) circuit for an open or poor connection.

7 If the earth circuit is good, refer to Wiring Diagrams at the end of this chapter and check the wiring between the components in the lighting circuit, and check the components themselves.

Sidelight

8 If the sidelight(s) fail(s) to work, first check the bulb(s) (see Section 6) then the fuse (see Section 4).

9 Next, disconnect the wiring connector and check for battery voltage on the supply side of the connector – connect the negative probe of a multimeter to the green wire (earth) terminal, and the positive probe to the brown wire terminal.

10 Turn the ignition and/or lighting switch ON – if no voltage is indicated, check for continuity between the green wire terminal and earth (ground). If there is no continuity, check the earth (ground) circuit for an open or poor connection.

11 If the earth circuit is good, refer to Wiring Diagrams at the end of this chapter and check the wiring between the components in the lighting circuit, and check the components themselves.

12 If voltage is indicated, check for continuity between the terminals on the sidelight side of the wiring connector and the corresponding terminals in the bulbholder – no continuity indicates a break in the circuit.

Tail light

13 If the tail light fails to work, first check the bulb (Section 8), then the fuse (Section 4).

14 If they are good, refer to Wiring Diagrams at the end of this chapter and check the wiring and connectors as follows.

15 On VT125C models, remove the right-hand side panel (see Chapter 8). Displace the wiring boot and identify the tail light wiring.

16 On XL125V models, displace the rear mudguard assembly to access the tail light wiring (see Chapter 8).

17 Disconnect the tail light wiring connectors and check for battery voltage on the supply side of the connectors – connect the negative probe of a multimeter to the green (earth) wire, and the positive probe to the brown wire.

18 Turn the ignition and/or lighting switch ON – if no voltage is indicated, check for continuity between the green wire terminal and earth (ground). If there is no continuity, check the earth (ground) circuit for an open or poor connection.

19 If the earth circuit is good, refer to Wiring Diagrams at the end of this chapter and check the wiring between the components in the lighting circuit, and check the components themselves.

20 If voltage is indicated, remove the tail light bulb (see Section 8) and check for continuity between the wiring connectors and the terminals in the bulbholder – no continuity indicates a break in the circuit.

Brake light

21 If the brake light fails to work, first check the bulb (Section 8), then the fuse (Section 4).

22 If they are good, follow the procedure in Step 14 to access the brake light wiring connectors. Refer to Wiring Diagrams at the end of this chapter and disconnect the connectors.

23 Check for battery voltage on the supply side of the connectors – connect the negative probe of a multimeter to the green (earth) wire, and the positive probe to the green/yellow wire. Turn the ignition ON. Check first with the front brake lever pulled in, then with the rear brake pedal pressed down.

24 If no voltage is indicated in either test, check the appropriate brake light switch (see Section 14), then the wiring between the brake light connector and the switches.

25 Check for continuity to earth (ground) in the green wire on the loom side of the wiring connector. If there is no continuity, check the earth (ground) circuit for a broken or poor connection.

26 If voltage is indicated, remove the bulb and check for continuity between the terminals on the tail light side of the wiring connectors and the corresponding terminals in the bulbholder – no continuity indicates a break in the circuit.

Licence plate light – XL125V-7

27 If the licence plate light fails to work, first check the bulb (Section 8), then the fuse (Section 4).

28 If they are good, follow the procedure in Section 9, to access the brake light wiring connectors. Refer to Wiring Diagrams at the end of this chapter and disconnect the connectors.

29 Check for battery voltage on the supply side of the connectors – connect the negative probe of a multimeter to the green wire (earth) terminal, and the positive probe to the brown wire terminal.

30 Turn the ignition ON – if no voltage is indicated, check for continuity between the green wire terminal and earth (ground). If there is no continuity, check the earth (ground) circuit for an open or poor connection.

31 If the earth circuit is good, refer to the Wiring Diagram at the end of this chapter and check the wiring between the components in the lighting circuit, and check the components themselves.

32 If voltage is indicated, remove the bulb and check for continuity between the terminals on the licence plate light side of the wiring connectors and the corresponding terminals in the bulbholder – no continuity indicates a break in the circuit.

Turn signals

33 See Section 11.

6	Headlight and sidelight bulbs

Note: The headlight bulbs are of the quartz-halogen type. Do not touch the bulb glass as skin acids will shorten the bulb's service life. If the bulb is accidentally touched, it should be wiped carefully when cold with a rag soaked in methylated spirit and dried before fitting. Use a paper towel or dry cloth when handling new bulbs to prevent injury if the bulb should break and to increase bulb life.

6.1 Note location of spacer on headlight screws

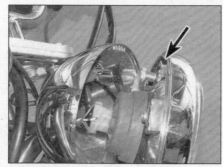

6.2 Release the tab (arrowed)

6.3 Disconnect wiring connector

6.4 Note the location of the dust cover

6.5a Release the retaining clip . . .

● Position the tab at the top of the rim under the lip on the shell, then press the lower edge of the rim in firmly.
● Ensure the spacers are fitted on the screws securing the headlight rim.
● Check the operation of the headlight before riding the motorcycle.

Sidelight

7 Follow the procedure in Steps 1 and 2, then pull the sidelight bulbholder out of the reflector **(see illustration)**
8 Push the bulb in and turn it anti-clockwise to release it. Check the terminals for corrosion and clean them if necessary.
9 Installation is the reverse of removal (see Step 6).

VT125C

Headlight

1 Undo the screws on the left and right-hand sides of the headlight shell, noting the location of the spacers **(see illustrations)**.
2 Draw out the headlight and release the tab on the top of the rim from the lip on the shell **(see illustration)**.
3 Pull the sidelight bulbholder out of the reflector **(see illustration 6.7)** then disconnect the headlight bulb wiring connector **(see illustration)**.

4 Note the location of the dust cover then remove it **(see illustration)**.
5 Release both sides of the retaining clip, noting how they fit, then lift out the bulb, noting how it locates in the reflector **(see illustrations)**.
6 Installation is the reverse of removal, noting the following:
● Ensure the bulb is correctly located in the reflector.
● Ensure the bulb retaining clip is secure and check that the dust cover is correctly installed.

XL125V-1 to V-6

Headlight

10 Follow the procedure in Chapter 8, Section 6, to remove the cockpit trim panel from the fairing, then remove the instrument cluster as described in Section 15, Step 53 of this Chapter. Access to the headlight and sidelight bulbs is gained from the rear of the headlight unit.

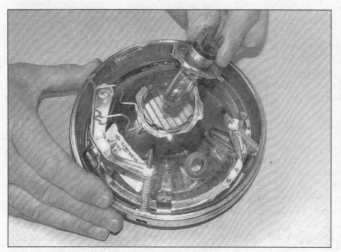

6.5b . . . and lift out the bulb

6.7 Pull out the sidelight bulbholder

6.11 Pull back the tab to remove the dust cover

6.12a Turn the bulbholder anti-clockwise . . .

6.12b . . . to release it from the headlight

6.16 Pull out the bulbholder

6.17 Pull out the capless bulb

6.20 Pull the tabs (arrowed) to remove the dust cover

11 Note the location of the dust cover, then pull back the tab to remove it **(see illustration)**.

12 Turn the bulbholder anti-clockwise to release it **(see illustrations)**.

13 Push the bulb in and turn it anti-clockwise to release it. Check the terminals for corrosion and clean them if necessary.

14 Installation is the reverse of removal, noting the following:

● Line up the pins of the new bulb with the slots in the bulbholder, then push the bulb in and turn it clockwise until it locks into place.

● Ensure the bulbholder is secure and check that the dust cover is correctly installed.

● Check the operation of the headlight before riding the motorcycle.

Sidelight

15 Refer to Step 10 to access the rear of the headlight unit.

16 Pull the left or right-hand sidelight bulbholder out of the headlight unit **(see illustration)**.

17 The bulb is of the capless type – pull it out of the bulbholder carefully **(see illustration)**.

18 Installation is the reverse of removal. Check the operation of the sidelight.

XL125V-7 onwards

Headlight

19 Follow the procedure in Chapter 8, Section 6, to remove the cockpit trim panel from the fairing, then remove the instrument cluster as described in Section 15, Step 90 of this Chapter. Access to the headlight bulbs is gained from the rear of the headlight unit.

20 Note the location of the dust cover, then pull back the tabs to remove it **(see illustration)**.

21 Release the retaining clip, noting how it fits, then lift out the bulbholder, noting how it locates in the headlight unit **(see illustrations)**.

6.21a Release the retaining clip . . .

6.21b . . . and lift out the bulbholder

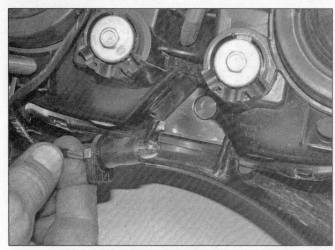

6.25 Pull out the bulbholder

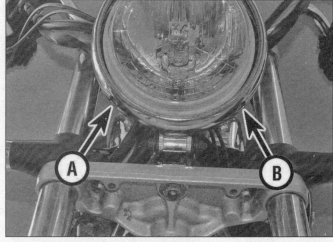

7.2 Vertical adjuster screw (A), horizontal adjuster screw (B) – VT125C

22 Push the bulb in and turn it anti-clockwise to release it. Check the terminals for corrosion and clean them if necessary.
23 Installation is the reverse of removal, noting the following:
● Line up the pins of the new bulb with the slots in the bulbholder, then push the bulb in and turn it clockwise until it locks into place.
● Ensure the bulbholder is correctly located in the headlight unit.
● Ensure the bulbholder is secure and check that the dust cover is correctly installed.
● Check the operation of the headlight before riding the motorcycle.

Sidelight

24 Follow the procedure in Chapter 8, Section 6, to remove the panel to the underside on the front fork bottom yoke.
25 Pull the sidelight bulbholder out of the centre of the headlight unit (see illustration).
26 The bulb is of the capless type – pull it out of the bulbholder carefully (see illustration 6.17).
27 Installation is the reverse of removal. Check the operation of the sidelight.

7 Headlight

Headlight aim

Note: *An improperly adjusted headlight may cause problems for oncoming traffic or provide poor, unsafe illumination of the road ahead. Before adjusting the headlight aim, be sure to consult with local traffic laws and regulations.*
1 Before making any adjustment, check that the tyre pressures are correct and the suspension is adjusted as required. Make any adjustments to the headlight aim with the machine on level ground, with the fuel tank half full and with an assistant sitting on the seat.

VT125C

2 Vertical adjustment is made by turning the adjuster screw on the right-hand side of the headlight rim (see illustration). Turn the screw clockwise to raise the beam, anti-clockwise to lower it.

3 Horizontal adjustment is made by turning the adjuster screw on the left-hand side of the headlight rim (see illustration 7.2). Turn the screw clockwise to move the beam to the right, anti-clockwise to move it to the left.
4 If either of the adjuster screws appears seized, remove the headlight (see Section 6) and lubricate the adjuster mechanism with WD-40.

XL125V-1 to V-6

5 The headlight beams can be adjusted vertically.
6 Adjustment is made by turning the single adjuster knob on the underside of the headlight unit. Access to the knob is through the aperture in the fairing bridging panel (see illustration). If required, follow the procedure in Chapter 8, Section 6, to remove the bridging panel.

XL125V-7 onwards

7 The headlight beams can be adjusted vertically.
8 Adjustment is made by turning the individual adjusters on the back of the headlight unit using a cross-head screwdriver (see illustration).

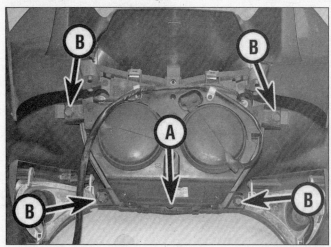

7.6 Location of the adjuster knob (A). Note the mounting bolts (B) – XL125V-1 to V-6

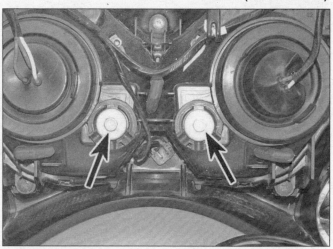

7.8 Location of the headlight adjusters – XL125V-7 onward

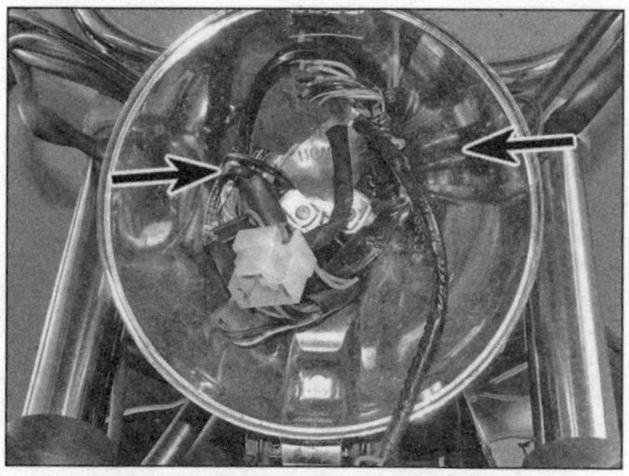

7.10 Release the wiring from the clips

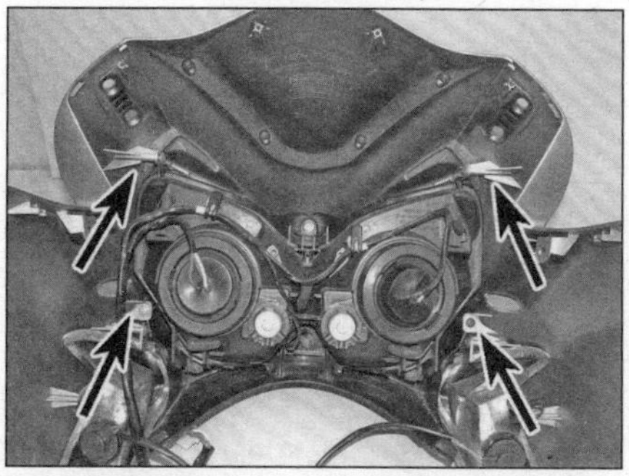

7.17a Undo the screws (arrowed) . . .

Three guides are provided on each adjuster to facilitate the use of the screwdriver. If required to improve access, follow the procedure in Chapter 8, Section 6, to remove the panel on the underside of the front fork bottom yoke.

Removal and installation

VT125C

9 Follow the procedure in Section 6, Steps 1 to 3, to remove the headlight reflector assembly.

10 Note the location of the wiring inside the headlight shell and release it from the wiring clips **(see illustration)**.

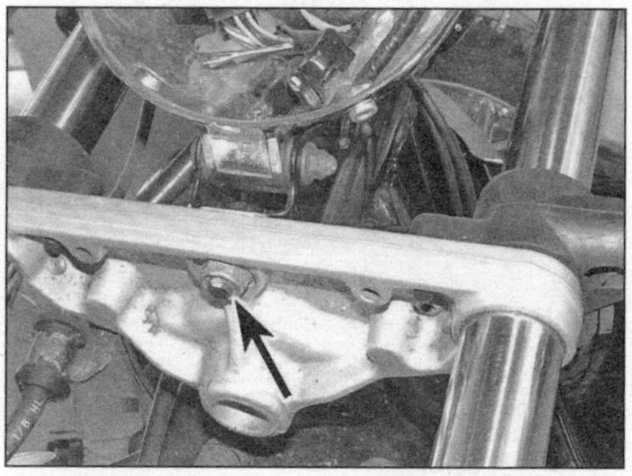

7.11 Location of the mounting nut

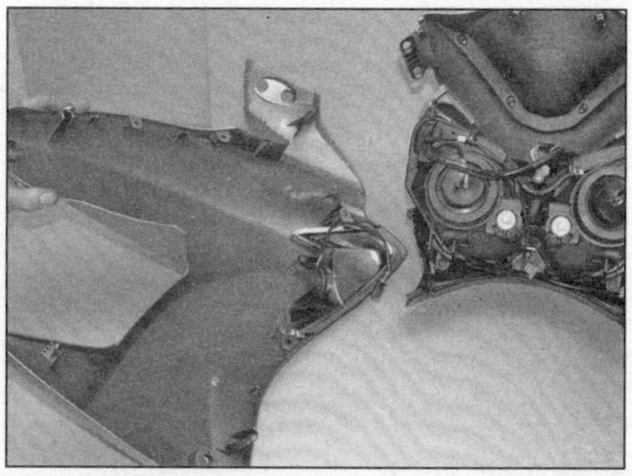

7.17b . . . and remove the side panels

11 Undo the mounting nut on the underside of the bottom front fork yoke **(see illustration)**, lift the headlight shell off and feed the wiring out through the back of the shell.

12 Installation is the reverse of removal, noting the following:

- Make sure all the wiring is correctly routed, connected and secured.
- Check the operation of the headlight and sidelight.
- Check the headlight aim.

XL125V-1 to V-6

13 Remove the fairing (see Chapter 8).

14 Undo the bolts securing the headlight assembly to the fairing and lift it out **(see illustration 7.6)**.

15 Installation is the reverse of removal, noting the following:

- Make sure all the wiring is correctly routed, connected and secured.
- Check the headlight aim.

XL125V-7 onwards

16 Remove the fairing (see Chapter 8).

17 The fairing comprises four separate panels secured to the headlight unit by screws. To disassemble the fairing, first undo the screws securing the left and right-hand side panels and ease them off, noting how the tabs for the mirror mountings interlock **(see illustrations)**.

18 Undo the screw securing the upper panel to the headlight unit, then undo the screws securing the lower panel **(see illustration)**.

19 Installation is the reverse of removal, noting the following:

- Ensure the side panels are correctly aligned with the upper and lower panels and headlight unit before tightening the fixing screws.
- Check the headlight aim.

8 Brake/tail light bulb and licence plate bulb

Note 1: *It is a good idea to use a paper towel or dry cloth when handling the new bulb to prevent injury if it breaks, and to increase bulb life.*

Note 2: *Take care not to over-tighten the lens screws as it is easy to strip the threads or crack the lens.*

VT125C

1 Undo the screws securing the tail light lens and lift it off, noting the location of the seal **(see illustration)**. **Note:** *A clear panel in the underside of the lens facilitates illumination of the licence plate.*

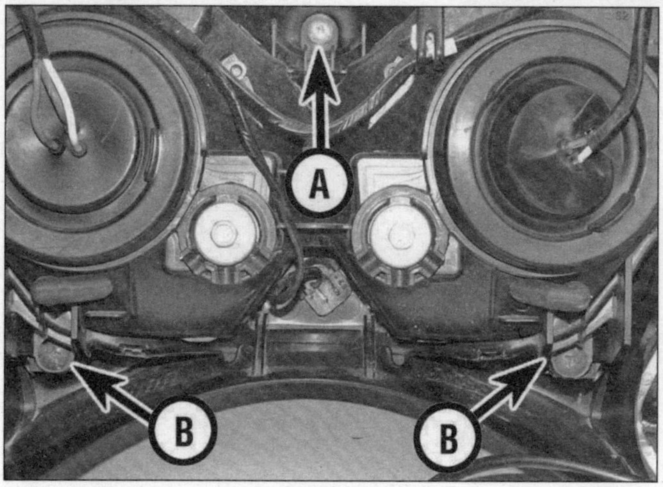

7.18 Screw (A) secures upper panel, screws (B) secure lower panel

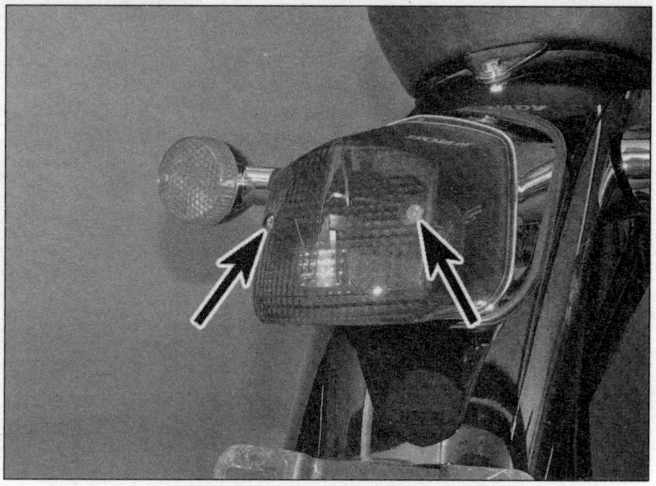

8.1 Screws secure tail light lens

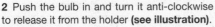

8.2 Push bulb in and turn anti-clockwise
to release

8.7a Undo the screws . . .

8.7b . . . and remove the tail light lens

2 Push the bulb in and turn it anti-clockwise to release it from the holder (see illustration).
3 Check the terminals for corrosion and clean them if necessary.
4 Line up the pins on the new bulb with the slots in the holder (the pins heights are different so that it can only be fitted one way), then push the bulb in and turn it clockwise, making sure it locates correctly.
5 Check the operation of the brake/tail light.
6 Ensure the seal is in place, then install the lens.

XL125V-1 to V-6

7 Undo the screws securing the tail light lens and lift it off, noting the location of the seal (see illustrations). Note: *A clear panel in the underside of the lens facilitates illumination of the licence plate.*
8 Push the bulb in and turn it anti-clockwise to release it from the holder.

9 Check the terminals for corrosion and clean them if necessary.
10 Line up the pins on the new bulb with the slots in the holder (the pins heights are different so that it can only be fitted one way), then push the bulb in and turn it clockwise, making sure it locates correctly.
11 Check the operation of the brake/tail light.
12 Ensure the seal is in place, then install the lens.

XL125V-7 onwards
Brake/tail light

13 To renew the brake/tail light bulb, undo the screws securing the tail light lens and lift it off, noting the location of the seal (see illustration).
14 Push the bulb in and turn it anti-clockwise to release it from the holder.
15 Check the terminals for corrosion and clean them if necessary.

16 Line up the pins on the new bulb with the slots in the holder (the pins heights are different so that it can only be fitted one way), then push the bulb in and turn it clockwise, making sure it locates correctly.
17 Check the operation of the brake/tail light.
18 Ensure the seal is in place, then install the lens.

Licence plate light

19 To renew the licence plate light bulb, first undo the screw securing the light and displace it from the mudguard (see illustrations).
20 Pull the bulbholder out of the back of the light (see illustration). The bulb is of the capless type – pull It out of the bulbholder carefully (see illustration 6.17).
21 Installation is the reverse of removal. Check the operation of the licence plate light.

8.13 Undo the screws and remove the tail light lens

8.19a Undo the screw . . .

9 Brake/tail light unit

VT125C

1 Remove the rear mudguard (see Chapter 8).
2 Release the brake/tail light wiring from the clips on the underside of the mudguard.
3 Undo the bolts securing the light unit, noting the location of the top-hat spacers and the grommets in the tail light support bracket (see illustration).

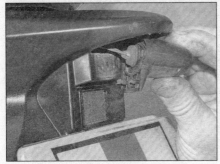

8.19b . . . and displace the light

8.20 Pull out the bulbholder

9.3 Bolts (arrowed) secure light unit

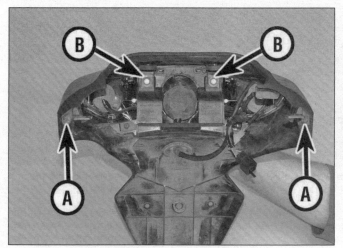

9.10a Undo screws (A) and bolts (B) . . .

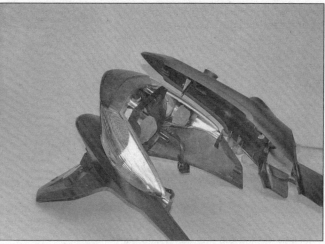

9.10b . . . then remove the top panel

4 Installation is the reverse of removal, noting the following:

● Ensure the wiring is secured by the clips.
● Check the operation of the tail and brake lights before riding the motorcycle.

XL125V-1 to V-6 models

5 Remove the rear mudguard/tail light unit assembly (see Chapter 8).
6 Disconnect the wiring connectors from the back of the brake/tail light unit.
7 Undo the screws securing the brake/tail light unit and lift it off. Note that the rear turn signals are separate to the brake/tail light unit.
8 Installation is the reverse of removal, noting the following:

● Ensure the wiring is securely connected.
● Check the operation of the tail and brake lights before riding the motorcycle.

XL125V-7 onward

9 Remove the rear mudguard/tail light unit assembly (see Chapter 8).
10 Undo the screws and bolts securing the top panel, then draw the panel back and separate it from the assembly, noting the location of the tabs **(see illustrations)**.
11 Release the licence plate light wiring from

the clip on the back of the tail light unit **(see illustration)**.
12 Undo the screws securing the tail light/turn signals assembly to the mudguard and lift it off **(see illustrations)**. Note that the rear turn signals are integral with the brake/tail light unit.
13 Installation is the reverse of removal, noting the following:

● Ensure the tail light/turn signals assembly is mounted securely on the mudguard.
● Ensure the top panel is correctly aligned.
● Secure the licence plate light wiring with the clip.
● Check the operation of the tail and brake lights and turn signals before riding the motorcycle.

10 Licence plate light unit – XL125V-7 onwards

1 XL125V-7 models onward are equipped with a separate licence plate light **(see illustration 8.19a)**.
2 To remove the light unit, first remove the rear mudguard/tail light assembly (see Chapter 8).

3 Release the licence plate light wiring from the clip on the back of the tail light unit **(see illustration 9.11)**.
4 Undo the screw securing the light and displace it from the mudguard, then draw the wiring through the mudguard **(see illustrations 8.19a and b)**.
5 Installation is the reverse of removal. Check the operation of the licence plate light.

11 Turn signal circuit check and relay

1 Most turn signal problems are the result of a burned out bulb or corroded socket. This is especially true when the turn signals function on one side (although possibly too quickly), but fail to work on the other side. If this is the case, first check the bulbs, the bulb sockets and the wiring connectors.
2 If all the turn signals fail to work, first check the fuse (see Section 4) and then the relay, relay wiring and connectors as follows (see *Wiring Diagrams* at the end of this Chapter). Refer to Section 17 for switch testing procedures.

9.11 Release the wiring from the clip

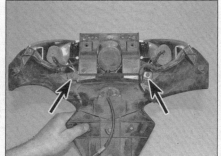

9.12a Undo the screws . . .

9.12b . . . and separate the tail light assembly from the mudguard

11.3 Location of the turn signal relay – VT125C

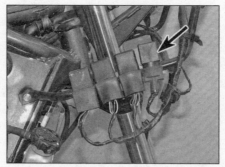

11.7 Location of the turn signal relay – XL125V-7 onward

11.8 Release the clip securing the connector

VT125C and XL125V-1 to V-6

3 On VT125C models the turn signal relay is located behind the right-hand side panel **(see illustration)** – remove the side panel for access (see Chapter 8). On XL125V-1 to V-6 models the turn signal relay is located on the left-hand side of the fairing bracket – remove the fairing for access (see Chapter 8).

4 To check the relay, disconnect the relay wiring connector. Using an insulated jumper wire, connect the black/brown and grey wire terminals on the loom side of the connector, then turn the ignition switch ON and select first the left and then right-hand turn signals. If the turn signals come on (but don't flash), the relay is confirmed faulty. Turn the ignition OFF.

5 If the turn signals on either side do not come on, check the wiring for continuity between the switch and the appropriate turn signals.

6 If none of the turn signals come on, check

the grey wire for continuity between the relay connector and the switch, then check the black/brown wire for continuity between the relay connector and the fusebox.

XL125V-7 onward

7 The turn signal relay is located on the right-hand side of the fairing bracket **(see illustration)** – remove the fairing for access (see Chapter 8).

8 To check the relay, first displace the relay from the fairing bracket, pull back the wiring boot and release the clip securing the connector **(see illustration)**.

9 Using an insulated jumper wire, connect the black/brown and grey wire terminals on the loom side of the connector, then turn the ignition switch ON and select first the left and then right-hand turn signals. Turn the ignition OFF.

10 If the turn signals do not come on, check

the black/brown for continuity between the relay connector and the fusebox, then check the grey wire for continuity between the relay connector and the switch.

11 If the turn signals come on (but don't flash), check the green wire for continuity between the relay connector and earth (ground).

12 If the green wire is good the relay is confirmed faulty.

12 Turn signal bulbs

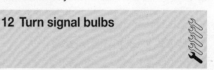

Note 1: *It is a good idea to use a paper towel or dry cloth when handling the new bulb to prevent injury if the bulb should break and to increase bulb life.*

Note 2: *Take care not to over-tighten the lens screws as it is easy to strip the threads or crack the lens.*

VT125C

1 Undo the screw securing the lens and detach the lens from the housing, noting how it fits **(see illustrations)**. Note that on some machines, the screw securing the lens is located on the underside of the turn signal body.

2 Push the bulb into the holder and turn it anti-clockwise to remove it.

3 Check the socket terminals for corrosion and clean them if necessary.

4 Line up the pins of the new bulb with the slots in the socket, then push the bulb in and turn it clockwise until it locks into place. Check the operation of the bulb.

5 Fit the lens onto the housing, locating the tab on the inner end into the cut-out in the housing, then install the screw **(see illustrations 12.1b and a)**.

XL125V-1 to V-6

Front

6 Undo the screw securing the lens and detach the lens from the housing, noting how it fits **(see illustrations)**.

7 Push the bulb into the holder and turn it anti-clockwise to remove it.

8 Check the socket terminals for corrosion and clean them if necessary.

12.1a Undo the screw

12.1b Note location of tab (arrowed)

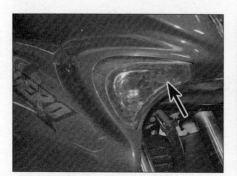

12.6a Undo the screw

12.6b Note location of tab (arrowed)

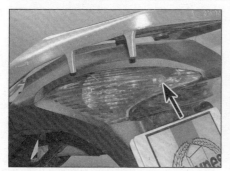

12.11 Undo the screw

12.13 Locate lower edge of lens first on installation

12.15 Remove the bulbholder from the back of the signal assembly

12.21 Detach the lens from the tail light assembly

13.2 Release the wiring from the clip (arrowed)

Rear

21 Undo the screw securing the lens and detach the lens from the housing, noting how it fits **(see illustration)**.
22 Follow the procedure in Steps 7 to 9 to remove the old bulb and fit the new one. Check the operation of the bulb.
23 Fit the lens onto the housing, locating the top edge first **(see illustration 12.21)**. Ensure the lens is correctly seated before installing the screw.

13 Turn signal assemblies

9 Line up the pins of the new bulb with the slots in the socket, then push the bulb in and turn it clockwise until it locks into place. Check the operation of the bulb.
10 Fit the lens onto the housing, locating the tab on the lower edge into the cut-out in the housing, then install the screw **(see illustrations 12.6b and a)**.

Rear

11 Undo the screw securing the lens and detach the lens from the housing, noting how it fits **(see illustration)**.
12 Follow the procedure in Steps 7 to 9 to remove the old bulb and fit the new one. Check the operation of the bulb.
13 Fit the lens onto the housing, locating the lower edge first **(see illustration)**. Ensure the lens is correctly seated before installing the screw.

XL125V-7 onwards

Front

14 Follow the procedure in Chapter 8, Section 6, to remove the panel from the underside of the front fork bottom yoke.
15 Turn the bulbholder anti-clockwise to release it **(see illustration)**.
16 Press the bulb in and turn it anti-clockwise to release it.
17 Check the socket terminals for corrosion and clean them if necessary.
18 Line up the pins of the new bulb with the slots in the socket, then push the bulb in and turn it clockwise until it locks into place. Check the operation of the bulb.
19 Install the bulbholder and turn it clockwise to lock it into place.
20 Install the panel on the underside of the front fork bottom yoke.

VT125C – Front

1 Follow the procedure in Section 6, Steps 1 to 3, to remove the headlight reflector assembly
2 Release the turn signal wiring from the clip on the mounting bracket **(see illustration)**, then trace it to the connectors inside the headlight shell and disconnect it **(see illustration 7.10)**. Feed the wiring back to the mounting bracket, noting its routing.
3 Loosen the mounting bracket pinch bolt and draw the bracket up off the front fork bottom yoke, noting how it locates **(see illustration)**.
4 Undo the screw securing the turn signal assembly to the bracket and displace the assembly **(see illustrations)**.
5 Feed the wiring through the bracket and remove the assembly.

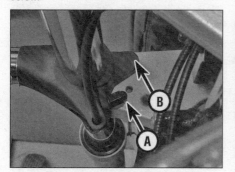

13.3 Loosen pinch bolt (A). Peg (B) locates in top of fork yoke

13.4a Undo the screw . . .

13.4b . . . and displace the turn signal assembly

13.9a Displace the wiring boot . . .

13.9b . . . and disconnect the wiring connectors

13.9c Turn signal connectors on right-hand side

6 The mounting bracket can only be removed once the appropriate front fork leg has been displaced (see Chapter 6).
7 Installation is the reverse of removal, noting the following:
● Ensure the wiring is correctly routed and secured.
● Check the operation of the turn signals before riding the motorcycle.

VT125C – Rear

8 Follow the procedure in Chapter 8 to remove the rear mudguard.
9 Trace the rear turn signal wiring along the inside of the frame and disconnect it at the connectors. The left-hand turn signal wiring connectors are located inside the wiring boot underneath the seat (see illustrations). The right-hand turn signal wiring connectors are located inside the wiring boot behind the right-hand side panel (see illustration). Release the wiring from any clips or ties and feed it back to the turn signal.
10 Undo the nut securing the turn signal assembly to the frame and remove the mounting plate and grommet (see illustration).
11 Support the chromed frame cover, feed the wiring through the frame and remove the assembly.
12 If required, undo the screw securing the turn signal to the mounting stem and separate the two items.
13 Installation is the reverse of removal, noting the following:

● Ensure the wiring is correctly routed and secured.
● Check the operation of the turn signals before riding the motorcycle.

XL125V-1 to V-6 – Front

14 Follow the procedure in Chapter 8 to remove the fairing.
15 Remove the headlight assembly (see Section 7).
16 Undo the screws securing the turn signal assembly and lift it off (see illustration).
17 Installation is the reverse of removal. Check the operation of the turn signals before riding the motorcycle.

XL125V-1 to V-6 – Rear

18 Remove the rear mudguard/tail light unit assembly (see Chapter 8).
19 Remove the brake/tail light unit (see Section 9).
20 Undo the screws securing the turn signal and lift it off.
21 Installation is the reverse of removal, noting the following:
● Ensure the wiring is securely connected.
● Check the operation of the turn signals before riding the motorcycle.

XL125V-7 onwards – Front

22 Follow the procedure in Chapter 8 to remove the fairing.
23 Remove the left and right-hand side panels (see Section 7).
24 Undo the screws securing the turn signal assembly and lift it off (see illustration).
25 Installation is the reverse of removal. Check the operation of the turn signals before riding the motorcycle.

XL125V-7 onwards – Rear

26 Follow the procedure in Section 9 to remove and install the tail light/turn signals assembly. Note that the rear turn signals are integral with the brake/tail light unit (see illustration).

13.10 Nut (arrowed) secures turn signal assembly

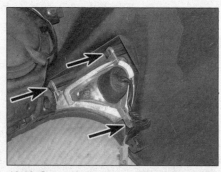

13.16 Screws secure turn signal assembly

13.24 Screws secure turn signal assembly

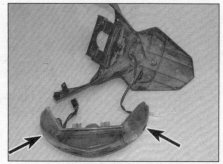

13.26 Turn signals (arrowed) are integral with the brake/tail light

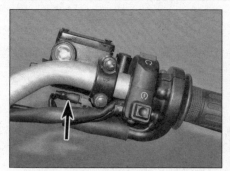

14.2 Front brake light switch connectors

14.6a Location of rear brake light switch . . .

14.6b . . . and brake light switch wiring connector – VT125C

14 Brake light switches

Check

1 Before checking the switches, and if not already done, check the brake light circuit (see Section 5).

2 The front brake light switch is mounted on the underside of the brake master cylinder. Disconnect the wiring connectors from the switch **(see illustration)**.

3 Using a continuity tester, connect the probes to the terminals of the switch. With the brake lever at rest, there should be no continuity. With the brake lever applied, there should be continuity.

4 If the switch does not behave as described, replace it with a new one – the front brake light switch cannot be adjusted (see Chapter 7, Section 5).

5 The rear brake light switch is mounted on the right-hand side of the frame behind the engine unit.

6 On VT125C models, remove the right-hand side panel (see Chapter 8) to access the switch, then trace the wiring to the connector inside the wiring boot on the right-hand side **(see illustrations)**.

7 On XL125V models, the switch is located behind the right-hand footrest bracket **(see illustration)**. Remove the seat and both side panels (see Chapter 8), then trace the wiring to the connector inside the wiring boot on the left-hand side **(see illustration)**.

8 Disconnect the wiring connector. Using a continuity tester, connect the probes to the terminals on the switch side of the connector. With the brake pedal at rest, there should be no continuity. With the brake pedal applied, there should be continuity. If the switch does not behave as described, first check that it is adjusted correctly (see Steps 10 and 11). If the switch still does not work, replace it with a new one.

9 If the switches are good, refer to *Wiring Diagrams* at the end of this chapter and check the wiring for continuity.

Adjustment

10 The rear brake light switch is connected either to the brake rod or the brake pedal by a short spring **(see illustration 14.12 or 13)**. When the pedal is applied the spring should pull the switch plunger down to turn the switch ON. The switch should be adjusted to ensure that the brake light comes on just before the rear brake takes effect.

11 If adjustment is necessary, hold the switch body and turn the adjuster until the brake light is activated correctly. If the brake light comes on too late or not at all, turn the adjuster clockwise so the switch threads out of its bracket. If the brake light comes on too soon or is permanently on, turn the ring anti-clockwise so the switch threads into its bracket.

Removal and installation

12 On VT125C models, remove the right-hand side panel (see Chapter 8) and disconnect the switch wiring connector **(see illustrations 14.6a and b)**. Feed the wiring down to the switch. Remove the rear wheel (see Chapter 7) and disconnect the brake light switch spring from the brake rod **(see illustration)**. Unscrew the switch from its adjuster and remove it.

13 On XL125V models, remove the seat and both side panels (see Chapter 8) and disconnect the switch wiring connector **(see illustrations 14.7a and b)**. Feed the wiring down to the switch. Remove the right-hand footrest bracket (see Chapter 6) and disconnect the brake light switch spring **(see illustration)**. Unscrew the switch from its adjuster and remove it.

14 Installation is the reverse of removal. Check and adjust the switch (see Steps 10 and 11).

14.7a Location of rear brake light switch – XL125V

14.7b Brake light switch wiring connector is inside boot

14.12 Disconnect the brake light switch spring from the brake rod – VT125C

14.13 Disconnect the brake light switch spring from the brake pedal – XL125V

15.1a Undo the screws . . .

15.1b . . . noting the washers

15.2 Disconnect the wiring connectors

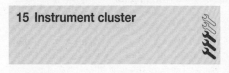

15 Instrument cluster

VT125C

Removal and installation

1 Undo the screws securing the instrument panel, noting the location of the washers **(see illustrations)**.

2 Lift the instrument panel up, displace the wiring boot and disconnect the wiring connectors **(see illustration)**.

3 If required, displace the warning lights and trip meter reset button from the panel **(see illustration 15.8)**. Undo the screws securing the speedometer in the panel, noting the location of the wiring clip **(see illustration)**.

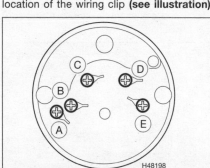

15.4 Speedometer terminal screw identification – light blue/white wire (A), black/yellow wire (B), pink wire (C), black/brown wire (D) and green/black wire (E)

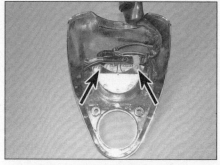

15.3a Screws (arrowed) secure speedometer

Lift the speedometer and wiring sub-loom out. Note the location of the speedometer seal – if it is damaged or deteriorated fit a new one on reassembly **(see illustration)**.

4 If required, undo the wiring sub-loom

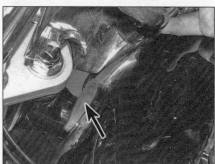

15.5a Check installation of rubber mount . . .

15.3b Note location of seal

terminal screws and disconnect the sub loom **(see illustration)**.

5 Installation is the reverse of removal, noting the following:

● Ensure the terminal screws are tightened securely.

● Secure the sub-loom with its clip.

● Ensure the rubber mount is in place on the front of the fuel tank **(see illustration)**.

● Locate the rear of the instrument cluster over the seal around the fuel filler cap and tighten the fixing screws securely **(see illustration)**.

Instrument and warning light bulbs

6 To renew a warning light bulb, first prise off the lens, taking care not to damage the rubber bulbholder **(see illustration)**.

7 Remove the instrument panel (see Steps 1 and 2).

8 Ease the bulbholder out from the panel **(see illustration)**.

15.5b . . . and seal around filler cap

15.6 Remove the lens carefully

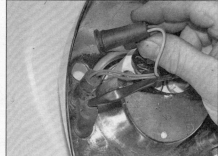

15.8 Remove the bulbholder from the inside

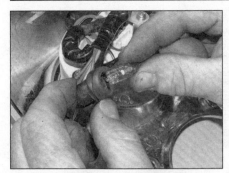

15.9 Pull the bulb out carefully

9 The bulb is of the capless type – pull it out of the bulbholder carefully **(see illustration)**.
10 Installation is the reverse of removal. Check the operation of the light.
11 The speedometer light is located in the back of the speedometer. Follow the procedure in Steps 8 to 10 to renew the speedometer bulb.

Speedometer – check

12 If the speedometer fails to work, first check the main fuse and the instrument cluster fuse (see Section 4).
13 If the fuses are good, remove the instrument panel and disconnect the wiring connectors (see Steps 1 and 2).
14 Using a multimeter, connect the positive (+) probe to the pink wire terminal on the loom side of the white connector and the negative (–) probe to the green/black wire terminal on the loom side of the red connector and check for battery voltage.
15 If there is no voltage, refer to *Wiring Diagrams* at the end of this Chapter and check the wiring for damage.
16 If there is battery voltage, connect the positive (+) probe to the black/brown wire terminal on the loom side of the white connector and the negative (–) probe to the green/black wire terminal on the loom side of the red connector. Turn the ignition ON and check for battery voltage. Turn the ignition OFF.
17 If there is no voltage, refer to *Wiring Diagrams* at the end of this Chapter and check the wiring for damage.
18 If the wiring is good, reconnect the white wire connector, turn the ignition ON, then check for continuity between the light blue/white wire terminal on the back of the speedometer **(see illustration 15.4)** and the green/black wire terminal on the speedometer side of the red connector.
19 There should be no continuity with the trip reset button released and continuity with the button depressed.
20 If the result is not as stated it is likely the speedometer is faulty – have it checked by a Honda dealer.

Speed sensor – check

Special tool: *An analogue voltmeter is required for this test (see Step 24).*
21 If not already done, check the main fuse and the instrument cluster fuse (see Section 4).
22 If the fuses are good, support the machine on an auxiliary stand with the rear wheel off the ground.
23 Remove the instrument panel to access the wire terminals on the back of the speedometer. Do not disconnect the wiring connectors. If necessary, undo the screw securing the wiring clip and displace the sub-loom.
24 Connect the positive (+) voltmeter probe to the black/yellow wire terminal on the back of the speedometer and the negative (–) probe to the green/black wire terminal **(see illustration 15.4)**.
25 With the ignition ON, turn the rear wheel slowly in the normal direction of rotation and observe the voltmeter. The reading should alternate between zero and 5.0 volts as the wheel turns. Turn the ignition OFF.
26 If the result is not as stated, connect the positive (+) probe of a multimeter to the black/brown wire terminal on the back of the speedometer and the negative (–) probe to the green/black wire terminal **(see illustration 15.4)**. Turn the ignition ON and check for battery voltage. Turn the ignition OFF.
27 If there is battery voltage, go to Step 30.
28 If there is no voltage, remove the front sprocket cover (see Chapter 7, Section 20) and the side panels (see Chapter 8). Trace the wiring from the speed sensor on the back of the transmission casing and disconnect it at the wiring connector **(see illustration)**.
29 Connect the positive (+) probe of a multimeter to the black/brown wire terminal on the loom side of the connector and the negative (–) probe to earth (ground). Turn the ignition ON and check for battery voltage. Turn the ignition OFF.
30 If there is battery voltage, disconnect the speedometer white wiring connector **(see illustration 15.2)**. Check for continuity in the black/yellow wire between the speedometer wiring connector and the speed sensor wiring connector. If there is no continuity, inspect the wire for damage. If there is continuity it is likely the speed sensor is faulty – have it checked by a Honda dealer.

Speed sensor – removal and installation

31 Remove the front sprocket cover (see Chapter 7, Section 20) and the side panels (see Chapter 8). Trace the wiring from the speed sensor on the back of the transmission casing and disconnect it at the wiring connector **(see illustration 15.28)**. Free the wiring from any clips or ties and feed it back to the sensor, noting its routing.
32 Remove the swingarm for access (see Chapter 6).
33 If the area around the speed sensor is dirty, clean it thoroughly before starting – this will make work much easier and rule out the possibility of dirt falling inside.
34 Undo the bolts securing the sensor, then draw the sensor out, noting the location of the O-ring **(see illustrations)**. Discard the O-ring as a new one must be fitted.
35 Lubricate the new O-ring with a smear of engine oil and fit it onto the sensor.
36 Ensure the recess in the crankcase is clean, then install the sensor and tighten the mounting bolts evenly.
37 Secure the wiring as noted on removal and connect the wiring connector.
38 Install the remaining components in the reverse order of removal

Coolant temperature warning light – check

39 When the ignition is turned ON, the coolant temperature warning light should come on briefly as part of a start-up system check. If the coolant light does not come on, first check that the neutral indicator light comes on, then follow Steps 40 to 44. If the neutral indicator

15.28 Location of the speed sensor

15.34a Undo the bolts . . .

15.34b . . . and remove the speed sensor. Note O-ring

15.53a Undo the bolts . . .

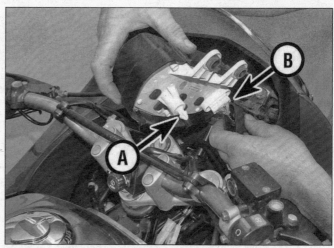

15.53b . . . release the peg (A) from the grommet and disconnect the wiring connector (B)

light does not come on, follow Steps 45 to 47. If the coolant temperature warning light does not go off, follow Steps 48 to 51.

40 Check the coolant temperature warning light bulb (see Steps 6 to 10). If the bulb is good, remove the left-hand cylinder head side cover and disconnect the thermo-switch wiring connector (see Chapter 3, Section 4). Connect the wiring connector to earth (ground) and turn the ignition ON.

41 If the warning light comes on, turn the ignition OFF and check that the wiring connector is a secure fit on the thermo-switch, then follow the procedure in Chapter 5, Section 6, to disconnect the ignition control unit (ICU) wiring connector. Check for continuity between the green wire terminal on the loom side of the ICU and earth (ground).

42 No continuity indicates a fault in the green wire (see *Wiring Diagrams* at the end of this Chapter). If there is continuity it is likely the ICU is faulty – have it checked by a Honda dealer.

43 If the warning light does not come on, turn the ignition OFF and disconnect the speedometer white wiring connector and the ICU wiring connector (see Chapter 5, Section 6). Leave the thermo-switch wiring connector disconnected. Check for continuity in the yellow/black wire between the speedometer

wiring connector and the ICU wiring connector, then check for continuity in the green/blue wire between the thermo-switch connector and the ICU connector.

44 No continuity indicates a fault in the wire (see *Wiring Diagrams* at the end of this Chapter). If the wiring is good it is likely the ICU is faulty – have it checked by a Honda dealer.

45 If the neutral indicator light does not come on, first check the bulb (see Steps 6 to 10), then check the fuse (see Section 4).

46 If the bulb and fuse are good, disconnect both speedometer wiring connectors. Using a multimeter, connect the positive (+) probe to the black/brown wire terminal on the loom side of the white connector and the negative (–) probe to earth (ground). Turn the ignition ON and check for battery voltage.

47 If there is no voltage, refer to *Wiring Diagrams* at the end of this Chapter and check the wire between the connector and the fusebox for damage.

48 If the coolant temperature warning light does not go off, ensure that the ignition is OFF, then disconnect the speedometer white wiring connector and the ICU wiring connector (see Chapter 5, Section 6). Check for continuity between the yellow/black wire terminals in both connectors and earth (ground). Continuity

indicates a short circuit in the yellow/black wire.

49 If the yellow/black wire is good, disconnect the thermo-switch wiring connector (see Chapter 3, Section 4) and check for continuity between the green blue/wire terminal and earth (ground). Continuity indicates a short circuit in the green/blue wire.

50 If the green/blue wire is good, test the operation of the thermo-switch (see Chapter 3, Section 4).

51 If the thermo-switch is good it is likely the ICU is faulty – have it checked by a Honda dealer.

XL125V-1 to V-6

Removal and installation

52 Remove the fairing cockpit trim panel (see Chapter 8).

53 Undo the bolts securing the instrument cluster, ease the instrument cluster out to release the peg on the underside from the grommet on the fairing bracket and disconnect the wiring connector **(see illustrations)**. If required, undo the screws on the back of the unit to separate the top half from the instrument panel and case – individual components are available.

54 Installation is the reverse of removal. Ensure the wiring connector is secure.

Instrument and warning light bulbs

55 Remove the instrument cluster (see Steps 52 and 53).

56 Prise out the rubber plug, then twist the bulbholder anti-clockwise to remove it **(see illustrations)**.

57 The bulb is of the capless type – pull it out of the bulbholder carefully.

58 Installation is the reverse of removal. Check the operation of the light.

Speed sensor – check

Special tool: *An analogue voltmeter is required for this test (see Step 62).*

Note: *The speed sensor is located on the*

15.56a Prise out the rubber plug . . .

15.56b . . . then twist the bulbholder anti-clockwise

15.65a Location of the speed sensor

15.65b Speed sensor wiring connector

left-hand side of the front wheel hub on all models except Type IIG German market models – on those machines the speed sensor is located on the back of the transmission casing (see Steps 65 to 67).

59 If the speedometer fails to work, first check the main fuse and the instrument cluster fuse (see Section 4).

60 If the fuses are good, support the machine on an auxiliary stand with the front wheel off the ground.

61 Remove the instrument cluster (see Steps 52 and 53).

62 Connect the positive (+) voltmeter probe to the black/yellow wire terminal on the loom side of the instrument cluster connector and the negative (–) probe to the green/black wire terminal.

63 Turn the front wheel slowly in the normal direction of rotation and observe the voltmeter. The reading should pulse as the wheel turns.

64 If the result is not as stated, inspect the wiring between the instrument cluster and the speed sensor for damage or poor connections in the connector (see Wiring Diagrams at the end of this Chapter). If the wiring is good it is likely the instrument cluster is faulty – have it checked by a Honda dealer.

65 On Type IIG German market models, remove the front sprocket cover (see Chapter 7, Section 20) and the left-hand side panel (see Chapter 8). Trace the wiring from the speed sensor on the back of the transmission casing and disconnect it at the wiring connector **(see illustrations)**.

66 Connect the positive (+) probe of a multimeter to the brown/black wire terminal on the loom side of the connector and the negative (–) probe to the green/black wire terminal. Turn the ignition ON and check for battery voltage. Turn the ignition OFF.

67 If there is no voltage, first check the main fuse and the instrument cluster fuse (see Section 4). If the fuses are good, follow the procedure in Chapter 5, Section 6, to disconnect the ignition control unit (ICU)

wiring connector. Check for continuity in the blue/orange wire between the speed sensor connector and the ICU connector. If there is no continuity, inspect the wire for damage.

Speed sensor – removal and installation

68 On all models except type IIG German market models, remove the front wheel and displace the speed sensor (see Chapter 7, Section 15).

69 Release the sensor wiring from the clips on the front fork leg and front mudguard, and the tie on the brake hose.

70 Trace the wiring to the connector and disconnect it.

71 Installation is the reverse of removal.

72 On Type IIG German market models, follow the procedure in Steps 31 to 38.

Tachometer – check

Special tool: To test the tachometer input voltage a multimeter with a minimum input resistance of 10 M ohms is required in conjunction with a peak voltage adapter. Honda provides a peak voltage adapter (Part No. 07HGJ-0020100 for this purpose. If the appropriate equipment is not available, the checks should be undertaken by a Honda dealer.

73 Remove the instrument cluster (see Steps 52 and 53).

74 Connect the positive (+) peak voltage adapter probe to the yellow/green wire terminal on the loom side of the instrument cluster connector and the negative (–) probe to earth (ground).

75 Start the engine and note the tachometer input voltage. Turn the engine OFF. Compare the result with the specification at the beginning of this Chapter.

76 If the input voltage is good it is likely the tachometer is faulty – have it checked by a Honda dealer.

77 In the input voltage is lower than the specified minimum it is likely the ICU is faulty – have it checked by a Honda dealer.

78 If no input voltage is recorded, follow

the procedure in Chapter 5, Section 6, to disconnect the ignition control unit (ICU) wiring connector. Check for continuity in the yellow/green wire between the instrument cluster connector and the ICU connector. If there is no continuity, inspect the wire for damage. If there is continuity it is likely the tachometer is faulty – have it checked by a Honda dealer.

Instrument cluster – check

79 If the instrument cluster is thought to be faulty, first check the operation of the speed sensor (see Steps 59 to 67) and the tachometer (see Steps 73 to 78).

80 If not already done, check the main fuse, the instrument cluster (meter) fuse and the clock fuse (see Section 4).

81 If the fuses are good, remove the instrument cluster (see Steps 52 and 53).

82 Using a multimeter, connect the positive (+) probe to the black/brown wire terminal on the loom side of the instrument cluster connector and the negative (–) probe to the green/black wire terminal. Turn the ignition ON – there should be battery voltage. Turn the ignition OFF.

83 Next, connect the positive (+) probe to the black/blue wire terminal on the loom side of the connector, turn the ignition ON and check for battery voltage. Turn the ignition OFF.

84 Finally, check for continuity between the green/black wire terminal on the loom side of the connector and earth (ground). There should be continuity.

85 If the results of all the tests are good, disconnect the battery positive lead (see Section 3) then reconnect it after a few seconds to reset the instrument cluster.

86 Turn the ignition ON and check the operation of the multi-function panel (coolant temperature, clock and odometer/trip displays).

87 Check the operation of the speedometer and tachometer.

88 If any of the instrument cluster functions fail to work it is likely the instrument cluster is faulty – have it checked by a Honda dealer.

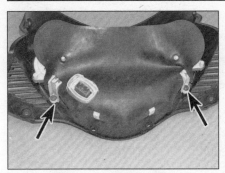

15.90a Undo the screws . . .

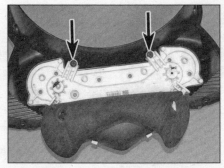

15.90b . . . securing the instrument cluster . . .

15.90c . . . and separate it from the trim panel

XL125V-7 onwards

Removal and installation

89 Remove the fairing cockpit trim panel (see Chapter 8).

90 Undo the screws securing the instrument cluster and separate it from the trim panel **(see illustrations)**. If required, unhook the cover. If required, undo the screws on the back of the unit to separate the clear cover, top half and bottom halves of the case and the instrument panel – individual components are available.

91 Installation is the reverse of removal. Ensure the wiring connector is secure.

Instrument and warning lights

92 All illumination is by LED. If a warning light fails to work, check the operation of the appropriate component first. If any part of the instrument cluster panel is faulty a new one will have to be fitted.

Power input – check

93 Before checking individual components in the instrument cluster, first ensure that the power supply is good.

94 Check the fuse (see Section 4) and the operation of the horn (common fuse with the instrument cluster).

95 Remove the cockpit trim panel (see Chapter 8).

96 Using a multimeter, connect the positive (+) probe to the black/brown wire terminal on the loom side of the instrument cluster connector and the negative (–) probe to earth (ground). Turn the ignition ON – there should be battery voltage. Turn the ignition OFF. If there is no voltage, inspect the black/brown wire for damage (see *Wiring Diagram* at the end of this Chapter).

97 Check for continuity between the green/black wire terminal on the loom side of the instrument cluster connector and earth (ground). If there is no continuity, inspect the wire for damage

98 Using a multimeter, connect the positive (+) probe to the red/green wire terminal on the loom side of the instrument cluster connector and the negative (–) probe to earth (ground). There should be battery voltage at all times (with the battery connected). If there is no voltage, check the red/green wire for damage, check the CLOCK

fuse, then disconnect the batter and check for continuity in the red wire between the fusebox and the starter relay (see *Wiring Diagram* at the end of this Chapter).

Speedometer and speed (VS) sensor – check

Note: *Under certain circumstances a faulty VS sensor will trigger the FI warning light (see Chapter 4B, Section 7).*

Special tool: *An analogue voltmeter and a needle probe are required to test the VS sensor output (see Step 106).*

99 When the ignition is first turned ON the speedometer, tachometer and coolant temperature gauge needles should all sweep across the faces of the instruments and return to rest as a start-up check.

100 If the speedometer needle does not move but the other two do, it is likely the speedometer is faulty – have it checked by a Honda dealer.

101 If none of the needles move, check the power input (see Steps 94 to 98).

102 If the speedometer performs the start-up check (see Step 99) but fails to work when the machine is ridden, check the VS sensor output as follows.

103 Support the machine on an auxiliary stand with the rear wheel off the ground.

104 Remove the cockpit trim panel (see Chapter 8) to access the wire terminals on the back of the instrument cluster. Do not disconnect the wiring connector.

105 Backprobe the pink/green wire terminal on the wiring connector with the positive (+) voltmeter probe and connect the negative (–) probe to earth (ground).

106 With the ignition ON, turn the rear wheel slowly in the normal direction of rotation and observe the voltmeter. The reading should alternate between zero and 12.0 volts as the wheel turns. Turn the ignition OFF.

107 If the result is as stated, but the speedometer fails to work when the machine is ridden, it is likely the speedometer is faulty – have it checked by a Honda dealer.

108 If the result is not as stated, remove the front sprocket cover (see Chapter 7, Section 20) and the left-hand side panel (see Chapter 8). Trace the wiring from the VS sensor on the back of the transmission casing and

disconnect it at the wiring connector **(see illustrations 15.65a and b)**.

109 Connect the positive (+) probe of a multimeter to the black/brown wire terminal on the loom side of the connector and the negative (–) probe to the green/black wire terminal. Turn the ignition ON and check for battery voltage. Turn the ignition OFF.

110 If there is no voltage, inspect the wire for damage (see *Wiring Diagrams* at the end of this Chapter).

111 If there is battery voltage, disconnect the instrument cluster wiring connector and check for continuity in the pink/green wire between the instrument cluster connector and the VS sensor wiring connector. If there is no continuity, inspect the wire for damage.

112 If there is continuity, disconnect the ECM grey wiring connector (see Chapter 4B, Section 7).

113 Check for continuity in the pink/green wire between the instrument cluster wiring connector and earth (ground). There should be no continuity – if there is, inspect the wire for damage.

114 If none of the above checks reveal a system fault it is likely the VS sensor is faulty – have it checked by a Honda dealer.

Speed (VS) sensor – removal and installation

115 Follow the procedure in Steps 31 to 38.

Tachometer – check

Special tool: *To test the tachometer input voltage a multimeter with a minimum input resistance of 10 M-ohms is required in conjunction with a peak voltage adapter. Honda provides a peak voltage adapter (Part No. 07HGJ-0020100 for this purpose. If the appropriate equipment is not available, the checks should be undertaken by a Honda dealer.*

116 Referring to Step 99, if the tachometer needle does not move but the other two do, it is likely the tachometer is faulty – have it checked by a Honda dealer.

117 If none of the needles move, check the power input (see Steps 94 to 98).

118 If the tachometer performs the start-up check (see Step 99) but fails to work when the machine is ridden, check the input voltage as follows.

15.130 ECT sensor wiring connector

119 Remove the instrument cluster (see Steps 89 and 90).

120 Connect the positive (+) peak voltage adapter probe to the yellow/green wire terminal on the loom side of the instrument cluster connector and the negative (–) probe to earth (ground).

121 Start the engine and note the tachometer input voltage. Turn the engine OFF. Compare the result with the specification at the beginning of this Chapter.

122 If the input voltage is good it is likely the tachometer is faulty – have it checked by a Honda dealer.

123 In the input voltage is lower than the specified minimum it is likely the engine control module (ECM) is faulty – have it checked by a Honda dealer (see Chapter 4B).

124 If no input voltage is recorded, disconnect the ECM grey wiring connector (see Chapter 4B, Section 7).

125 Check for continuity in the yellow/green wire between the instrument cluster connector and the ECM connector. If there is no continuity, inspect the wire for damage. If there is continuity it is likely the ECM is faulty – have it checked by a Honda dealer.

Coolant temperature gauge – check

126 Referring to Step 99, if the temperature gauge needle does not move but the other two do, it is likely the gauge is faulty – have it checked by a Honda dealer.

127 If none of the needles move, check the power input (see Steps 94 to 98).

128 If the temperature gauge performs the start-up check (see Step 99) but fails to work when the machine is ridden, check the gauge as follows.

129 Refer to Chapter 4B, Section 7, to access the engine control module (ECM) and disconnect the grey wiring connector.

130 Disconnect the ECT sensor wiring connector **(see illustration)**. Using an insulated jumper wire, connect the green/blue wire terminal on the connector to earth (ground) and turn the ignition ON.

131 If the gauge needle moves, check the operation of the sensor (see Chapter 4B, Section 13). **Note:** *Under certain circumstances a faulty ECT sensor will trigger the FI warning light (see Chapter 4B, Section 7).*

132 If the needle does not move, disconnect the instrument cluster wiring connector and check for continuity in the green/blue wire between the instrument cluster connector and the sensor wiring connector. If there is no continuity, inspect the wire for damage.

133 If there is continuity it is likely the gauge is faulty – have it checked by a Honda dealer.

Low fuel level warning light

134 Follow the procedure in Chapter 4B, Section 6 to check the warning light.

16 Ignition switch

⚠ *Warning: To prevent the risk of short circuits, disconnect the battery negative (–) lead before making any ignition switch checks.*

VT125C

1 The ignition switch is located on the left-hand side of the machine behind the rear cylinder **(see illustration)**.

2 To test the switch, first remove the seat and left-hand side panel (see Chapter 8).

3 Trace the wiring from the back of the switch to the wiring boot and disconnect the 3-pin wiring connector **(see illustration)**.

4 Using a multimeter, check for continuity between the wire terminals on the switch side of the connector. There should be no continuity between any of the terminals with the switch in the OFF position and continuity between all three terminals with the switch ON.

5 To remove the switch, undo the screw securing the cover and lift it off, then undo the bolts securing the switch to the frame. Release the wiring from any clips or ties

6 Installation is the reverse of removal. Make sure the wiring connector is secure.

XL125V

7 The ignition switch is located on the front of the front fork top yoke, below the steering lock.

8 To test the switch, first remove the fairing (see Chapter 8), the fuel tank and the air filter housing (see Chapter 4A or 4B as applicable).

9 Trace the wiring from the underside of the switch to the wiring boot behind the steering head and disconnect the wiring connector **(see illustration)**.

10 Using a multimeter, check for continuity between the wire terminals on the switch side of the connector. There should be no continuity between any of the terminals with the switch in the OFF position and continuity between all terminals with the switch ON. Note that on XL125V-1 to V-6 models there are three terminals in the connector, on XL125V-7 models onward there are two terminals.

11 To remove the switch, first remove the fork top yoke (see Chapter 6, Section 9).

12 Undo the screws securing the switch to the steering lock and remove the switch **(see illustration)**.

13 Installation is the reverse of removal. Make sure the wiring is correctly routed and securely connected.

16.1 Location of the ignition switch – VT125C

16.3 Ignition switch wiring connector

16.9 Ignition switch wiring connector – XL125V

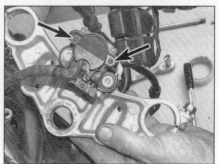

16.12 Screws (arrowed) secure ignition switch

17.9a Undo the screws . . .

17.9b . . . and split the housing

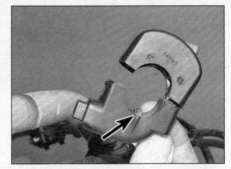

17.11 Right-hand switch housing – XL125V. Note locating pin (arrowed)

17 Handlebar switches

Check

1 Generally speaking, the switches are reliable and trouble-free. Most troubles, when they do occur, are caused by dirty or corroded contacts, but wear and breakage of internal parts is a possibility that should not be overlooked. If breakage does occur, the entire switch and related wiring harness will have to be replaced with a new one, as individual parts are not available.

2 The switches can be checked for continuity using a multimeter or a continuity test light. Always disconnect the battery negative (–) lead, which will prevent the possibility of a short circuit, before making the checks.

3 On VT125C models, remove the headlight reflector assembly (see Section 6, Steps 1 to 3). Note the location of the wiring inside the headlight shell and release it from the wiring clips **(see illustration 7.10)**. Trace the wiring from the switch to be tested and disconnect it at the connector.

4 On XL125V models, remove the fairing (see Chapter 8), the fuel tank and the air filter housing (see Chapter 4A or 4B as applicable). Trace the wiring from the switch to be tested to the wiring boot behind the steering head and disconnect the wiring connector **(see illustration 16.9)**.

5 Check for continuity between the terminals

of the switch connector with the switch in the various positions i.e. switch off – no continuity, switch on – continuity (see the *Wiring Diagrams* at the end of this Chapter). Continuity should exist between the terminals connected by a solid line on the diagram when the switch is in the indicated position.

6 If the check indicates a problem exists, displace the switch housing and spray the switch contacts with electrical contact cleaner (there is no need to remove the switch completely). If they are accessible, the contacts can be scraped clean with a small knife. If switch components are damaged or broken, it will be obvious when the switch is disassembled.

Removal and installation

7 Follow the procedure in Steps 3 or 4 as applicable to disconnect the appropriate wiring connector. Feed the wiring back to the switch, freeing it from any clips or ties and noting its routing.

8 If removing the right-hand switch, disconnect the wires from the front brake light switch **(see illustration 14.2)**. If removing the left-hand switch, disconnect the wires from the clutch switch **(see illustration 20.2)**.

9 To remove the left-hand switch, undo the screws on the underside of the housing and free the switch from the handlebar by separating the two halves **(see illustrations)**. On VT125C models, note the location of the spacer inside the housing – the spacer cannot be removed unless the handlebar grip is removed first.

10 On VT125C models, to remove the right-hand housing, follow the procedure in Chapter 4A, Section 7, to separate the two halves of the switch/twistgrip housing and detach the throttle cables from the twistgrip pulley.

11 On XL125V models, to remove the right-hand housing, undo the screws on the underside of the housing and free the switch from the handlebar by separating the two halves **(see illustration)**.

12 Note the location of the switch housing screws – if they are different lengths they must be returned to their correct positions.

13 Installation is the reverse of removal. Make sure the locating pin in the switch housing locates in the hole in the handlebar. Check the operation of the switches before riding the motorcycle.

18 Neutral switch

1 The neutral switch is part of the starter safety circuit which prevents or stops the engine running if the transmission is in gear whilst the sidestand is down, and prevents the engine from starting if the transmission is in gear unless the sidestand is up and the clutch lever is pulled in.

Check

2 Before checking the electrical circuit, check the neutral indicator bulb on VT125C and XL125V-1 to V-6 models (Section 15) and the fuse on all models (see Section 4).

3 The switch is located in the lower left-hand side of the crankcase forward of the gearchange shaft **(see illustration)**. Remove the front sprocket cover for access (see Chapter 7, Section 20) and clean the area around the switch thoroughly before starting – this will make work much easier and rule out the possibility of dirt falling inside.

4 Displace the boot from the switch terminal, undo the nut and disconnect the wire **(see illustration)**.

5 Connect the wire to earth (ground) and turn the ignition ON – the neutral indicator light on

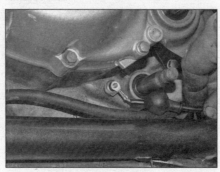

18.3 Location of the neutral switch

18.4 Disconnect the wire from the switch terminal

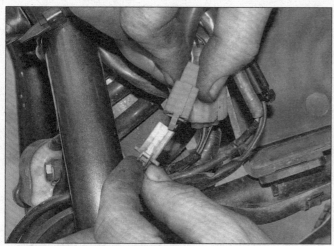

19.2 Sidestand switch wiring connector

20.2 Location of the clutch switch – VT125C

the instrument cluster should come on. Turn the ignition OFF. If the light does not come on, check the wire for damage (see the *Wiring Diagrams* at the end of this Chapter) and check the diode (see Section 21).

6 Check for continuity between the switch terminal and the crankcase. With the transmission in neutral, there should be continuity. With the transmission in gear, there should be no continuity. If the switch does not perform as described it is faulty and must be renewed.

Removal and installation

7 Follow the procedure in Steps 3 and 4, then unscrew the switch from the crankcase and discard the sealing washer.

8 Fit a new sealing washer to the switch then install it and tighten it to the torque setting specified at the beginning of this Chapter.

9 Connect the wire to the switch terminal and tighten the nut securely, then install the boot.

10 Install the front sprocket cover.

19 Sidestand switch

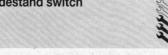

1 The sidestand switch is part of the starter safety circuit which prevents or stops the engine running if the transmission is in gear whilst the sidestand is down, and prevents the engine from starting if the transmission is in gear unless the sidestand is up and the clutch lever is pulled in.

Check

2 The switch is mounted on the stand pivot (see Chapter 6, Section 4). To check the operation of the switch, remove the seat and the left-hand side panel (see Chapter 8). Trace the wiring from the switch to the wiring boot and disconnect it at the connector **(see illustration)**.

3 Using a multimeter, check for continuity between the wire terminals on the switch side

of the connector. There should be no continuity with the stand DOWN and continuity with the stand UP. If the switch does not perform as described it is faulty and must be renewed.

Removal and installation

4 Remove the front sprocket cover (see Chapter 7, Section 20).

5 Disconnect the switch wiring connector (see Step 2), then feed the wiring down to the switch, releasing it from any clips or ties.

6 Follow the procedure in Chapter 6, Section 4, to undo the bolt securing the switch and remove the switch and wiring. If required, check the operation of the sidestand.

7 On installation, ensure the peg on the switch locates in the hole on the stand. Tighten the switch bolt securely. Check the operation of the switch (see Step 3).

8 Secure the wiring as noted on removal and ensure the connector is secure

9 Install the remaining components in the reverse order of removal.

20 Clutch switch

1 The clutch switch is part of the starter safety circuit which prevents or stops the

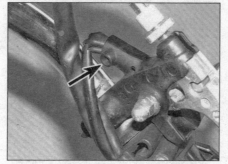

20.5a Depress tab to release the switch

engine running if the transmission is in gear whilst the sidestand is down, and prevents the engine from starting if the transmission is in gear unless the sidestand is up and the clutch lever is pulled in.

Check

2 The switch is located in the clutch lever bracket **(see illustration)**.

3 To check the switch, disconnect the wiring connectors, then using a multimeter, check for continuity between the wire terminals on the switch. There should be no continuity with the lever out and continuity with it pulled in. If the switch does not perform as described it is faulty and must be renewed.

Removal and installation

4 Disconnect the switch wiring connectors.

5 On some machines, the switch is secured by a spring tab inside the lever bracket – depress the tab with a small screwdriver and pull the switch out **(see illustration)**. On other machines, the switch is secured by a small screw – undo the screw and pull the switch out **(see illustration)**. In some cases it is first necessary to remove the clutch lever (see Chapter 6, Section 5), then withdraw the switch from inside the lever bracket.

6 Installation is the reverse of removal.

20.5b Screw (arrowed) secures clutch switch

21 Starter diode

1 The diode for the starter safety circuit is located in the fusebox **(see illustration)**.
2 To check the diode, unclip the fusebox lid (see Section 4) and pull the diode out.
3 Using a multimeter, connect the positive (+) probe to the diode A terminal and the negative (–) probe to the diode B terminal **(see illustration)**. The diode should show continuity. Now reverse the probes. The diode should show no continuity.
4 Repeat the test between the C and B terminals. Connect the positive (+) probe to the C terminal and the negative (–) probe to the B terminal. The diode should show continuity. Now reverse the probes. The diode should show no continuity.
5 If the results are not as stated, the diode is faulty and a new one must be fitted.

22 Horn

Check

1 The horn is located at the front of the machine on the left-hand side **(see illustration)**. On XL125V models, remove the fairing inner panel for access (see Chapter 8).
2 Disconnect the wiring connectors from the back of the horn. Using two jumper wires, apply voltage from a fully-charged 12V battery directly to the terminals on the horn. If the horn doesn't sound, replace it with a new one.
3 If the horn works, check the fuse (Section 4), then refer to *Wiring Diagrams* at the end of this Chapter and check for battery voltage in the wire from the horn button to the horn with the ignition ON and the horn button pressed. If voltage is present, check the other wire to the horn for continuity to earth (ground).
4 If no voltage was present, check for continuity in the wire between the horn and the horn button, and the horn button and the fuse.

22.1 Location of the horn

21.1 Starter safety circuit diode

5 If all the wiring and connectors are good, check the button contacts in the switch housing (see Section 17).

Removal and installation

6 On XL125V models, remove the fairing inner panel (see Chapter 8).
7 Disconnect the wiring connectors from the back of the horn, then undo the mounting bolt.
8 Installation is the reverse of removal. Ensure the wiring connectors are secure and check the operation of the horn before riding the motorcycle.

23 Starter relay

Relay check

1 If the starter circuit is faulty, first check the fuses (see Section 4).
2 On VT125C models, the starter relay is located behind the rear cylinder head – remove the left-hand side panel (see Chapter 8) for access **(see illustration 4.3a)**. On XL125V models, the starter relay is located behind the left-hand side panel – remove the seat and left-hand side panel (see Chapter 8) for access **(see illustration 4.3b)**.
3 Lift the terminal cover and unscrew the bolt securing the starter motor lead **(see illustration)**. Position the lead away from the relay terminal. With the ignition switch ON, the engine kill switch in the RUN position and

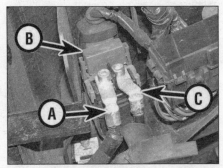
23.3 Starter motor lead (A). Note wiring connector (B) and battery lead (C)

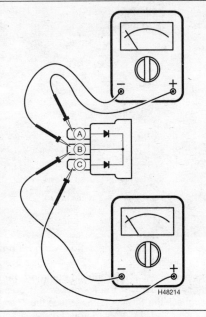
21.3 Diode check – connect the meter probes as described

the transmission in neutral, press the starter button – the relay should be heard to click. Turn the ignition OFF.
4 If the relay doesn't click, remove the relay and test it as follows.
5 Disconnect the battery negative (–) lead (see Section 3).
6 Disconnect the relay wiring connector and unscrew the bolts securing the starter motor and battery leads and detach the leads **(see illustration 23.3)**. Remove the relay from its holder.
7 Using a multimeter, check for continuity between the relay's starter motor and battery lead terminals **(see illustration)**. There should be no continuity.
8 Using a fully-charged 12 volt battery, connect the positive (+) terminal to the yellow/red wire terminal of the relay, and the negative (–) terminal to the green/red wire terminal of the relay **(see illustration 23.7)**. There should now be continuity between the starter motor and battery lead terminals.

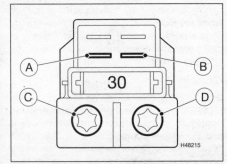
23.7 Starter relay terminal identification – green/red wire (A), yellow/red wire (B), starter motor lead (C), and battery lead (D)

9 If the results are not as stated, the relay is faulty and a new one must be fitted.

10 Installation is the reverse of removal. Ensure the terminal bolts are tightened securely. If a new relay is being fitted, don't forget to fit the main fuse. Connect the negative (–) lead last when reconnecting the battery.

Relay circuit check

11 Disconnect the relay wiring connector **(see illustration 23.3)**. Check for continuity between the green/red wire terminal on the loom side of the connector and earth (ground). Note that the components of the starter safety circuit must be in their correct positions (see Sections 18, 19 and 20). If there is no continuity, check the wiring and components of the starter safety circuit.

12 Reconnect the relay wiring connector, then displace the wiring boot to access the rear of the connector. Using a multimeter, backprobe the yellow/red wire terminal on the relay connector with the meter positive (+) probe and connect the meter negative (–) probe to earth (ground). Turn the ignition ON and press the starter button – there should be battery voltage. If there is no voltage, check the wiring between the relay wiring connector and the starter button (see *Wiring Diagrams* at the end of this Chapter).

24 Starter motor removal and installation

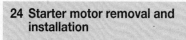

Removal

1 The starter motor is mounted on the front of the crankcase.

2 Disconnect the battery negative (–) lead (see Section 3).

3 On VT125C models, undo the bolts securing the starter motor cover and lift the cover off, noting how it fits **(see illustrations)**.

4 Peel back the terminal cover, unscrew the nut securing the starter lead and detach the lead from the terminal **(see illustrations)**.

5 Undo the bolts securing the starter motor to the crankcase and draw the starter motor out **(see illustrations)**. On VT125C models,

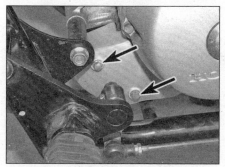

24.3a Unscrew the bolts . . .

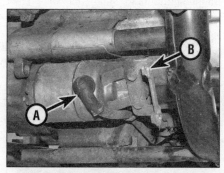

24.4a Terminal cover (A) – XL125V. Note cover bracket (B)

note the location of the cover bracket **(see illustration 24.4a)**.

6 Clean the area around the front of the crankcase to prevent any dirt falling inside.

7 Remove the O-ring on the end of the starter motor and discard it as a new one must be used **(see illustration)**.

Installation

8 Ensure the mounting face of the crankcase is clean. Fit a new O-ring onto the end of the starter motor, making sure it is seated in its groove. Apply a smear of engine oil to the O-ring.

9 Manoeuvre the starter motor into position, ensuring the teeth on the shaft mesh correctly with those of the starter reduction gear (see Chapter 2). Install the mounting bolts and tighten them securely.

10 Connect the starter lead to the terminal

24.3b . . . and remove the cover

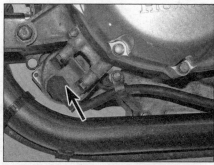

24.4b Terminal cover – VT125C

and secure it with the nut. Tighten the nut to the torque setting specified at the beginning of this Chapter. Fit the cover over the terminal.

11 On VT125C models, install the starter motor cover **(see illustrations 24.3a and b)**.

12 Connect the battery negative (–) lead.

25 Starter motor overhaul

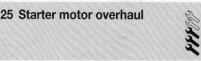

VT125C and XL125V-1 to V-6 models

Disassembly

1 Remove the starter motor (see Section 24).

2 Note the alignment marks between the main housing and the front and rear covers, or make

24.5a Undo the mounting bolts . . .

24.5b . . . and draw the starter motor out

24.7 Remove the O-ring

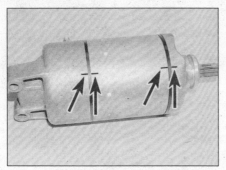

25.2 Note alignment marks

25.3 D-shaped washer (A) and O-ring (B)

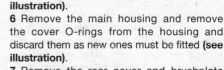

25.4 Remove front cover and tabbed washer (arrowed)

your own if they arenít clear **(see illustration)**.
3 Unscrew the two long bolts, noting the location of the D-shaped washers **(see illustration)**. Discard the O-rings as new ones must be used.
4 Wrap some insulating tape around the teeth

on the starter motor shaft – this will protect the oil seal from damage as the front cover is removed. Remove the front cover from the motor and remove the tabbed washer from inside the front cover **(see illustration)**.
5 Remove the insulating washer and shims

from the front end of the armature shaft, noting the order in which they are fitted **(see illustration)**.
6 Remove the main housing and remove the cover O-rings from the housing and discard them as new ones must be fitted **(see illustration)**.
7 Remove the rear cover and brushplate assembly from the armature commutator **(see illustration)**. Remove the shims from the rear end of the armature shaft **(see illustration)**.
8 Noting the order in which they are fitted, undo the nut on the terminal and remove the washer, insulating washers and O-ring **(see illustrations)**.
9 Withdraw the terminal and brushplate assembly from the rear cover and remove the square insulating washer from the terminal **(see illustrations)**.
10 Lift the brush springs and slide the brushes out from their holders, noting that one brush

25.5 Insulating washer (A) and shims (B)

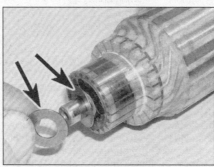

25.6 Remove the main housing and O-rings

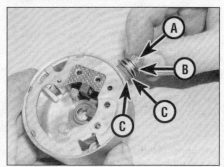

25.8a Terminal nut (A), washer (B), insulating washers (C) . . .

25.7a Separate the commutator (arrowed) from the brushplate . . .

25.7b . . . and remove the shims from the end of the shaft

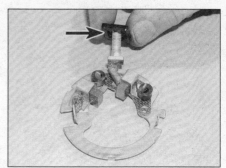

25.8b . . . and O-ring

25.9a Withdraw the brushplate assembly . . .

25.9b . . . and remove the insulating washer

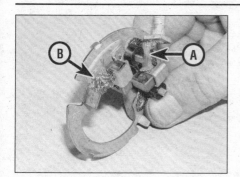

25.10 Brush (A) is attached to terminal, brush (B) is attached to brushplate

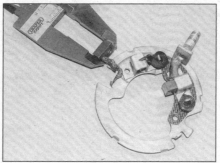

25.11 Measure brush length

25.13 Checking for continuity between the commutator bars

is attached to the terminal and the other is attached to the brushplate **(see illustration)**.

Inspection

11 Check the general condition of all the starter motor components. Some parts, such as brushes, brush holder, springs and O-rings are available separately, otherwise a new starter motor will have to be fitted. The parts that are most likely to require attention are the brushes. Measure the length of the brushes and compare the result with the specification at the beginning of this Chapter **(see illustration)**. If either of the brushes is worn beyond the service limit, renew the brushplate and terminal brush assembly. If the brushes are not worn excessively or otherwise damaged, they may be re-used.

12 Inspect the commutator bars on the armature for scoring, scratches and discoloration. The commutator can be cleaned and polished with crocus cloth – but do not use sandpaper or emery paper. After cleaning, wipe away any residue with a cloth soaked in electrical system cleaner or denatured alcohol.

13 Using an ohmmeter or continuity test light, check for continuity between the commutator bars **(see illustration)**. Continuity (zero resistance) should exist between each bar and all of the others.

14 Also, check for continuity between the commutator bars and the armature shaft **(see illustration)**. There should be no continuity (infinite resistance). If the checks indicate otherwise, the armature is defective.

15 Check for continuity between the positive brush and the brush terminal. There should be continuity (zero resistance). Check for continuity between the terminal and the housing (when assembled). There should be no continuity (infinite resistance).

16 Check the front end of the armature shaft for worn, cracked or broken teeth. If the shaft is damaged or worn, a new starter motor will have to be fitted.

17 Inspect the front and rear covers for signs of cracks or wear.

18 Inspect the front cover oil seal and bearing **(see illustration)**.

Reassembly

19 Slide the brushes back into position in their holders and place the brush spring ends onto the brushes.

20 Ensure that the square insulating washer is in place on the terminal, then insert the terminal through the rear cover from the inside. Fit the O-ring, insulating washers and plain washer on the terminal and then fit and tighten the nut **(see illustrations 25.8b and 25.8a)**.

21 Ensure the brushplate is correctly fitted into the cover – align the tab on the brushplate with the slot in the cover **(see illustration)**.

22 Slide the shims onto the rear end of the armature shaft **(see illustration 25.7b)**. Lubricate the shaft with a smear of grease, then insert the shaft into the rear cover, locating the brushes on the commutator as you do, taking care not to damage the brushes. Check that each brush is securely pressed against the commutator by its spring and is free to move easily in its holder.

23 Fit new O-rings onto the main housing, then fit the housing over the armature and

onto the rear cover, aligning the marks made on removal (see Step 2).

24 Slide the shims and then the insulating washer onto the front end of the armature shaft and lubricate the shaft with a smear of grease. Apply a smear of grease to the inside of the front cover oil seal and fit the tabbed washer into the cover, making sure the tabs locate correctly **(see illustration 25.4)**. Wrap some insulating tape around the teeth on the starter motor shaft to protect the oil seal, then install the cover onto the main housing, aligning the marks made on removal (see Step 2).

25 Ensure that the D-shaped washers are in place on the long bolts and slide a new O-ring onto each of the bolts. Check the marks made on removal are correctly aligned, then install the long bolts and tighten them to the torque setting specified at the beginning of this Chapter, making sure the flat edge on each D-washer is correctly fitted against the front cover **(see illustration)**.

25.14 Checking for continuity between commutator bars and the armature shaft

25.18 Check the oil seal (arrowed) and bearing

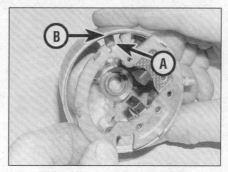

25.21 Align tab (A) with slot (B)

25.25 Ensure D-washers are correctly installed

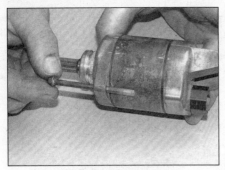

25.29a Unscrew the long bolts ...

25.29b ... and remove the front cover

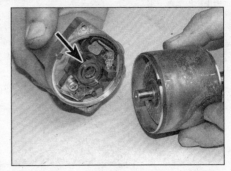

25.30 Draw off the rear cover and brush holder (arrowed)

26 Remove the protective tape from the shaft and install the starter motor (see Section 24).

XL125V-7 onwards

Disassembly

27 Remove the starter motor (see Section 24).

28 Note any alignment marks between the main housing and the front and rear covers, or make your own if they aren't clear **(see illustration 25.2)**.

29 Unscrew the two long bolts then remove the front cover from the motor along with its sealing ring **(see illustrations)**. Discard the sealing ring as a new one must be used.

30 Hold the main housing and draw off the rear cover and brush holder assembly **(see illustration)**. Discard the sealing ring as a new one must be used.

31 Draw the main housing off the armature –

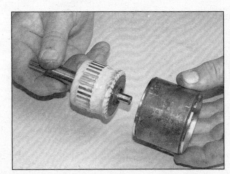

25.31 Draw the main housing off the armature

note that there will be some resistance due to the attraction of the magnets **(see illustration)**.

32 Note the location of the brushes in the brush holder – lift the brushes out and remove the brush springs **(see illustrations)**.

25.32a Remove the brushes (arrowed) ...

33 Check for continuity between the positive brush and the brush terminal **(see illustration)**. There should be continuity (zero resistance). Check for continuity between the terminal and the housing. There should be no continuity (infinite resistance).

34 Undo the screw and remove the negative brush **(see illustration 25.33)**.

35 Noting the order in which they are fitted, undo the nut on the terminal and remove the plain washer, insulating washer, insulator and O-ring **(see illustrations)**.

36 Withdraw the terminal and positive brush assembly from the rear cover, then lift out the brush holder **(see illustrations)**.

Inspection

37 Check the general condition of all the starter motor components. Some parts,

25.32b ... and the springs

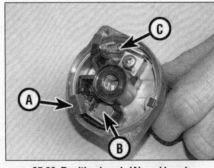

25.33 Positive brush (A) and brush terminal (B). Negative brush and terminal (C)

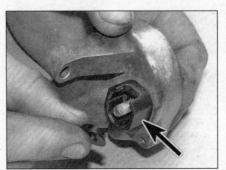

25.35a Remove the nut and plain washer (arrowed)

25.35b Remove the insulating washer and insulator (arrowed)

25.35c Remove the O-ring

25.36a Remove the terminal and positive brush

25.36b Lift out the brush holder

25.37 Measure brush length

such as brushes, brush holder, springs and O-rings are available separately, otherwise a new starter motor will have to be fitted. The parts that are most likely to require attention are the brushes. Measure the length of the brushes and compare the result with the specification at the beginning of this Chapter **(see illustration)**. If either of the brushes is worn beyond the service limit, renew both brushes and springs. If the brushes are not worn excessively or otherwise damaged, they may be re-used.

38 Inspect the commutator bars on the armature for scoring, scratches and discoloration. The commutator can be cleaned and polished with crocus cloth – but do not use sandpaper or emery paper. After cleaning, wipe away any residue with a cloth soaked in electrical system cleaner or denatured alcohol.

39 Using an ohmmeter or continuity test light,

check for continuity between the commutator bars **(see illustration)**. Continuity should exist between each bar and all of the others.

40 Also, check for continuity between the commutator bars and the armature shaft **(see illustration)**. There should be no continuity (infinite resistance). If the checks indicate otherwise, the armature is defective.

41 Check the front end of the armature shaft for worn, cracked or broken teeth **(see illustration)**. If the shaft is damaged or worn, a new starter motor will have to be fitted.

42 Inspect the front and rear covers for signs of cracks or wear.

43 Inspect the front cover oil seal and bearing **(see illustration)**.

Reassembly

44 Fit the brush holder into the rear cover and install the terminal and positive brush **(see illustrations 25.36b and a)**.

45 Fit the O-ring and press it into place between the terminal and the cover **(see illustration 25.35c)**.

46 Fit the insulator, insulating washer and plain washer, then secure them with the nut **(see illustrations 25.35b and a)**.

47 Install the negative brush and secure it with the screw **(see illustration 25.33)**.

48 Install the springs and brushes in the brush holder **(see illustrations 25.32b and a)**.

49 Insert the armature into main housing, then fit the new sealing rings onto the housing **(see illustration)**.

50 Apply a smear of grease to the rear end of the shaft, then fit the rear cover ensuring the marks between the cover and housing align **(see illustration)**.

51 Apply a smear of grease to the front cover oil seal, then fit the front cover ensuring the marks between the cover and housing align **(see illustration 25.29b)**.

25.39 Checking for continuity between the commutator bars

25.40 Checking for continuity between commutator bars and the armature shaft

25.41 Examine the shaft for worn or broken teeth

25.43 Check the cover seal and bearing

25.49 Fit the new sealing rings

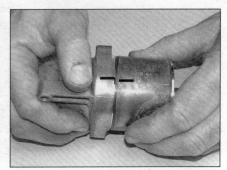

25.50 Ensure cover and housing marks align

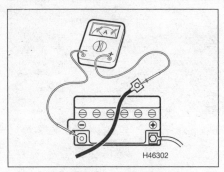

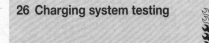

26.5 Set-up for checking current leakage

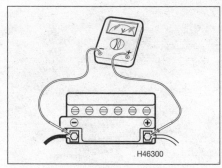

26.9 Set-up for regulated voltage output check

52 Check the marks made on removal are correctly aligned (see Step 28), then fit the long bolts and tighten them to the torque setting specified at the beginning of this Chapter.

53 Install the starter motor (see Section 24).

26 Charging system testing

1 If the performance of the charging system is suspect, the system as a whole should be checked first, followed by testing of the individual components. **Note:** *Before beginning the checks, make sure the battery is fully charged and that all system connections are clean and tight.*

2 Checking the output of the charging system and the performance of the various components within the charging system requires the use of a multimeter. If a multimeter is not available, the job of checking the charging system should be left to a Honda dealer.

3 When making the checks, follow the procedures carefully to prevent incorrect connections or short circuits resulting in irreparable damage to electrical system components.

Leakage test

Caution: Always connect an ammeter in series, never in parallel with the battery, otherwise it will be damaged. Do not turn the ignition ON or operate the starter motor when the ammeter is connected – a sudden surge in current will blow the meter's fuse.

4 Ensure the ignition is OFF, then disconnect the battery negative (–) lead (see Section 3).

5 Set the multimeter to the Amps function and connect its negative (–) probe to the battery negative (–) terminal, and positive (+) probe to the disconnected negative (–) lead **(see illustration)**. Always set the meter to a high amps range initially and then bring it down to the mA (milli Amps) range; if there is a high current flow in the circuit it may blow the meter's fuse.

6 Battery current leakage should not exceed the maximum limit (see *Specifications* at the beginning of this Chapter). If a higher leakage rate is shown there is a short circuit in the wiring, although if an after-market immobiliser or alarm is fitted, its current draw should be taken into account. Disconnect the meter and reconnect the battery negative (–) lead.

7 If leakage is indicated, refer to *Wiring Diagrams* at the end of this Chapter to systematically disconnect individual electrical components and repeat the test until the source is identified.

Regulated output test

8 Remove the rider's seat and, if necessary, the left-hand side panel to access the battery (see Chapter 8). Start the engine and warm it up to operating temperature. Turn the engine OFF.

9 Connect a multimeter set to the 0 - 20 volts DC scale to the terminals of the battery – positive (+) meter probe to battery positive (+) terminal and the negative (–) meter probe to battery negative (–) terminal **(see illustration)**.

10 Start the engine, switch the headlight high beam ON, then slowly increase the engine speed to 5000 rpm and note the reading obtained.

11 Compare the result with the specification at the beginning of this Chapter. If the regulated voltage output is outside the specification, check the alternator and the regulator (see Sections 27 and 28).

> **HAYNES HiNT** *Clues to a faulty regulator are constantly blowing bulbs, with brightness varying considerably with engine speed, and battery overheating.*

27 Alternator

Special tool: *A rotor strap and rotor puller are necessary to remove the alternator rotor from the crankshaft (see Steps 10 and 12).*

Check

1 Remove the seat and the left-hand side panel (see Chapter 8). Remove the front sprocket cover (see Chapter 7, Section 20).

2 Trace the wiring from the back of the alternator cover on the left-hand side of the engine to the wiring boot and disconnect the 3-pin connector **(see illustrations)**.

27.2a Trace the alternator wiring from the cover . . .

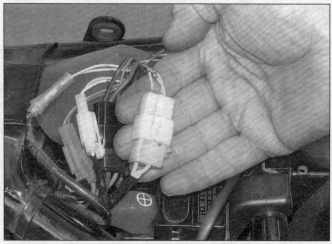

27.2b . . . and disconnect the 3-pin connector

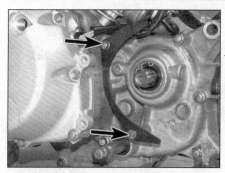

27.6 Bolts (arrowed) secure chain guide

27.7 Disconnect the 2-pin wiring connector

27.8 Location of the alternator cover bolts

3 Using a multimeter set to the ohms scale, connect the meter probes to one pair of terminals at a time on the alternator side of the wiring connector and measure the resistance between the terminals. Note the three readings obtained. Now check for continuity between each terminal and earth (ground).

4 If the stator coil windings are in good condition the three readings should be within the range shown in *Specifications* at the beginning of this Chapter and there should be no continuity (infinite resistance) between any of the terminals and earth (ground). If not, the alternator stator coil assembly is faulty and should be renewed. **Note:** *Before condemning the stator coils, check the fault is not due to damaged wiring between the connector and coils.*

Removal

5 Drain the engine oil (see Chapter 1). Position a suitable receptacle underneath the alternator cover to catch any residual oil when the cover is removed.

6 If not already done, disconnect the alternator wiring connector (see Steps 1 and 2) then free the wiring from any clips or ties and feed it back to the alternator cover. Undo the bolts securing the chain guide and remove it **(see illustration)**.

7 Trace the CKP sensor or ignition pulse generator wiring (see Chapter 4B or 5 as

applicable) from the back of the alternator cover to the wiring boot and disconnect the 2-pin wiring connector **(see illustration)**. Feed the wiring back of the alternator cover.

8 Working in a criss-cross pattern, loosen the alternator cover bolts evenly, then remove the bolts, noting where they fit **(see illustration)**.

9 Draw the cover off the engine, noting that it will be restrained by the force of the rotor magnets **(see illustration)**. Discard the cover gasket as a new one must be fitted **(see illustration)**. Note the location of the cover dowels and remove them for safekeeping if they are loose **(see illustrations)**.

10 To loosen the rotor nut it is necessary to stop the rotor from turning. Honda produces

a service tool (Part No. 07725-0040001) to do this. Alternatively, use a commercially available rotor strap. Clean the outside of the rotor with a suitable solvent before installing the strap. If a rotor strap is not available, and the engine is in the frame, place the transmission in gear and have an assistant apply the rear brake hard.

11 With the rotor held, loosen the nut **(see illustration)**. Unscrew the nut and remove the washer **(see illustration)**.

12 To remove the rotor from the crankshaft taper it is necessary to use a rotor puller. Honda produces a service tool (Part No. 07KMC-HE00100) to do this. Alternatively, use a commercially available puller. Thread the puller onto the centre of the rotor, then counter-hold it using a spanner on the flats

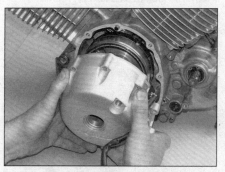

27.9a Draw off the cover . . .

27.9b . . . and discard the gasket

27.9c Note location of cover dowels

27.11a Using a rotor strap to hold the rotor

27.11b Remove the nut and washer

27.12a Install the puller on the centre of the rotor

27.12b Counter-hold the puller and tighten the centre bolt . . .

27.12c . . . until the rotor is displaced

and tighten the centre bolt until the rotor is displaced **(see illustrations)**.

13 Remove the Woodruff key from its slot in the crankshaft if it is loose **(see illustration)**.

14 To remove the stator from the cover on VT125C and XL125V-1 to V-6 models, first displace the ignition pulse generator wiring grommet, then undo the bolts securing the stator and lift it out.

15 To remove the stator from the cover on XL125V-7 models onward, first undo the bolts securing the CKP sensor and the wiring clamp **(see illustration)**. Undo the bolts securing the stator and lift it out together with the CKP sensor and wiring sub-loom **(see illustration)**.

Installation

16 Remove all traces of old gasket and sealant from the crankcase and cover surfaces.

17 Apply a suitable sealant to the wiring grommet(s), then fit the stator into the cover, aligning the grommet(s) with the slot **(see illustration)**.

18 On VT125C and XL125V-1 to V-6 models, clean the threads of the stator bolts and apply a suitable non-permanent thread-locking compound.

19 On all models, install the stator bolts and tighten them to the torque setting specified at the beginning of this Chapter.

20 On XL125V-7 models onward, install the wiring clamp and the CKP sensor and tighten the mounting bolts to the specified torque setting.

21 Clean the tapered end of the crankshaft and the corresponding mating surface on the inside of the rotor with a suitable solvent. Fit the Woodruff key into its slot in the crankshaft if removed **(see illustration 27.13)**.

22 Make sure that no metal objects have attached themselves to the magnet on the inside of the rotor. Slide the rotor onto the shaft, making sure the groove on the inside of the rotor is aligned with and fits over the Woodruff key **(see illustration)**.

23 Fit the washer and nut, then tighten the nut to the torque setting specified at the beginning of this Chapter, using the method employed on removal to prevent the rotor from turning **(see illustration)**.

24 If removed, fit the dowels into the crankcase, then locate a new gasket onto the dowels **(see illustrations 27.9c and b)**.

25 Install the alternator cover, ensuring it locates onto the dowels **(see illustration 27.9a)**. Install the cover bolts as noted on removal and tighten them evenly in a criss-cross pattern.

26 Secure the wiring as noted on removal

27.13 Location of the Woodruff key (arrowed)

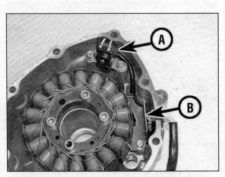

27.15a CKP sensor (A) and wiring clamp (B)

27.15b Bolts (arrowed) secure alternator stator

27.17 Align wiring grommet(s) with slot in cover

27.22 Align groove (arrowed) with Woodruff key

27.23 Tighten rotor nut to the specified torque

28.1a Location of the regulator/rectifier –
VT125C

28.1b Location of the regulator/rectifier –
XL125V-1 to V-6. Note earth wire (arrowed)

28.1c Location of the regulator/rectifier –
XL125V-7 onward

and reconnect the wiring connectors. Install the chain guide **(see illustration 27.6)**.

27 Install the remaining components in the reverse order of removal.

28 Refill the engine with the recommended grade and type of oil (see Chapter 1).

28 Regulator/rectifier

Check

1 On VT125C models, the regulator/rectifier is located inside the frame behind the steering head **(see illustration)** – remove the fuel tank for access (see Chapter 4A). On XL125V-1 to V-6 models, the regulator/rectifier is located behind the fusebox **(see illustration)** – remove the left-hand side panel for access (see Chapter 8). On XL125V-7 models onward, the regulator/rectifier is located behind the engine unit **(see illustration)** – remove the left-hand side panel for access (see Chapter 8).

2 If, after checking the charging system (see

28.12a Alternator wiring connector –
XL125V-7 onward

Section 26) and the alternator (see Section 27), the regulator/rectifier is thought to be faulty, check the wiring as follows.

3 On VT125C models, disconnect the regulator/rectifier wiring connector from the underside of the unit **(see illustration 28.1a)**.

4 On XL125V-1 to V-6 models, first displace the fusebox, then disconnect the regulator/rectifier wiring connector from the underside of the unit.

5 On XL125V-7 models onward, trace the red and green wires from the regulator/rectifier to the wiring boot to the rear of the fusebox and disconnect the wiring connector.

6 Using a multimeter, connect the meter positive (+) probe to the red wire terminal on the loom side of the connector and the negative (–) probe to earth (ground) and check for battery voltage. There should be battery voltage at all times.

7 Check for continuity between the green wire terminal on the loom side of the connector and earth (ground). There should be continuity.

8 To check the wiring between the regulator/rectifier and the alternator on VT125C and

28.12b Regulator/rectifier mounting bolts

XL125V-1 to V-6 models, measure the resistance between the yellow wire terminals (see Section 27, Steps 3 and 4).

9 If the wiring is good, it is likely the regulator/rectifier unit is faulty – have it checked by a Honda dealer.

Removal and installation

10 On VT125C models, remove the fuel tank and the air filter housing (see Chapter 4A). Disconnect the wiring connector **(see illustration 28.1a)**, then undo the mounting bolts, noting the location of the earth wire, and remove the regulator/rectifier.

11 On XL125V-1 to V-6 models, remove the left-hand side panel (see Chapter 8) and displace the fusebox. Disconnect the wiring connector from the underside of the unit, then undo the mounting bolts, noting the location of the earth wire **(see illustration 28.1b)**, and remove the regulator/rectifier.

12 On XL125V-7 models onward, remove the left and right-hand side panels (see Chapter 8). Trace the three yellow wires from the regulator/rectifier and disconnect them at the alternator wiring connector inside the wiring boot on the left-hand side of the machine **(see illustration)**. Trace the red and green wires from the regulator/rectifier and disconnect them at the 2-pin connector inside the wiring boot to the rear of the fusebox. Release the wiring from any clips or ties and feed it back to the regulator/rectifier. Undo the mounting bolts and remove the regulator/rectifier **(see illustration)**.

13 Installation is the reverse of removal. Tighten the mounting bolts securely, not forgetting to connect the earth wire if applicable. Secure the wiring as noted on removal and reconnect the wiring connector(s).

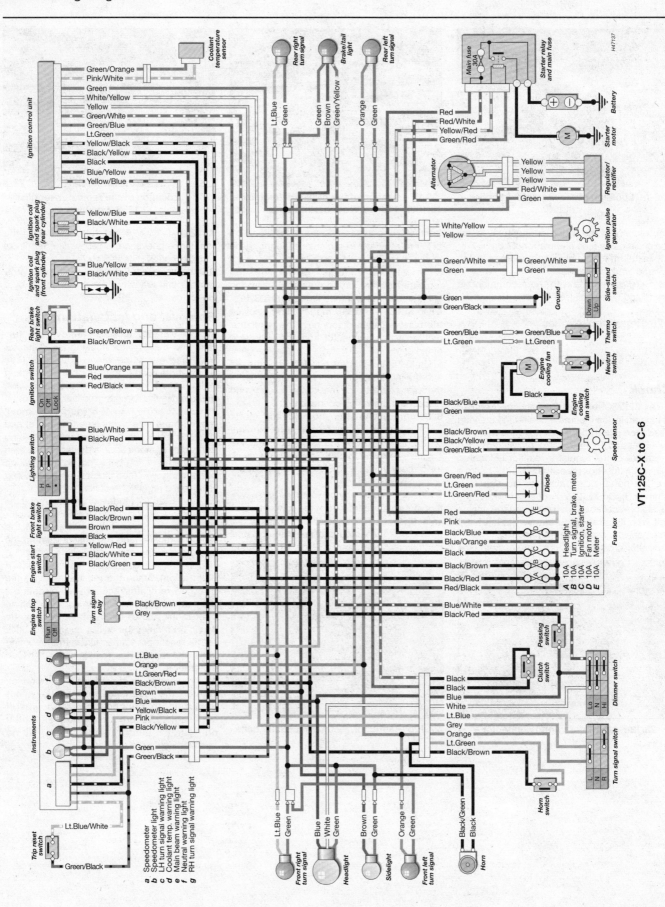

VT125C-X to C-6

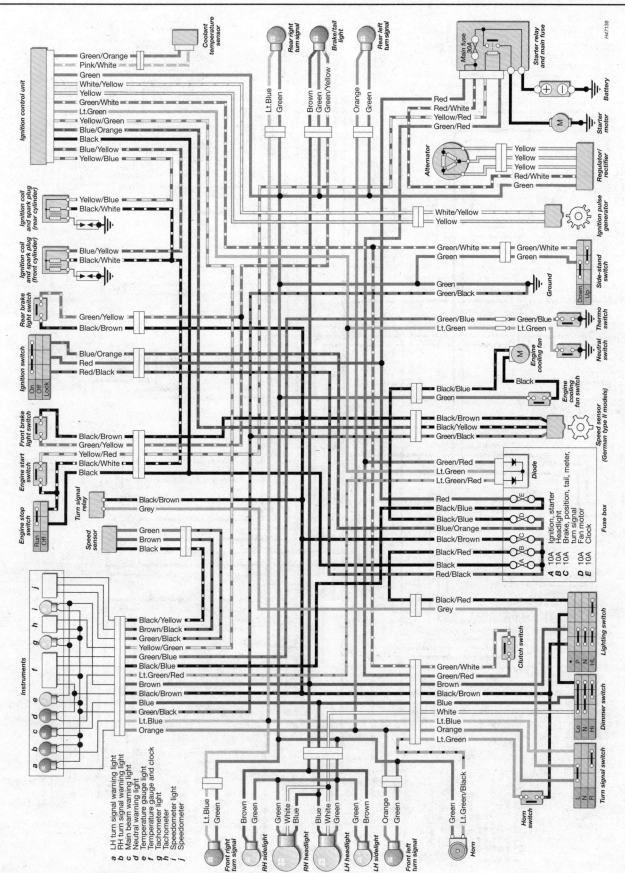

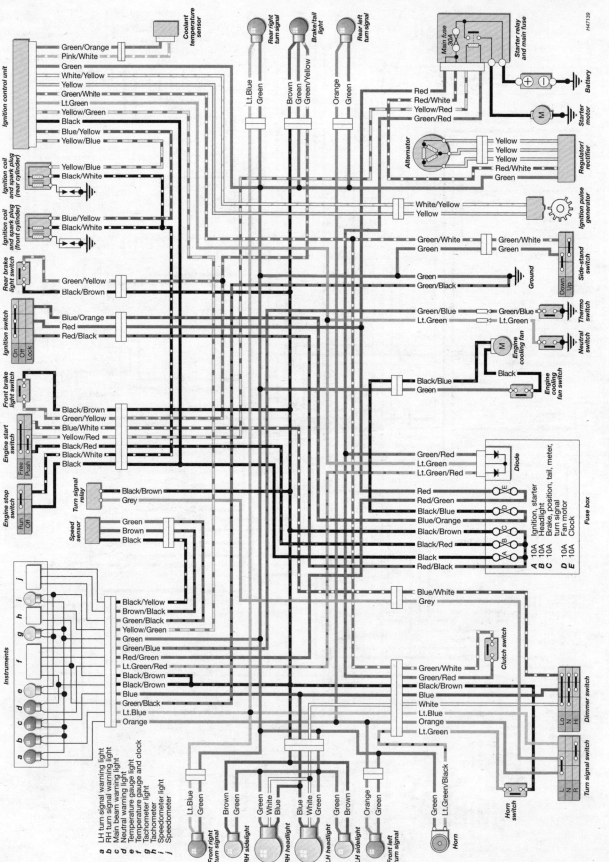

XL125V-4 to V-6

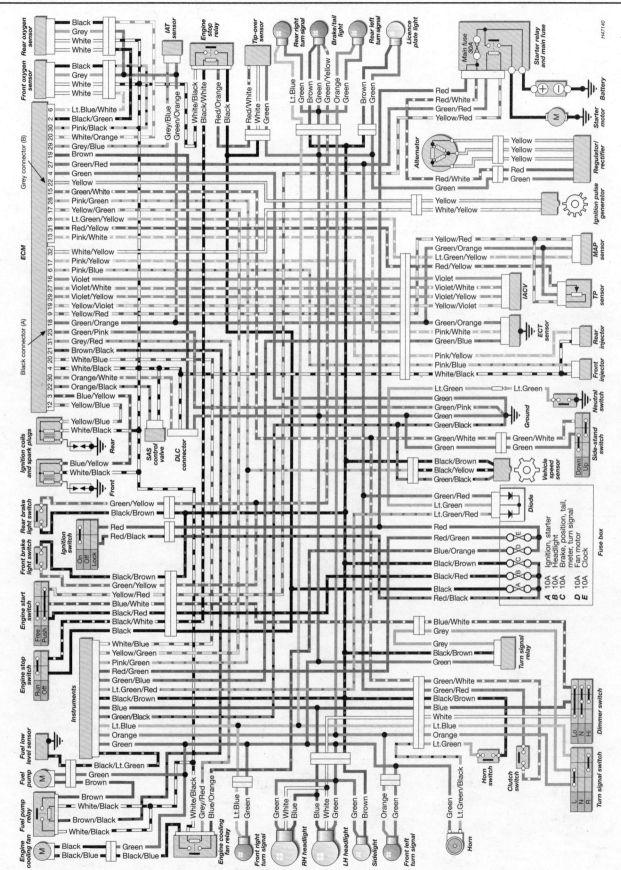

XL125V-7 onwards

Notes

Buying tools

A toolkit is a fundamental requirement for servicing and repairing a motorcycle. Although there will be an initial expense in building up enough tools for servicing, this will soon be offset by the savings made by doing the job yourself. As experience and confidence grow, additional tools can be added to enable the repair and overhaul of the motorcycle. Many of the specialist tools are expensive and not often used so it may be preferable to hire them, or for a group of friends or motorcycle club to join in the purchase.

As a rule, it is better to buy more expensive, good quality tools. Cheaper tools are likely to wear out faster and need to be renewed more often, nullifying the original saving.

Warning: To avoid the risk of a poor quality tool breaking in use, causing injury or damage to the component being worked on, always aim to purchase tools which meet the relevant national safety standards.

The following lists of tools do not represent the manufacturer's service tools, but serve as a guide to help the owner decide which tools are needed for this level of work. In addition, items such as an electric drill, hacksaw, files, hammers, soldering iron and a workbench equipped with a vice, may be needed. Although not classed as tools, a selection of bolts, screws, nuts, washers and pieces of tubing always come in useful.

For more information about tools, refer to the Haynes *Motorcycle Workshop Practice TechBook* (Bk. No. 3470).

Manufacturer's service tools

Inevitably certain tasks require the use of a service tool. Where possible an alternative tool or method of approach is recommended, but sometimes there is no option if personal injury or damage to the component is to be avoided. Where required, service tools are referred to in the relevant procedure.

Service tools can usually only be purchased from a motorcycle dealer and are identified by a part number. Some of the commonly-used tools, such as rotor pullers, are available in aftermarket form from mail-order motorcycle tool and accessory suppliers.

Maintenance and minor repair tools

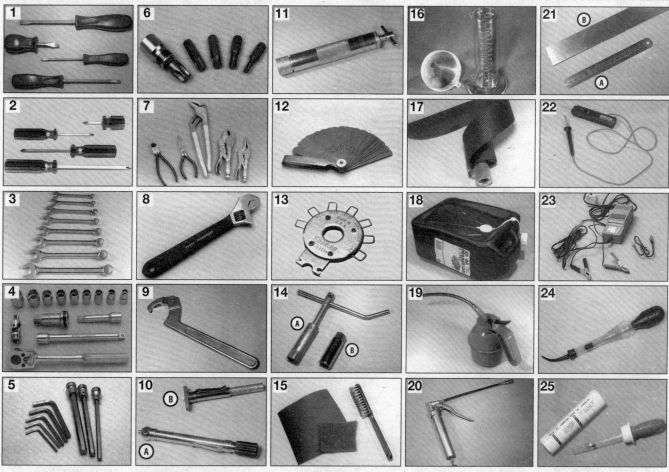

1 Set of flat-bladed screwdrivers
2 Set of Phillips head screwdrivers
3 Combination open-end & ring spanners
4 Socket set (3/8 inch or 1/2 inch drive)
5 Set of Allen keys or bits
6 Set of Torx keys or bits
7 Pliers and self-locking grips (Mole grips)
8 Adjustable spanner
9 C-spanner (ideally adjustable type)
10 Tyre pressure gauge (A) & tread depth gauge (B)
11 Cable pressure oiler
12 Feeler gauges
13 Spark plug gap measuring and adjusting tool
14 Spark plug spanner (A) or deep plug socket (B)
15 Wire brush and emery paper
16 Funnel and measuring vessel
17 Strap wrench, chain wrench or oil filter removal tool
18 Oil drainer can or tray
19 Pump type oil can
20 Grease gun
21 Steel rule (A) and straight-edge (B)
22 Continuity tester
23 Battery charger
24 Hydrometer (for battery specific gravity check)
25 Anti-freeze tester (for liquid-cooled engines)

Repair and overhaul tools

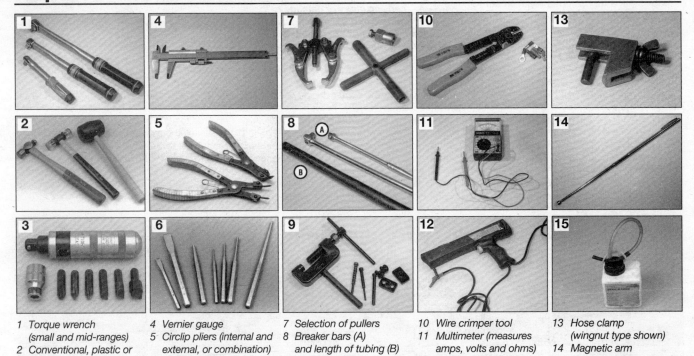

1 Torque wrench
   (small and mid-ranges)
2 Conventional, plastic or
   soft-faced hammers
3 Impact driver set

4 Vernier gauge
5 Circlip pliers (internal and
   external, or combination)
6 Set of punches
   and cold chisels

7 Selection of pullers
8 Breaker bars (A)
   and length of tubing (B)
9 Chain breaking/
   riveting tool

10 Wire crimper tool
11 Multimeter (measures
   amps, volts and ohms)
12 Stroboscope (for
   dynamic timing checks)

13 Hose clamp
   (wingnut type shown)
14 Magnetic arm
   (telescopic type shown)
15 One-man brake/clutch
   bleeder kit

Specialist tools

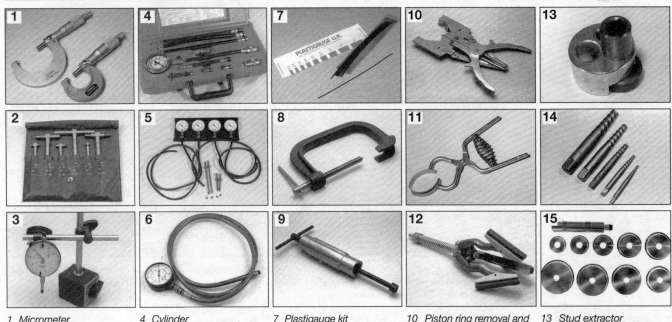

1 Micrometer
   (external type)
2 Telescoping gauges or
   small-hole gauges
3 Dial gauge

4 Cylinder
   compression gauge
5 Vacuum gauges (shown)
   or manometer
6 Oil pressure gauge

7 Plastigauge kit
8 Valve spring compressor
   (4-stroke engines)
9 Piston pin drawbolt tool

10 Piston ring removal and
   installation tool
11 Piston ring clamp
12 Cylinder bore hone
   (stone type shown)

13 Stud extractor
14 Screw extractor set
15 Bearing driver set

1 Workshop equipment and facilities

The workbench

● Work is made much easier by raising the bike up on a ramp - components are much more accessible if raised to waist level. The hydraulic or pneumatic types seen in the dealer's workshop are a sound investment if you undertake a lot of repairs or overhauls (see illustration 1.1).

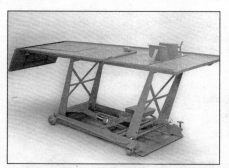

1.1 Hydraulic motorcycle ramp

● If raised off ground level, the bike must be supported on the ramp to avoid it falling. Most ramps incorporate a front wheel locating clamp which can be adjusted to suit different diameter wheels. When tightening the clamp, take care not to mark the wheel rim or damage the tyre - use wood blocks on each side to prevent this.
● Secure the bike to the ramp using tie-downs (see illustration 1.2). If the bike has only a sidestand, and hence leans at a dangerous angle when raised, support the bike on an auxiliary stand.

1.2 Tie-downs are used around the passenger footrests to secure the bike

● Auxiliary (paddock) stands are widely available from mail order companies or motorcycle dealers and attach either to the wheel axle or swingarm pivot (see illustration 1.3). If the motorcycle has a centrestand, you can support it under the crankcase to prevent it toppling whilst either wheel is removed (see illustration 1.4).

1.3 This auxiliary stand attaches to the swingarm pivot

1.4 Always use a block of wood between the engine and jack head when supporting the engine in this way

Fumes and fire

● Refer to the Safety first! page at the beginning of the manual for full details. Make sure your workshop is equipped with a fire extinguisher suitable for fuel-related fires (Class B fire - flammable liquids) - it is not sufficient to have a water-filled extinguisher.
● Always ensure adequate ventilation is available. Unless an exhaust gas extraction system is available for use, ensure that the engine is run outside of the workshop.
● If working on the fuel system, make sure the workshop is ventilated to avoid a build-up of fumes. This applies equally to fume build-up when charging a battery. Do not smoke or allow anyone else to smoke in the workshop.

Fluids

● If you need to drain fuel from the tank, store it in an approved container marked as suitable for the storage of petrol (gasoline) (see illustration 1.5). Do not store fuel in glass jars or bottles.

1.5 Use an approved can only for storing petrol (gasoline)

● Use proprietary engine degreasers or solvents which have a high flash-point, such as paraffin (kerosene), for cleaning off oil, grease and dirt - never use petrol (gasoline) for cleaning. Wear rubber gloves when handling solvent and engine degreaser. The fumes from certain solvents can be dangerous - always work in a well-ventilated area.

Dust, eye and hand protection

● Protect your lungs from inhalation of dust particles by wearing a filtering mask over the nose and mouth. Many frictional materials still contain asbestos which is dangerous to your health. Protect your eyes from spouts of liquid and sprung components by wearing a pair of protective goggles (see illustration 1.6).

1.6 A fire extinguisher, goggles, mask and protective gloves should be at hand in the workshop

● Protect your hands from contact with solvents, fuel and oils by wearing rubber gloves. Alternatively apply a barrier cream to your hands before starting work. If handling hot components or fluids, wear suitable gloves to protect your hands from scalding and burns.

What to do with old fluids

● Old cleaning solvent, fuel, coolant and oils should not be poured down domestic drains or onto the ground. Package the fluid up in old oil containers, label it accordingly, and take it to a garage or disposal facility. Contact your local authority for location of such sites or ring the oil care hotline.

OIL CARE

Note: It is illegal and anti-social to dump oil down the drain. To find the location of your local oil recycling bank in the UK, call 03708 506 506 or visit www.oilbankline.org.uk

In the USA, note that any oil supplier must accept used oil for recycling.

2 Fasteners -
screws, bolts and nuts

Fastener types and applications

Bolts and screws

● Fastener head types are either of hexagonal, Torx or splined design, with internal and external versions of each type **(see illustrations 2.1 and 2.2)**; splined head fasteners are not in common use on motorcycles. The conventional slotted or Phillips head design is used for certain screws. Bolt or screw length is always measured from the underside of the head to the end of the item **(see illustration 2.11)**.

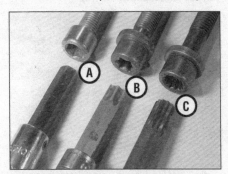

2.1 Internal hexagon/Allen (A), Torx (B) and splined (C) fasteners, with corresponding bits

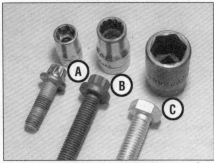

2.2 External Torx (A), splined (B) and hexagon (C) fasteners, with corresponding sockets

● Certain fasteners on the motorcycle have a tensile marking on their heads, the higher the marking the stronger the fastener. High tensile fasteners generally carry a 10 or higher marking. Never replace a high tensile fastener with one of a lower tensile strength.

Washers (see illustration 2.3)

● Plain washers are used between a fastener head and a component to prevent damage to the component or to spread the load when torque is applied. Plain washers can also be used as spacers or shims in certain assemblies. Copper or aluminium plain washers are often used as sealing washers on drain plugs.

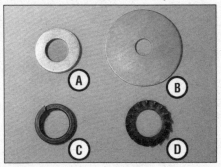

2.3 Plain washer (A), penny washer (B), spring washer (C) and serrated washer (D)

● The split-ring spring washer works by applying axial tension between the fastener head and component. If flattened, it is fatigued and must be renewed. If a plain (flat) washer is used on the fastener, position the spring washer between the fastener and the plain washer.

● Serrated star type washers dig into the fastener and component faces, preventing loosening. They are often used on electrical earth (ground) connections to the frame.

● Cone type washers (sometimes called Belleville) are conical and when tightened apply axial tension between the fastener head and component. They must be installed with the dished side against the component and often carry an OUTSIDE marking on their outer face. If flattened, they are fatigued and must be renewed.

● Tab washers are used to lock plain nuts or bolts on a shaft. A portion of the tab washer is bent up hard against one flat of the nut or bolt to prevent it loosening. Due to the tab washer being deformed in use, a new tab washer should be used every time it is disturbed.

● Wave washers are used to take up endfloat on a shaft. They provide light springing and prevent excessive side-to-side play of a component. Can be found on rocker arm shafts.

Nuts and split pins

● Conventional plain nuts are usually six-sided **(see illustration 2.4)**. They are sized by thread diameter and pitch. High tensile nuts carry a number on one end to denote their tensile strength.

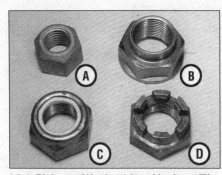

2.4 Plain nut (A), shouldered locknut (B), nylon insert nut (C) and castellated nut (D)

● Self-locking nuts either have a nylon insert, or two spring metal tabs, or a shoulder which is staked into a groove in the shaft - their advantage over conventional plain nuts is a resistance to loosening due to vibration. The nylon insert type can be used a number of times, but must be renewed when the friction of the nylon insert is reduced, ie when the nut spins freely on the shaft. The spring tab type can be reused unless the tabs are damaged. The shouldered type must be renewed every time it is disturbed.

● Split pins (cotter pins) are used to lock a castellated nut to a shaft or to prevent slackening of a plain nut. Common applications are wheel axles and brake torque arms. Because the split pin arms are deformed to lock around the nut a new split pin must always be used on installation - always fit the correct size split pin which will fit snugly in the shaft hole. Make sure the split pin arms are correctly located around the nut **(see illustrations 2.5 and 2.6)**.

2.5 Bend split pin (cotter pin) arms as shown (arrows) to secure a castellated nut

2.6 Bend split pin (cotter pin) arms as shown to secure a plain nut

Caution: If the castellated nut slots do not align with the shaft hole after tightening to the torque setting, tighten the nut until the next slot aligns with the hole - never slacken the nut to align its slot.

● R-pins (shaped like the letter R), or slip pins as they are sometimes called, are sprung and can be reused if they are otherwise in good condition. Always install R-pins with their closed end facing forwards **(see illustration 2.7)**.

2.7 Correct fitting of R-pin. Arrow indicates forward direction

Circlips (see illustration 2.8)

● Circlips (sometimes called snap-rings) are used to retain components on a shaft or in a housing and have corresponding external or internal ears to permit removal. Parallel-sided (machined) circlips can be installed either way round in their groove, whereas stamped circlips (which have a chamfered edge on one face) must be installed with the chamfer facing away from the direction of thrust load **(see illustration 2.9)**.

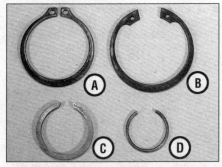

2.8 External stamped circlip (A), internal stamped circlip (B), machined circlip (C) and wire circlip (D)

● Always use circlip pliers to remove and install circlips; expand or compress them just enough to remove them. After installation, rotate the circlip in its groove to ensure it is securely seated. If installing a circlip on a splined shaft, always align its opening with a shaft channel to ensure the circlip ends are well supported and unlikely to catch **(see illustration 2.10)**.

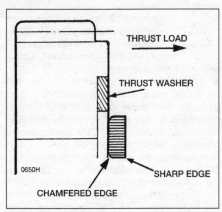

2.9 Correct fitting of a stamped circlip

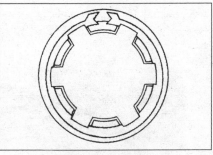

2.10 Align circlip opening with shaft channel

● Circlips can wear due to the thrust of components and become loose in their grooves, with the subsequent danger of becoming dislodged in operation. For this reason, renewal is advised every time a circlip is disturbed.

● Wire circlips are commonly used as piston pin retaining clips. If a removal tang is provided, long-nosed pliers can be used to dislodge them, otherwise careful use of a small flat-bladed screwdriver is necessary. Wire circlips should be renewed every time they are disturbed.

Thread diameter and pitch

● Diameter of a male thread (screw, bolt or stud) is the outside diameter of the threaded portion **(see illustration 2.11)**. Most motorcycle manufacturers use the ISO (International Standards Organisation) metric system expressed in millimetres, eg M6 refers to a 6 mm diameter thread. Sizing is the same for nuts, except that the thread diameter is measured across the valleys of the nut.

● Pitch is the distance between the peaks of the thread **(see illustration 2.11)**. It is expressed in millimetres, thus a common bolt size may be expressed as 6.0 x 1.0 mm (6 mm thread diameter and 1 mm pitch). Generally pitch increases in proportion to thread diameter, although there are always exceptions.

● Thread diameter and pitch are related for conventional fastener applications and the following table can be used as a guide. Additionally, the AF (Across Flats), spanner or socket size dimension of the bolt or nut **(see illustration 2.11)** is linked to thread and pitch specification. Thread pitch can be measured with a thread gauge **(see illustration 2.12)**.

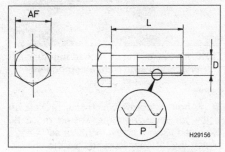

2.11 Fastener length (L), thread diameter (D), thread pitch (P) and head size (AF)

2.12 Using a thread gauge to measure pitch

AF size	Thread diameter x pitch (mm)
8 mm	M5 x 0.8
8 mm	M6 x 1.0
10 mm	M6 x 1.0
12 mm	M8 x 1.25
14 mm	M10 x 1.25
17 mm	M12 x 1.25

● The threads of most fasteners are of the right-hand type, ie they are turned clockwise to tighten and anti-clockwise to loosen. The reverse situation applies to left-hand thread fasteners, which are turned anti-clockwise to tighten and clockwise to loosen. Left-hand threads are used where rotation of a component might loosen a conventional right-hand thread fastener.

Seized fasteners

● Corrosion of external fasteners due to water or reaction between two dissimilar metals can occur over a period of time. It will build up sooner in wet conditions or in countries where salt is used on the roads during the winter. If a fastener is severely corroded it is likely that normal methods of removal will fail and result in its head being ruined. When you attempt removal, the fastener thread should be heard to crack free and unscrew easily - if it doesn't, stop there before damaging something.

● A smart tap on the head of the fastener will often succeed in breaking free corrosion which has occurred in the threads **(see illustration 2.13)**.

● An aerosol penetrating fluid (such as WD-40) applied the night beforehand may work its way down into the thread and ease removal. Depending on the location, you may be able to make up a Plasticine well around the fastener head and fill it with penetrating fluid.

2.13 A sharp tap on the head of a fastener will often break free a corroded thread

● If you are working on an engine internal component, corrosion will most likely not be a problem due to the well lubricated environment. However, components can be very tight and an impact driver is a useful tool in freeing them **(see illustration 2.14)**.

2.14 Using an impact driver to free a fastener

● Where corrosion has occurred between dissimilar metals (eg steel and aluminium alloy), the application of heat to the fastener head will create a disproportionate expansion rate between the two metals and break the seizure caused by the corrosion. Whether heat can be applied depends on the location of the fastener - any surrounding components likely to be damaged must first be removed **(see illustration 2.15)**. Heat can be applied using a paint stripper heat gun or clothes iron, or by immersing the component in boiling water - wear protective gloves to prevent scalding or burns to the hands.

2.15 Using heat to free a seized fastener

● As a last resort, it is possible to use a hammer and cold chisel to work the fastener head unscrewed **(see illustration 2.16)**. This will damage the fastener, but more importantly extreme care must be taken not to damage the surrounding component.

Caution: Remember that the component being secured is generally of more value than the bolt, nut or screw - when the fastener is freed, do not unscrew it with force, instead work the fastener back and forth when resistance is felt to prevent thread damage.

2.16 Using a hammer and chisel to free a seized fastener

Broken fasteners and damaged heads

● If the shank of a broken bolt or screw is accessible you can grip it with self-locking grips. The knurled wheel type stud extractor tool or self-gripping stud puller tool is particularly useful for removing the long studs which screw into the cylinder mouth surface of the crankcase or bolts and screws from which the head has broken off **(see illustration 2.17)**. Studs can also be removed by locking two nuts together on the threaded end of the stud and using a spanner on the lower nut **(see illustration 2.18)**.

2.17 Using a stud extractor tool to remove a broken crankcase stud

2.18 Two nuts can be locked together to unscrew a stud from a component

● A bolt or screw which has broken off below or level with the casing must be extracted using a screw extractor set. Centre punch the fastener to centralise the drill bit, then drill a hole in the fastener **(see illustration 2.19)**. Select a drill bit which is

2.19 When using a screw extractor, first drill a hole in the fastener . . .

approximately half to three-quarters the diameter of the fastener and drill to a depth which will accommodate the extractor. Use the largest size extractor possible, but avoid leaving too small a wall thickness otherwise the extractor will merely force the fastener walls outwards wedging it in the casing thread.

● If a spiral type extractor is used, thread it anti-clockwise into the fastener. As it is screwed in, it will grip the fastener and unscrew it from the casing **(see illustration 2.20)**.

2.20 . . . then thread the extractor anti-clockwise into the fastener

● If a taper type extractor is used, tap it into the fastener so that it is firmly wedged in place. Unscrew the extractor (anti-clockwise) to draw the fastener out.

Warning: Stud extractors are very hard and may break off in the fastener if care is not taken - ask an engineer about spark erosion if this happens.

● Alternatively, the broken bolt/screw can be drilled out and the hole retapped for an oversize bolt/screw or a diamond-section thread insert. It is essential that the drilling is carried out squarely and to the correct depth, otherwise the casing may be ruined - if in doubt, entrust the work to an engineer.

● Bolts and nuts with rounded corners cause the correct size spanner or socket to slip when force is applied. Of the types of spanner/socket available always use a six-point type rather than an eight or twelve-point type - better grip

2.21 Comparison of surface drive ring spanner (left) with 12-point type (right)

is obtained. Surface drive spanners grip the middle of the hex flats, rather than the corners, and are thus good in cases of damaged heads **(see illustration 2.21)**.

● Slotted-head or Phillips-head screws are often damaged by the use of the wrong size screwdriver. Allen-head and Torx-head screws are much less likely to sustain damage. If enough of the screw head is exposed you can use a hacksaw to cut a slot in its head and then use a conventional flat-bladed screwdriver to remove it. Alternatively use a hammer and cold chisel to tap the head of the fastener round to slacken it. Always replace damaged fasteners with new ones, preferably Torx or Allen-head type.

HAYNES HiNT

A dab of valve grinding compound between the screw head and screw-driver tip will often give a good grip.

Thread repair

● Threads (particularly those in aluminium alloy components) can be damaged by overtightening, being assembled with dirt in the threads, or from a component working loose and vibrating. Eventually the thread will fail completely, and it will be impossible to tighten the fastener.

● If a thread is damaged or clogged with old locking compound it can be renovated with a thread repair tool (thread chaser) **(see illustrations 2.22 and 2.23)**; special thread

2.22 A thread repair tool being used to correct an internal thread

2.23 A thread repair tool being used to correct an external thread

chasers are available for spark plug hole threads. The tool will not cut a new thread, but clean and true the original thread. Make sure that you use the correct diameter and pitch tool. Similarly, external threads can be cleaned up with a die or a thread restorer file **(see illustration 2.24)**.

2.24 Using a thread restorer file

● It is possible to drill out the old thread and retap the component to the next thread size. This will work where there is enough surrounding material and a new bolt or screw can be obtained. Sometimes, however, this is not possible - such as where the bolt/screw passes through another component which must also be suitably modified, also in cases where a spark plug or oil drain plug cannot be obtained in a larger diameter thread size.

● The diamond-section thread insert (often known by its popular trade name of Heli-Coil) is a simple and effective method of renewing the thread and retaining the original size. A kit can be purchased which contains the tap, insert and installing tool **(see illustration 2.25)**. Drill out the damaged thread with the size drill specified **(see illustration 2.26)**. Carefully retap the thread **(see illustration 2.27)**. Install the

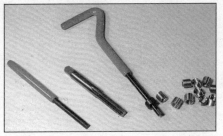

2.25 Obtain a thread insert kit to suit the thread diameter and pitch required

2.26 To install a thread insert, first drill out the original thread . . .

2.27 . . . tap a new thread . . .

2.28 . . . fit insert on the installing tool . . .

2.29 . . . and thread into the component . . .

2.30 . . . break off the tang when complete

insert on the installing tool and thread it slowly into place using a light downward pressure **(see illustrations 2.28 and 2.29)**. When positioned between a 1/4 and 1/2 turn below the surface withdraw the installing tool and use the break-off tool to press down on the tang, breaking it off **(see illustration 2.30)**.

● There are epoxy thread repair kits on the market which can rebuild stripped internal threads, although this repair should not be used on high load-bearing components.

Thread locking and sealing compounds

● Locking compounds are used in locations where the fastener is prone to loosening due to vibration or on important safety-related items which might cause loss of control of the motorcycle if they fail. It is also used where important fasteners cannot be secured by other means such as lockwashers or split pins.

● Before applying locking compound, make sure that the threads (internal and external) are clean and dry with all old compound removed. Select a compound to suit the component being secured - a non-permanent general locking and sealing type is suitable for most applications, but a high strength type is needed for permanent fixing of studs in castings. Apply a drop or two of the compound to the first few threads of the fastener, then thread it into place and tighten to the specified torque. Do not apply excessive thread locking compound otherwise the thread may be damaged on subsequent removal.

● Certain fasteners are impregnated with a dry film type coating of locking compound on their threads. Always renew this type of fastener if disturbed.

● Anti-seize compounds, such as copper-based greases, can be applied to protect threads from seizure due to extreme heat and corrosion. A common instance is spark plug threads and exhaust system fasteners.

3 Measuring tools and gauges

Feeler gauges

● Feeler gauges (or blades) are used for measuring small gaps and clearances (see illustration 3.1). They can also be used to measure endfloat (sideplay) of a component on a shaft where access is not possible with a dial gauge.

● Feeler gauge sets should be treated with care and not bent or damaged. They are etched with their size on one face. Keep them clean and very lightly oiled to prevent corrosion build-up.

3.1 Feeler gauges are used for measuring small gaps and clearances - thickness is marked on one face of gauge

● When measuring a clearance, select a gauge which is a light sliding fit between the two components. You may need to use two gauges together to measure the clearance accurately.

Micrometers

● A micrometer is a precision tool capable of measuring to 0.01 or 0.001 of a millimetre. It should always be stored in its case and not in the general toolbox. It must be kept clean and never dropped, otherwise its frame or measuring anvils could be distorted resulting in inaccurate readings.

● External micrometers are used for measuring outside diameters of components and have many more applications than internal micrometers. Micrometers are available in different size ranges, eg 0 to 25 mm, 25 to 50 mm, and upwards in 25 mm steps; some large micrometers have interchangeable anvils to allow a range of measurements to be taken. Generally the largest precision measurement you are likely to take on a motorcycle is the piston diameter.

● Internal micrometers (or bore micrometers) are used for measuring inside diameters, such as valve guides and cylinder bores. Telescoping gauges and small hole gauges are used in conjunction with an external micrometer, whereas the more expensive internal micrometers have their own measuring device.

External micrometer

Note: *The conventional analogue type instrument is described. Although much easier to read, digital micrometers are considerably more expensive.*

● Always check the calibration of the micrometer before use. With the anvils closed (0 to 25 mm type) or set over a test gauge (for

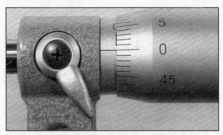

3.2 Check micrometer calibration before use

the larger types) the scale should read zero (see illustration 3.2); make sure that the anvils (and test piece) are clean first. Any discrepancy can be adjusted by referring to the instructions supplied with the tool. Remember that the micrometer is a precision measuring tool - don't force the anvils closed, use the ratchet (4) on the end of the micrometer to close it. In this way, a measured force is always applied.

● To use, first make sure that the item being measured is clean. Place the anvil of the micrometer (1) against the item and use the thimble (2) to bring the spindle (3) lightly into contact with the other side of the item (see illustration 3.3). Don't tighten the thimble down because this will damage the micrometer - instead use the ratchet (4) on the end of the micrometer. The ratchet mechanism applies a measured force preventing damage to the instrument.

● The micrometer is read by referring to the linear scale on the sleeve and the annular scale on the thimble. Read off the sleeve first to obtain the base measurement, then add the fine measurement from the thimble to obtain the overall reading. The linear scale on the sleeve represents the measuring range of the micrometer (eg 0 to 25 mm). The annular scale

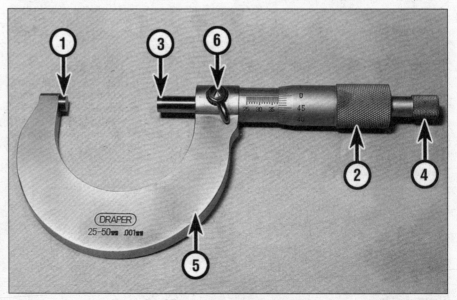

3.3 Micrometer component parts

1	Anvil	3	Spindle	5	Frame
2	Thimble	4	Ratchet	6	Locking lever

on the thimble will be in graduations of 0.01 mm (or as marked on the frame) - one full revolution of the thimble will move 0.5 mm on the linear scale. Take the reading where the datum line on the sleeve intersects the thimble's scale. Always position the eye directly above the scale otherwise an inaccurate reading will result.

In the example shown the item measures 2.95 mm **(see illustration 3.4)**:

Linear scale	2.00 mm
Linear scale	0.50 mm
Annular scale	0.45 mm
Total figure	**2.95 mm**

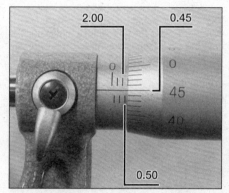

3.4 Micrometer reading of 2.95 mm

Most micrometers have a locking lever (6) on the frame to hold the setting in place, allowing the item to be removed from the micrometer.
● Some micrometers have a vernier scale on their sleeve, providing an even finer measurement to be taken, in 0.001 increments of a millimetre. Take the sleeve and thimble measurement as described above, then check which graduation on the vernier scale aligns with that of the annular scale on the thimble **Note:** *The eye must be perpendicular to the scale when taking the vernier reading - if necessary rotate the body of the micrometer to ensure this.* Multiply the vernier scale figure by 0.001 and add it to the base and fine measurement figures.

In the example shown the item measures 46.994 mm **(see illustrations 3.5 and 3.6)**:

Linear scale (base)	46.000 mm
Linear scale (base)	00.500 mm
Annular scale (fine)	00.490 mm
Vernier scale	00.004 mm
Total figure	**46.994 mm**

Internal micrometer

● Internal micrometers are available for measuring bore diameters, but are expensive and unlikely to be available for home use. It is suggested that a set of telescoping gauges and small hole gauges, both of which must be used with an external micrometer, will suffice for taking internal measurements on a motorcycle.

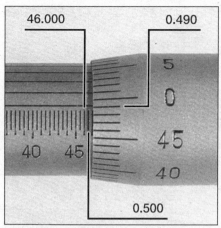

3.5 Micrometer reading of 46.99 mm on linear and annular scales . . .

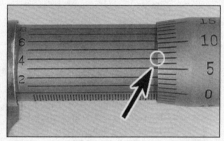

3.6 . . . and 0.004 mm on vernier scale

● Telescoping gauges can be used to measure internal diameters of components. Select a gauge with the correct size range, make sure its ends are clean and insert it into the bore. Expand the gauge, then lock its position and withdraw it from the bore **(see illustration 3.7)**. Measure across the gauge ends with a micrometer **(see illustration 3.8)**.

3.7 Expand the telescoping gauge in the bore, lock its position . . .

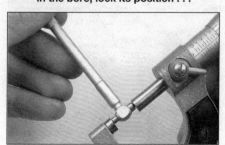

3.8 . . . then measure the gauge with a micrometer

3.9 Expand the small hole gauge in the bore, lock its position . . .

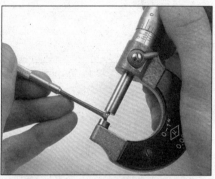

3.10 . . . then measure the gauge with a micrometer

● Very small diameter bores (such as valve guides) are measured with a small hole gauge. Once adjusted to a slip-fit inside the component, its position is locked and the gauge withdrawn for measurement with a micrometer **(see illustrations 3.9 and 3.10)**.

Vernier caliper

Note: *The conventional linear and dial gauge type instruments are described. Digital types are easier to read, but are far more expensive.*
● The vernier caliper does not provide the precision of a micrometer, but is versatile in being able to measure internal and external diameters. Some types also incorporate a depth gauge. It is ideal for measuring clutch plate friction material and spring free lengths.
● To use the conventional linear scale vernier, slacken off the vernier clamp screws (1) and set its jaws over (2), or inside (3), the item to be measured **(see illustration 3.11)**. Slide the jaw into contact, using the thumb-wheel (4) for fine movement of the sliding scale (5) then tighten the clamp screws (1). Read off the main scale (6) where the zero on the sliding scale (5) intersects it, taking the whole number to the left of the zero; this provides the base measurement. View along the sliding scale and select the division which lines up exactly with any of the divisions on the main scale, noting that the divisions usually represents 0.02 of a millimetre. Add this fine measurement to the base measurement to obtain the total reading.

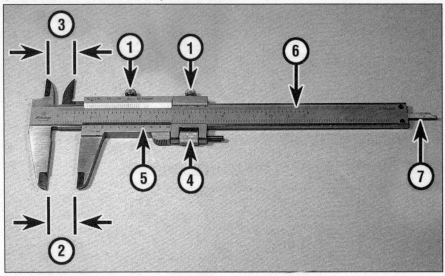

3.11 Vernier component parts (linear gauge)

1 Clamp screws	3 Internal jaws	5 Sliding scale	7 Depth gauge
2 External jaws	4 Thumbwheel	6 Main scale	

In the example shown the item measures 55.92 mm **(see illustration 3.12)**:

Base measurement	55.00 mm
Fine measurement	00.92 mm
Total figure	**55.92 mm**

3.12 Vernier gauge reading of 55.92 mm

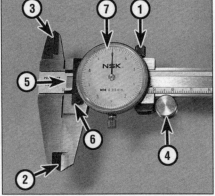

3.13 Vernier component parts (dial gauge)

1 Clamp screw	5 Main scale
2 External jaws	6 Sliding scale
3 Internal jaws	7 Dial gauge
4 Thumbwheel	

● Some vernier calipers are equipped with a dial gauge for fine measurement. Before use, check that the jaws are clean, then close them fully and check that the dial gauge reads zero. If necessary adjust the gauge ring accordingly. Slacken the vernier clamp screw (1) and set its jaws over (2), or inside (3), the item to be measured **(see illustration 3.13)**. Slide the jaws into contact, using the thumbwheel (4) for fine movement. Read off the main scale (5) where the edge of the sliding scale (6) intersects it, taking the whole number to the left of the zero; this provides the base measurement. Read off the needle position on the dial gauge (7) scale to provide the fine measurement; each division represents 0.05 of a millimetre. Add this fine measurement to the base measurement to obtain the total reading.

In the example shown the item measures 55.95 mm **(see illustration 3.14)**:

Base measurement	55.00 mm
Fine measurement	00.95 mm
Total figure	**55.95 mm**

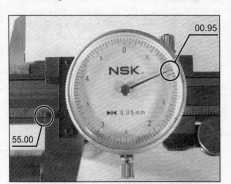

3.14 Vernier gauge reading of 55.95 mm

Plastigauge

● Plastigauge is a plastic material which can be compressed between two surfaces to measure the oil clearance between them. The width of the compressed Plastigauge is measured against a calibrated scale to determine the clearance.

● Common uses of Plastigauge are for measuring the clearance between crankshaft journal and main bearing inserts, between crankshaft journal and big-end bearing inserts, and between camshaft and bearing surfaces. The following example describes big-end oil clearance measurement.

● Handle the Plastigauge material carefully to prevent distortion. Using a sharp knife, cut a length which corresponds with the width of the bearing being measured and place it carefully across the journal so that it is parallel with the shaft **(see illustration 3.15)**. Carefully install both bearing shells and the connecting rod. Without rotating the rod on the journal tighten its bolts or nuts (as applicable) to the specified torque. The connecting rod and bearings are then disassembled and the crushed Plastigauge examined.

3.15 Plastigauge placed across shaft journal

● Using the scale provided in the Plastigauge kit, measure the width of the material to determine the oil clearance **(see illustration 3.16)**. Always remove all traces of Plastigauge after use using your fingernails. *Caution: Arriving at the correct clearance demands that the assembly is torqued correctly, according to the settings and sequence (where applicable) provided by the motorcycle manufacturer.*

3.16 Measuring the width of the crushed Plastigauge

Dial gauge or DTI (Dial Test Indicator)

● A dial gauge can be used to accurately measure small amounts of movement. Typical uses are measuring shaft runout or shaft endfloat (sideplay) and setting piston position for ignition timing on two-strokes. A dial gauge set usually comes with a range of different probes and adapters and mounting equipment.

● The gauge needle must point to zero when at rest. Rotate the ring around its periphery to zero the gauge.

● Check that the gauge is capable of reading the extent of movement in the work. Most gauges have a small dial set in the face which records whole millimetres of movement as well as the fine scale around the face periphery which is calibrated in 0.01 mm divisions. Read off the small dial first to obtain the base measurement, then add the measurement from the fine scale to obtain the total reading.

In the example shown the gauge reads 1.48 mm (see illustration 3.17):

Base measurement	1.00 mm
Fine measurement	0.48 mm
Total figure	**1.48 mm**

3.17 Dial gauge reading of 1.48 mm

● If measuring shaft runout, the shaft must be supported in vee-blocks and the gauge mounted on a stand perpendicular to the shaft. Rest the tip of the gauge against the centre of the shaft and rotate the shaft slowly whilst watching the gauge reading (see illustration 3.18). Take several measurements along the length of the shaft and record the

3.18 Using a dial gauge to measure shaft runout

maximum gauge reading as the amount of runout in the shaft. **Note:** *The reading obtained will be total runout at that point - some manufacturers specify that the runout figure is halved to compare with their specified runout limit.*

● Endfloat (sideplay) measurement requires that the gauge is mounted securely to the surrounding component with its probe touching the end of the shaft. Using hand pressure, push and pull on the shaft noting the maximum endfloat recorded on the gauge (see illustration 3.19).

3.19 Using a dial gauge to measure shaft endfloat

● A dial gauge with suitable adapters can be used to determine piston position BTDC on two-stroke engines for the purposes of ignition timing. The gauge, adapter and suitable length probe are installed in the place of the spark plug and the gauge zeroed at TDC. If the piston position is specified as 1.14 mm BTDC, rotate the engine back to 2.00 mm BTDC, then slowly forwards to 1.14 mm BTDC.

Cylinder compression gauges

● A compression gauge is used for measuring cylinder compression. Either the rubber-cone type or the threaded adapter type can be used. The latter is preferred to ensure a perfect seal against the cylinder head. A 0 to 300 psi (0 to 20 Bar) type gauge (for petrol/gasoline engines) will be suitable for motorcycles.

● The spark plug is removed and the gauge either held hard against the cylinder head (cone type) or the gauge adapter screwed into the cylinder head (threaded type) (see illustration 3.20). Cylinder compression is measured with the engine turning over, but not running - carry out the compression test as described in

3.20 Using a rubber-cone type cylinder compression gauge

Fault Finding Equipment. The gauge will hold the reading until manually released.

Oil pressure gauge

● An oil pressure gauge is used for measuring engine oil pressure. Most gauges come with a set of adapters to fit the thread of the take-off point (see illustration 3.21). If the take-off point specified by the motorcycle manufacturer is an external oil pipe union, make sure that the specified replacement union is used to prevent oil starvation.

3.21 Oil pressure gauge and take-off point adapter (arrow)

● Oil pressure is measured with the engine running (at a specific rpm) and often the manufacturer will specify pressure limits for a cold and hot engine.

Straight-edge and surface plate

● If checking the gasket face of a component for warpage, place a steel rule or precision straight-edge across the gasket face and measure any gap between the straight-edge and component with feeler gauges (see illustration 3.22). Check diagonally across the component and between mounting holes (see illustration 3.23).

3.22 Use a straight-edge and feeler gauges to check for warpage

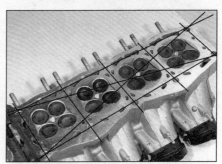

3.23 Check for warpage in these directions

● Checking individual components for warpage, such as clutch plain (metal) plates, requires a perfectly flat plate or piece or plate glass and feeler gauges.

4 Torque and leverage

What is torque?

● Torque describes the twisting force about a shaft. The amount of torque applied is determined by the distance from the centre of the shaft to the end of the lever and the amount of force being applied to the end of the lever; distance multiplied by force equals torque.

● The manufacturer applies a measured torque to a bolt or nut to ensure that it will not slacken in use and to hold two components securely together without movement in the joint. The actual torque setting depends on the thread size, bolt or nut material and the composition of the components being held.

● Too little torque may cause the fastener to loosen due to vibration, whereas too much torque will distort the joint faces of the component or cause the fastener to shear off. Always stick to the specified torque setting.

Using a torque wrench

● Check the calibration of the torque wrench and make sure it has a suitable range for the job. Torque wrenches are available in Nm (Newton-metres), kgf m (kilograms-force metre), lbf ft (pounds-feet), lbf in (inch-pounds). Do not confuse lbf ft with lbf in.

● Adjust the tool to the desired torque on the scale **(see illustration 4.1)**. If your torque wrench is not calibrated in the units specified, carefully convert the figure (see *Conversion Factors*). A manufacturer sometimes gives a torque setting as a range (8 to 10 Nm) rather than a single figure - in this case set the tool midway between the two settings. The same torque may be expressed as 9 Nm ± 1 Nm. Some torque wrenches have a method of locking the setting so that it isn't inadvertently altered during use.

● Install the bolts/nuts in their correct location and secure them lightly. Their threads must be clean and free of any old locking compound. Unless specified the threads and flange should be dry - oiled threads are necessary in certain circumstances and the manufacturer will take this into account in the specified torque figure. Similarly, the manufacturer may also specify the application of thread-locking compound.

● Tighten the fasteners in the specified sequence until the torque wrench clicks, indicating that the torque setting has been reached. Apply the torque again to double-check the setting. Where different thread diameter fasteners secure the component, as a rule tighten the larger diameter ones first.

● When the torque wrench has been finished with, release the lock (where applicable) and fully back off its setting to zero - do not leave the torque wrench tensioned. Also, do not use a torque wrench for slackening a fastener.

Angle-tightening

● Manufacturers often specify a figure in degrees for final tightening of a fastener. This usually follows tightening to a specific torque setting.

● A degree disc can be set and attached to the socket **(see illustration 4.2)** or a protractor can be used to mark the angle of movement on the bolt/nut head and the surrounding casting **(see illustration 4.3)**.

4.2 Angle tightening can be accomplished with a torque-angle gauge . . .

4.1 Set the torque wrench index mark to the setting required, in this case 12 Nm

4.3 . . . or by marking the angle on the surrounding component

Loosening sequences

● Where more than one bolt/nut secures a component, loosen each fastener evenly a little at a time. In this way, not all the stress of the joint is held by one fastener and the components are not likely to distort.

● If a tightening sequence is provided, work in the REVERSE of this, but if not, work from the outside in, in a criss-cross sequence **(see illustration 4.4)**.

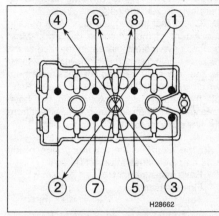

4.4 When slackening, work from the outside inwards

Tightening sequences

● If a component is held by more than one fastener it is important that the retaining bolts/nuts are tightened evenly to prevent uneven stress build-up and distortion of sealing faces. This is especially important on high-compression joints such as the cylinder head.

● A sequence is usually provided by the manufacturer, either in a diagram or actually marked in the casting. If not, always start in the centre and work outwards in a criss-cross pattern **(see illustration 4.5)**. Start off by securing all bolts/nuts finger-tight, then set the torque wrench and tighten each fastener by a small amount in sequence until the final torque is reached. By following this practice,

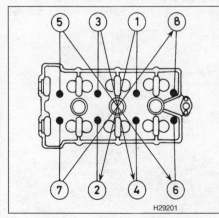

4.5 When tightening, work from the inside outwards

the joint will be held evenly and will not be distorted. Important joints, such as the cylinder head and big-end fasteners often have two- or three-stage torque settings.

Applying leverage

● Use tools at the correct angle. Position a socket wrench or spanner on the bolt/nut so that you pull it towards you when loosening. If this can't be done, push the spanner without curling your fingers around it **(see illustration 4.6)** - the spanner may slip or the fastener loosen suddenly, resulting in your fingers being crushed against a component.

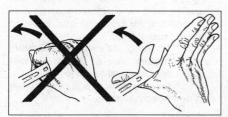

4.6 If you can't pull on the spanner to loosen a fastener, push with your hand open

● Additional leverage is gained by extending the length of the lever. The best way to do this is to use a breaker bar instead of the regular length tool, or to slip a length of tubing over the end of the spanner or socket wrench.
● If additional leverage will not work, the fastener head is either damaged or firmly corroded in place (see *Fasteners*).

5 Bearings

Bearing removal and installation

Drivers and sockets

● Before removing a bearing, always inspect the casing to see which way it must be driven out - some casings will have retaining plates or a cast step. Also check for any identifying markings on the bearing and if installed to a certain depth, measure this at this stage. Some roller bearings are sealed on one side - take note of the original fitted position.
● Bearings can be driven out of a casing using a bearing driver tool (with the correct size head) or a socket of the correct diameter. Select the driver head or socket so that it contacts the outer race of the bearing, not the balls/rollers or inner race. Always support the casing around the bearing housing with wood blocks, otherwise there is a risk of fracture. The bearing is driven out with a few blows on the driver or socket from a heavy mallet. Unless access is severely restricted (as with wheel bearings), a pin-punch is not recommended unless it is moved around the bearing to keep it square in its housing.

● The same equipment can be used to install bearings. Make sure the bearing housing is supported on wood blocks and line up the bearing in its housing. Fit the bearing as noted on removal - generally they are installed with their marked side facing outwards. Tap the bearing squarely into its housing using a driver or socket which bears only on the bearing's outer race - contact with the bearing balls/rollers or inner race will destroy it **(see illustrations 5.1 and 5.2)**.
● Check that the bearing inner race and balls/rollers rotate freely.

5.1 Using a bearing driver against the bearing's outer race

5.2 Using a large socket against the bearing's outer race

Pullers and slide-hammers

● Where a bearing is pressed on a shaft a puller will be required to extract it **(see illustration 5.3)**. Make sure that the puller clamp or legs fit securely behind the bearing and are unlikely to slip out. If pulling a bearing

5.3 This bearing puller clamps behind the bearing and pressure is applied to the shaft end to draw the bearing off

off a gear shaft for example, you may have to locate the puller behind a gear pinion if there is no access to the race and draw the gear pinion off the shaft as well **(see illustration 5.4)**. *Caution: Ensure that the puller's centre bolt locates securely against the end of the shaft and will not slip when pressure is applied. Also ensure that puller does not damage the shaft end.*

5.4 Where no access is available to the rear of the bearing, it is sometimes possible to draw off the adjacent component

● Operate the puller so that its centre bolt exerts pressure on the shaft end and draws the bearing off the shaft.
● When installing the bearing on the shaft, tap only on the bearing's inner race - contact with the balls/rollers or outer race with destroy the bearing. Use a socket or length of tubing as a drift which fits over the shaft end **(see illustration 5.5)**.

5.5 When installing a bearing on a shaft use a piece of tubing which bears only on the bearing's inner race

● Where a bearing locates in a blind hole in a casing, it cannot be driven or pulled out as described above. A slide-hammer with knife-edged bearing puller attachment will be required. The puller attachment passes through the bearing and when tightened expands to fit firmly behind the bearing **(see illustration 5.6)**. By operating the slide-hammer part of the tool the bearing is jarred out of its housing **(see illustration 5.7)**.
● It is possible, if the bearing is of reasonable weight, for it to drop out of its housing if the casing is heated as described below. If this

5.6 Expand the bearing puller so that it locks behind the bearing . . .

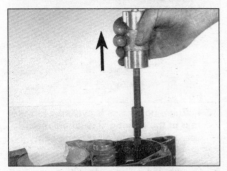

5.7 . . . attach the slide hammer to the bearing puller

method is attempted, first prepare a work surface which will enable the casing to be tapped face down to help dislodge the bearing - a wood surface is ideal since it will not damage the casing's gasket surface. Wearing protective gloves, tap the heated casing several times against the work surface to dislodge the bearing under its own weight **(see illustration 5.8)**.

5.8 Tapping a casing face down on wood blocks can often dislodge a bearing

● Bearings can be installed in blind holes using the driver or socket method described above.

Drawbolts

● Where a bearing or bush is set in the eye of a component, such as a suspension linkage arm or connecting rod small-end, removal by drift may damage the component. Furthermore, a rubber bushing in a shock absorber eye cannot successfully be driven out of position. If access is available to a engineering press, the task is straightforward. If not, a drawbolt can be fabricated to extract the bearing or bush.

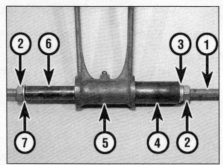

5.9 Drawbolt component parts assembled on a suspension arm

1 Bolt or length of threaded bar
2 Nuts
3 Washer (external diameter greater than tubing internal diameter)
4 Tubing (internal diameter sufficient to accommodate bearing)
5 Suspension arm with bearing
6 Tubing (external diameter slightly smaller than bearing)
7 Washer (external diameter slightly smaller than bearing)

5.10 Drawing the bearing out of the suspension arm

● To extract the bearing/bush you will need a long bolt with nut (or piece of threaded bar with two nuts), a piece of tubing which has an internal diameter larger than the bearing/bush, another piece of tubing which has an external diameter slightly smaller than the bearing/bush, and a selection of washers **(see illustrations 5.9 and 5.10)**. Note that the pieces of tubing must be of the same length, or longer, than the bearing/bush.
● The same kit (without the pieces of tubing) can be used to draw the new bearing/bush back into place **(see illustration 5.11)**.

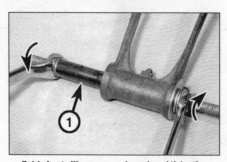

5.11 Installing a new bearing (1) in the suspension arm

Temperature change

● If the bearing's outer race is a tight fit in the casing, the aluminium casing can be heated to release its grip on the bearing. Aluminium will expand at a greater rate than the steel bearing outer race. There are several ways to do this, but avoid any localised extreme heat (such as a blow torch) - aluminium alloy has a low melting point.
● Approved methods of heating a casing are using a domestic oven (heated to 100°C) or immersing the casing in boiling water **(see illustration 5.12)**. Low temperature range localised heat sources such as a paint stripper heat gun or clothes iron can also be used **(see illustration 5.13)**. Alternatively, soak a rag in boiling water, wring it out and wrap it around the bearing housing.

⚠ **Warning: All of these methods require care in use to prevent scalding and burns to the hands. Wear protective gloves when handling hot components.**

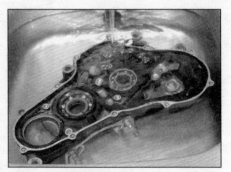

5.12 A casing can be immersed in a sink of boiling water to aid bearing removal

5.13 Using a localised heat source to aid bearing removal

● If heating the whole casing note that plastic components, such as the neutral switch, may suffer - remove them beforehand.
● After heating, remove the bearing as described above. You may find that the expansion is sufficient for the bearing to fall out of the casing under its own weight or with a light tap on the driver or socket.
● If necessary, the casing can be heated to aid bearing installation, and this is sometimes the recommended procedure if the motorcycle manufacturer has designed the housing and bearing fit with this intention.

● Installation of bearings can be eased by placing them in a freezer the night before installation. The steel bearing will contract slightly, allowing easy insertion in its housing. This is often useful when installing steering head outer races in the frame.

Bearing types and markings

● Plain shell bearings, ball bearings, needle roller bearings and tapered roller bearings will all be found on motorcycles (see illustrations 5.14 and 5.15). The ball and roller types are usually caged between an inner and outer race, but uncaged variations may be found.

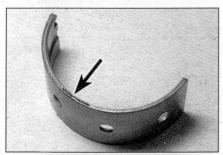

5.14 Shell bearings are either plain or grooved. They are usually identified by colour code (arrow)

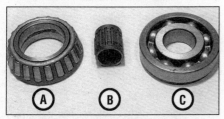

5.15 Tapered roller bearing (A), needle roller bearing (B) and ball journal bearing (C)

● Shell bearings (often called inserts) are usually found at the crankshaft main and connecting rod big-end where they are good at coping with high loads. They are made of a phosphor-bronze material and are impregnated with self-lubricating properties.

● Ball bearings and needle roller bearings consist of a steel inner and outer race with the balls or rollers between the races. They require constant lubrication by oil or grease and are good at coping with axial loads. Taper roller bearings consist of rollers set in a tapered cage set on the inner race; the outer race is separate. They are good at coping with axial loads and prevent movement along the shaft - a typical application is in the steering head.

● Bearing manufacturers produce bearings to ISO size standards and stamp one face of the bearing to indicate its internal and external diameter, load capacity and type (see illustration 5.16).

● Metal bushes are usually of phosphor-bronze material. Rubber bushes are used in suspension mounting eyes. Fibre bushes have also been used in suspension pivots.

5.16 Typical bearing marking

Bearing fault finding

● If a bearing outer race has spun in its housing, the housing material will be damaged. You can use a bearing locking compound to bond the outer race in place if damage is not too severe.

● Shell bearings will fail due to damage of their working surface, as a result of lack of lubrication, corrosion or abrasive particles in the oil (see illustration 5.17). Small particles of dirt in the oil may embed in the bearing material whereas larger particles will score the bearing and shaft journal. If a number of short journeys are made, insufficient heat will be generated to drive off condensation which has built up on the bearings.

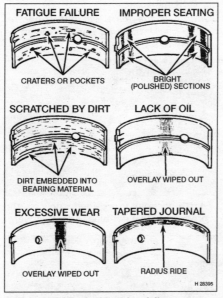

5.17 Typical bearing failures

● Ball and roller bearings will fail due to lack of lubrication or damage to the balls or rollers. Tapered-roller bearings can be damaged by overloading them. Unless the bearing is sealed on both sides, wash it in paraffin (kerosene) to remove all old grease then allow it to dry. Make a visual inspection looking to dented balls or rollers, damaged cages and worn or pitted races (see illustration 5.18).

● A ball bearing can be checked for wear by listening to it when spun. Apply a film of light oil to the bearing and hold it close to the ear - hold the outer race with one hand and spin the inner

5.18 Example of ball journal bearing with damaged balls and cages

5.19 Hold outer race and listen to inner race when spun

race with the other hand (see illustration 5.19). The bearing should be almost silent when spun; if it grates or rattles it is worn.

6 Oil seals

Oil seal removal and installation

● Oil seals should be renewed every time a component is dismantled. This is because the seal lips will become set to the sealing surface and will not necessarily reseal.

● Oil seals can be prised out of position using a large flat-bladed screwdriver (see illustration 6.1). In the case of crankcase seals, check first that the seal is not lipped on the inside, preventing its removal with the crankcases joined.

6.1 Prise out oil seals with a large flat-bladed screwdriver

● New seals are usually installed with their marked face (containing the seal reference code) outwards and the spring side towards the fluid being retained. In certain cases, such as a two-stroke engine crankshaft seal, a double lipped seal may be used due to there being fluid or gas on each side of the joint.

● Use a bearing driver or socket which bears only on the outer hard edge of the seal to install it in the casing - tapping on the inner edge will damage the sealing lip.

Oil seal types and markings

● Oil seals are usually of the single-lipped type. Double-lipped seals are found where a liquid or gas is on both sides of the joint.
● Oil seals can harden and lose their sealing ability if the motorcycle has been in storage for a long period - renewal is the only solution.
● Oil seal manufacturers also conform to the ISO markings for seal size - these are moulded into the outer face of the seal (see illustration 6.2).

6.2 These oil seal markings indicate inside diameter, outside diameter and seal thickness

7 Gaskets and sealants

Types of gasket and sealant

● Gaskets are used to seal the mating surfaces between components and keep lubricants, fluids, vacuum or pressure contained within the assembly. Aluminium gaskets are sometimes found at the cylinder joints, but most gaskets are paper-based. If the mating surfaces of the components being joined are undamaged the gasket can be installed dry, although a dab of sealant or grease will be useful to hold it in place during assembly.
● RTV (Room Temperature Vulcanising) silicone rubber sealants cure when exposed to moisture in the atmosphere. These sealants are good at filling pits or irregular gasket faces, but will tend to be forced out of the joint under very high torque. They can be used to replace a paper gasket, but first make sure that the width of the paper gasket is not essential to the shimming of internal components. RTV sealants should not be used on components containing petrol (gasoline).
● Non-hardening, semi-hardening and hard setting liquid gasket compounds can be used with a gasket or between a metal-to-metal joint. Select the sealant to suit the application: universal non-hardening sealant can be used on virtually all joints; semi-hardening on joint faces which are rough or damaged; hard setting sealant on joints which require a permanent bond and are subjected to high temperature and pressure. **Note:** *Check first if*

the paper gasket has a bead of sealant impregnated in its surface before applying additional sealant.
● When choosing a sealant, make sure it is suitable for the application, particularly if being applied in a high-temperature area or in the vicinity of fuel. Certain manufacturers produce sealants in either clear, silver or black colours to match the finish of the engine. This has a particular application on motorcycles where much of the engine is exposed.
● Do not over-apply sealant. That which is squeezed out on the outside of the joint can be wiped off, whereas an excess of sealant on the inside can break off and clog oilways.

Breaking a sealed joint

● Age, heat, pressure and the use of hard setting sealant can cause two components to stick together so tightly that they are difficult to separate using finger pressure alone. Do not resort to using levers unless there is a pry point provided for this purpose (see illustration 7.1) or else the gasket surfaces will be damaged.
● Use a soft-faced hammer (see illustration 7.2) or a wood block and conventional hammer to strike the component near the mating surface. Avoid hammering against cast extremities since they may break off. If this method fails, try using a wood wedge between the two components.
Caution: If the joint will not separate, double-check that you have removed all the fasteners.

7.1 If a pry point is provided, apply gently pressure with a flat-bladed screwdriver

7.2 Tap around the joint with a soft-faced mallet if necessary - don't strike cooling fins

Removal of old gasket and sealant

● Paper gaskets will most likely come away complete, leaving only a few traces stuck on

Most components have one or two hollow locating dowels between the two gasket faces. If a dowel cannot be removed, do not resort to gripping it with pliers - it will almost certainly be distorted. Install a close-fitting socket or Phillips screwdriver into the dowel and then grip the outer edge of the dowel to free it.

the sealing faces of the components. It is imperative that all traces are removed to ensure correct sealing of the new gasket.
● Very carefully scrape all traces of gasket away making sure that the sealing surfaces are not gouged or scored by the scraper (see illustrations 7.3, 7.4 and 7.5). Stubborn deposits can be removed by spraying with an aerosol gasket remover. Final preparation of

7.3 Paper gaskets can be scraped off with a gasket scraper tool . . .

7.4 . . . a knife blade . . .

7.5 . . . or a household scraper

7.6 Fine abrasive paper is wrapped around a flat file to clean up the gasket face

7.7 A kitchen scourer can be used on stubborn deposits

the gasket surface can be made with very fine abrasive paper or a plastic kitchen scourer **(see illustrations 7.6 and 7.7)**.
● Old sealant can be scraped or peeled off components, depending on the type originally used. Note that gasket removal compounds are available to avoid scraping the components clean; make sure the gasket remover suits the type of sealant used.

8 Chains

Breaking and joining final drive chains

● Drive chains for all but small bikes are continuous and do not have a clip-type connecting link. The chain must be broken using a chain breaker tool and the new chain securely riveted together using a new soft rivet-type link. Never use a clip-type connecting link instead of a rivet-type link, except in an emergency. Various chain breaking and riveting tools are available, either as separate tools or combined as illustrated in the accompanying photographs - read the instructions supplied with the tool carefully.

 Warning: The need to rivet the new link pins correctly cannot be overstressed - loss of control of the motorcycle is very likely to result if the chain breaks in use.

● Rotate the chain and look for the soft link. The soft link pins look like they have been deeply centre-punched instead of peened over

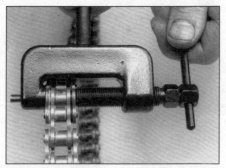

8.1 Tighten the chain breaker to push the pin out of the link . . .

8.2 . . . withdraw the pin, remove the tool . . .

8.3 . . . and separate the chain link

like all the other pins **(see illustration 8.9)** and its sideplate may be a different colour. Position the soft link midway between the sprockets and assemble the chain breaker tool over one of the soft link pins **(see illustration 8.1)**. Operate the tool to push the pin out through the chain **(see illustration 8.2)**. On an O-ring chain, remove the O-rings **(see illustration 8.3)**. Carry out the same procedure on the other soft link pin.
Caution: Certain soft link pins (particularly on the larger chains) may require their ends to be filed or ground off before they can be pressed out using the tool.
● Check that you have the correct size and strength (standard or heavy duty) new soft link - do not reuse the old link. Look for the size marking on the chain sideplates **(see illustration 8.10)**.
● Position the chain ends so that they are engaged over the rear sprocket. On an O-ring chain, install a new O-ring over each pin of the link and insert the link through the two chain

8.4 Insert the new soft link, with O-rings, through the chain ends . . .

8.5 . . . install the O-rings over the pin ends . . .

8.6 . . . followed by the sideplate

ends **(see illustration 8.4)**. Install a new O-ring over the end of each pin, followed by the sideplate (with the chain manufacturer's marking facing outwards) **(see illustrations 8.5 and 8.6)**. On an unsealed chain, insert the link through the two chain ends, then install the sideplate with the chain manufacturer's marking facing outwards.
● Note that it may not be possible to install the sideplate using finger pressure alone. If using a joining tool, assemble it so that the plates of the tool clamp the link and press the sideplate over the pins **(see illustration 8.7)**. Otherwise, use two small sockets placed over

8.7 Push the sideplate into position using a clamp

8.8 Assemble the chain riveting tool over one pin at a time and tighten it fully

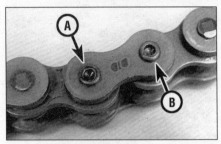

8.9 Pin end correctly riveted (A), pin end unriveted (B)

the rivet ends and two pieces of the wood between a G-clamp. Operate the clamp to press the sideplate over the pins.

● Assemble the joining tool over one pin (following the maker's instructions) and tighten the tool down to spread the pin end securely **(see illustrations 8.8 and 8.9)**. Do the same on the other pin.

 Warning: Check that the pin ends are secure and that there is no danger of the sideplate coming loose. If the pin ends are cracked the soft link must be renewed.

Final drive chain sizing

● Chains are sized using a three digit number, followed by a suffix to denote the chain type **(see illustration 8.10)**. Chain type is either standard or heavy duty (thicker sideplates), and also unsealed or O-ring/ X-ring type.

● The first digit of the number relates to the pitch of the chain, ie the distance from the centre of one pin to the centre of the next pin **(see illustration 8.11)**. Pitch is expressed in eighths of an inch, as follows:

8.10 Typical chain size and type marking

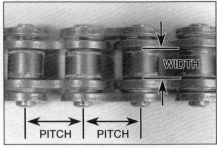

8.11 Chain dimensions

Sizes commencing with a 4 (eg 428) have a pitch of 1/2 inch (12.7 mm)

Sizes commencing with a 5 (eg 520) have a pitch of 5/8 inch (15.9 mm)

Sizes commencing with a 6 (eg 630) have a pitch of 3/4 inch (19.1 mm)

● The second and third digits of the chain size relate to the width of the rollers, again in imperial units, eg the 525 shown has 5/16 inch (7.94 mm) rollers **(see illustration 8.11)**.

9 Hoses

Clamping to prevent flow

● Small-bore flexible hoses can be clamped to prevent fluid flow whilst a component is worked on. Whichever method is used, ensure that the hose material is not permanently distorted or damaged by the clamp.

a) A brake hose clamp available from auto accessory shops **(see illustration 9.1)**.
b) A wingnut type hose clamp **(see illustration 9.2)**.

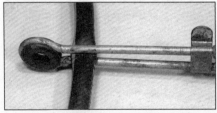

9.1 Hoses can be clamped with an automotive brake hose clamp . . .

9.2 . . . a wingnut type hose clamp . . .

c) Two sockets placed each side of the hose and held with straight-jawed self-locking grips **(see illustration 9.3)**.
d) Thick card each side of the hose held between straight-jawed self-locking grips **(see illustration 9.4)**.

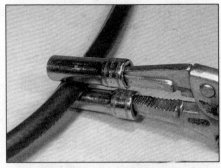

9.3 . . . two sockets and a pair of self-locking grips . . .

9.4 . . . or thick card and self-locking grips

Freeing and fitting hoses

● Always make sure the hose clamp is moved well clear of the hose end. Grip the hose with your hand and rotate it whilst pulling it off the union. If the hose has hardened due to age and will not move, slit it with a sharp knife and peel its ends off the union **(see illustration 9.5)**.

● Resist the temptation to use grease or soap on the unions to aid installation; although it helps the hose slip over the union it will equally aid the escape of fluid from the joint. It is preferable to soften the hose ends in hot water and wet the inside surface of the hose with water or a fluid which will evaporate.

9.5 Cutting a coolant hose free with a sharp knife

Length (distance)

Inches (in)	x 25.4	= Millimetres (mm)	x 0.0394	=	Inches (in)
Feet (ft)	x 0.305	= Metres (m)	x 3.281	=	Feet (ft)
Miles	x 1.609	= Kilometres (km)	x 0.621	=	Miles

Volume (capacity)

Cubic inches (cu in; in³)	x 16.387	= Cubic centimetres (cc; cm³)	x 0.061	=	Cubic inches (cu in; in³)
Imperial pints (Imp pt)	x 0.568	= Litres (l)	x 1.76	=	Imperial pints (Imp pt)
Imperial quarts (Imp qt)	x 1.137	= Litres (l)	x 0.88	=	Imperial quarts (Imp qt)
Imperial quarts (Imp qt)	x 1.201	= US quarts (US qt)	x 0.833	=	Imperial quarts (Imp qt)
US quarts (US qt)	x 0.946	= Litres (l)	x 1.057	=	US quarts (US qt)
Imperial gallons (Imp gal)	x 4.546	= Litres (l)	x 0.22	=	Imperial gallons (Imp gal)
Imperial gallons (Imp gal)	x 1.201	= US gallons (US gal)	x 0.833	=	Imperial gallons (Imp gal)
US gallons (US gal)	x 3.785	= Litres (l)	x 0.264	=	US gallons (US gal)

Mass (weight)

Ounces (oz)	x 28.35	= Grams (g)	x 0.035	=	Ounces (oz)
Pounds (lb)	x 0.454	= Kilograms (kg)	x 2.205	=	Pounds (lb)

Force

Ounces-force (ozf; oz)	x 0.278	= Newtons (N)	x 3.6	=	Ounces-force (ozf; oz)
Pounds-force (lbf; lb)	x 4.448	= Newtons (N)	x 0.225	=	Pounds-force (lbf; lb)
Newtons (N)	x 0.1	= Kilograms-force (kgf; kg)	x 9.81	=	Newtons (N)

Pressure

Pounds-force per square inch (psi; lbf/in²; lb/in²)	x 0.070	= Kilograms-force per square centimetre (kgf/cm²; kg/cm²)	x 14.223	=	Pounds-force per square inch (psi; lbf/in²; lb/in²)
Pounds-force per square inch (psi; lbf/in²; lb/in²)	x 0.068	= Atmospheres (atm)	x 14.696	=	Pounds-force per square inch (psi; lbf/in²; lb/in²)
Pounds-force per square inch (psi; lbf/in²; lb/in²)	x 0.069	= Bars	x 14.5	=	Pounds-force per square inch (psi; lbf/in²; lb/in²)
Pounds-force per square inch (psi; lbf/in²; lb/in²)	x 6.895	= Kilopascals (kPa)	x 0.145	=	Pounds-force per square inch (psi; lbf/in²; lb/in²)
Kilopascals (kPa)	x 0.01	= Kilograms-force per square centimetre (kgf/cm²; kg/cm²)	x 98.1	=	Kilopascals (kPa)
Millibar (mbar)	x 100	= Pascals (Pa)	x 0.01	=	Millibar (mbar)
Millibar (mbar)	x 0.0145	= Pounds-force per square inch (psi; lbf/in²; lb/in²)	x 68.947	=	Millibar (mbar)
Millibar (mbar)	x 0.75	= Millimetres of mercury (mmHg)	x 1.333	=	Millibar (mbar)
Millibar (mbar)	x 0.401	= Inches of water (inH₂O)	x 2.491	=	Millibar (mbar)
Millimetres of mercury (mmHg)	x 0.535	= Inches of water (inH₂O)	x 1.868	=	Millimetres of mercury (mmHg)
Inches of water (inH₂O)	x 0.036	= Pounds-force per square inch (psi; lbf/in²; lb/in²)	x 27.68	=	Inches of water (inH₂O)

Torque (moment of force)

Pounds-force inches (lbf in; lb in)	x 1.152	= Kilograms-force centimetre (kgf cm; kg cm)	x 0.868	=	Pounds-force inches (lbf in; lb in)
Pounds-force inches (lbf in; lb in)	x 0.113	= Newton metres (Nm)	x 8.85	=	Pounds-force inches (lbf in; lb in)
Pounds-force inches (lbf in; lb in)	x 0.083	= Pounds-force feet (lbf ft; lb ft)	x 12	=	Pounds-force inches (lbf in; lb in)
Pounds-force feet (lbf ft; lb ft)	x 0.138	= Kilograms-force metres (kgf m; kg m)	x 7.233	=	Pounds-force feet (lbf ft; lb ft)
Pounds-force feet (lbf ft; lb ft)	x 1.356	= Newton metres (Nm)	x 0.738	=	Pounds-force feet (lbf ft; lb ft)
Newton metres (Nm)	x 0.102	= Kilograms-force metres (kgf m; kg m)	x 9.804	=	Newton metres (Nm)

Power

Horsepower (hp)	x 745.7	= Watts (W)	x 0.0013	=	Horsepower (hp)

Velocity (speed)

Miles per hour (miles/hr; mph)	x 1.609	= Kilometres per hour (km/hr; kph)	x 0.621	=	Miles per hour (miles/hr; mph)

Fuel consumption*

Miles per gallon (mpg)	x 0.354	= Kilometres per litre (km/l)	x 2.825	=	Miles per gallon (mpg)

Temperature

Degrees Fahrenheit = (°C x 1.8) + 32   Degrees Celsius (Degrees Centigrade; °C) = (°F - 32) x 0.56

It is common practice to convert from miles per gallon (mpg) to litres/100 kilometres (l/100km), where mpg x l/100 km = 282

This Section provides an easy reference-guide to the more common faults that are likely to afflict your machine. Obviously, the opportunities are almost limitless for faults to occur as a result of obscure failures, and to try and cover all eventualities would require a book. Indeed, a number have been written on the subject.

Successful troubleshooting is not a mysterious 'black art' but the application of a bit of knowledge combined with a systematic and logical approach to the problem. Approach any troubleshooting by first accurately identifying the symptom and then checking through the list of possible causes, starting with the simplest or most obvious and progressing in stages to the most complex.

Take nothing for granted, but above all apply liberal quantities of common sense.

The main symptom of a fault is given in the text as a major heading below which are listed the various systems or areas which may contain the fault. Details of each possible cause for a fault and the remedial action to be taken are given, in brief, in the paragraphs below each heading. Further information should be sought in the relevant Chapter.

1 Engine doesn't start or is difficult to start

- [ ] Starter motor doesn't rotate
- [ ] Starter motor rotates but engine does not turn over
- [ ] No fuel flow
- [ ] Engine flooded
- [ ] No spark or weak spark
- [ ] Compression low
- [ ] Stalls after starting
- [ ] Rough idle

2 Poor running at low speed

- [ ] Spark weak
- [ ] Fuel/air mixture incorrect
- [ ] Compression low
- [ ] Poor acceleration

3 Poor running or no power at high speed

- [ ] Firing incorrect
- [ ] Fuel/air mixture incorrect
- [ ] Compression low
- [ ] Knocking or pinking
- [ ] Miscellaneous causes

4 Overheating

- [ ] Firing incorrect
- [ ] Fuel/air mixture incorrect
- [ ] Compression too high
- [ ] Engine load excessive
- [ ] Lubrication inadequate
- [ ] Miscellaneous causes

5 Clutch problems

- [ ] Clutch slipping
- [ ] Clutch not disengaging completely

6 Gearchange problems

- [ ] Doesn't go into gear, or lever doesn't return
- [ ] Jumps out of gear
- [ ] Overselects

7 Abnormal engine noise

- [ ] Knocking or pinking
- [ ] Piston slap or rattling
- [ ] Valve noise
- [ ] Other noise

8 Abnormal driveline noise

- [ ] Clutch noise
- [ ] Transmission noise
- [ ] Final drive noise

9 Abnormal frame and suspension noise

- [ ] Front end noise
- [ ] Shock absorber noise
- [ ] Brake noise

10 Excessive exhaust smoke

- [ ] White smoke
- [ ] Black smoke
- [ ] Brown smoke

11 Poor handling or stability

- [ ] Handlebar hard to turn
- [ ] Handlebar shakes or vibrates excessively
- [ ] Handlebar pulls to one side
- [ ] Poor shock absorbing qualities

12 Braking problems

- [ ] Brakes are spongy or don't hold
- [ ] Brake lever or pedal pulsates
- [ ] Brakes drag

13 Electrical problems

- [ ] Battery dead or weak
- [ ] Battery overcharged

1 Engine doesn't start or is difficult to start

Starter motor doesn't rotate

- [ ] Fuse blown. Check main fuse (Chapter 9).
- [ ] Battery voltage low. Check and recharge battery (Chapter 9).
- [ ] Starter motor defective. Make sure the wiring to the starter is secure. Make sure the starter relay clicks when the start button is pushed. If the relay clicks, then the fault is probably in the wiring or motor.
- [ ] Starter relay faulty. Check it according to the procedure in Chapter 9.
- [ ] Starter button not contacting. The contacts could be wet, corroded or dirty. Disassemble and clean the switch (Chapter 9).
- [ ] Wiring open or shorted. Check all wiring connections and harnesses to make sure that they are dry, tight and not corroded. Also check for broken or frayed wires that can cause a short to earth (see *Wiring Diagrams*, Chapter 9).
- [ ] Ignition switch defective. Check the switch according to the procedure in Chapter 9. Replace the switch with a new one if it is defective.
- [ ] Engine stop switch defective. Check for wet, dirty or corroded contacts. Clean or renew the switch as necessary (Chapter 9).
- [ ] Faulty neutral/sidestand/clutch switch or starter diode. Check the wiring to each switch and the switch itself, and check the diode, according to the procedures in Chapter 9.
- [ ] Fuel injection system shutdown due to system fault – XL125V-7 onward (see Chapter 4B).

Starter motor rotates but engine does not turn over

- [ ] Starter clutch defective. Inspect and repair or replace (Chapter 2).
- [ ] Damaged idle/reduction or starter gears. Inspect and replace the damaged parts (Chapter 2).

No fuel flow

- [ ] No fuel in tank.
- [ ] Breather hose obstructed. Usually caused by dirt or a trapped hose.
- [ ] Fuel tap filter clogged (VT125C and XL125V-1 to V-6). Remove the tap and clean the strainer (Chapter 4A).
- [ ] Fuel pump strainer clogged (XL125V-7 onward). Remove the pump and clean the strainer (Chapter 4B).
- [ ] Fuel pump failure or fuel injection system fault (XL125V-7 onward) (Chapter 4B).
- [ ] Fuel hose clogged. Detach the fuel hose and carefully blow through it.

Engine flooded (carburettor engines)

- [ ] Float height too high. Check as described in Chapter 4A.
- [ ] Inlet needle valve worn or stuck open. A piece of dirt, rust or other debris can cause the inlet needle to seat improperly, causing excess fuel to be admitted to the float bowl. In this case, the float chamber should be cleaned and the needle and seat inspected. If the needle and seat are worn, then the leaking will persist and the parts should be replaced with new ones (Chapter 4A).
- [ ] Starting technique incorrect. Under normal circumstances (e.g., if all the carburettor functions are sound) the machine should start with little or no throttle. When the engine is cold, the choke should be operated and the engine started without opening the throttle. When the engine is at operating temperature, only a very slight amount of throttle should be necessary. If the engine is flooded, hold the throttle fully open while cranking the engine. This will allow additional air to reach the cylinders.

Engine flooded (fuel injected engines)

- [ ] Injector needle valve worn or stuck open. A piece of dirt, rust or other debris can cause the needle to seat improperly, causing excess fuel to be admitted to the throttle body. In this case, the injector should be cleaned (Chapter 4B). If the injector is damaged it must be renewed.
- [ ] Starting technique incorrect. Under normal circumstances (i.e. if all the components of the fuel injection system are good) the machine should start with the throttle closed.

No spark or weak spark

- [ ] Ignition switch OFF. Engine stop switch OFF.
- [ ] Battery voltage low. Check and recharge battery as necessary (Chapter 9).
- [ ] Spark plug dirty, defective or worn out. Locate reason for fouled plug using spark plug condition chart and follow the plug maintenance procedures in Chapter 1.
- [ ] Spark plug cap or lead faulty. Check condition. Replace either or both components if cracks or deterioration are evident.
- [ ] Spark plug cap not making good contact. Make sure that the plug cap fits snugly over the plug end.
- [ ] Ignition system fault. Refer to Chapter 4B or 5 as applicable for details.
- [ ] Ignition HT coil defective. Check the coil, referring to Chapter 4B or 5.
- [ ] Ignition switch shorted. This is usually caused by water, corrosion, damage or excessive wear. If cleaning with electrical contact cleaner does not help, renew the switch (Chapter 9).
- [ ] Wiring shorted or broken. Make sure that all wiring connections are clean, dry and tight. Look for chafed and broken wires.

Compression low

- [ ] Spark plugs loose. Remove the plugs and inspect the threads. Reinstall and tighten to the specified torque (Chapter 1).
- [ ] Cylinder head not sufficiently tightened down. If a cylinder head is suspected of being loose, then there's a chance that the gasket or head is damaged if the problem has persisted for any length of time. The cylinder head nuts should be tightened to the correct torque in the correct sequence (Chapter 2).
- [ ] Improper valve clearance. This means that the valve is not closing completely and compression pressure is leaking past the valve. Check and adjust the valve clearances (Chapter 1).
- [ ] Cylinders and/or pistons worn. Excessive wear will cause compression pressure to leak past the rings. This is usually accompanied by worn rings as well. A top-end overhaul is necessary (Chapter 2).
- [ ] Piston rings worn, weak, broken, or sticking. Broken or sticking piston rings usually indicate a lubrication or carburetion problem that causes excess carbon deposits or seizures to form on the pistons and rings. Top-end overhaul is necessary (Chapter 2).
- [ ] Cylinder head gasket damaged. If the head is allowed to become loose, or if excessive carbon build-up on the piston crown and combustion chamber causes extremely high compression, the head gasket may leak. Retorquing the head is not always sufficient to restore the seal, so gasket replacement is necessary (Chapter 2).
- [ ] Cylinder head warped. This is caused by overheating or improperly tightened head nuts. Machine shop resurfacing or head replacement is necessary (Chapter 2).
- [ ] Valve spring broken or weak. Caused by component failure or wear; the valve springs must be replaced as a set (Chapter 2).
- [ ] Valve not seating properly. This is caused by a bent valve (from over-revving or improper valve adjustment), burned valve or seat (improper carburetion) or an accumulation of carbon deposits on the seat (from carburetion or lubrication problems). The valves must be cleaned and/or replaced and the seats serviced if possible (Chapter 2).

1 Engine doesn't start or is difficult to start (continued)

Stalls after starting

- [ ] Ignition malfunction. See Chapter 4B or 5 as applicable.
- [ ] Improper choke action – VT125C and XL125V-1 to V-6 models. Make sure the choke action is not restricted and stays in set position (Chapter 4A).
- [ ] Carburettor malfunction. See Chapter 4A.
- [ ] Faulty fast idle control – XL125V-7 onward. Check the operation of the idle air control valve (Chapter 4B).
- [ ] Fuel injection system malfunction – see Chapter 4B.
- [ ] Fuel contaminated. The fuel can be contaminated with either dirt or water, or can change chemically if the machine is allowed to sit for several months or more. Drain the tank and clean the carburettor or throttle body (Chapter 4A or 4B).
- [ ] Intake air leak. Check the carburettor or throttle body connection with the cylinder head (Chapter 4A or 4B).
- [ ] Engine idle speed incorrect. On VT125C and XL125V-1 to V-6 models it is possible to turn throttle stop screw until the engine idles at the specified rpm (Chapter 1).

Rough idle

- [ ] Ignition malfunction. See Chapter 4B or 5 as applicable.
- [ ] Idle speed incorrect (VT125C and XL125V-1 to V-6 models). See Chapter 1.
- [ ] Carburettor malfunction or fuel injection system fault. See Chapter 4A or 4B.
- [ ] Fuel contaminated. The fuel can be contaminated with either dirt or water, or can change chemically if the machine is allowed to sit for several months or more. Drain the tank and clean the carburettor or throttle body (Chapter 4A or 4B).
- [ ] Intake air leak. Check the carburettor or throttle body connection with the cylinder head (Chapter 4A or 4B).
- [ ] Air filter clogged. Renew the air filter element (Chapter 1).
- [ ] Air induction system fault. Check the system (Chapters 1 and 4A or 4B).
- [ ] Fuel injection system fault. See Chapter 4B.

2 Poor running at low speed

Spark weak

- [ ] Battery voltage low. Check and recharge battery (Chapter 9).
- [ ] Spark plug fouled, defective or worn out. Refer to Chapter 1 for spark plug maintenance.
- [ ] Spark plug cap or lead defective. Refer to Chapter 4B or 5 for details on the ignition system.
- [ ] Spark plug cap not making contact.
- [ ] Incorrect spark plug. Wrong type, heat range or cap configuration. Check and install correct plug listed in Chapter 1.
- [ ] Ignition system defective. See Chapter 4B or 5 as applicable.
- [ ] Ignition HT coil defective. See Chapter 4B or 5.

Fuel/air mixture incorrect (carburettor models)

- [ ] Pilot screw out of adjustment (Chapter 4A).
- [ ] Pilot jet or air passage clogged. Remove and overhaul the carburettors (Chapter 4A).
- [ ] Air bleed holes clogged. Remove carburettors, clean and blow out all passages (Chapter 4A).
- [ ] Air filter clogged, poorly sealed or missing (Chapter 1).
- [ ] Air filter housing poorly sealed. Look for cracks, holes or loose clamps and replace or repair defective parts.
- [ ] Fuel level too high or too low. Check the fuel level and float height (Chapter 4A).
- [ ] Fuel tank air vent obstructed. Make sure the breather hose is not blocked.
- [ ] Carburettor intake duct loose. Check for cracks, breaks, tears or loose clamps.

Compression low

- [ ] Spark plug loose. Remove the plugs and inspect their threads. Reinstall and tighten to the specified torque (Chapter 1).
- [ ] Cylinder head not sufficiently tightened down. If a cylinder head is suspected of being loose, then there's a chance that the gasket and head are damaged if the problem has persisted for any length of time. The cylinder head nuts should be tightened to the correct torque in the correct sequence (Chapter 2).
- [ ] Improper valve clearance. This means that the valve is not closing completely and compression pressure is leaking past the valve. Check and adjust the valve clearances (Chapter 1).
- [ ] Cylinders and/or pistons worn. Excessive wear will cause compression pressure to leak past the rings. This is usually accompanied by worn rings as well. A top-end overhaul is necessary (Chapter 2).

- [ ] Piston rings worn, weak, broken, or sticking. Broken or sticking piston rings usually indicate a lubrication or carburetion problem that causes excess carbon deposits or seizures to form on the pistons and rings. Top-end overhaul is necessary (Chapter 2).
- [ ] Cylinder head gasket damaged. If the head is allowed to become loose, or if excessive carbon build-up on the piston crown and combustion chamber causes extremely high compression, the head gasket may leak. Retorquing the head is not always sufficient to restore the seal, so gasket replacement is necessary (Chapter 2).
- [ ] Cylinder head warped. This is caused by overheating or improperly tightened head nuts. Machine shop resurfacing or head replacement is necessary (Chapter 2).
- [ ] Valve spring broken or weak. Caused by component failure or wear; the springs should be renewed as a set (Chapter 2).
- [ ] Valve not seating properly. This is caused by a bent valve (from over-revving or improper valve adjustment), burned valve or seat (improper carburetion) or an accumulation of carbon deposits on the seat (from carburetion, lubrication problems). The valves must be cleaned and/or replaced and the seats serviced if possible (Chapter 2).

Poor acceleration

- [ ] Carburettor leaking or dirty (VT125C and XL125V-1 to V-6). Overhaul the carburettors (Chapter 4A).
- [ ] Throttle bodies leaking or dirty (VT125V-7 onward). Overhaul the throttle bodies (Chapter 4B).
- [ ] Fuel flow restricted (VT125C and XL125V-1 to V-6). Check the tap and its filter and all the hoses from the tank (Chapter 4A). If the breather hose is blocked a vacuum can form in the tank which will restrict flow.
- [ ] Fuel flow restricted (VT125V-7 onward). Check the pump and strainer and all the hoses from the tank (Chapter 4B). If the breather hose is blocked a vacuum can form in the tank which will restrict flow.
- [ ] Carburettors not synchronised (VT125C and XL125V-1 to V-6). Adjust them with a vacuum gauge set or manometer (Chapter 1).
- [ ] Engine oil viscosity too high. Using a heavier oil than that recommended in Chapter 1 can damage the oil pump or lubrication system and cause drag on the engine.
- [ ] Brakes dragging. Usually caused by debris which has entered the brake piston seals (disc brake), sticking brake operating mechanism or badly adjusted brake (drum brake), or from a warped disc or bent axle. Repair as necessary (Chapter 7).

3 Poor running or no power at high speed

Firing incorrect

- ☐ Air filter restricted. Renew filter element (Chapter 1).
- ☐ Spark plug fouled, defective or worn out. See Chapter 1 for spark plug maintenance.
- ☐ Spark plug cap or lead wiring defective. See Chapter 4B or 5 for details of the ignition system.
- ☐ Spark plug cap not in good contact.
- ☐ Incorrect spark plug. Wrong type, heat range or cap configuration. Check and install correct plug listed in Chapter 1.
- ☐ Ignition system defective. See Chapter 4B or 5 as applicable.
- ☐ Ignition HT coil defective. See Chapter 4B or 5.
- ☐ Fuel injection system fault. See Chapter 4B.

Fuel/air mixture incorrect

- ☐ Main jet clogged (VT125C and XL125V-1 to V-6). Dirt, water or other contaminants can clog the main jet. Clean the fuel tap strainer, the float bowl area and the jets and carburettors (Chapter 4A).
- ☐ Main jet wrong size (VT125C and XL125V-1 to V-6). The standard jetting is for sea level atmospheric pressure and oxygen content.
- ☐ Air filter clogged, poorly sealed, or missing (Chapter 1).
- ☐ Air filter housing poorly sealed. Look for cracks, holes or loose clamps, and replace or repair defective parts.
- ☐ Fuel level too high or too low (VT125C and XL125V-1 to V-6). Check the fuel level and float height (Chapter 4A).
- ☐ Fuel pump faulty, or the fuel strainer is blocked (XL125V-7 onward) (see Chapter 4B).
- ☐ Fuel injector clogged (XL125V-7 onward). For both injectors to be clogged, either a very bad batch of fuel with an unusual additive has been used, or some other foreign material has entered the tank. Check the fuel strainer. In some cases, if a machine has been unused for several months, the fuel turns to a varnish-like liquid which can cause an injector needle to stick to its seat. Drain the tank and fuel system (Chapter 4B).
- ☐ Fuel tank breather hose blocked.
- ☐ Intake duct loose. Check for cracks, breaks, tears or loose clamps.
- ☐ Fuel hose clogged. Detach the fuel hose and carefully blow through it.

Compression low

- ☐ Spark plug loose. Remove the plugs and inspect their threads. Reinstall and tighten to the specified torque (Chapter 1).
- ☐ Cylinder head not sufficiently tightened down. If a cylinder head is suspected of being loose, then there's a chance that the gasket and head are damaged if the problem has persisted for any length of time. The cylinder head nuts should be tightened to the proper torque in the correct sequence (Chapter 2).
- ☐ Improper valve clearance. This means that the valve is not closing completely and compression pressure is leaking past the valve. Check and adjust the valve clearances (Chapter 1).
- ☐ Cylinders and/or pistons worn. Excessive wear will cause compression pressure to leak past the rings. This is usually accompanied by worn rings as well. A top-end overhaul is necessary (Chapter 2).
- ☐ Piston rings worn, weak, broken, or sticking. Broken or sticking piston rings usually indicate a lubrication or carburetion problem that causes excess carbon deposits or seizures to form on the pistons and rings. Top-end overhaul is necessary (Chapter 2).
- ☐ Cylinder head gasket damaged. If the head is allowed to become loose, or if excessive carbon build-up on the piston crown and combustion chamber causes extremely high compression, the head gasket may leak. Retorquing the head is not always sufficient to restore the seal, so gasket replacement is necessary (Chapter 2).
- ☐ Cylinder head warped. This is caused by overheating or improperly tightened head nuts. Machine shop resurfacing or head replacement is necessary (Chapter 2).
- ☐ Valve spring broken or weak. Caused by component failure or wear; renew the springs as a set (Chapter 2).
- ☐ Valve not seating properly. This is caused by a bent valve (from over-revving or improper valve adjustment), burned valve or seat (improper carburetion) or an accumulation of carbon deposits on the seat (from carburetion, lubrication problems). The valves must be cleaned and/or replaced and the seats serviced if possible (Chapter 2).

Knocking or pinking

- ☐ Carbon build-up on the piston and in the combustion chamber. Remove the cylinder heads and clean the pistons and combustion chambers (Chapter 2).
- ☐ Incorrect or poor quality fuel. Old or improper grades of fuel can cause detonation. This causes the piston to rattle, thus the knocking or pinking sound. Drain old fuel and always use the recommended fuel grade.
- ☐ Spark plug heat range incorrect. Uncontrolled detonation indicates the plug heat range is too hot. The plug in effect becomes a glow plug, raising cylinder temperatures. Install the proper heat range plug (Chapter 1).
- ☐ Improper air/fuel mixture (carburettor models). This will cause the cylinder to run hot, which leads to detonation. Clogged jets or an air leak can cause this imbalance (Chapter 4A).
- ☐ Fuel injection system fault (Chapter 4B).

Miscellaneous causes

- ☐ Throttle valve doesn't open fully. Adjust the cable freeplay (Chapter 1).
- ☐ Clutch slipping. May be caused by loose or worn clutch components. Refer to Chapter 2 for clutch overhaul procedures.
- ☐ Engine oil viscosity too high. Using a heavier oil than the one recommended in Chapter 1 can damage the oil pump or lubrication system and cause drag on the engine.
- ☐ Brakes dragging. Usually caused by debris which has entered the brake piston seals (disc brake), sticking brake operating mechanism or badly adjusted brake (drum brake), or from a warped disc or bent axle. Repair as necessary.

4 Overheating

Engine overheats

☐ Coolant level low. Check and add coolant (Chapter 1).
☐ Leak in cooling system. Check cooling system hoses and radiator for leaks and other damage. Repair or renew parts as necessary (Chapter 3).
☐ Thermostat sticking closed. Check and renew as described in Chapter 3.
☐ Faulty radiator cap. Have the cap pressure tested.
☐ Coolant passages clogged. Drain and flush the entire system, then refill with fresh coolant (Chapter 3).
☐ Water pump defective. Remove the pump and check the components (Chapter 3).
☐ Clogged radiator fins. Clean them by blowing compressed air through the fins from the rear of the radiator, and straighten any bent fins that restrict air flow.
☐ Cooling fan or operating circuit fault (Chapter 3).

Firing incorrect

☐ Spark plug fouled, defective or worn out. See Chapter 1 for spark plug maintenance.
☐ Incorrect spark plug.
☐ Faulty HT ignition coil (Chapter 4B or 5, as applicable).

Fuel/air mixture incorrect

☐ Main jet clogged (VT125C and XL125V-1 to V-6). Dirt, water and other contaminants can clog the main jets. Clean the fuel tap strainer, the float bowl area and the jets and carburettors (Chapter 4A).
☐ Main jet wrong size (VT125C and XL125V-1 to V-6). The standard jetting is for sea level atmospheric pressure and oxygen content.
☐ Air filter clogged, poorly sealed or missing (Chapter 1).
☐ Air filter housing poorly sealed. Look for cracks, holes or loose clamps and replace or repair.
☐ Fuel level too low (VT125C and XL125V-1 to V-6). Check fuel level and float height (Chapter 4A).
☐ Fuel pump faulty, or the fuel strainer is blocked (XL125V-7 onward) (see Chapter 4B).
☐ Fuel injector clogged (XL125V-7 onward). For both injectors to be clogged, either a very bad batch of fuel with an unusual additive

has been used, or some other foreign material has entered the tank. Check the fuel strainer. In some cases, if a machine has been unused for several months, the fuel turns to a varnish-like liquid which can cause an injector needle to stick to its seat. Drain the tank and fuel system (Chapter 4B).
☐ Fuel tank breather hose blocked.
☐ Intake duct loose. Check for cracks, breaks, tears or loose clamps.

Compression too high

☐ Carbon build-up on the piston and in the combustion chamber. Remove the cylinder heads and clean the pistons and combustion chambers (Chapter 2).
☐ Improperly machined head surface.

Engine load excessive

☐ Clutch slipping. Can be caused by damaged, loose or worn clutch components. Refer to Chapter 2 for overhaul procedures.
☐ Engine oil level too high. The addition of too much oil will cause pressurisation of the crankcase and inefficient engine operation. Check the level (Pre-ride checks).
☐ Engine oil viscosity too high. Using a heavier oil than the one recommended in Chapter 1 can damage the oil pump or lubrication system as well as cause drag on the engine.
☐ Brakes dragging. Usually caused by debris which has entered the brake piston seals (disc brake), sticking brake operating mechanism or badly adjusted brake (drum brake), or from a warped disc or bent axle. Repair as necessary.

Lubrication inadequate

☐ Engine oil level too low. Friction caused by intermittent lack of lubrication or from oil that is overworked can cause overheating. The oil provides a definite cooling function in the engine. Check the oil level (Pre-ride checks).
☐ Poor quality engine oil or incorrect viscosity or type. Oil is rated not only according to viscosity but also according to type. Some oils are not rated high enough for use in this engine. Check the Specifications section and change to the correct oil (Chapter 1).
☐ Faulty oil pump causing reduced pressure in system. Check the pump for wear (see Chapter 2).

5 Clutch problems

Clutch slipping

☐ Cable freeplay insufficient. Check and adjust cable (Chapter 1).
☐ Friction plates worn or warped. Overhaul the clutch assembly (Chapter 2).
☐ Plain plates worn or warped (Chapter 2).
☐ Clutch spring(s) broken or weak. Old or heat-damaged (from slipping clutch) springs should be replaced with new ones (Chapter 2).
☐ Clutch release mechanism defective. Replace any defective parts (Chapter 2).
☐ Clutch centre or housing unevenly worn. This causes improper engagement of the plates. Replace the damaged or worn parts (Chapter 2).

Clutch not disengaging completely

☐ Cable freeplay excessive. Check and adjust cable (Chapter 1).
☐ Clutch plates warped or damaged. This will cause clutch drag, which in turn will cause the machine to creep. Overhaul the clutch assembly (Chapter 2).

☐ Clutch spring tension uneven. Usually caused by a sagged or broken spring. Check and replace the springs as a set (Chapter 2).
☐ Engine oil deteriorated. Old, thin, worn out oil will not provide proper lubrication for the discs, causing the clutch to drag. Change the oil and filter (Chapter 1).
☐ Engine oil viscosity too high. Using a heavier oil than recommended in Chapter 1 can cause the plates to stick together, putting a drag on the engine. Change to the correct weight oil (Chapter 1).
☐ Clutch housing seized on input shaft. Lack of lubrication, severe wear or damage can cause the housing to seize on the shaft. Overhaul of the clutch, and perhaps transmission, may be necessary to repair the damage (Chapter 2).
☐ Clutch release mechanism defective. Worn or damaged release mechanism parts can stick and fail to apply force to the pressure plate. Overhaul the clutch cover components (Chapter 2).
☐ Loose clutch centre nut. Causes drum and centre misalignment putting a drag on the engine. Engagement adjustment continually varies. Overhaul the clutch assembly (Chapter 2).

6 Gearchange problems

Doesn't go into gear or lever doesn't return

- [ ] Clutch not disengaging.
- [ ] Selector fork(s) bent or seized due to lack of lubrication. Overhaul the transmission (Chapter 2).
- [ ] Gear(s) stuck on shaft. Most often caused by a lack of lubrication or excessive wear in transmission bearings and bushes. Overhaul the transmission (Chapter 2).
- [ ] Selector drum binding. Caused by lubrication failure or excessive wear. Replace the drum and bearings (Chapter 2).
- [ ] Gearchange lever return spring weak or broken (Chapter 2).
- [ ] Gearchange lever broken. Splines stripped out of lever or shaft, caused by allowing the lever to get loose or from dropping the machine. Replace necessary parts (Chapter 2).
- [ ] Gearchange mechanism stopper arm broken or worn. Full engagement and rotary movement of selector drum results. Replace the arm (Chapter 2).
- [ ] Stopper arm spring broken. Allows arm to float, causing sporadic selector operation. Replace spring (Chapter 2).

Jumps out of gear

- [ ] Selector fork(s) worn. Overhaul the transmission (Chapter 2).
- [ ] Gear groove(s) worn in selector drum. Overhaul the transmission (Chapter 2).
- [ ] Gear dogs or dog slots worn or damaged. The gears should be inspected and replaced. No attempt should be made to service the worn parts.

Overselects

- [ ] Stopper arm spring weak or broken (Chapter 2).
- [ ] Gearchange shaft return spring post broken or distorted (Chapter 2).

7 Abnormal engine noise

Knocking or pinking

- [ ] Carbon build-up on the pistons and in the combustion the chamber. Remove the cylinder heads and clean the pistons and combustion chambers (Chapter 2).
- [ ] Incorrect or poor quality fuel. Old or improper fuel can cause detonation. This causes the piston to rattle, thus the knocking or pinking sound. Drain the old fuel and always use the recommended grade fuel (Chapter 4A or 4B).
- [ ] Spark plug heat range incorrect. Uncontrolled detonation indicates that the plug heat range is too hot. The plug in effect becomes a glow plug, raising cylinder temperatures. Install the proper heat range plug (Chapter 1).
- [ ] Improper air/fuel mixture (carburettor models). This will cause the cylinder to run hot and lead to detonation. Clogged jets or an air leak can cause this imbalance. See Chapter 4A.
- [ ] Fuel injection system fault. See Chapter 4B.

Piston slap or rattling

- [ ] Cylinder-to-piston clearance excessive. Inspect and overhaul top-end parts (Chapter 2).
- [ ] Connecting rod bent. Caused by over-revving, piston seizure or broken valve. Replace the damaged parts (Chapter 2).
- [ ] Piston pin or piston pin bore worn or seized from wear or lack of lubrication. Replace damaged parts (Chapter 2).
- [ ] Piston ring(s) worn, broken or sticking. Overhaul the top-end (Chapter 2).
- [ ] Piston seizure damage. Usually from lack of lubrication or overheating. Replace the piston and bore the cylinder, as necessary (Chapter 2).

- [ ] Connecting rod small or big-end clearance excessive. Caused by excessive wear or lack of lubrication. Replace worn parts.

Valve noise

- [ ] Incorrect valve clearances. Adjust the clearances by referring to Chapter 1.
- [ ] Valve spring broken or weak. Renew the valve springs as a set (Chapter 2).
- [ ] Camshaft, camshaft bearings or cylinder head worn or damaged. Lack of lubrication at high rpm is usually the cause of damage. Insufficient oil or failure to change the oil at the recommended intervals are the chief causes (Chapter 2).

Other noise

- [ ] Cylinder head gasket leaking.
- [ ] Exhaust pipe leaking at cylinder head connection. Caused by improper fit of pipe or loose exhaust flange. Renew the seal and ensure all exhaust fasteners are tightened evenly. Failure to do this will lead to a leak (Chapter 4A or 4B as appropriate).
- [ ] Crankshaft runout excessive. Caused by a bent crankshaft (from over-revving) or damage from an upper cylinder component failure.
- [ ] Engine mounting bolts loose. Tighten all engine mount bolts to the specified torque (Chapter 2).
- [ ] Crankshaft bearings worn (Chapter 2).
- [ ] Cam chain tensioner defective. Replace according to the procedure in Chapter 2.
- [ ] Cam chain, sprockets or guides worn (Chapter 2).

8 Abnormal driveline noise

Clutch noise

- [ ] Clutch housing/friction plate clearance excessive (Chapter 2).
- [ ] Loose or damaged clutch pressure plate and/or bolts (Chapter 2).
- [ ] Broken or incorrectly fitted anti-judder spring (Chapter 2).

Transmission noise

- [ ] Shaft bearings or gear pinion bushes worn. Also includes the possibility that the shafts are worn. Overhaul the transmission (Chapter 2).
- [ ] Gears worn or chipped (Chapter 2).
- [ ] Metal chips jammed in gear teeth. Probably pieces from a broken clutch, gear or selector mechanism that were picked up by the gears. This will cause early bearing failure (Chapter 2).
- [ ] Engine oil level too low. Causes a howl from transmission. Also affects engine power and clutch operation (Pre-ride checks).

Final drive noise

- [ ] Chain not adjusted properly (Chapter 1).
- [ ] Front or rear sprocket loose. Tighten fasteners (Chapter 7).
- [ ] Sprocket(s) worn. Renew sprockets and chain as a set (Chapter 7).
- [ ] Rear sprocket warped. Replace (Chapter 7).
- [ ] Sprocket coupling worn. Check coupling, dampers and bearing (Chapter 7).

9 Abnormal frame and suspension noise

Front end noise

☐ Low oil level or improper viscosity oil in forks. This can sound like spurting and is usually accompanied by irregular fork action (Chapter 6).

☐ Fork spring weak or broken. Makes a clicking or scraping sound. Fork oil, when drained, will have a lot of metal particles in it (Chapter 6).

☐ Steering head bearings loose or damaged. Clicks when braking. Check and adjust or replace as necessary (Chapters 1 and 6).

☐ Fork clamp bolts loose. Make sure all fork clamp bolts are tightened to the specified torque (Chapter 6).

☐ Fork tube bent. Good possibility if machine has been in an accident. Have both tubes checked for runout. Replace defective tube(s) with a new one (Chapter 6).

☐ Front axle or clamp bolt loose. Tighten to the specified torque (Chapter 7).

Shock absorber noise

☐ Fluid level incorrect caused by defective seal. Rear shock will be covered with oil. Replace shock on XL125V models, and both shocks on VT125C models (Chapter 6).

☐ Defective shock absorber with internal damage. This is in the body of the shock and can't be remedied. The shock must be replaced with a new one – on VT125C models, renew the shocks as a pair (Chapter 6).

☐ Bent or damaged shock body. Replace the shock with a new one (Chapter 6).

Brake noise

Disc brake

☐ Worn brake pads – if there is no friction material left there will be a metal-on-metal grinding sound, and the disc will be damaged (Chapter 1).

☐ Squeal caused by dust on brake pads. Usually found in combination with glazed pads. Clean caliper area using brake cleaning solvent and dust off pads (Chapter 7).

☐ Contamination of brake pads. Oil or brake fluid causing brake to chatter or squeal. Fit a new set of pads (Chapter 7).

☐ Pads glazed. Caused by excessive heat from prolonged use or from contamination. A very fine flat file can be used to roughen the pad surfaces, but pad replacement is recommended as a cure (Chapter 7).

☐ Disc warped. Can cause a chattering, clicking or intermittent squeal. Usually accompanied by a pulsating lever/pedal and uneven braking. Replace the disc (Chapter 7).

Drum brake

☐ Accumulation of dust inside brake drum. Braking efficiency may also be affected. Remove rear wheel and clean drum.

☐ Worn brake shoes – if there is no friction material left there will be a metal-on-metal grinding sound, and the brake drum will be damaged (Chapter 1).

☐ Loose or worn wheel bearings. Check and replace as needed (Chapter 7).

10 Excessive exhaust smoke

White smoke

☐ Piston oil control ring worn. The ring(s) may be broken or damaged, causing oil from the crankcase to be pulled past the piston into the combustion chamber. Replace the piston rings as a set (Chapter 2).

☐ Cylinder worn or scored. Caused by overheating or oil starvation. The cylinders will have to be rebored and a new pistons and rings installed.

☐ Valve oil seal damaged or worn. Replace oil seals with new ones (Chapter 2).

☐ Valve guide worn. Perform a complete valve job (Chapter 2).

☐ Engine oil level too high, which causes the oil to be forced past the rings. Drain oil to the proper level (Chapter 1 and *Pre-ride checks*).

☐ Head gasket broken between oil return and cylinder. Causes oil to be pulled into the combustion chamber. Replace the head gasket and check the head for warpage (Chapter 2).

☐ Abnormal crankcase pressurisation, which forces oil past the rings. Clogged breather or hose usually the cause (Chapter 2).

Black smoke

☐ Air filter clogged. Renew the element (Chapter 1).

☐ Carburettor main jet too large or loose (VT125C and XL125V-1 to V-6 models). Compare the jet size to the *Specifications* (Chapter 4A).

☐ Choke stuck, causing fuel to be pulled through choke circuit (VT125C and XL125V-1 to V-6 models) (Chapter 4A).

☐ Fuel level too high (VT125C and XL125V-1 to V-6 models). Check and adjust the float height as necessary (Chapter 4A).

☐ Float needle valve held off needle seat (VT125C and XL125V-1 to V-6 models). Clean the float bowls and fuel line and replace the float needles if necessary (Chapter 4A).

☐ Fuel injection system malfunction (XL125V-7 onward) (Chapter 4B).

Brown smoke

☐ Air filter poorly sealed or not installed (Chapter 1).

☐ Carburettor main jet too small or clogged (VT125C and XL125V-1 to V-6 models). Lean condition caused by wrong size main jet or by a restricted orifice. Clean float bowl and jets and compare jet size to *Specifications* (Chapter 4A).

☐ Fuel flow insufficient (VT125C and XL125V-1 to V-6 models). Fuel inlet needle valve stuck closed due to chemical reaction with old fuel. Fuel level incorrect. Restricted fuel line. Clean line and float bowl and adjust float height if necessary (Chapter 4A).

☐ Intake duct loose (Chapter 4A or 4B as applicable).

☐ Fuel injection system malfunction (XL125V-7 onward) (Chapter 4B).

11 Poor handling or stability

Handlebar hard to turn

☐ Steering head bearing adjustment too tight (Chapter 1).

☐ Bearings damaged. Roughness can be felt as the bars are turned from side-to-side (Chapter 1). Replace bearings and races (Chapter 6).

☐ Races dented or worn. Denting results from wear in only one position (e.g. straight-ahead), from a collision or hitting a pothole or from crashing the machine. Replace races and bearings (Chapter 6).

☐ Steering stem lubrication inadequate. Causes are grease getting hard from age or being washed out by high pressure washers. Disassemble steering head and grease the bearings (Chapter 6).

☐ Steering stem bent. Caused by a collision, hitting a pothole or by crashing the machine. Replace damaged part. Don't try to straighten the steering stem (Chapter 6).

☐ Front tyre air pressure very low (*Pre-ride checks*).

11 Poor handling or stability (continued)

Handlebar shakes or vibrates excessively

- [ ] Tyres worn or out of balance (*Pre-ride checks*).
- [ ] Swingarm bearings worn. Replace worn bearings by referring to Chapter 6.
- [ ] Wheel rim(s) warped or damaged. Inspect wheels for runout (Chapter 7).
- [ ] Wheel bearings worn. Worn front or rear wheel bearings can cause poor tracking. Worn front bearings will cause wobble (Chapter 7).
- [ ] Handlebar clamp bolts loose (Chapter 6).
- [ ] Steering stem or fork clamp bolts loose. Tighten them to the specified torque (Chapter 6).
- [ ] Engine mounting bolts loose. Will cause excessive vibration with increased engine rpm (Chapter 2).

Handlebar pulls to one side

- [ ] Frame bent. Definitely suspect this if the machine has been crashed. May or may not be accompanied by cracking near the bend. Replace the frame (Chapter 6).
- [ ] Wheels out of alignment. Caused by incorrect attention to wheel alignment during chain tension adjustment, improper location of axle spacers (Chapter 7) or from bent steering stem or frame (Chapter 6). Check wheel alignment (Chapter 7).
- [ ] Swingarm bent or twisted. Caused by age (metal fatigue) or impact damage. Replace the swingarm (Chapter 6).

- [ ] Steering stem bent. Caused by a collision, hitting a pothole or by crashing the machine. Replace damaged part. Don't try to straighten the steering stem (Chapter 6).
- [ ] Fork leg bent. Disassemble the forks and replace the damaged parts (Chapter 6).
- [ ] Fork oil level uneven. Caused by leaking oil seals. Renew seals and fill forks to the correct level (Chapter 6).

Poor shock absorbing qualities

- [ ] Too hard:
  - a) Fork oil level too high (Chapter 6).
  - b) Fork oil viscosity too thick. Use a lighter oil (see the Specifications in Chapter 6).
  - c) Fork tube bent. Causes a harsh, sticking feeling (Chapter 6).
  - d) Fork internal damage (Chapter 6).
  - e) Rear shock shaft or body bent or damaged (Chapter 6).
  - f) Shock internal damage.
  - g) Tyre pressure too high (Pre-ride checks).
- [ ] Too soft:
  - a) Fork or shock oil insufficient and/or leaking (Chapter 6).
  - b) Fork oil level too low (Chapter 6).
  - c) Fork oil viscosity too thin (Chapter 6).
  - d) Fork springs weak or broken (Chapter 6).
  - e) Rear shock internal damage or leakage (Chapter 6).
  - f) Shock spring weak or broken (Chapter 6).

12 Braking problems

Brakes are spongy or don't hold (disc brake)

- [ ] Air in brake line or brake fluid leak. Caused by inattention to master cylinder fluid level or by leakage. Locate problem and bleed brakes (Chapter 7 and *Pre-ride checks*).
- [ ] Pads or disc worn (Chapters 1 and 7).
- [ ] Contaminated pads. Caused by contamination with oil, grease, brake fluid, etc. Replace pads. Clean disc and caliper thoroughly with brake cleaner (Chapter 7).
- [ ] Brake fluid deteriorated. Fluid is old or contaminated. Drain system, replenish with new fluid and bleed the system (Chapter 7).
- [ ] Master cylinder internal parts worn or damaged causing fluid to bypass (Chapter 7).
- [ ] Master cylinder bore scratched by foreign material or broken spring. Repair or replace master cylinder (Chapter 7).
- [ ] Disc warped. Replace disc (Chapter 7).

Brake doesn't hold (drum brake)

- [ ] Brake incorrectly adjusted (Chapter 1).
- [ ] Brake shoes worn. Renew shoes (Chapter 7).

Brake lever or pedal pulsates (disc brake)

- [ ] Disc warped. Replace disc (Chapter 7).
- [ ] Wheel axle bent. Replace axle (Chapter 7).
- [ ] Brake caliper bolts loose (Chapter 7).

- [ ] Wheel warped or otherwise damaged (Chapter 7).
- [ ] Wheel bearings damaged or worn (Chapters 1 and 7).

Brake pedal pulsates (drum brake)

- [ ] Brake drum out of round. Renew rear wheel or seek advice on having the drum skimmed (Chapter 7).
- [ ] Wheel bearings damaged or worn (Chapter 7).

Brakes drag (disc brake)

- [ ] Master cylinder piston seized. Caused by wear or damage to piston or cylinder bore (Chapter 7).
- [ ] Lever/pedal balky or stuck. Check pivot and lubricate (Chapter 6).
- [ ] Brake caliper piston seized in bore. Caused by wear or ingestion of dirt past deteriorated seal (Chapter 7).
- [ ] Brake caliper slider pins damaged or sticking, causing caliper to bind. Lube the slider pins (Chapter 7).
- [ ] Brake pad damaged. Pad material separated from backing plate. Usually caused by faulty manufacturing process or from contact with chemicals. Replace pads (Chapter 7).
- [ ] Pads improperly installed (Chapter 7).

Brakes drag (drum brake)

- [ ] Brake pedal freeplay insufficient (Chapter 1).
- [ ] Brake shoe springs weak or broken (Chapter 7).
- [ ] Brake shoe operating cam sticking due to lack of lubrication (Chapter 7).

13 Electrical problems

Battery dead or weak

- [ ] Battery faulty or worn out. Check the terminal voltage and renew battery if recharging doesn't work (Chapter 9).
- [ ] Battery leads making poor contact. Clean and reconnect (Chapter 9).
- [ ] Load excessive. Caused by addition of high wattage lights or other electrical accessories.
- [ ] Ignition switch defective. Switch either earths internally or fails to shut off system. Replace the switch (Chapter 9).
- [ ] Regulator/rectifier defective (Chapter 9).

- [ ] Alternator stator coil open or shorted (Chapter 9).
- [ ] Wiring faulty. Wiring earthed or connections loose in ignition, charging or lighting circuits (Chapter 9).

Battery overcharged

- [ ] Regulator/rectifier defective. Overcharging is noticed when battery gets excessively warm (Chapter 9).
- [ ] Battery defective. Replace battery with a new one (Chapter 9).
- [ ] Battery amperage too low, wrong type or size. Install manufacturer's specified amp-hour battery to handle charging load (Chapter 9).

Note: *References throughout this index are in the form - "Chapter number" • "Page number"*

Preserving Our Motoring Heritage

< The Model J Duesenberg Derham Tourster. Only eight of these magnificent cars were ever built – this is the only example to be found outside the United States of America

Almost every car you've ever loved, loathed or desired is gathered under one roof at the Haynes Motor Museum. Over 300 immaculately presented cars and motorbikes represent every aspect of our motoring heritage, from elegant reminders of bygone days, such as the superb Model J Duesenberg to curiosities like the bug-eyed BMW Isetta. There are also many old friends and flames. Perhaps you remember the 1959 Ford Popular that you did your courting in? The magnificent 'Red Collection' is a spectacle of classic sports cars including AC, Alfa Romeo, Austin Healey, Ferrari, Lamborghini, Maserati, MG, Riley, Porsche and Triumph.

A Perfect Day Out

Each and every vehicle at the Haynes Motor Museum has played its part in the history and culture of Motoring. Today, they make a wonderful spectacle and a great day out for all the family. Bring the kids, bring Mum and Dad, but above all bring your camera to capture those golden memories for ever. You will also find an impressive array of motoring memorabilia, a comfortable 70 seat video cinema and one of the most extensive transport book shops in Britain. The Pit Stop Cafe serves everything from a cup of tea to wholesome, home-made meals or, if you prefer, you can enjoy the large picnic area nestled in the beautiful rural surroundings of Somerset.

> John Haynes O.B.E., Founder and Chairman of the museum at the wheel of a Haynes Light 12.

< The 1936 490cc sohc-engined International Norton – well known for its racing success

The Museum is situated on the A359 Yeovil to Frome road at Sparkford, just off the A303 in Somerset. It is about 40 miles south of Bristol, and 25 minutes drive from the M5 intersection at Taunton.
Open 9.30am - 5.30pm (10.00am - 4.00pm Winter) 7 days a week, *except Christmas Day, Boxing Day and New Years Day*
Special rates available for schools, coach parties and outings Charitable Trust No. 292048